The Amazing Treasury of the Sakya Lineage

The Amazing Treasury of the Sakya Lineage

VOLUME 1

Ameshab Ngakwang
Kunga Sönam

Translated and Introduced by

Khenpo Kunga Sherab and Matthew W. King

Foreword by

His Holiness the Sakya Trichen

Wisdom

Wisdom Publications
132 Perry Street
New York, NY 10014 USA
wisdom.org

Library of Congress Cataloging-in-Publication Data
Names: Ngag-dbang-kun-dga'-bsod-nams, 'Jam-mgon A-myes-zhabs, 1597– approximately 1662, author. | Ngag-dbang-kun-dga'-bsod-nams, 'Jam-mgon A-myes-zhabs, 1597– approximately 1662. Dpal ldan Sa-skya'i gdung rabs rin po che ngo mtshar bang mdzod. | Kunga Sherab, Khenpo, translator. | King, Matthew W. (Matthew William), translator. | Ngag-dbang-kun-dga'-theg-chen-dpal-'bar, Sa-skya Khri-'dzin XLI, 1945– writer of foreword.
Title: The amazing treasury of the Sakya lineage / Ameshab Ngakwang Kunga Sönam; translated and Introduced by Khenpo Kunga Sherab and Matthew W. King; foreword by His Holiness the Sakya Trichen.
Other titles: Sa-skya gdung rabs chen mo. English
Description: First edition. | New York: Wisdom Publications, 2024– | Includes bibliographical references and index.
Identifiers: LCCN 2024006947 (print) | LCCN 2024006948 (ebook) | ISBN 9781614299196 (paperback) | ISBN 9781614299332 (ebook)
Subjects: LCSH: Sa-skya-pa lamas—China—Tibet Autonomous Region—Biography. | Sa-skya-pa (Sect)—History.
Classification: LCC BQ7672.9.A2 N3313 2024 (print) | LCC BQ7672.9.A2 (ebook) | DDC 294.3/92—dc23/eng/20240604
LC record available at https://lccn.loc.gov/2024006947
LC ebook record available at https://lccn.loc.gov/2024006948

ISBN 978-1-61429-919-6 ebook ISBN 978-1-61429-933-2

28 27 26 25 24
5 4 3 2 1

Cover image: Khön Könchok Gyalpo. Image courtesy of His Holiness the Forty-Second Sakya Trizin, Ratna Vajra Rinpoché.
Cover design by Gopa & Ted 2. Interior design by Tony Lulek.

Printed on acid-free paper that meets the guidelines for permanence and durability of the Production Guidelines for Book Longevity of the Council on Library Resources.

Printed in Canada.

Contents

Foreword by His Holiness the Sakya Trichen vii
Acknowledgments ix
List of Conventions xiii
Illustrations xv
Translators' Introduction 1

The Wondrous Precious Treasury Fulfilling All Wishes:
Biographies of the Precious Lineage of the Glorious Sakya, the Great Regents of the Buddha in the North of Jambudvīpa

Offering of Veneration 29
Explanation of the Lineage Succession from the Luminous Gods 33
Explanation of the Lineage Succession of the Stainless Khön 39
The Celestial Family of the Khön Sakyapa Lineage 53

1. Sachen Kunga Nyingpo 59
2. The Precious Master, Sönam Tsemo 99
3. Jetsun Rinpoché Drakpa Gyaltsen 107
4. Palchen Öpo 125
5. The Lord of Dharma Sakya Paṇḍita Kunga Gyaltsen 127
6. Sangtsa Sönam Gyaltsen 193
7. Guoshi Drogön Chögyal Phakpa Lodrö Gyaltsen 197
8. Drogön Chakna Dorjé 291

9. Dishi Rinchen Gyaltsen 295
10. Master Yeshé Jungné 299
11. The Dishi Dharmapālarakṣita 301
12. The Kinsman Ratnabhadra 303
13. Guoshi Mahātmā Sangpo Pal 305

Notes 313
Bibliography 365
Index 373
About the Authors 379

HIS HOLINESS
THE SAKYA TRICHEN

SAKYA TSECHEN
KUNCHAB LING

FOREWORD

THE *SAKYA DUNGRAB CHENMO*, translated in part here in this first volume of *The Amazing Treasury of the Sakya Lineage*, is one of the Sakya order's most important historical texts. It records the biographies of the hereditary lineage of the holy family of the Khön Sakyapa from its earliest ancestors over a thousand years ago until contemporary times. It includes the biographies of the masters who were the throne holders of the lineage, as well as many of their brothers and sisters. Their great lives illuminate the history of the Sakya order and demonstrate the Khön family's continuous dedication to the study, practice, teaching, and preservation of the Buddhadharma.

It is said that the Khön Sakya lineage has three names. The first, *Lharik*, means "celestial race." The second, *Khön*, literally means "disagreement," referring to an ancient disagreement between sons of the celestial race and demons known as *rakshas*. The celestial race was victorious in the disagreement and the leader took as a wife one of the raksha daughters, and it is from his union that the Khön lineage began. But figuratively, *Khön* indicates the victory of Manjushri's wisdom light in overpowering the darkness of ignorance. The third and most well-known name of the Khön lineage is *Sakyapa*, which is the name of both the region in Tibet where the Khön masters built their original monastery and the great tradition of religious practice that originated there.

As the centuries have passed, more and more biographies have been added to the *Dungrab Chenmo*, recording the holy lives of successive generations. The first *Dungrab Chenmo* was written in the seventeenth century by Ameshab Ngakwang Kunga Sönam, who was the twenty-seventh throne holder of the Sakya order. It included the biographies of the Khön masters up until that time. In the eighteenth century, a supplementary volume was added by the thirty-first throne holder, Sachen Kunga Lodrö, which added biographies up until that time. Early in the twentieth century, a third volume was composed by my grandfather, Dakshul Trinley Rinchen, the thirty-ninth throne holder, adding biographies up until contemporary times.

Now two scholars have begun the important work of translating these three volumes into English for the benefit of the wider world. The first of two volumes of Ameshab Ngakwang Kunga Sönam's history is presented here. I rejoice in the translators' activities and wish them every success in their endeavors.

May the accounts of the holy lives preserved in the *Dungrab Chenmo* inspire future generations of practitioners to follow in these great masters' footsteps, and may the future generations of the Khön Sakyapa continue to uphold the Buddhadharma for countless generations to come.

The Sakya Trichen
June 8, 2023

Acknowledgments

In 2018, the Second Annual North American Sakya Monlam festival was held in Minneapolis. At that time, Khenpo Kunga Sherab, Ani Vajra Rinpoché, Dakmo Chimé, and others attended a dinner with His Holiness Sakya Trichen Rinpoché, who was staying at Silvia Yueh's house. During the meal, His Holiness shared a delightful narrative pulled from the vast history of the Sakya tradition. When he had finished, Silvia Yueh, president of the Sachen Foundation, asked His Holiness where he had heard this story. His Holiness replied that it was from *The Amazing Treasury of the Sakya Tradition*, often glossed in shorthand as *The Succession History of Glorious Sakya*, or simply *The Great Succession History*. Ms. Yueh inquired if this text was available anywhere in English. His Holiness replied that, regretfully, it was not. Because of its significance and its unique content, His Holiness continued, he hoped that in the future it would be translated and made widely available for scholars and practitioners.

His Holiness' comments planted a seed in Khenpo Kunga Sherab, who at first thought to begin fundraising to pay for a translation. Khenpo Kunga consulted His Holiness Sakya Trizin Ratna Vajra Rinpoché, who generously offered to fund this translation via the Sachen Foundation. Inspired, Khenpo Kunga then decided that he would himself undertake the translation. Given that the early Sakya school was so deeply connected to the Mongols, Khenpo Kunga Sherab contacted Professor Matthew King, who researches Buddhism along the Tibet-Mongol interface, and asked whether he would like to work on this text. Matthew was delighted at the opportunity, and now, a couple of years later, the result is volume 1 of *The Amazing Treasury of the Sakya Lineage*, cotranslated here with full scholarly annotation and introduction. Volume 2, also generously funded by the Sachen Foundation, is currently in preparation and will find its way into print with Wisdom Publications soon.

To acknowledge our debts and thank the many interlocutors who helped with this challenging project, it is necessary to briefly offer readers a few general notes about the literary qualities of *The Amazing Treasury*. Like most Tibetan monastic histories of the last millennia, whether prose or verse history (e.g., *chos 'byung*), chronicle (*lo rgyus*), or succession narrative (*gdung rabs, gdan rabs, rgyal rabs*, etc.), *The Amazing Treasury* is best thought of as a critical, selective compilation of hundreds of excerpted sections from older texts deemed by its author to have historical worth.[1] Jamgön Ameshab Ngakwang Kunga Sönam, the author of the present text to whom we will be introduced below, intervenes often in the narrative to summarize his points, to compare and assess contradictory evidence, and to articulate his original historical arguments. Beyond such scattered authorial interventions, the bulk of *The Amazing Treasury* is an intertextual collection of other works, heavily weighted toward genealogies and biographies, but also philosophical tracts, meditation instructions, legal documents, letters, and much more besides.

Despite their historical significance, many of the larger works quoted so extensively in *The Amazing Treasury* are no longer extant. Even in the seventeenth century, when this work was written, many of these sources were barely attested. Now, three centuries later and across the chasm of the upheavals and erasures that so severely affected Tibetans in the twentieth century, we have less access to even fewer of these precious sources. The historical remoteness, rarity, and genre conventions of many of these early excerpted works have posed steep interpretative challenges not only for the translators of the present volume, but also for generations of highly educated native Tibetan readers deeply trained in the Sakya tradition! This is because many excerpts in the early sections of *The Amazing Treasury* are pithy, technical, and deeply braided with colloquial shorthand from another age. These excerpted sources are also sometimes representative of regional and historically specific understandings of the doctrine and practice of sūtra and tantra, often as this was explained (and debated) in the circles of charismatic teachers many centuries ago. Finally, befitting New Translation period conventions, much early excerpted material in *The Amazing Treasury* draws in complicated ways upon Sanskrit poetics and literary convention and Indian mythology—evidence of the high regard given to those few Tibetans of the period who could show their mastery of Indian literary arts and tradition, of whom many Sakya hierarchs were preeminent examples. Similarly, narratives about Khön patriarchs, whose lives became deeply entwined with the sprawling structures of the Mongol Empire and Yuan dynasty, often make obscure reference to imperial sites and administrative structures.

Hence His Holiness' comment about the great value and inimitability of this text for scholars and practitioners today. And hence our need to thank the many Tibetan monastic specialists who have helped us in innumerable ways to interpret difficult passages. We, Khenpo Kunga Sherab and Matthew King, must first express our immense gratitude for the guidance and kindness given by His Holiness Gongma Trichen Rinpoché, the Forty-First Sakya Trizin, His Holiness the Forty-Second Sakya Trizin Ratna Vajra Rinpoché, and Asanga Rinpoché, with whom we were in regular conversation over the entire course of this project.

We next wish to humbly thank the community of Sakya scholars from inside Tibetan regions of the PRC and in exile who took up our many queries about dozens of particularly challenging sections and references in *The Amazing Treasury*, usually through a lively WeChat group called "Questions on Doubts" (*Bka' 'dri zhu tshom*). We would also like to acknowledge Barbara Hazelton, a colleague of Khenpo Kunga's at the University of Toronto. Barbara translated a few of the early pages of this text, for which we are grateful. We are also very thankful to Dr. Gareth Sparham, professor emeritus at the University of Michigan, who kindly helped correct our rendering of the long Sanskrit title of this text. We are also endebted to Khenpo Chenyang Gyatso, who was born in the vicinity of Sakya and who generously helped identify many regional references in the text.

We must also thank Khenchen Diphu Palden Gyatso, who generously offered to sponsor the production of original artwork of the thirty-five major protagonists of the first half of *The Amazing Treasury*. We are also most grateful to the talented Tibetan artist Urgyen Gyalpo, now based in Toronto's Tibetan refugee community, for the original artwork he created for this volume. In many cases, we needed to make decisions about the appropriate iconography for these figures, many of whom are not widely represented in extant images. For this, we relied upon Sachen Kunga Lodrö's instructions for how to draw the Sakya lineage lamas (as carefully prescribed in the *'Dzam gling byang phyogs kyi thub pa'i rgyal tshab dpal ldan sa skya pa'i gdung rabs rin po che'i bris thang bzhengs tshul ngo mtshar rgya mtsho'i gter*). These wonderful and historically significant images are included in the text below.

We are also very grateful to the current vajra master of Sakya Monastery in Tibet, the most venerable Palden Doyön, who has been enormously generous and supportive over the course of this project. For example, he helped identify many little-known texts referenced in *The Amazing Treasury*, offered much advice about complex passages, and provided pictures of hard-to-access wall murals at Sakya as references for the aforementioned artwork.

We, the translators, are most indebted to the ongoing support given by the Sachen Foundation for this project. We offer our heartfelt thanks to all the hardworking directors, as well as to the sponsors—a global community of devotees of the Sakya tradition whose generosity has made this translation possible. Finally, we thank Daniel Aitken, Brianna Quick, and the production team at Wisdom Publications for their support, editorial prowess, and encouragement as we collectively bring this project into print.

Khenpo Kunga Sherab, Toronto, Ontario
Matthew King, Claremont, California

List of Conventions

Tibetan

The transcription of Tibetan words in this book follows the Wisdom Publications system. The Wylie transliteration is given on first usage, either as a note or in parentheses in the text as appropriate. If it is not otherwise marked, transliterations are always of the Tibetan.

Mongolian

Keeping the spelling of Mongolian words consistent and not overly technical for the sake of nonspecialists is always challenging. This book follows classical Mongolian spelling (marked in notes and parentheses as "Mong."). We follow the Tibetan and Himalayan Library (THL)'s vertical script Mongolian transcription system, developed by Prof. Christopher Atwood, except that we retain *γ* instead of *ġ* or *gh* on the old Mostaert and Lessing models.

Foreign Terminology

Certain English terms, Buddhist technical language, and proper nouns are followed by transliterated equivalents in Tibetan and, as the case may be, Mongolian, Sanskrit, Chinese, etc. In each case, transliterated equivalents are given in parentheses or as notes with the respective language clearly marked, separated by a semicolon: for example, "... fields of knowledge in logic and epistemology (Skt. *pramāṇa*; Tib. *tshad ma*; Mong. *kemjiy-e*)...".

Illustrations

Succession Lineage of the Luminous Gods

1. Chiring (Spyi ring) 33
2. Yuring (G.yu ring) 35
3. Yusé (G.yu se) 36
4. Masang Chijé (Ma sangs spyi rje) 36
5. Pawo Tak (Dpa' bo stag) 37
6. Takpo Öchen (Stag po 'od can) 37
7. Yapang Kyé (G.ya' spang skyes, ca. eighth cent.) 38

Succession Lineage of the Stainless Khön

8. Khön Barkyé ('Khon bar skyes, ca. eighth cent.) 41
9. Khön Palpoché ('Khon dpal po che, ca. eighth–ninth cent.) 42
10. Khön Lui Wangpo ('Khon klu'i dbang po, ca. eighth–ninth cent.) 43
11. Khön Dorjé Rinchen ('Khon rdo rje rin chen, ca. eighth–ninth cent.) 44
12. Khön Sherab Yönten ('Khon shes rab yon tan, ca. ninth cent.) 46
13. Khön Yönten Jungné ('Khon yon tan 'byung gnas, ca. ninth cent.) 46
14. Khön Tsültrim Gyalpo ('Khon tshul khrims rgyal po, ca. ninth–tenth cent.) 47
15. Khön Tsuktor Sherab ('Khon gtsug tor shes rab, ca. tenth cent.) 47

16. Khön Gekyab ('Khon dge skyabs, ca. tenth century) 48
17. Khön Getong ('Khon dge mthong, ca. tenth cent.) 48
18. Khön Tön Balpo ('Khon ston bal po, ca. tenth cent.) 49
19. Khön Shākya Lodrö
('Khon shākya blo gros, ca. eleventh cent.) 49

Succession Lineage of the Khön of Glorious Sakya
20. Khön Konchok Gyalpo
('Khon dkon mchog rgyal po, 1034–1102) 55
21. Sachen Kunga Nyingpo
(Sa chen kun dga' snying po, 1092–1158) 58
22. Lopön Sönam Tsemo
(Slob dpon bsod nams rtse mo, 1142–82) 100
23. Jetsun Drakpa Gyeltsen
(Rje btsun grags pa rgyal mtshan, 1147–1216) 108
24. Sangdak Palchen Öpo
(Gsang bdag dpal chen 'od po, 1150–1203) 124
25. Sakya Paṇḍita Kunga Gyaltsen
(Sa skya paṇdita kun dga' rgyal mtshan, 1182–1251) 126
26. Sangtsa Sönam Gyaltsen
(Zang tsha bsod nams rgyal mtshan, 1184–1239) 194
27. Guoshi Drogön Chögyal Phakpa Lodrö Gyaltsen
('Gro mgon chos rgyal 'phags pa blo gros
rgyal mtshan, 1235–80) 196
28. Drogön Chakna Dorjé ('Gro mgon phyag na rdo rje, 1239–67) 292
29. Dishi Rinchen Gyeltsen (Rin chen rgyal mtshan, 1238–79) 296
30. Yeshé Jungné (Ye shes 'byung gnas, 1238–74) 298
31. Dishi Dharmapālarakṣita
(Bdag nyid chen po dharma pā la rak shi ta, 1268–87) 300
32. Dungsé Ratnabhadra
(Gdung sras ratna bhadra, ca. late thirteenth century) 303
33. Guoshi Mahātmā Sangpo Pal
(Bdag nyid chen po bzang po dpal, 1262–1324) 304

Translators' Introduction

The Amazing Treasury is one of the most capacious Buddhist histories to have ever been written in the Tibetan and Mongolian heartlands of Asia. As its title suggests, this is a work brimming with the wealth of rare and otherwise lost stories. Its author was Jamgön Ameshab Ngakwang Kunga Sönam ('Jam mgon A myes zhabs ngag dbang kun dga' bsod nams, 1597–1659), a member of the Khön family lineage and the twenty-seventh throne holder, or "Sakya Trizin," of Sakya Monastery (r. 1620–51). Ameshab completed *The Amazing Treasury* in 1629, little more than a decade before the power and influence of the Khön family and Sakya school began a precipitous decline. This came following the deposition of their patron, the Tsang Desi Karma Tenkyong Wangpo,[2] who was defeated in the Tsang-Mongol war that concluded in 1642. The decentering of Sakya power and influence was only quickened by the concurrent rise of the Geluk (Dge lugs) school of Tibetan Buddhism and the Ganden Phodrang state of the Dalai Lamas and their powerful patrons, the Qošud Mongolian Empire and the Manchu ruling elite of the Qing Empire (1644–1912).[3]

Volume 1 of this translation is focused not on events from the author's seventeenth century, but an earlier transformational period spanning the tenth to fourteenth centuries. *The Amazing Treasury* widely illuminates that long era of innovation and upheaval across East, Inner, and South Asia. In the generations that followed the collapse of the Tibetan empire in the ninth century, the emergent Sakya tradition, with the Khön family lineage at its core, abounded with translators, adopters, arbiters, and innovators of Indic Buddhist traditions newly circulating into Tibet. In time, the Sakya transported their Dharma transmission and unique form of kin and monastic authority from the southern Tibetan plateau to the heart of a radically transformed Eurasian geopolitics. In the thirteenth century, the Mongol Empire forever transformed medieval Eurasia, and the Sakya school became confidants, tutors, and preceptors to some of its most powerful leaders. Khön luminaries like Sakya Paṇḍita and Phakpa Lodrö Gyaltsen, along with their Mongol patrons and disciples such as Köden Ejen and Qubilai Qaγan, innovated new forms of trans-Asian patronage, systematized study, and practice of Indian-derived scholasticism and tantrism, Buddhist aesthetic cultures, and moral models of religious and political authority that have endured over the last eight centuries down to today.

It is to Ameshab's spacious and enthralling seventeenth-century account of those events that the present volume is dedicated. To tell its story, *The Amazing Treasury* compiles and critically compares a vast collection of eyewitness accounts, oral traditions, songs and poems, philosophical treatises, and biographies. As readers explore his rich reconstruction of the Khön family and its special reception of Indian Mahāyāna Buddhist scholasticism and tantricism that began a thousand years ago, remember that this text was written at a time when the Sakya school was facing an uncertain future. Indeed, one imagines that Ameshab hoped that a literary reconstruction of the Sakya's "golden age" would ensure its continuity through the complex and often bloody upheavals of seventeenth-century Tibet.

As readers will see below, the Khön patriarchs and their Sakya Buddhist tradition were emblematic of, and a catalyst for, much of the religious, social, and political developments at the center of what Ronald Davidson lastingly called the "Tibetan Renaissance" (ca. ninth to thirteenth centuries CE).[4] This was a prolonged Tibetan mediation of newly circulating Central and South Asian scholastic and tantric movements that dramatically and enduringly transformed the transmission, translation, canonization, and practice of the Buddhadharma in Inner Asia. *The Amazing Treasury* uniquely documents this movement from sources thought to derive from the very center of the Renaissance era.

This remarkable work shatters any remnants of "Tibet as Shangri-la" outside of Eurasian history, for here we see the Sakya shaping, and being dramatically shaped in turn by, broader geopolitical theater and intellectual currents. This is especially true of the frame of Mongolian and Chinese history, which comes to surround the lives and writing of the thirteenth- and fourteenth-century Sakya forefathers whose life stories make up the bulk of volume 1. For this reason, *The Amazing Treasury* is something of a global history, or at least an example of global literature, as this was conceived by the seventeenth-century Tibetan luminaries like Ameshab in the Eurasian throughways of Inner Asia.

It is not only for scholars and practitioners of today that *The Amazing Treasury* is so illuminating. For several centuries after it was written, this text was closely read by Buddhist monastic historians well outside of cultural Tibet. In Mongolia and Siberia, for example, Ameshab's account of the Sakya patriarchs (and the histories upon which it drew) had enormous effect. Readers need only open classical works of Mongolian monastic historians to see the imprint of these narratives—historians such as Saγan Sečen, Rasipunsuγ, Thuken Chökyi Nyima, Güng Gombojab, Dharmatāla Damchö Gyatso, and Zava Damdin Lubsangdamdin. They, like Mongolian and Siberian Buddhists today who are reviving their Buddhist traditions after some seven decades of socialist state repression, understood their reception of the Buddhadharma to be owed in fundamental ways to Sakya lamas at the courts of the sons and grandsons of Činggis Qan.[5] So, too, generations of Manchu emperors and their legions of Tibetan and Mongolian Buddhist preceptors, scribes, ritualists, artists, and historians who, beginning in the seventeenth century, projected Qing imperial authority into Inner Asia on the strategic memory of the Sakya–Mongol relations of the thirteenth and fourteenth centuries.

All this is to say that, if one wishes to understand the form, scope, and content of Buddhism in Inner Asia over the last millennium, one must develop a thorough understanding of the history of the Sakya tradition and of the succession history of the Khön family that is its core. To that end, there is no better premodern guide than Ameshab's *Amazing Treasury* translated and annotated below.

The remainder of this introduction offers readers a brief overview of the Khön family lineage and the Sakya school of Tibetan Buddhism. It then summarizes the narrative arc of *The Amazing Treasury* and the historical traditions upon which it was based, followed by a short account of its author, the fraught times in which he lived, and his stated reasons for composing this text. The extensively annotated and illustrated translation then follows in full.

The Khön Sakyapa

According to the memory of its millennia-old tradition, the Sakya school of Tibetan Buddhism is distantly rooted in celestial ancestors referred to as the Lharik, or "celestial generation" (Lha rigs).[6] In time, those divine beings were remembered to have materialized as the prominent Khön ('Khon) aristocratic family who were active in the pseudo-historical Yarlung dynasty (*yar klung*, ca. second century BCE–seventh century CE) and the powerful Tibetan Empire that followed (seventh–ninth centuries CE).[7] The Tibetan Empire period begins with early *tsenpo* kings like Namri Songtsen (Gnam ri srong btsan, ca. 570–618), in whose courts the Khön were also remembered to have served. Indeed, Ameshab identified his Khön ancestors populating the royal circles of the Pugyal (*spur rgyal*) ruling elite.[8] They appeared to him in the textual records as courtly confidants and ministers, and especially among the early patrons and practitioners of Indian Buddhist tantrism and monasticism that began arriving in Tibet in the seventh century.

Owing to the exemplary lives of persons like Khön Barkyé and Khön Jekungdak—the latter served as minister to the famous Tibetan Dharma king Trisong Detsen—this "royal generation" (*rgyal rigs*) became known collectively as the "Khön family" (*'Khon gyi gdung*). Their political and religious authority, continuous over the last thousand years and more, was at the heart of the genesis of the Sakya tradition and of what we now gloss as Tibetan Buddhism generally. It remains so today.

From among the many tributaries of the Khön family, it was the "Sakya" branch (*sa skya*, meaning "Pale Earth" for reasons described below) that formed a major school of Inner Asian Buddhism and that are the dominant protagonists of *The Amazing Treasury*. According to later monastic historians like Ameshab, the Sakya Buddhist school was founded by a Khön patriarch very precisely in 1073 CE. That year, a temple complex that would become Sakya Monastery was raised in the Sakya Valley of Tsang (Gtsang), Central Tibet. The man responsible was Khön Könchok Gyalpo ('Khon dkon mchog rgyal po, 1034–1102). Könchok Gyalpo was a quintessential figure in the transition from the older tantric traditions of the Tibetan Empire (which had collapsed two centuries earlier, in 842 CE) to the flush of new tantric and Mahāyāna Buddhist transmission washing over Tibet in the generations that followed. This latter transmission of the Dharma, the so-called "Later Spread" (Phyi dar) or "New Translation" (Gsar ma) period, is usually dated to the career of the illustrious Western Tibetan translator Rinchen Sangpo (Rin chen bzang po, 958–1055).

Khön Könchok Gyalpo was both a contemporary of Rinchen Sangpo and a lineage holder of more ancient Khön tantric transmissions descended from imperial times. On the advice of his brother, Könchok Gyalpo began to study the new Buddhist movements circulating through the Himalayas and the Tibetan plateau. He and other Tibetans did so at the feet of mostly itinerant South and Central Asian translators, charismatic teachers, and tantric practitioners with ties to great northern Indian monastic universities like Vikramaśīla[9] and Nālandā.[10] They were also intermediaries for the non-institutionalized tantric transmissions of South Asian adepts like Tilopa, Nāropa, Kṛṣṇācārya, Saraha, and Virūpa, mahāsiddhas who never visited Tibet but whose life stories, songs of realization, and teaching and practice lineages transformed Buddhist life in the Land of Snows.

Among the many mahāsiddhas, or "great [tantric] adepts," who populate the Tibetan imagination, Virūpa[11] is considered the original progenitor of the unique tantric transmission of the Sakya school. Virūpa, "the Ugly One," is remembered to have previously served in the illustrious position of abbot of Nālandā monastery. Performing his abbatial duties by day, Virūpa secretly pursued his practice of tantra at night. Progress in his practice, however, was slow. In time, Nairātmyā,[12] the consort of the buddha Hevajra (Tib. Kye rdo rje; Ch. Jingangwang), appeared to him in visions and bestowed instructions and initiations. Inspired, Virūpa abandoned his post and adopted the lifestyle of a siddha to accomplish the "quick path" of the Hevajra tantric system. Centuries later, Tibetans understood Virūpa as the authoritative wellspring for the Lamdré, or "path and result" (*lam 'bras*), method. His teaching lineages on this technique were, and remain, the specialty inheritance of the Sakya school.[13]

The founder of Sakya Monastery, Könchok Gyalpo, personally encountered the dispensation of these new siddha movements via the great translator and yogi Drokmi Lotsāwa Śākya Yeshé ('Brog mi lo tsā ba shākya ye shes, ca. 992–1072). Drokmi Lotsāwa was a Tibetan who had studied extensively in what is now Nepal and India with South Asian masters such as Prajñendraruci and Gayadhāra. According to later biographical traditions about him, Drokmi received transmissions of the *Hevajra Tantra*[14] and its explanatory tantras from these two masters, along with specialist teachings on the aforementioned path and result, or Lamdré. Such were the more immediate tantric ecologies in which the Sakya school, so named, took shape in the eleventh century.[15]

The *Hevajra Tantra* is itself a prominent protagonist of Ameshab's *Amazing Treasury*, and the Lamdré and Hevajra corpus generally was a major preoccupation of Ameshab's prodigious historical scholarship beyond the pages of the present historical work.[16] Given its importance, it will be useful to share a little about the literary history of this tantra as it became known and practiced in Tibet, especially among the Sakya and Kagyü schools, via Renaissance-era figures like Drokmi, Könchok Gyalpo, and Marpa Lotsāwa.[17]

The *Hevajra Tantra*, known also by its longer Sanskrit title, *Hevajra-ḍākinījālasaṃvara Tantra*, was classified and canonized over time by Tibetan exegetes and doxographers as one of the many yoginī tantras (*rnal 'byor ma'i rgyud*) belonging to the unexcelled yoga tantra class (Skt. *anuttarayogatantra*; Tib. *rnal 'byor bla na med pa'i rgyud*). Among "New Translation" Buddhist movements in Inner Asia such as the Sakya, the unexcelled yoga tantra corpus was considered to be the highest tantric teachings of the historical Buddha Śākyamuni (given privately, in different forms, across a vast swath of time). Some New Translation schools (such as the later Geluk tradition) classified the Hevajra corpus as a mother tantra (Skt. *mātṛtantra*: Tib. *ma rgyud*), recognizing an emphasis on the cultivation of wisdom via the "mind of clear light" (Skt. *prabhās-varacitta*; Tib. *'od gsal gyi sems*).

By contrast, it seems that since at least the time of Phakpa Lodrö's thirteenth-century *Catalogue of the Tantras* (*Rgyud sde'i dkar chag*), the Sakya school has categorized the Hevajra system as nondual tantra (Skt. *advayatantra*; Tib. *gnyis med kyi rgyud*). In general, nondual tantras were often so classified for privileging neither the cultivation of wisdom via the mind of clear light nor the cultivation of method via the illusory body (Skt. *māyādeha;* Tib. *sgyu lus*), the emphasis of so-called father tantra (Skt. *pitṛtantra;* Tib. *pha rgyud*).[18] However, the Sakya school seems to have historically classified the *Hevajra Tantra* corpus as nondual for another reason: its practice and explanatory lineages balance generation stage (Skt. *utpattikrama;* Tib. *bskyed rim*) practices with those of the completion stage (Skt. *niṣpannakrama;* Tib. *rdzogs rim*).

The version of the *Hevajra Tantra* that became best known and translated in Tibet contained 750 stanzas. Contemporary scholars have tended to date its composition to the eighth century CE.[19] The canonized *Hevajra Tantra* arrived in Tibet made up of two segments, the first with eleven chapters and the second with twelve. For this reason, Tibetan authors like Ameshab often refer to the *Hevajra Tantra* in shorthand as the "*Two-Part*" tantra (Skt. *Dvikalparāja;* Tib. *Brtag gnyis*).[20] As with many other tantric works compiled in the Tibetan canon, Tibetan scholars considered the extant *Hevajra Tantra* to be only an abridged exposition of a lost complete work in thirty-two chapters and five hundred thousand verses.

The *Hevajra Tantra* is notable for its use of its so-called coded or "twilight" language (Skt. *sandhyābhāṣā;* Tib. *dgongs skad*), which purposefully remains illegible without the guidance of a qualified guru and the associated oral lineage. Like other tantras that became popular in Tibet during the "five forefathers of the Sakya" period (such as the *Cakrasaṃvara Tantra*), the *Hevajra Tantra* presents methods for accomplishing both "common attainments" (Skt. *sādhāraṇasiddhi;* Tib. *thun mong gi dngos grub*) and the "supreme attainment" of complete enlightenment (Skt. *uttamasiddhi;* Tib. *mchog gi dngos grub*). Very much in common with other yoginītantras arriving in Tibet during this period, the *Hevajra Tantra* presents a path to supreme attainment organized through the generation of great bliss (Skt. *mahāsukha;* Tib. *bde ba chen po*), meditation upon the channels (Skt. *nāḍi;* Tib. *rtsa*), winds (Skt. *prāṇa;* Tib. *rlung*), and drops (Skt. *bindu;* Tib. *thig le*), as well as the yoga of sexual union (Skt. *sampuṭa;* Tib. *yang dag par sbyor ba*). Though it was translated into Chinese in 1055 by Dharmapāla (Ch. Fahu 法護), the Hevajra system was never widely adopted in East Asia.[21] Its post-Indic life was largely in the Tibetan cultural world, from where it later spread among Mongol, Manchu, Siberian, and Han practitioners.

In the early eleventh century, nearly contemporaneously with Dharmapāla, the aforementioned Drokmi Lotsāwa translated the *Hevajra Tantra* into Tibetan. Based upon commentaries attributed to the Indian siddha Nāropa, the *Hevajra Tantra* was widely promoted in the teachings of the early Kagyü tradition. Indeed, Drokmi is remembered to have returned to Tibet and taught Sanskrit to the translator-adept Marpa Chökyi Lodrö (Mar pa chos kyi blo gros, ca. 1002–97), progenitor of the Kagyü school (*bka' brgyud*) and guru to Tibet's famous yogin Milarepa (Mi la ras pa, 1040–1123). But most impactfully, Drokmi helped transmit Virūpa's Hevajra system to the early Khön patriarchs of the Sakya school.

The Hevajra system generally and the Lamdré path and result method specifically became central to the institutional and doctrinal identities of the Sakya Buddhist tradition. As Ameshab copiously describes below, in the hands of Sakya hierarchs during the thirteenth century, the Hevajra system was transposed into the heart of Eurasian geopolitics. Phakpa Lodrö Gyaltsen, a Khön master practitioner and holder of the throne of Sakya, initiated no less than the Mongol emperor Qubilai Qaγan and his principal consort, Čabui, into the Hevajra system.[22] These were truly epochal events for Ameshab and countless other Tibetan and Mongolian Buddhist historians who have retold its story over the centuries; though it must be noted that, contra such memorialization, this was not in fact the first initiation by a Tibetan master of a Mongolian qaγan. As Johan Elverskog points out, "We know from Situ Panchen's *History of the Kagyu Sect* [i.e., the *Sgrub brgyud karma kam tshang brgyud pa rin po che'i rnam par thar pa rab 'byam nor bu zla ba chu shel gyi phreng ba*] that Karma Pakshi (1204 or 1206–1283/4) the second Black Hat Karmapa had initiated Möngke Khan into the Cakrasamvara mandala already in 1256."[23] In any case, as we shall see in abundant narrative detail below, from receiving Hevajra initiation and transmission from this Khön master, two of the most powerful individuals in premodern world history were transformed into devotees of this tantra and into disciples of the Sakya tradition.[24]

Gilded in Hevajra-centered ritualism and based on an earlier Tangut model, the Sakya tradition and its Mongolian patrons developed a lasting model of "preceptor-patron" (*yon mchod*) sovereignty and relationality known most simply as "the Two Systems" (Tib. *lugs gnyis;* Mong. *qoyar yosu*). This model of unified Dharmic and political authority has remained central to Inner Asian Buddhist institutional life, diplomacy, historical consciousness, and moral authority into the present century. Indeed, understanding how *yon mchod* is constructed historically is important if one is to understand the broad contours of Buddhist history and communal relation in Inner Asia after the thirteenth century (very much including the contrasting claims of sovereignty and dominion made by the People's Republic of China and the Tibetan exile community over the last seven decades). The *Amazing Treasury* is an invaluable resource in this regard.

Returning to the genesis of the early Sakya, Drokmi Lotsāwa is said to have taught not only Könchok Gyalpo but also the shepherd Sé Karchungwa (Se 'khar chung ba, 1029–1116), *alias* Setön Kunrik (Se ston kun rig), along with the latter's student, Zhangtön Chöbar (Zhang ston chos 'bar, 1053–1135). Zhangtön Chöbar was, like Könchok Gyalpo, emblematic of the synthetic religiosity of many early masters of the New Translation movement. For example, Zhangtön Chöbar was a dedicated practitioner of the Great Perfection (Rdzogs chen) teachings of the older transmission cycle, which only in time and in contrast to the new transmissions would be grouped together as the "Old" [Translation] schools, or "Nyingma" (Rnying ma). He is said to have continued his great perfection practice by day and then turned to his new practice of Lamdré by night, a wonderfully personal example of the syncretism and improvisation of this period.

At the confluence of these many streams was Könchok Gyalpo's son, Sachen Kunga Nyingpo (Sa chen kun dga' snying po, 1092–1158). Drokmi, Setön Kunrik, and Zhangtön Chöbar all transmitted the Lamdré to Sachen. He additionally studied under the great translator and tantric guru of his father, Mel Lotsāwa Lodrö Drakpa (Mal lo tsā ba blo gros grags pa, ca. eleventh century). Mel Lotsāwa was a proponent of New Translation tantric systems, such as the Cakrasaṃvara[25] and Mahākāla,[26] and Sachen received initiation into both systems from him, along with those of Vajrabhairava[27] and Vajrayoginī.[28] Sachen synthesized all these with older, imperial-era Viśuddhaheruka[29] and Vajrakīlaya[30] systems maintained by his Khön family lineage.[31] In time, Sachen also received a complete transmission of the Lamdré from Chöbar, accompanied by a command to neither teach nor even reference the tradition for a period of eighteen years.

The early Sakya tradition was thus shaped by Tibetan regional powers still rooted in powerful clans and aristocratic families connected to the imperial period that had ended in the mid-ninth century. By the tenth and eleventh centuries, these groups were apparently awash in enough gold and aspiration to fund sustained transmissions and translations from Indian tantric masters and to establish enduring networks with the large Buddhist monastic universities of northern India. The 1073 founding of the Sakya temple complex was emblematic of such developments across the central and western Tibetan plateau.

Sakya monastic historians like Ameshab long understood that Könchok Gyalpo's choice for the site of Sakya had been foretold by none other than Atiśa Dīpaṃkara Śrījñāna (A ti sha mar me mdzad dpal ye shes, 982–1055). Atiśa was a great Bengali master who came to Tibet in 1042 at the invitation of the king of western Tibet, Yeshé Ö (Ye shes 'od, 947–1024), and his nephew Jangchub Ö (Byang chub 'od, late tenth century). Atiśa's teaching in Tibet was a watershed moment for all the New Translation movements (such as the Sakya, Kagyü, and later Geluk). His disciples would later found the widely influential Kadampa (*Bka' gdams pa*) school, which also figures prominently in Ameshab's history below. According to tradition, in the year of his arrival Atiśa had gazed upon a lion-shaped patch of pale or gray earth (*sa skya*) marking the slopes of Mount Pönpo in southern Tibet. He prophesied to those in his company that in the future, emanations of Avalotikeśvara, Mañjuśrī, and Vajrapāṇi would all come to dwell there.[32] As predicted, four decades later, in 1073, the Sakya complex was founded. It would remain the institutional center of the Sakya school until the Chinese annexation of the Tibetan Plateau in the 1950s, when it was largely destroyed. Along with hundreds of thousands of other Tibetans, the Khön family leadership fled into exile, where they remain still. Today, networks of Sakya monasteries and Dharma centers are found across Asia, Europe, and North America. The original Sakya complex upon the slopes of Mount Pönpo in Tibet has been partially rebuilt and functions within the restricted structures of the People's Republic of China.

The Five Forefathers of the Sakya

Beginning with Sachen Kunga Nyingpo, the "five forefathers of the Sakya" (*sa skya'i gong ma rnam lnga*) together solidifed the institutional and sectarian foundations of the Sakya school.[33] These five are the dominant protagonists of volume 1 of the *Treasury* translated here. They were the third to the seventh throne holders of Sakya, or Sakya Trizin (*Sa skya khri 'dzin*). Sakya Trizin is a hereditary title that has endured in a continuous lineage since the death of Khön Könchok Gyalpo in 1102. In 2017, His Holiness the Forty-Second Sakya Trizin, Ratna Vajra Rinpoché (b. 1974) inherited the title from his long-serving father, His Holiness the Forty-First Sakya Trizin, Ngakwang Kunga Tekchen Pelbar (Ngag dbang kun dga' theg chen dpal 'bar, r. 1951–2017), now referred to as the Kyabgön Gongma Trichen Rinpoché. In 2022, the throne of the Sakya was passed from Ratna Vajra Rinpoché to his brother, Khöndung Gyana Vajra Rinpché (b. 1979), who serves as the Forty-Third Sakya Trizin. As mentioned already, our author Ameshab Ngakwang Kunga Sönam served as the Twenty-Seventh Sakya Trizin.

The layman Sachen Kunga Nyingpo, the first of the five forefathers, is remembered to have been the first to press into writing the quintessential Lamdré instructions, which had until then been consigned to a highly secretive and exclusively oral transmission. Sachen was also the first to write down Virūpa's *Vajra Verses*,[34] which had similarly circulated only orally. He additionally authored a collection of eleven commentaries, each originally intended for only a single disciple (among them were three women and eight men). Exemplifying the mixed form of familial and monastic authority that has uniquely reproduced the Sakya tradition over the last thousand years, Sachen Kunga Nyingpo had two famous sons: Sönam Tsemo (Bsod nams rtse mo, 1142–82) and Jetsun Drakpa Gyaltsen (Rje btsun Grags pa rgyal mtshan, 1147–1216). These two would become the fourth and fifth Sakya Trizins and the second and third forefathers.

Sönam Tsemo is remembered to have been a gifted child. He could recite by heart the entire *Cakrasaṃvara Tantra* before the age of five and the *Hevajra Tantra* by sixteen. He was a disciple of his father's tantric lineages, including the Lamdré, but brought the Sakya school into a new constellation by also being educated in the Indian Mahāyāna philosophical traditions at the important but still little-researched Sangphu Neuthok Monastery (Gsang phu ne'u thog).[35] Founded in 1072 by Ngok Lekpai Sherab, a disciple of Atiśa, Sangphu was by the twelfth century a famous seat of Kadampa learning in central Tibet, just south of Lhasa. At Sangphu, Sönam Tsemo became an accomplished disciple of the luminary Chapa Chökyi Sengé (Phya pa chos kyi seng ge, 1109–69).[36] It is said that Sönam Tsemo excelled in Madhyamaka philosophy and *pramāṇa* traditions of logic and epistemology, developed proficiency in reading Sanskrit, became a gifted exegete of *Ascertaining Valid Cognition*,[37] one of Dharmakīrti's seven treatises on logic and epistemology,[38] and mastered Śāntideva's famous *Introduction to the Bodhisattva's Practice*.[39] One of Sönam Tsemo's compositions, a pithy work from 1167 entitled *Entranceway to the Dharma*,[40] would later have a particularly strong influence upon his nephew Kunga Gyaltsen, memorialized more famously as Sakya Paṇḍita, another of the five forefathers who would take the burgeoning Sakya reputation for scholastic achievement to the global stage.[41]

Sachen Kunga Nyingpo's other son (i.e., Sönam Tsemo's younger brother) was Drakpa Gyaltsen. He, too, was recognized while still a child for his remarkable and apparently inborn abilities. By twelve years old, it is said he could recite the *Hevajra Tantra* by heart. Much to the amazement of the assembly at Sakya, at that tender age he also gave a large public teaching on this tantra. Like his father and older brother, Drakpa Gyaltsen remained a layman throughout his life, though he is remembered for revering the monastic community and yearning to one day ordain as a Buddhist monk. Instead, Drakpa Gyaltsen received the lay vows of an *upāsaka* (*dge bsnyen*) when he was eight years old.[42] His commitment to purely guarding the lay precepts remains legendary in the Inner Asian Buddhist world, as does his commitment to avoiding alcohol or meat—by all accounts, a quite notable degree of asceticism for a lay tantrika in twelfth-century Tibet. Like his brother and father, Drakpa Gyaltsen received a rigorous education in the literature and contemplative techniques of Mahāyāna grounds and paths as well as in tantrism. Alongside his brother, he was among the first to receive Lamdré teachings from their father, Sachen, who transmitted the tradition to his sons as soon as his eighteen-year pledge to secrecy had expired. Drakpa Gyaltsen's celebrated commitment to meditation practice, his popular teaching, his work to record and preserve the Lamdré tradition, and his long tenure as Sakya Trizin helped solidify the burgeoning doctrinal and institutional identity of the Sakya school.

In the long shadow of Drakpa Gyaltsen, the remaining two forefathers of the Sakya would become caught up in the radical upheavals of early-thirteenth century Eurasia. These two together are the dominant focus of the history translated below. Originally under duress, they would bring the Sakya school into the heart of the largest and most powerful pre-modern land empire in world history: the Mongol Empire, another of the major settings of *The Amazing Treasury*.

"Two Reds" at the Heart of the Mongolian Empire

The two final forefathers were Drakpa Gyaltsen's nephew Sakya Paṇḍita Kunga Gyaltsen (Sa skya paṇdita kun dga' rgyal mtshan, 1182–1251) and his grandnephew Phakpa Lodrö Gyaltsen ('Phags pa blo gros rgyal mtshan, 1235–80).[43] Unlike the three Sakya forefathers that came before, Sakya Paṇḍita (or Sapaṇ, as he is known) and Phakpa were Khön hierarchs who took the vows of Buddhist monks. The five Sakya forefathers are thus often glossed in Inner Asian Buddhist histories for the color of their robes as the "Three Whites and Two Reds" (*Dkar gsum dmar gnyis*): three laymen and two monks who transformed the face of Tibetan Buddhism in the New Translation period.

The two "reds," Sapaṇ and Phakpa, not only elevated monasticism among the Khön leadership, but they also widely promoted vast learning in tantric self-cultivation and in the so-called "five [major] sciences" known to classical Buddhist scholasticism in South Asia.[44] Indeed, as Jonathan Gold has argued, Sakya Paṇḍita was the nexus from which the Sakya school became a model for the scholastic cultures that have since organized all Inner Asian Buddhist traditions generally, but especially the Sakya and Geluk traditions, over the last eight centuries.[45] Readers of *The Amazing Treasury* will be delighted to find a very detailed biographical portrait of Sapaṇ, which highlights the unique education and scholasticism then being promoted at Sakya Monastery, and the impacts his model had on generations of Khön hierarchs who later led the Sakya tradition.

The textual legacy of Sapaṇ has also remained a major touchstone for literary and intellectual life in Buddhist Inner Asia down to today. The most popular and widely read of his works clarify and schematize Buddhist ethics and philosophical inquiry. They tend to present the gradual path of Buddhist self-cultivation in both high prose meant for advanced scholastics as well as pithy verse meant for popular consumption. Some of the most well-known of his more than one hundred extant works include: *Clarifying the Sage's Intent* (*Thub pa'i dgongs pa rab tu gsal ba*), *Entrance Gate for the Wise* (*Mkhas pa rnam 'jug pa'i sgo*), *Treasury of Epistemology* (*Tshad ma rigs pa'i gter*), *Treasury of Aphoristic Jewels* (*Legs par bshad pa rin po che'i gter*), and *Clear Differentiation of the Three Vows* (*Sdom gsum rab dbye*).[46]

Sakya Paṇḍita's illustrious scholarly accomplishments also helped periodize an entirely new era in the history of Buddhism in Tibet: a transition from some six centuries of dutiful Tibetans understanding themselves as disciples and translators of the Indian Buddhist tradition to a new era of being recognized as Buddhist masters in their own right. Such recognition came to Sapaṇ not only from Central and Inner Asian scholars, practitioners, and patrons, but also, in a significant reversal, from Indians. This epochal development is often distilled in Tibetan Buddhist histories like *The Amazing Treasury* as a singular event: Sapaṇ's defeat of the Indian scholar Harinanda in debate at Kyirong (Skyid grong) in 1240.

When Sakya Paṇḍita was already an old man and Phakpa still a child, the Mongol Empire literally came knocking at Sakya Monastery's door. The period of Mongolian hegemony in Eurasia began in 1206 with the rise to power of Temujin, known to the world as Činggis Qan (i.e., Genghis Khan, ca. 1167–1227), at the head of a quickly growing tribal conquest empire.[47] Two years after Činggis Qan's death in 1227, his third son Ögedei was elected as *qa'yan*, or "Supreme Qan," of the quickly expanding Mongol Empire. A year later, allied Mongolian forces occupied territories bounding Tibetan societies on three sides. In 1227, the Mongols had conquered the Tangut Empire, a great patron of Buddhism that hosted many Tibetan and Uyghur monks at court.[48]

In the years that followed, Mongol forces sought any strategic advantage in their conquest of Song-dynasty China, including military campaigns in the Gansu and Sichuan provinces spanning the Sino-Tibetan frontiers.[49] Within a few years of Činggis Qan's elevation as *qan*, Tibetans began encountering the Mongol Empire while serving in the courts of the Tanguts.[50] It appears that as early as 1209, the master Dishi Repa Sherab Sengé (Ti shri Ras pa Shes rab seng ge, 1164–1236) performed "Mongol repelling" rituals (*hor gyi dmag bzlog*) at Liangzhou.[51] While Činggis Qan died during the Tangut campaign, his sons and armies continued to push deeper into the Tibetan cultural sphere in Yunnan and Sichuan. It was only a matter of time before Buddhist institutions in Central Tibet such as Sakya would come face-to-face with this globalizing imperial force transforming Eurasia.[52] That encounter came with the arrival of Köden Ejen, one of Činggis Qan's grandsons, to the eastern frontiers of the Tibetan cultural world during campaigns against the faltering Song Dynasty in China.[53]

Köden Ejen, the second son of Činggis Qan's son and successor Ögedei Qaγan (r. 1229–1241), was tasked with managing Mongol campaigns along the Sino-Tibetan frontiers. Köden played a relatively minor military role in the Sino-Tibetan frontiers that is far outsized by his place in Mongolian and Tibetan monastic historiography, very much including in *The Amazing Treasury.* In the memory of later Buddhist historians in Inner Asia, Köden is usually misidentified as the Mongol ruler. Often, he is even assumed to have been the emperor of China.[54] In 1235, Köden led Mongol forces into southern Gansu province and then Sichuan, sacking Chengdu in November of 1236.[55] For the effort, Köden was given regional leadership around the aforementioned Liangzhou, contemporary Wuwei, which had been the second largest city of the Tangut Empire until a Mongol occupation began in 1226.

In 1240, Köden sent a reconnaissance mission to Central Tibet headed by a pitiless Tangut commander of the Mongol army named Dorta Darqan. Even the generally rosy depictions of later Tibetan and Mongolian historians underscore the bloodiness of Dorta's expedition.[56] Radreng (Rwa sgreng) and Gyal Lhakhang (Rgyal lha khang), both Kadampa monasteries, were razed. Hundreds of their monks, an abbot, and a regional leader were murdered.[57]

Following their salvo, the Mongols suddenly retreated from Tibet's violated cultural borders. In the wake of the initial campaign, Köden's father, Ögedei Qaγan, had died. According to Mongolian imperial custom, Köden and the rest of the dispersed Činggisid nobility left the frontlines to convene a grand *quraltai* assembly in Qaraqorum to elect the new *qaγan*. Köden, according to Christopher Atwood, had designs on his father's throne, but "the other princes considered [him] too sickly and elected his elder brother Güyüg instead."[58] In 1244, while Köden was being overlooked in the heart of empire, his forces once again departed Liangzhou for Central Tibet. Their orders were apparently to return with a Tibetan Buddhist lama who could act as teacher and tantric preceptor to Köden and who possessed enough political clout to credibly submit the Tibetan plateau to the Mongols (there was no unified Tibetan state at this time, only a constellation of polities). The Mongols appear to have initially contacted monastic leaders in the Drikung Kagyü tradition ('Bris gung bka' brgyud). Unwilling to accompany them, the Kagyü monks strategically redirected the Mongols to the ruling Khön family and their base at Sakya.

The Mongol party arrived at Sakya Monastery in Tsang that very year, likely realizing that the unique family-based hereditary system of the Khön Sakya was a good candidate for a meaningful and continuous submission to the Mongol empire. A certain Dorsi Gön (Rdor sri mgon) and the notorious Dorta Darqan presented Sakya Paṇḍita with an official letter (*gser yig*) summoning him to Köden's court. In blunt terms memorialized in the translation below, the Khön and their Sakya tradition were commanded to Liangzhou where they would enter the global stage in a staggering new imperial context spread between the Pacific and the Black Sea.

According to later Inner Asian historical tradition, when faced with the menace of this Mongol summons, Sapaṇ recalled a prophecy delivered to him by his uncle and primary religious teacher Drakpa Gyaltsen. In this recollection, Drakpa Gyaltsen had foretold the emissaries of "King Köden," a representative of the Mongol Empire "ruled by the descendants of Činggis, the Heavenly, the Beneficial." Bolstered by prophetic vision, Sakya Paṇḍita prepared to depart Sakya for the court of Köden.

Whether he undertook the journey out of devotion or fear, Sapaṇ apparently did not rush to Köden's encampment at Liangzhou as ordered. Along his long route northeast past Lake Kokonor, he paused often to teach and to confer ordination and tantric initiation. Nor did he travel alone. The Mongol party had also required two young members of the Khön family to report to the Mongol encampment (apparently recognizing them as heirs and, thus, as useful hostages). These were Sapaṇ's nephews, Phakpa Lodrö Gyaltsen ('Phags pa blo gros rgyal mtshan, 1235–80) and Chakna Dorjé (Phyag na rdo rje, 1239–67). As the *Amazing Treasury* abundantly describes, both of these young Khön family members would grow up to play widely impactful religious and political roles between the grand Mongol courts and the Tibetan world.[59]

Sakya Paṇḍita and his party finally arrived in Liangzhou in 1246, when Sapaṇ was sixty-five years old. They remained there for some time while awaiting Köden's return from Qaraqorum. Denied the throne of the Mongol empire, the sickly Köden returned to Liangzhou only in 1247, there to find the Tibetans still waiting. According to tradition, though Köden had previously met some Tibetan monks, they had not roused his faith since they could not describe the Buddha's qualities in any compelling detail. *The Amazing Treasury* and similar accounts describe how Sapaṇ first offered teachings on points of doctrine and then proved his supernormal ability by recognizing and then materializing a magically conjured temple (in some versions, a magical palace or city).

Still, Köden was skeptical. And quite sick. Köden finally confided to Sapaṇ that he was afflicted by a skin ailment (*sha khra*) that may have been leprosy. His court shamanists had failed in curing it, even when they resorted to animal sacrifice. Köden begged for the tantric techniques uniquely possessed by the Sakya master. Sapaṇ agreed and cured Köden by way of wrathful tantric ritual. In Tibetan and Mongolian Buddhist histories from the last eight centuries, Sapaṇ's intervention into the bodily health of the Činggisid noblemen became a narrative event that stands in for the initial conversions of the Mongols to Buddhism.[60] The body natural of Köden is the body politic of the Mongols. Readers of the translation below will see how Ameshab uses the space of Köden's body to tell a much wider story about Sakya ascension in Eurasia, and more specifically, about their role in correcting and purifying the violence of the Mongol's rise to power. By the subjugating power of the Khön, these previously "red-faced" enemies of the Dharma were transformed into dutiful disciples and exuberant patrons. The authority that the Mongols bestowed upon Sapaṇ and the Khön lineage remained a model for religious and political life in Inner Asia for centuries, referenced for example in the creation of the Dalai Lama institution in the sixteenth century and the rise of the Qing Empire in the seventeenth.

The Sakya-Mongol alliance only grew after the deaths of Sakya Paṇḍita and Köden Ejen in 1251. In 1253, Phakpa and Chakna were summoned to the courts of Qubilai in Qanbaliq, or Dadu, contemporary Beijing.[61] The former was appointed as seventh Sakya Trizin, though still a child and a long way from the safety of Sakya. At the time of their meeting, Qubilai was part of a marginalized branch of the Činggisid lineage who was tasked with managing Mongol-Chinese relations, including settling Daoist-Buddhist disputes.[62] During their relationship, however, Qubilai would rise precipitiously to become supreme qaγan during the apex of the Mongol Empire's sovereignty in Eurasia. Though he was proclaimed qaγan in 1261, he needed to overcome rival branches of the sprawling Činggisid nobility to consolidate his power. In 1271, Qubilai founded the Great Yuan Dynasty (Mong. Yeke Yuwan Ulus), though he did not defeat the remnants of the Song Dynasty until 1279. The Sakya school rose along with the Yuan Dynasty, with Phakpa at the side of its powerful qaγan and his family.

The details of all this are provided by Ameshab below and need not detain us here. Readers will be interested to know that Phakpa wrote several works addressed specifically to the imperial family, including to some of Qubilai's sons whose education he was responsible for, which are now available in English.[63] In the course of Phakpa and Qubilai's evolving relationship, which famously involved three initiations of the imperial family into the Hevajra tantric system, the Yuan dynasty came to administer Tibetan affairs via the Sakya school, including setting up the Bureau for Promoting Governance, or Xuanzheng Yuan. This was in effect a bureau of Buddhist and Tibetan affairs in Dadu, established by Qubilai in 1264.[64] That office, it should be noted, also ties together the lives of the Sakya forefathers described in *The Amazing Treasury* and the quickly changing imperial landscape during Ameshab's time. The Lifan

Yuan, the official administrative office of the Qing Empire to deal with Tibetan and Uyghur (and, early on, Russian) administration and relations, was built explicitly on the model of Qubilai's Xuanzheng Yuan.

Specifically, Sakya lamas like Phakpa and his spiritual heirs (and Khön kinsmen and kinswomen) for generations supported the "golden lineage" (Mong. Altan uraγ) of the Borjigid descendents of Činggis Qan. This was the fuller expression of the so-called unification of Dharma and state (*chos srid zung 'brel*), the aforementioned "Two Systems" (*lugs gnyis*). This became the foundation not only for New Translation institution building and relationality within and outside the Sakya school in the thirteenth to fourteenth centuries, as described above. It was also a dominant model for later Tibetan, Mongol, Chinese, Russian, and Manchu relationality that would bind Buddhist lineages and institutions with political structures and sovereign forms across Inner and East Asia. Two such partnerships were the ascension of the Dalai Lama institution and its Qošud Mongol allies during the lifetime of Ameshab, and the concurrent rise of the Qing Empire that would widely promote the Geluk school for centuries to come.[65]

With Mongolian support, the Sakya Khön family ruled Tibet until the collapse of the Yuan Dynasty in 1368 and the rise of the Phakmodru Dynasty in the middle of the fourteenth century. In that time, several independent lineages and institutions emerged that shared Sakya doctrinal tradition, including the Jonang (Jo nang), which would be widely suppressed following the rise of the Mongol-Geluk alliance that came within decades of *The Amazing Treasury*. Other relevant Sakya-affiliated traditions included the Bodong (Bo dong) and Buluk (Bu lugs, alias Zhwa lu), though a survey of these subtraditions is unfortunately beyond the scope of this introduction.

Ameshab and the Long Seventeenth Century

We now turn to the collapse of the Phakmodru Dynasty in Tibet, who had become patrons of the Sakya, and to the upheaval of Tibetan religious and political life in the seventeenth century. It was during these complex times that a distant heir of Sapaṇ and Phakpa Lama, the Twenty-Seventh Sakya Trizin Ameshab, was tasked with leading the Sakya tradition during another period of Mongol-driven upheaval and transformation in Tibet. Amid all this, Ameshab set ink to paper and wrote *The Amazing Treasury*, a detailed story of his family and Buddhist tradition that by then enfolded Eurasia itself.

Jamgön Ameshab Ngakwang Kunga Sönam was born into the illustrious Khön family in 1597, the Fire Bird Year of the tenth rabjung.[66] His mother was Lhasé Sönam Gyalmo[67] (1567–1613) and his father Ngakchang Drakpa Lodrö (1563–1617),[68] the Twenty-Fifth Sakya Trizin.[69] Ameshab's paternal uncle was the Twenty-Fourth Sakya Trizin, Jamyang Sönam Wangpo.[70] The eldest of Ameshab's two brothers was Jamyang Tutop Wangchuk (1588–1637).[71] The next was Ngakwang Kunga Wangyal (1592–1620),[72] who in 1617 was enthroned as the Twenty-Sixth Sakya Trizin, following their father's death.

As a young boy, Ngakwang Kunga (as he was then known) became a dutiful disciple of his father, with whom he began to study reading and writing. When he was just five or six years old, his father began to bestow upon him the major tantric transmissions of the Sakya school, such as those of the Cakrasaṃvara, Vajrakīlaya, and, of course, Hevajra systems. In addition to his father, Ngakwang Kunga studied various subjects with prominent Sakya masters of the early seventeenth century, including Sönam Palsang[73] and the elderly Thirteenth Ngor Khenchen, Namkha Palsang.[74]

During this youthful tutelage, Ngakwang Kunga developed a reputation for studiousness and a serene demeanor. He was thus nicknamed "grandfather," or *ameshab* in the local Tsangpa dialect. By this he has been known for the last four centuries. Amid a flurry of instruction and transmission, when he was six years old, Ameshab was enthroned at Duchö Labrang (*dus mchod bla brang*), one of what was then four palatial residences at Sakya and the only one to still exist today. When Ameshab was ten years old, he and his brothers were given, among other rarified tantric transmissions, the precious Lamdré initiations and teachings. Within a few years, he entered long-term retreat with his family to cultivate meditative experience of the transmissions he had received. Soon after, when he was eleven years old, Ameshab was ordained first as a layman and then as a novice monk (Skt. *śrāmaṇera*; Tib. *dge tshul*) in the hallowed confines of the Ütsé Temple at Sakya Monastery (*sa skya dbu rtse*).

In 1614, Ameshab became a disciple of the great Muchen Sangyé Gyaltsen (1542–1618).[75] This guru-disciple relationship became one of several competing poles of affiliation and responsibility during Ameshab's illustrious life. At the center of this tension was Ameshab's apparent desire to lead a scholastic and contemplative career as a Buddhist monk and the inflexible requirement that he shoulder his inherited responsibilities, which, most centrally, required him to reproduce the institutional power of Sakya by disrobing and fathering male heirs. He largely pursued the former in the sphere of influence of prominent lamas such as Muchen Sangyé Gyaltsen. Eventually, he turned to the latter under the watchful eye of the Khön family and the administration of Sakya Monastery.

Ameshab's elder brother, Ngakwang Kunga Wangyal, was enthroned as Sakya Trizin in 1617 but held the position for only a short while; he died suddenly in 1620. It was in that year, in grief over his dead brothers and father, that Ameshab was elevated and enthroned as the Twenty-Seventh throne holder of Sakya. In the decades that followed, Ameshab extensively promoted the preservation and transmission of the Sakya school. He also became a confidant and preceptor of the Tsang ruler (Gtsang sde srid) Karma Tenkyong Wangpo (Karma bstan skyong dbang po, 1606-1642), and in that role acted as a public peace builder across multiple military conflicts that led up to the 1642 seige of Shigaste and the disposition of Karma Tenkyong at the hands of the Qošut Mongols and their Geluk allies. While Sakya Monastery itself was not destroyed, power and influence shifted from Shigatse and Sakya in Tsang Province to the newly established Ganden Phodrang government and the institution of the Dalai Lamas in Lhasa, Ü Province.

Four decades after his enthronment, by the time Sakya power passed to Ameshab's son following his death in 1659, not only the Tibetan cultural world but Inner and East Asia generally had been thoroughly remade. As it was for the Mongol Empire in the thirteenth century, one of the primary drivers of this seventeenth-century change was newly centralized and powerful Mongolian confederacies. During Ameshab's lifetime, the Ming Dynasty (1368–1644) that had succeeded the Yuan had been defeated by a coalition of Jurchen (Manchu), Mongol, and Han bannermen. In its ruins, they established the Qing Empire. As mentioned, in 1642 the Tsang-Mongol war concluded with the defeat of the Tsang ruling house, who had been important Sakya patrons. The victorious Qošud Mongols, a branch of the Oirats, elevated the Fifth Dalai Lama, his regents, and the Ganden Potrang government. Opponents of the Dalai Lama's Geluk tradition (and of some branches of the Nyingma school from whose association his claim to power was derived) were widely repressed. The Sakya were largely spared forced conversion and institutional erasure, apparently because of their history with the Mongols, but their support networks were upturned. (The Jonang branch of the Sakya, however, were not so lucky and were thoroughly repressed in Central Tibet).

Ameshab thus died with his tradition splintered, its patronage network in disarray, and the future of the Sakya school uncertain. Likely because of the impoverishment of Sakya after 1642, it was a very long time after Ameshab's death before his *Collected Works* were compiled or printed. While the record is scant, Jan-Ulrich Sobisch argues that "the lack of funds for a certainly expensive carving and printing project [...] was to some degree connected with the [Gelukpa] political hegemony, starting in 1642."[76] In any case, over time Ameshab's life and prodigious scholarly projects were collected and carved into woodblocks, printed, and widely disseminated, very much including his most renowned work: *The Amazing Treasury.*

The Amazing Treasury of the Sakya Lineage

Scattered throughout the text, Ameshab left a few short reflections about his motivation to write the *Amazing Treasury*. For example, in its concluding verses we read:

> I think that long ago, spiritual masters who upheld the Sakya teachings
> occupied themselves when teaching and writing
> in expressing the everlasting good qualities
> of the precious succession lineage of the incomparably kind [Sakya lamas].

> Nowadays, even the intelligent who are otherwise devoted
> are greatly distracted by other activities
> and neglect the collected writings of the previous masters of this tradition.
> Seeing this, I have composed this text.[77]

Earlier in *The Amazing Treasury*, Ameshab shares a little more about his intentions with the text:

> Later, the wisdom of all the Conquerors was unified when Mañjughoṣa himself took form in the Khön family lineage. From then on, the complete teaching and practice of the outer and inner sūtras and tantras were upheld, protected, and increased. Later, they were widely spread. Everywhere across the northern reaches of Jambudvīpa to the shores of the eastern ocean, all beings are completely sustained by an excellent abundance of the Dharma and material well-being. Having become extremely grateful for this marvel, one should understand the great purpose of exerting oneself in explaining and studying the succession of those beings and their enlightened life stories.[78]

As several Sakya monastic scholars reminded us during the translation of this book, *The Amazing Treasury* is defined by its unique reliance upon texts that privilege eyewitness accounts of the events described, or else accounts as near to events as possible. As we shall see below, the sharp critic Ameshab develops his historical points by appraising and comparing major succession histories and other historical materials that came before.

Some of the historical works that readers will see Ameshab using most frequently include: Butön Rinchen Drup's (Bu ston rin chen grub, 1290–1364) *Sakya Succession History* (*Sa skya pa'i gdung rabs*), Taktsang Lotsāwa Sherab Rinchen's (Stag tshang lo tsa ba shes rab rin chen, 1405–77) *Ocean of All Desirables: A Succession History of Sakya* (*Sa skya pa'i gdung rabs 'dod dgu'i rgya mtsho*); Tsang Jampa Dorjé Gyaltsen's (Gtsang byams pa rdo rje rgyal mtshan 1424–98) *Tsang Jampa's Succession History* (*Gtsang byams pa'i gdung rabs*); Ngorchen Könchok Lhundrup's (Ngor chen dkon mchog lhun grub, 1497–1557) *Ornament Adorning the Mouths of the Noble* (*Sa skya pa'i gdung rabs ya rabs kyi kha rgyan*); Nyi Dewa Namkha Palsang's (Nyi lde ba nam mkha' dpal bzang, ca. fourteenth cent.) *Succession History Composed by Nyi Dewa* (*Chos rje nyi lde bas mdzad pa'i gdung rabs*); and Khenchen Sherab Dorjé's (Mkhan chen shes rab rdo rje, ca. fourteenth cent.) *The Direct Disciple Holy Lama Sherab Dorjé's Succession History* (*Bla ma dam pa'i dngos slob shes rab rdo rje'i gdung rabs*).

In the centuries after it was finally published, *The Amazing Treasury* circulated in more than twenty different editions. In time, two later Sakya Trizins composed extensive supplements that extended its story about the Khön and the Sakya beyond Ameshab's seventeenth-century account. The Thirty-First Sakya Trizin, Ngakwang Kunga Sönam Drakpa (r. 1741–83), composed the *Supplement to the Amazing Treasury of the Precious Sakya Lineage* (*Gdung rabs rin chen bang mdzod kyi kha skong*). And then in the twentieth century, the Thirty-Ninth Sakya Trizin, Drakshul Trinlé Rinchen (r. 1915–36), composed the *Extra Supplement to the Amazing Treasury of the Precious Sakya Lineage* (*Gdung rabs rin chen bang mdzod yang skor*). Together, these two texts are equally vital reference works on not only the Sakya tradition, but also on Inner Asian Buddhism generally, through the complex upheavals of the eighteenth to twentieth centuries. The translators hope at some point to also make these two supplements available in English.

Our translation of volume 1 has been done in consultation with several editions of the Tibetan text. To aid readers who may wish to consult the Tibetan original, throughout the translation we have provided pagination to one specific edition of the *Amazing Treasury* that is widely available in North American and European research libraries. Those page numbers appear in square brackets at the exact word in which a new page begins in the Tibetan. The Library of Congress has catalogued that edition as follows: Ṅag-dbaṅ-kun-dga' -bsod-nams, 'Jam-mgon A-myes-zabs, *'Dzam gliṅ byaṅ phyogs kyi Thub pa'i rgyal tshab chen po Dpal ldan Sa skya pa'i gduṅ rabs rin po che ji ltar byon pa'i tshul gyi rnam par thar pa ṅo tshar rin po che'i baṅ mdzod dgos 'dod kun 'byuṅ* (Delhi; Tashi Dorji; Dolanji, H.P.: Tibetan Bonpo Monastic Centre, 1975).

In summary, Ameshab's *Amazing Treasury*—a work that more than any other documents and celebrates the literary traces of the Sakya's Golden Age—was written in the twilight of Sakya position and influence. Between 1640 and the Tibetan refugee exodus of the 1950s and 1960s, the Sakya school experienced a steep descent in institutional power, though certainly not matched by a decline in the rigor of its scholastic and contemplative traditions. As such, *The Amazing Treasury*, like all histories, must be read not as a final account of history "as it was," but as a representation of the past serving the needs and interests of authors and readers in the present: whether of Ameshab's tumultuous seventeenth century, or of the Sakya school today, which is once again thriving as a truly global tradition, thanks to the leadership of the last three Sakya Trizins and all the Dungsé. It is to their long lives, and to the next chapter of the Sakya school, that this translation is dedicated!

The Wondrous Precious Treasury Fulfilling All Wishes

Biographies of the Precious Lineage of the Glorious Sakya, the Great Regents of the Buddha in the North of Jambudvīpa

Part 1

Jamgön Ameshab Ngakwang
Kunga Sönam

Translated by
Khenpo Kunga Sherab and Matthew King

Offering of Veneration

[2] The Sanskrit title: *Śrīvāṃbhūmipaṇdos madgurudharmasya svamī sarvasatvānām śāstānuttarebhyo anusārikamayābhīkṣṇapraṇamāmi.*

The Tibetan title: *Palden sakyapai lama dampa chökyi jé semchen tamchékyi tönpa lanamepa namla jésu drangwa dak yangyang chak gyi.*[79]

To the holy lamas of the glorious Sakyapa, Lords of the Dharma, unsurpassable teachers for all sentient beings: I follow you and make prostrations again and again!

> Unobscured wisdom surveying each of the limitless fields of knowledge,
> minds moistened by loving-kindness toward the numberless sentient beings without exception,
> and marvelous deeds capable of overcoming the vast, immeasurable armies of Māra's hordes:
> victory to the lamas who are gods among gods, inseparable from such supreme deities as inconceivable Mañjughoṣa and Sarasvastī!

> O' you learned ones renowned as supreme upholders of the Lord of Subduer's teachings,
> refuge of northerly sentient beings, offering the supreme protection of wisdom, love, and power,
> the lineage that returns again and again as emanations of the eminent lords of the Three Families:

to the succession of the stainless lineage, with devotion I pay homage!

That supreme deity with five knotted hairlocks of blue utpala,
manifested as luminous gods appearing in such guises
as the immortal three siblings, the four divine sons, and the seven siblings of Masang[80]:
to the emanated actors of the divine lineage such as these, I offer whatsoever suitable praise!

In inner aspect, vajra holders named "Khön" bearing malice toward ignorance;
in outer aspect, widely renowned [4] as "Khön" with malice toward demons;
bearing the supreme meaning of the name "Khön," stainless descendants of the Khön teachers:
to those highest of beings who are lords of Khön, adepts of secret mantra, I pay homage![81]

To the enlightened activities of the Sakya, like rays of the sun,[82]
arisen elegantly out of the gray earth of the mountainside,
whose renown as the "Sakyapa" shines brightly everywhere:
I pay devotion from my heart to the Exalted Ones of the Sakyapa![83]

After drawing near to the lotus feet of those great beings,
formidably powerful rulers then relied upon them.[84]
At that time, like the pairing of the sun and moon in the sky here upon earth,
they were likewise renowned as "patronized and patron."

Even so, on occasion a few of their kinsmen with deranged minds
engaged in all manner of disturbing and shameful behavior

and disrupted the teachings, doctrine holders, and monasteries of the Sakya;
so many actions revealing the signs of our degenerate age.

E ma! How wonderful!—At that time, emanated bodies of the mantra holders—
E ma! How wonderful!—used miraculous powers beyond all conception—
E ma! How wonderful!—to overcome the demonic maras, and from this rekindled—
E ma! How wonderful!—the teachings of glorious Sakya from extinguished embers.

To he who performed such immeasurably kind acts,
the mantra holder Lama Kunga Rinchen,
and to his heart disciples, the Mañjuśrī siblings:[85]
from the depths of my heart, respectfully I pay homage with my palms pressed together!

Specifically, to the mantra holder supreme regent,
the great bodhisattva who is the beautifying ornament of Jambudvīpa,
the father of the infinite conquerors without exception [Sachen Kunga Nyingpo]:
to he who is endowed with immeasurable kindness, respectfully I pay homage.

The Promise to Compose and Advice on Study

I will explain this great jewel treasury
of the marvelous life stories of the lineage succession [5] of the Sakyapa,
supreme regents of the Sage in northern Jambudvīpa:
those with a sincere interest, joyfully draw near and listen!

Following this expression of veneration and the promise to compose comes advice on study. [5]

Herein is *The Wondrous Precious Treasury Fulfilling All Wishes: Biographies of the Precious Lineage of the Glorious Sakya, the Great Regents of the Buddha in the North of Jambudvīpa.* It is explained in five sections:

1. Explanation of the lineage succession from the luminous gods
2. Explanation of the lineage succession of the stainless Khön
3. Explanation of the lineage succession of the celestial Khön of Sakya
4. Explanation of the lineage succession of the division of the four lama residences
5. Explanation of other relevant topics

Part 1
Explanation of the Lineage Succession from the Luminous Gods

The first section, the explanation of the lineage succession from the luminous gods, has two parts:

1. A brief explanation given in verse
2. An extensive explanation upon the meaning of those verses

Fig. 1. Chiring

As for the first, it is taken from the scholar Könchok Lhundrup's[86] *Ornament Adorning the Mouths of the Noble: The Lineage Succession of the Sakya*[87]:

> The lineage of glorious Sakyapa, emanations of Mañjughoṣa,
> came originally from the realm of divine luminosity
> and appeared as three brothers: Chiring, Yuring, and Yusé.[88]
> Yusé reigned as lord of humans and bore four sons.

Yuring, [Yusé's] elder brother, emerged as his ally.
The sons of Yuring and his wife Musa Dembu[89]
became known as "the seven siblings of the good mother."
The six eldest of those brothers, along with their father,
departed for the celestial realms.

The youngest of the seven, named Masang Chijé,[90]
And his wife, Tokcham Urmo,[91] had a son named Pawo [6]
Tak.[92]
He and his wife, Lucham Drama,[93] later bore a son
who was named Lutsa Takpo Öchen.[94]

Lutsa resided with Mönsa Tsomogyal,[95] and they bore a son
into their mantra lineage[96]
at the juncture of a rocky and a grass-covered mountain.[97]
For that reason, the boy was named Yapang Kyé,[98]
and he became famous as a hero inviolable by others.

As for the second part, "the extensive explanation upon the meaning of the above verses," it is as follows: In general, the Dharma kings and bodhisattvas who were manifestations of the Lords of the Three Families newly established the Conqueror's teachings in the Land of Snow, which were previously unknown there. The three—Tsang [Rapsel], Yo [Gejung], and Mar [Shakyamuné][99]—along with the preceptor lineage of Lachen [Gongpa Rabsel][100] restored [the Dharma in Tibet] after a period of degeneration.[101]

[The Dharma] was widely spread [in Tibet] by such figures as: the devoted royal uncle and nephew [Lama Yeshé Ö and Lhatsün Jangchup Ö];[102] the Jowo master [Atiśa] and disciple [Dromtönpa];[103] the three Drok[mi Śākya Yeshé], Gö [Khupa Lhetsé],[104] and Mar[pa Lotsāwa Chökyi Lodrö];[105] Pa[tsap Lotsāwa Nyima Drakpa], Ngok [Lotsāwa Loden Sherab], and Khyung [Rinchen Drak];[106] and Ra [Lotsāwa Dorjé Drakpa] and Dro [Lotsāwa Sherab Drakpa].[107] Though indeed this was true, for the most part this amounted to a transmission of sūtra and only a partial transmission of mantra.

Later, the wisdom of all the Conquerors was unified when Mañjughoṣa

Fig. 2. Yuring

himself took form within the Khön succession lineage. From then on, the complete teaching and practice of the outer and inner sūtras and tantras increased and was upheld and protected. Later, it was widely spread. Everywhere, across the northern reaches of Jambudvīpa to the shores of the eastern ocean, all beings became completely sustained by the excellent abundances of the Dharma and material well-being. Having become extremely grateful for this marvel, one should understand the great purpose [7] of exerting oneself in explaining and studying the succession lineage of those beings and their liberated life stories.

Regarding their hereditary line (*rigs*), a brāhmaṇa caste never existed in Tibet. Even so, instances of a royal caste, a merchant caste, and a caste of commoners did indeed exist here.[108] From among them, the Zhang ministers (*zhang blon*) were of the merchant caste. We must correctly identify the famed [Khön] Könpa Jé Gungtak[109] as the progenitor of their human lineage. The paternal descendants of their bone lineage,[110] moreover, did not originate from among the famous four great clans or the six human tribes of Tibet.[111] They were, instead, a lineage descended from the immaculate gods of the celestial realms.

It was in reality Mañjuśrī himself who manifested as the famous celestial divine siblings Chiring, Yuring, and Yusé[112] in order to tame beings. From another perspective, however, those three are considered emanations in the lineage of the deities of celestial luminosity. They descended to the human realm, where they were requested to become sovereigns.

Fig. 3. Yusé

As a result, Yusé, the youngest of the celestial siblings, was made ruler of humans. It is well-known that he had four sons, who together became known as the "Sijilé siblings."[113] They, in turn, came to fight against the eighteen great Dong clans.[114] The middle celestial sibling, Yuring, arrived to help his comrade [Yusé]. They together conquered the Dong and then enslaved them. This middle celestial sibling, Yuring, took as his wife a daughter of the Mu clan[115] named Musa Dembu.[116] Together they bore seven sons who became well known as the "seven brothers of Masang."

Fig. 4. Masang Chijé

Fig. 5. Pawo Tak

That being so, the six eldest of the seven brothers, along with their father, departed to the god realms. The seventh son, named Masang Chijé,[117] remained in the human realm. He later took as his wife Tokcham Urmo,[118] the daughter of Toklha Öchen.[119] They bore a son who became well known as Toktsa Pawo Tak.[120] He, in turn, married the daughter of a nāga named Lucham Drama.[121] Lutsa Takpo Öchen[122] was born as their son. It is said [8] that all those before him departed to dwell in the

Fig. 6. Takpo Öchen

celestial realms. Lutsa took Mönsa Tsomo Gyal as his wife.[123] A son was born to them at the border of Ya and Pang. This was very rare indeed,

Fig. 7. Yapang Kyé (ca. eighth cent.)

and so he was named Yapang Kyé, "Born Between Rock and Grass."[124] They resided together upon a beautiful peak among all the high northern mountains to the northwest of Yeru Shang.[125] That mountain is also well known by the name Yapang.[126]

This concludes the explanation of the lineage succession from the luminous gods. With this account:

> The supreme deity, venerable Mañjuśrī, elegantly arose
> as an emanation body in order to be perceived by others and
> by which to benefit them.
> It is said that whosoever explains this wondrous true story,
> detailing their excellent origins and descent, is truly
> resplendent!

So goes the intermediary verse.

Part 2
Explanation of the Lineage Succession of the Stainless Khön

[This section is in two parts:]

1. A brief explanation given in verse
2. An extensive explanation upon the meaning of those verses

As for the first, the *Ornament Adorning the Mouths of the Noble: The Lineage Succession of the Sakya* describes what occurred up to the time of Yapang Kyé and immediately thereafter:

> Yapang Kyé killed the demon Kyareng the Bloodless[127]
> and kidnapped his consort Yadrum Silima[128]
> so that she would become his wife.
> They bore a son who became well known as Khön Barkyé.[129]
> He, in turn, bore a son with Tsensa Chambu Drön.[130]
> His beauty and intelligence had rarely been seen before
> among humans
> and he was named Könpa Jegungtak.[131]
> He became known as Khön Tön Palpoché[132] and later traveled
> to Nyentsé.[133]
> Palpoché and Langsa Nechung[134] had four sons
> named Trizé, Lhalek, Tselha [9] Wangchuk,
> and the supremely knowledgeable Luyi Wangpo Tsezin.[135]

[Commentary:][136] As we see in this explanation from the *Ornament Adorning the Mouths of the Noble*, one tradition claims that Khön Palpoché had four sons. A different tradition claims he had only two sons, named

Lui Wangpo and Dorjé Rinchen.[137] Here, I follow the second tradition and provide greater detail below.

> Tsezin's son was Dorjé Rinpoché.

[Commentary:] Some lineage succession texts, including Könchok Lhundrup's verses, among others, claim that Khön Dorjé Rinchen was Tsezin's son. However, these mistakenly follow [spelling] errors in Jetsun [Drakpa Gyaltsen] Rinpoché's biography of Sachen [Kunga Nyingpo]. Others assert that Dorjé Rinpoché was the younger brother of Lui Wangpo.[138] They follow authentic texts, such as Jetsun Rinpoché's lineage succession of the Khön as well as [Drakpa Gyaltsen's letter to] Garing Gyalpo[139] on the comparative study of dates and numeration.[140] In these pages, I follow this latter interpretation.

> Dorjé Rinpoché married queen Drosa Yalön Kyé.[141]
> She gave birth to the seven Drotsa siblings,[142]
> most of whom departed to various regions to benefit sentient beings,
> but the sixth, Tatak Sherab Yönten,[143] went off to Drompa.[144]
> Later came Yönten Jungné, Tsultrim Gyal,
> Tsuktor Sherab, Gekyab, Getong,
> Khön Tön Belpo, and Shākya Lodrö[145]:
> following in order, each of these is the father to the next.
> Shakya Lodrö had two sons: the elder was named
> Sherab Tsultrim and the younger Könchok Gyalpo.[146]
> Up to the former, they practiced secret mantra according to the Old School.

Second, "an extensive explanation of the meaning of those verses": That great hero known as Ya Pangkyé fought and then killed the demon named Kyareng the Bloodless [10] who had an exceptionally beautiful consort named Yadrum Silima. Yapang Kyé took her as his wife and together they bore a son. Because he was born (*kyé*) from the enmity (*khön*) between (*bar*) a demon and a god, he was named Yatruk Khön

Barkyé.[147] The name "Khön" arose in this family lineage in that way, very much like the story of the Śākya clan.

Fig. 8. Khön Barkyé (ca. eighth cent.)

Mother and son dwelled upon a very beautiful and soaring mountain named Sheltsa Gyalmö Gang,[148] surrounded by a great range of snow mountains to the northwest of Yapang. There was also a Sakyapa spirit lake[149] to the south of Yapang. Furthermore, it is said that when the luminous celestial gods first came to the human realm, they alighted on the peak of Sheltsa Gyalmö Gang. This is according to the oral tradition of Ngakchang Chökyi Gyalpo,[150] about which I heard directly from my lama, Mañjuśrī, and his brother.[151] Some other lineage histories mention that they descended upon the elevated and unsoiled earth of Ngari.[152]

Khön Barkyé, that child of the gods, would marry Tsensa Chambu Drön.[153] A superior being was born to them who possessed power and magical ability, clear awareness and sharp intelligence, and bodily splendor. He had a charisma[154] that captivated everyone. Such a being is found but rarely (*kön*) among humans, and so he was named Könpa Jé Gungtak. He was sent off to find his own dwelling place and discovered that land at Samyé[155] was endowed with the ten excellent qualities. That land, however, was owned already by a king. He then determined that Ya Chang, in Latö Nyentsé Tar, possessed eight excellent qualities and so he took ownership of it. Moreover, as for the eight excellent qualities: [11] the excellent earth was parceled into great and small valleys, ideal for cultivation and house building. The excellent water of its vast lakes and waterways was ideal for drinking and irrigation. The excellent trees in the Gunta and Gunmuk forests[156] were ideal for house beams and firewood. The excellent grasslands of Targyi Yachang,[157] with its fine grazing pastures, was ideal for the [nomads closer to the city known as] Gamdrok, as well as [for those more distant nomads called] Gyangdrok.[158]

Regarding the ten excellent qualities of land, Taktsang Lotsāwa [Sherab Rinchen][159] has mentioned that in addition to the eight described above, some claim that one may add the good qualities of pathways across mountain ridges and navigable waterways in lower valleys. These two, however, are good qualities of the beings within an environment,[160] and so he argues that it is incorrect to include them. More properly in accord with the other eight, which are each good qualities of the environment itself,[161] [Taktsang Lotsāwa] adds the excellent qualities of stones, which are ideal for house foundations and for millstones. It is exceedingly difficult to find deposits of these two types of stones together in any given place, since usually wherever one is found, the other is absent. For this reason, to find these ten excellent qualities of land together in their entirety is extremely difficult.

Fig. 9. Khön Palpoché (ca. eighth–ninth cent.)

This lord [Könpa Jé Gungtak] had a close relationship with the Dharma King of Samyé, Trisong Detsen,[162] who appointed him as an inner minister. Thereafter, his wealth grew plentifully and so he became widely known as Khön Palwo Ché, "Khön with Great Wealth."[163] So began the fame of the Khön family name.

Khön Palwo Ché would marry Lang Khampa Lotsāwa's sister,[164] Langsa Nechungma,[165] to whom two sons were born. The eldest was named Lui Wangpo Sungwa, translator of the Khön, and the youngest was named Khön Dorjé Rinpoché.[166] It is written in Jetsun Drakpa Gyaltsen's biography of Sachen that among the three youngest of the seven translators for testing[167] was a very learned man named Khön Lui Wangpo. Some other lineage histories record that this younger brother was just an ordinary person, and that it was in fact his son who became known as Dorjé Rinpoché [12] with all these wonderful qualities. Some lineage histories follow this version of events, including *The Ornament*

Fig. 10. Khön Lui Wangpo
(ca. eighth–ninth cent.)

Adorning the Mouths of the Noble, the *Lineage Succession of Nyidé*, the *Lineage Succession of Müsé*, *Illuminating the Wondrous*, and so forth.[168] In them, [it is written that Dorjé Rinpoché had four sons] named Trizé Lhalek, Tselha Wangchuk, Lui Wangpo, and Tsezin.[169] Some other histories have Tsezin and Dorjé Rinchen as the same person.[170] Still other histories[171]—like *The Ornament Adorning the Mouths of the Noble*, *Illuminating the Wondrous*, and *The Lineage Succession of Tsang Jampa*[172]—make many different claims about them, such as that they were father and son. In *The Lineage Succession of the Khön*, Jetsun [Drakpa Gyaltsen] Rinpoché wrote:

> He who was named the Protector Khön Lui Wangpo was counted among the seven men to be tested. His younger brother, Khön Dorjé Rinpoché, was a disciple of Master Padmasambhava who lived as a tāntrika.

According to the Great Omniscient One's *Clarifying the Intention of the Discourses,*[173] both Lhopa Kunkhyen and Dewa Chenpa Yeshé Gönpo[174] accept that Dorjé Rinpoché should be identified as Lui Wangpo's younger brother. This is also, moreover, recorded in a few elaborate lineage histories, such as Taktsang's work and that of the direct disciple of Lama Dampa [Sönam Gyaltsen] Sherab Dorjé, as well as in a great many minor histories.

Fig. 11. Khön Dorjé Rinchen
(ca. eighth–ninth cent.)

Jetsun Drakpa Gyaltsen's biography of Lama Sachen clarifies that the phrase "that ordinary younger brother" is in reference to Dorjé Rinchen, who was the son of Lui Wangpo. If that is so, we would have to accept that Tsezin was ordinary but that his son was not. In that case, we would be required to distinguish between what is and is not "ordinary," but this is an exceedingly difficult task. [13] Taking all this into consideration, we must explain the phrase "an ordinary younger brother" as either a typographical error or else a claim that Lui Wangpo's younger brother was born to an ordinary mother, yet still possessed a wealth of excellent qualities and was named Dorjé Rinchen. However, in both Jetsun Drakpa Gyaltsen's *Lineage Succession* and his letter to Garing Gyalpo comparing the enumeration of dates, he refers to Dorjé Rinchen as Lui Wangpo's younger brother. It is impossible, moreover, for the holy speech of the Jetsun to be marked by any internal contradiction. And so, for that reason, Ngakchang Chökyi Gyalpo and his spiritual sons came to accept the view of the great Sakya translators that Dorjé Rinchen was indeed the younger brother of Lui Wangpo.

Moving along, let us come to Lui Wangpo Sungpa.[175] The great scholar-adept from Zahor in eastern India, the glorious benefactor of the Land of Snows, the mahāpaṇḍita Śāntarakṣita,[176] investigated whether it would be suitable or not for Tibetans to ordain as novice monks.[177] Seeing that it would indeed be suitable, he permitted such ordination to proceed in Tibet. Among the seven emanated beings who were extraordinary translators and who became known as the seven men to be tested, the first to receive *pravrajitaḥ* ordination in Tibet, were three elder, three younger, and one middling candidate. The second of the three youngest was Khön Nāgendrarakṣita, or "Lui Wangpo Sungpa" in Tibetan.[178]

Some claim that Lui Wangpo received his novice vows from his uncle.[179] This, however, contradicts the assertion that he should be counted among the men to be tested. As for the rationale of the terms "men to be tested" in the phrase "seven men to be tested," the Great Abbot Śāntarakṣita tested whether it would be suitable to ordain monastics in Tibet. Determining that it would be, he ordained them in his presence, and it is said [14] that they became Tibet's first Buddhist monks. Lang Khampa Lotsāwa was the middling one among the seven men to be tested. He was, however, also known by the name Deshek Gocha Sungpa.[180] If [Khön Lui Wangpo] received his novice vows from [Lang Khampa Lotsāwa], he would not have been among those ordained in Śāntarakṣita's presence. We must, however, accept that he was indeed among the seven men to be tested.[181] For this reason, it is correct to say that he became a lineage holder of the Great Abbot's monastic vows.

Lui Wangpo received a great many teachings from both the Great Abbot and his uncle. He developed superb knowledge in the art of translation. He also received oral instructions from the great master Padmasambhava. He pursued his meditation practice at Yerpai Drak[182] and

Fig. 12. Khön Sherab Yönten (ca. ninth cent.)

there accomplished realization. He became a famous scholar-adept and was the first great Dharma practitioner of the Khön lineage.

His younger brother, Dorjé Rinpoché, also listened to and studied many of the old mantric teachings from Master Padmasambhava. He, too, attained some realizations and developed a name for himself. Back in his father's homeland, he married Dro Dradul's daughter named

Fig. 13. Khön Yönten Jungné (ca. ninth cent.)

Drosa Yanglön Kyi, and together they had seven sons.[183] Their uncle being from a lineage of Tibetan athletes, they all became very skilled in their uncle's sports. On one occasion, a three-day athletic festival was

Fig. 14. Khön Tsültrim Gyalpo (ca. ninth–tenth cent.)

held at Drok Nyentsé.[184] All seven brothers entered the competition, changing their horses and their clothing each day. On the first day, they rode white horses and wore white cloaks; on the second day, they rode red horses and wore red cloaks; on the third day, they rode black horses and wore black cloaks; and they competed in all the horse races. The villagers gathered for the spectacle. Their uncle became upset, believing they were challenging him, and so he gathered an army to attack them.

Fig. 15. Khön Tsuktor Sherab (ca. tenth cent.)

In response, the brothers said: "In the first place, he is our uncle. In the second place, we have been neighbors for a long time. In addition,

Fig. 16. Khön Gekyab (c. tenth century)

[15] there is no reason to bring violence to the entire kingdom!" The eldest son then departed for Ngari Mangyul.[185] The next eldest went to Ngari Gungthang.[186] The next eldest left for Sé,[187] the next eldest for Nyal Loro,[188] and the fifth eldest for Nyang Shab.[189] In time, the brothers would rule over these regions. From their progeny, many branches of the

Fig. 17. Khön Getong (c. tenth cent.)

Khön family would spread widely, but none attained much renown. The youngest remained in his homeland. He also fought against the Dro. At

Nyentsé, his sons became known as the three groups of Matrik.[190] The sixth son, Sherab Yönten,[191] resided at Drompa Yalung.[192] The youngest

Fig. 18. Khön Tön Balpo (c. tenth cent.)

of his two sons went to Khabso Taktok.[193] The upper north Khön lineage spread from him. The older son, Yönten Jungné,[194] held the Dharma lineage of his fathers and ancestors. He had three sons, from among whom Tsultrim Gyalpo[195] settled at Drompa[196] and nurtured disciples there by

Fig. 19. Khön Shākya Lodrö (c. eleventh cent.)

means of the Dharma. He in turn had three sons, from among whom the middle one departed for Delchang Tsang.[197] His eldest son was named Tsuktor Sherab,[198] while his youngest son resided at Yalung.[199]

Tsuktor Sherab had seven sons of his own, and those seven plus his younger brother became famous altogether as the "assembly of the eight Khön." The fifth of the seven sons was named Khön Gekyab.[200] He went to Chishab[201] and had two sons. All of those who became known as the "Khön of Upper Shab"[202] are descendants of the youngest of those sons. The elder son, named Getong,[203] bore only one son. He was named Khön Tön Belpo and meditated upon Viśuddha Heruka and Vajrakīlaya[204] at the craggy mountain called Tsamo Rong.[205] He obtained siddhi,[206] and the twelve Tenma goddesses became his personal attendants. Khön Tön Belpo had a son named Shākya Lodrö,[207] who captured Jaru Valley [16] along with upper and lower Shab.[208] He became famous for his remarkable Dharma activities in those regions. Late in life, he came to rule his father's homeland, Yalung Khartab,[209] and there had two sons. The eldest was named Khön Rok Sherab Tsultrim and the youngest Khön Könchok Gyalpo.[210] In his youth, the elder brother received the gōmi upāsakā lay vows[211] from Shutön Tsöndrü,[212] abbot of Lotön Dorjé Wangchuk.[213] Thereafter, he kept pure conduct and so bore no children. He became well versed in the Dharma of his father and ancestors. He accomplished the siddhi of Vajrakīlaya and became famous for his unimaginable power and miraculous abilities.

In this way, the Khön ancestors up to the time of Sherab Tsultrim were somewhat knowledgeable in a few philosophical traditions, such as those of the Perfection Vehicle.[214] They were extremely knowledgeable in the secret mantra systems of the Earlier Translation School,[215] including the six sections of newly translated tantras, the five early translations, the thirteen later translations, and the twenty-one subsequent translations. Many of them intensely practiced the essence of the Viśuddha Heruka[216] and Vajrakīlaya[217] tantric systems and achieved realizations. They also practiced devotions to the Dharma protectors Karmo Nyida and Dügön,[218] and all of them attained supernormal powers.[219]

With this, the explanation of the lineage succession of the stainless Khön is complete.

The powerful Khöntön, with malice against ignorance:
coming to see the manner of their elegant procession,
a rosary of jewel-like lineal succession,
who could not but realize that this is a marvelous, astonishing subject!

So goes the intermediary verse.

Part 3
The Celestial Family of the Khön Sakyapa Lineage

This has two parts:

1. A brief explanation in verse
2. An extensive [17] explanation of the meaning of those verses.

As for the first, it is said in *The Ornament Adorning the Mouths of the Noble: A History of the Sakya Lineage*:

> Up until the life of the eldest of the two siblings, Khön Rok Sherab Tsultrim and his brother, [the Khön] practiced the secret mantra of the Old Translation School.

Immediately after providing a description, the following explanatory verses are given:

> His younger brother promoted the New Translation system
> and founded Sakya.[220]
> He and Shangmo Sönam Kyi[221] had a son
> renowned as Sakya's Great Lama, Kunga Nyingpo.[222]
> That great lama and his first wife, Jo Cham Purmo from
> Tsharong,[223]
> had a son named Kunga Bar.[224]
> Kunga Nyingpo's second wife, Jo Cham Ö Drön,[225] had three
> sons
> named Lopön Tsemo, Jetsun Drakpa, and Palchen Öpo.[226]
> Pelchen Öpo's wife, Nyitri Cham from Garpu,[227]
> bore two sons: Sakya Paṇchen and Sangtsa Sönam Gyaltsen.[228]

Sangtsa's first wife, Machik Kunkyi from Doktö Tsana,[229]
bore two sons: Phakpa and Drogön Chakna Dorjé.[230]
Sangtsa's second wife, Jodrö from Sakya's Chu Do,[231]
bore a son named Lopön Ringyal.[232]
The son of Sangtsa's third wife, Machik Dorjé Dén,[233]
was the great master Yeshé Jungné.[234]
Drogön Chakna's wife, Machik Khandro Bum from Shalu,[235]
bore a son named Dharmapāla.
Dharmapāla and his wife, Tak Bum,[236]
had a son named Ratnābhadrā, who died as a child.
Yeshé Jungné's wife, Machik Chösin Kyi from Khabmé,[237]
bore a son named Mahātmā.[238]

Secondly, "an extensive explanation of the meaning of these verses." Khönrok [18] Sherab Tsultrim's younger brother, Khön Könchok Gyalpo,[239] was known as the first Khön Sakyapa. He was born in the Wood Male Dog Year (1034). Beginning in his youth, he received many initiations, teachings, and quintessential instructions from his father and brother. He trained diligently to master the Dharma of his forefathers. Though he was dedicated to the secret mantra of the New Translation School, he went to the great festival of Drölung.[240] Among the various performances there, in one he watched many tantric practitioners wearing the masks of the twenty-eight Wangchukma.[241] They held the individual hand implements and danced about in the wrathful manner of female deities with matted hair. Theirs was the best performance and the most popular, since a large crowd gathered around to watch.

He related all this to his brother, who responded, "It is now coming to pass that secret mantra is being misused! In the future, it will be very rare indeed for there to be any fully qualified and accomplished masters of the secret mantra of the Old Translation systems! I am in control of my possessions, and so I will now hide away my texts and three supports in the treasury." With these words, he did so. However, because the Dharma protectors Yangdak Heruka and Phurpa Dorjé Shönu were so very powerful, he was unable to hide [his ritual texts]. It is for that reason that the future lineage holders of [Sakya] continually practiced the sādhanas of these two deities, and that on regular occasions they made torma offerings to the Dharma protector Karmo Nyida Chamsing.[242]

Later, his brother told him, "I am becoming old, but you are still young. As such, you should train in the secret mantra of the New Translation system. Moreover, nowadays Drokmi Shakya Yeshé[243] is very knowledgeable in this, and so you should go and study with him." With these words, Könchok Gyalpo departed. He requested the initiation of Hevajra and commentary from Khyin Lotsāwa.[244] However, Khyin Lotsāwa passed away before he could receive the complete cycle of teachings on this tantra. Before he died, Khyin Lotsāwa told Könchok Gyalpo, "You should request the remaining teachings from [19] Drokmi." [Könchok Gyalpo] then took his leave to follow those instructions exactly.

[After he had made his request, Drokmi] told him: "Since your father passed away, are you now appropriately following after your grandfather?" Saying this, he became very happy. Later, [Könchok Gyalpo] sold his fields and bought seventeen horses with the profits. To provide grass for them, he offered up a jeweled rosary. Because he had requested the precious teachings (of Lamdré), he received instructions on a few of its

Fig. 20. Khön Konchok Gyalpo (1034–1102)

ancillary paths. Specifically, he received extensive explanations of the three tantras. Among [Drokmi's] five great sons who upheld his commentary transmission, [Könchok Gyalpo] became the supreme one.

In addition, he heard teachings on the *Guhyasamāja Tantra* cycle from

Gö Lotsāwa [Shönu Pal].[245] From the paṇḍita of Uḍḍiyāna, Sherab Sangwa,[246] he received teachings on the cycle of the Five Nectars.[247] From Ma Lotsāwa,[248] he received teachings on the *Cakrasaṃvara Tantra*, on the essence of its practice, and so forth. Furthermore, from a great many holy lamas—such as Mal Lotsāwa [Lodrö Drakpa]; Bari Lotsāwa [Rinchen Drak]; Puhrang Lotsāwa; Nam Khaupa and his brother, Khön Gyichuwa; and Kyura Aseng[249]—he received innumerable teachings on bodhicitta, empowerments, commentaries, and quintessential instructions. As a result, he became lord of all the tantras of the New and Old Translation systems.

[Könchok Gyalpo] later built outer supports[250] for his deceased father and brother at Shangyul Jakshong.[251] Therein he installed blessed phurba daggers made of *sengdeng* wood. In Drabo Lung,[252] he built a small monastery and resided there a few years. Later, this monastery became known as Sakya Gokpo.[253]

During this period, this master and his disciples departed on a picnic. Gazing from atop a mountain pass, Mount Pönpo[254] appeared to him as if it were reclining elephant. He discerned a small cavern on its right slope, which appeared extremely white and shiny to him. Seeing this mountain marked by a great many auspicious and beneficial signs, such as water coursing down the right slope, he thought, "If I build a monastery there, it will greatly benefit the Buddha's teachings and sentient beings." [20]

[Könchok Gyalpo] beseeched Jowo Dong Nakpa,[255] the lord of that general area, for permission to build a monastery there, which was granted. The individual local owners of that land were Shang Shung Gurawa, Bandé Drong Shi, and Lhami Drong Dun.[256] He said to them, "I wish to build a monastery there. If there are no disagreements among you, I will compensate you. It would be wonderful if you would give me this land." They told him that he need not pay them and offered him the land. The lama insisted, telling them, "It will be better in the future [for me to pay you]." He gave them one white mare, a jewel rosary, women's garments, and so on. Then all the land from below Mön Drok[257] to above Bal Drok[258] became the property of the lama.

Glorious Sakya Monastery, the Bodhgayā of Tibet, was constructed when this lama was forty years old, in the two-hundred-and-seventh year of the seventh of the ten five-hundred-year periods of the Buddha's teachings, known as "the period of Abhidharma," during the waxing moon of the eighth month of the Water Female Ox Year [1073 CE].

Up to and including Khön Könchok Gyalpo, the succession of this lineage is known as the "celestial family of the Khön Sakyapa."

Fig. 21. Sachen Kunga Nyingpo (1092–1158)

1. Sachen Kunga Nyingpo (1092–1158)

Concerning the story of [Könchok Gyalpo's] son: When Jowo Lhachik's [i.e., Atiśa Dīpaṃkaraśrījñāna][259] student, the bodhisattva monk otherwise known as Jinpa Pal,[260] was in the intermediate state (*bar srid*), he appeared in a vision to Nam Khaupa [Darma Sengé][261] as Avalokiteśvara in the aspect of Khasarpāṇi.[262] Nam Khaupa knew that Könchok Gyalpo's older wife, Dorjé Chukmo, had never produced an heir to the Khön line. And, further, he understood that there was an auspicious connection that bound Könchok Gyalpo to Machik Shangmo.[263] He therefore advised Khön Könchok Gyalpo that this [21] path of skillful means would be sufficient. It came auspiciously to fruition, and the bardo being Avalokiteśvara took up residence in Machik Shangmo's womb. That child became renowned as the great exalted one of the Sakya, Kunga Nyingpo, the supreme crown ornament of all vajra holders in the Land of Snows.

Furthermore, as for how the great Nam Khaupa arranged the auspicious circumstances for the birth of Khön Könchok Gyalpo's lineage heir (*gdung sras*): At that time, at Khau Kyé Lhé Monastery,[264] the Venerable Lord of Siddhas, "Victory Banner of the Dharma" [Nam Khaupa], abided in single-pointed meditation upon clear light.[265] In a vision, he saw a bardo being appearing in the sky over Kargong Lung[266] under a tent of coiled rainbow light. He was in the aspect of Avalokiteśvara Khasarpāṇi, with one face and two arms. His right hand was held in the mudrā of supreme generosity. His left clasped an utpala flower between the thumb and ring fingers. He was draped with silk and jewels. He stood with his two feet together, side by side. [Lama Khaupa] beheld all as if by direct perception. Later, when reflecting upon this vision, he understood that an actual incarnation of Avalokiteśvara would soon appear.

To establish the necessary auspicious circumstances for this to occur, Venerable Khaupa began repeatedly requesting Khön Könchok Gyalpo, who then resided at Sakya, to visit. The latter did so many times, usually returning home in the evenings. On one such occasion, they held a discussion that lasted until the sun had almost set. [Lama Khaupa] then offered barley for the price of chang,[267] telling [Könchok Gyalpo], "Tonight, you should pay for chang using this [barley], and you ought to stay the night at Kargong Lung." [22] Hearing this, Khön [Könchok Gyalpo] thought to himself, "It has become so late, and yet he did not even invite me to stay the night at his house!" He thus took his leave filled with disappointment. Upon the slopes of Mount Truma[268] he looked back in the direction of Kyelhé Monastery and grumbled to himself, "I am an old man, and yet he sent me off! This lama is truly unkind!" Though disillusioned, he carried on down the path. Later, he came to the slopes of a mountain known as Tukjé Dong and a narrow path that was later called Yiché Trang.[269] By the time he had passed through, he had decided that he would thereafter do whatever his lama asked of him.

When the sun had nearly set, he arrived. At that very moment, Machik was approaching from the opposite direction, out to draw water from the spring of Kargong Lungma. Though they had made no prior arrangement to do so, because of auspicious codependent origination, they met. Khön requested a place to spend the night. With much reverence, Machik invited him to her home. The lama then said, "Sell me some *chang*!" In a cup with neither crack nor flaw, she brought the lama the choicest helping with a delicious flavor. Thinking to himself that this was a very auspicious sign, the lama took a drink. Following his lama's instructions, he stayed the night and the abundant excellence of coemergent dependent origination occurred. A bardo being then appeared within her womb.

After several months had passed, Venerable Khaupa told [Khön Könchok Gyalpo] "Now, you should invite her to come stay at my residence. I will do whatever is appropriate on her behalf, such as healing rituals and offering service for her." Later, when Könchok Gyalpo was fifty-nine years old, in the Male Water Monkey Year [23] known as "Angir" (1092), the pinnacle of compassionate ones, Kunga Nyingpo,[270] was born accompanied by many amazing signs. His birthplace is nowadays marked by the Taming Mara Stūpa at Truma,[271] built by Ngakchang Chökyi Gyalpo[272] and others based upon instructions in the *Kālacakra Tantra*.

Previously, that area had nothing other than a few old houses. The Ngakchang Lama then newly established the marvelous Truma Monastery.[273] Later, when [Könchok Gyalpo's] son was born, Nam Khaupa held him in his lap and showered him with praise: "This must be either the actual Avalokiteśvara or the bodhisattva Jinpa Pal![274] And it is without contradiction to say that he is also the Lord of Yogins [Virūpa]!"

The boy grew quickly, and whoever saw him became overjoyed. He was also strikingly handsome. For these reasons, they named him Kunga Nyingpo, "Essence Liked by All."[275] For a short while, they kept the boy a secret from Dorjé Chukmo.[276] In time, however, she came to know about him. She said to the great teacher of the Khön [Könchok Gyalpo], "Were your lineage to become severed, it would be a tremendous loss. Still, it is no good that you have kept Shangmo's child hidden from me! Now you have a son, and that is very good. I have no need for wealth; it is your son's mother who is now in need of it." And so, Könchok Gyalpo gave all the property of Sakya Monastery to the mother and son, other than the front fields. Those fields appear differently in various lineage succession texts: they are sometimes called Jatra Ma[277] and identified as the lower fields.

It is incorrect to identify the homeland of the Lord Sachen [Kunga Nyingpo]'s [24] mother is Khargo Lung;[278] Kargong Lung is the correct name.[279] The reason is that there is a gold mine (*gser kha*) there. At a certain point, white quartz began to appear at the mouth of the mine. Because of this, the whole area became known by this name [Kargong Lung, the "Quartz Region"]. Several old histories mention this.

Furthermore, as for how Lord Jowo, Master Padmasambhava, and others prophesied that the Lords of the Three Families[280] would emanate continually in this region, including those incarnations of Avalokiteśvara, the great lords of the Sakyapa, as well as about how their great monastic seat and their Dharma protectors would arise, it is as follows. Moreover, Jowo Atiśa came to Tibet and resided for three years in such places as Upper Ngari.[281] Upon Dromtönpa's[282] invitation, he then came to Central Tibet. Along the path, he passed over the peak of Mount Drong Nu.[283] From there he gazed out upon Mount Pönpo[284] and beheld two wild yaks grazing upon its slopes. He described what he had seen to his retinue, and they asked him to interpret its significance. He told them, "This is a sign that in the future the two Mahākālas will perform activities here." This prophecy was in reference to the two Dharma protectors of Sakya, the Gur and Shal [Mahākālas].

Atiśa later arrived in Chaktsal Gang.[285] When he dismounted, he asked his entourage to arrange offerings. He then made extensive prostrations toward the white earth of that place. His retinue asked him why he had done this, to which he replied: "Did you not see? Seven *dhī* syllables, a *hṛi* syllable, and a *hūṃ* syllable appeared on the surface of that white earth! I therefore prostrated and made offerings." [25] "What do these signify?" his retinue asked. "This is a sign," he told them, "that in the future, seven manifestations of Mañjuśrī, one manifestation of Avalokiteśvara, and one manifestation of Vajrapāni, these nine, will appear here. And that then, in addition, other manifestations of the Lords of the Three Families will appear continuously at this place to perform activities on behalf of sentient beings."

Moreover, as Master Padmasambhava prophesied in the *Whispered Lineage of the Ḍākinīs of Luminous Space*:[286]

> The three Lords of the Three Families will appear in Tsang:
> named Kunga Nyingpo, the translator of Sakya,
> Sönam Tsemo, and Drakpa Gyaltsen.

And elsewhere it is said:

> At Sakya, the two translators
> named Kunga and Phakpa will appear.
> They will improve the well-being of Tibetans.
> They will uphold all the Buddha's teachings.[287]
> They will be manifestations of Mañjughoṣa.

In *Praise to Sachen*,[288] Lopön Rinpoché [Sönam Tsemo] explains the meaning of those prophecies as follows:

You, O Lord, are no other than
actual Vajradhara and Mañjuśrī.

Furthermore, the Great Jetsun [Drakpa Gyaltsen] has written:

Mañjuśrī assuming a human form.

And elsewhere:

O supreme lama, indistinguishable
from Vajradhara and Mañjunātha:[289]
I cannot make even the slightest distinction between you.

In this way, Khön Könchok Gyalpo, father of Lord Sachen, founded the glorious Sakya Monastery. He held this seat for many years and extensively spread [26] the explanation of the tantric lineage of Lama Drokmi. He set many students upon the path to ripening and liberation. He greatly benefited the teachings and then, in the Male Water Horse Year (1102), when he was sixty-nine years old, he passed into nirvāṇa at Gorum[290] accompanied by many amazing signs. Just before he passed into nirvāṇa, he offered this final testament: "Sakya was built atop a nāga palace. In the future it will become wealthier, but since nāgas have a rude manner, it is also possible that harm might arise. As such, build a stūpa atop Drokpo Dungtsuk[291] and install my entire corpse inside." This stūpa is today known as Khön Kumbüm.

As mentioned, Khön Könchok Gyalpo was married to two wives. His older wife, Dorjé Chukmo, did not bear him a son. His younger wife, Machik Shangmo, who hailed from Kargong Lungma in Khaui Do[292] and whose father was named Shang Shung Gurawa,[293] bore him one son named Kunga Nyingpo, the Great Sakyapa. The circumstances of his birth were elaborately described above. Beginning with the birth of that holy superior being onward, the abundance of his riches and power increased exponentially, such that he eventually acquired the seven qualities of a higher rebirth.[294]

Just so, that great lama possessed the knowledge of scripture and realization. As for the first, there are two [i.e., common and uncommon knowledge of scripture]. As for how he first acquired common knowledge: he originally delighted in the study of all worldly knowledge, such as studying the commentarial traditions on reading, writing, and astrology, as well as becoming learned in examining the qualities of men, women, animals, and jewels, practicing visual art, medical treatment, the Sanskrit language, [27] poetry, composition, and so forth. From all this, he could satisfy and delight the world's beings.

As for the second, how he acquired uncommon knowledge, this has two parts: [how he studied in general and how he studied the Lamdré tradition specifically.]

In the first place, he received the Hevajra initiation from his father and heard a few of the minor teachings that he knew. Later, when he was eleven years old, his father went to bliss.[295] An astrological reading indicated that if the funeral was done, the foundation for the stūpa laid, and the seat holder enthroned in a single day, there would be an abundance of prosperity for those left behind. His mother told him, "It is said that your father had an extremely strong connection with [Bari] Lotsāwa and that his Dharma is authentic. Since your father's teacher was a translator, you ought to also study the Dharma with one. However, because you are so young you cannot yet direct the monastery. It will be best to entrust the main seat to Bari Lotsāwa." Bari was dully invited from Yukharmo.[296] A group of monks from both Trang and Drakmar[297] performed the funeral ritual. On the same day, they laid the stūpa's foundation and enthroned Bari Lotsāwa at the main seat. Other than the great field in front of the monastery, everything was entrusted to Lama Bari Lotsāwa.

The Lama said, "The son of that noble father must study. To do so effectively he will need wisdom, for which Ārya Mañjuśrī is the deity. He should thus meditate upon the *a ra pa tsa na* [mantra]."[298] While Sachen Kunga Nyingpo was engaged in this practice, sometimes a man like a big conch shell[299] and other times a man like a large lion appeared to him. When he reported this [28], his lama told him, "The demon Pekar[300] wants to cause obstacles for you, so you should immediately undertake the meditation and recitation of Jowo Miyowa."[301] Then the lama gave him the authorizing empowerment together with the complete sādhana of Chui Sungwa[302] along with its ancillary practices. By undertaking these practices, Sachen Kunga Nyingpo pacified all his obstacles. After six months, he accomplished his meditation and beheld the face of Mañjuśrī. Today, that retreat center is well known as Jampal Drakhung,[303] in the middle of east Labrang.

In that way, Mañjuśrī revealed his actual face and gave [Sachen Kunga Nyingpo] the teaching of "Parting from the Four Attachments."[304] In his vision, seven swords continually emanated from Mañjuśrī's heart and were absorbed into the lama's heart. It is said that future generations of his lineage would all be manifestations of Mañjuśrī, and specifically that these Mañjuśrī descendants would all succeed one another auspiciously.

From being truly blessed by the holy yidam deity, [Sachen Kunga Nyingpo] understood most fields of knowledge effortlessly. Even so, to appear in accord with holy conduct and to match the expectations of future generations, he made the appearance of studying extensively. Later, when he was twelve years old, it became apparent that this noble son (*jo sras*) ought to be sent off for an education. Those around him conferred and decided: "Since the Abhidharma is fundamental to all the teachings, he should be dispatched to study it."

Sachen Kunga Nyingpo then departed for Rong Ngurmik.[305] However, since the monks of Drang Tiba[306] had congregated there, he could find no place to live. On a back street, he found an old cave. He hung a curtain in front of it and stayed there. Next to his cave, a monk from Yardrok Khoblé[307] was afflicted by smallpox.[308] He had no one to nurse him, [29] and Sachen Kunga Nyingpo could not bear to see his suffering. The lama took care of the monk. Eventually he recovered, but then the lama himself contracted smallpox.

At that time, there was a clairvoyant (*mig mthong mkhan*) at Sakya named Apho Paktön.[309] Early in the morning, he came outside into the sun and said "From Drachung Gongkha[310] in the east, a man appeared riding a dark brown horse and wearing a plain hat with lines on it and trim. Whipping his horse on the way to Sakya, he said, 'Kunga Nyingpo is sick! What will you Sakyapas do about this?' He is known as Dügyal Thötreng Chen."[311] When news of this [vision] circulated, the community agreed that what Apho had reported was likely true.

That evening, a messenger arrived. Machik thought to herself, "If Kunga Nyingpo is not yet dead, that is fine. But if he is, I too, am no longer of benefit to Sakya." She sold some of her possessions for gold and so forth, and with that departed. When mother and son reconnected, the lama cried since he was still so young and had been sick all alone in a faraway place. His mother told him, "The son of a noble father [such as yours] must remain brave! Fortified with courage, were you to die amid an ocean of monks such as this, you would feel that it was for a purpose!" Then, in the company of his mother, the great lama's body made an imprint in the rock of his cave. This famously still exists today.

Later, when he had recovered from his illness, Kunga Nyingpo received teachings on the Abhidharma from Ngurmikpa Drangti Darma Nyingpo.[312] Upon hearing this teaching just once, he understood everything. Everyone was amazed at this extraordinary feat. After that, [30] following the death of Geshé Drangti, Kunga Nyingpo studied with his foremost pupil, Jang Chepa Khyung.[313] He received teachings on Asaṅga's *Five Sections on the Bhūmis*[314] and the two compendia.[315] Later on, at Nyang Tö,[316] he received teachings from Khyung Rinchen Drak[317] on such texts as [Dharmakīrti's] *Ascertaining Valid Cognition*[318] and *Drop of Reasoning*.[319] At that time, the lama's foremost pupil was Medikpa.[320]

Then the head of Sakya sent a letter to Kunga Nyingpo that read: "There will be future opportunities for you to study the texts on logic. By contrast, since the Bari Lama is now so old, you will not be able to study with him much longer. Therefore, return here." The lama then departed. From Bari Lama he received teachings upon the textual traditions of the Prajñāpāramitā, including works like *The Heap of Jewels Sūtra*[321] and *The Buddha's Flower Adornment Sūtra*[322] along with their respective quintessential instructions.

From among the action tantras,[323] Kunga Nyingpo received transmission of some two hundred sections from [various] tantras along with their supplementary texts, ornamented by detailed oral instructions. From among the performance tantras,[324] he received transmission of Yamāntaka[325] and Wrathful All-Victorious[326] together with their supplementary texts.

As for the mahayoga tantras,[327] he received transmissions of the five root and expository tantras of Śrī Guhyasamāja[328] together with the commentaries of Master [Nāgārjuna] and his two spiritual sons and their detailed supplements; the Buddhajñānapāda[329] commentary and its detailed supplement; the three Yamāntaka tantras together with Palzin's[330] commentary and its supplements; the *Śrī Vajracatuhpitha*[331] commentary along with its supplements; the *Sarvabuddhasamāyoga*[332] commentary along with its supplements; as well as the *Hundreds of Sādhanas* collection[333] and its detailed quintessential instructions. He received [31] more transmission than can be recorded here and completely understood all of them.

In summary, Lama Bariwa held the main seat for eight years. During that time, he built the All Victorious Stūpa,[334] inside of which he installed earth collected from many blessed places in India, a piece of the Bodhi tree, and relics of the Tathāgata and many paṇḍitas and siddhas, including especially Buddha Kāśyapa's[335] monastic robe. He built this stūpa, which became the foundation of the teachings, accompanied by many auspicious signs. Inside this stūpa, he installed 370,000 vijaya dhāraṇi.[336] It was consecrated with two thousand vijaya rituals. On the eighth day, when they threw flowers upon it, the bell radiated yellow light the color of refined gold. This pervaded all that was visible of the earth and sky and made the sound of a bell. A gentle voice was heard softly saying four times, "Well done! Well done!" Everyone gathered there saw and heard all this and was amazed. Ever since, unimaginably propitious omens emit continuously from this stūpa in all directions and times. Lopön Sönam Tsemo's[337] collected writing notes that this is all described in the biography of Bariwa.

Furthermore, from among the Four Commissioned Oral Lineages of Mahākāla,[338] this lama bestowed upon Lord Sachen the body oral transmission of the "Wish-Fulfilling Jewel Stone Mahākāla."[339] Soon after, Bari Lotsāwa passed away at Bar Cave.[340]

After that, Lama [Sachen] went to Drompa Yutsé Jipu.[341] There, with Melhang Tsho,[342] [32] he studied *Ascertaining Valid Cognition*, the *Drop of Reasoning*, along with the fifteenth chapter of its commentary, and the three treatises of the eastern Svātantrika Mādhyamikas.[343] Upon hearing all these teachings, he understood them completely.

He then went to study with Lama Nam Khaupa [Darma Sengé].[344] Of the texts he studied, among action class tantras were such texts as the *The Great Tantra of Supreme Knowledge*,[345] the *Tantra of Subāhu's Questions*,[346] the *Empowerment of Vajrapāṇi*,[347] the *Secret Tantra of the General Rituals of All Maṇḍalas*,[348] the *Later Concentration Tantra*,[349] and the *Trisamayavyūharāja*

Tantra,[350] each of them accompanied by commentaries and their supplementary texts. Among performance class [tantras] were such works as the *The Tantra of the Complete Enlightenment of Vairocana*[351] together with its minor commentaries. Among the yoga class [tantras], he studied the *Compendium of Suchness Tantra*[352] along with its commentary, *Illuminating Suchness,*[353] and the *Extensive Explanation of the Compendium of Suchness Tantra called "The Ornament of Kosala";*[354] the glorious *Supreme*[355] and its commentary, the *2,500 Verses;*[356] the *Vajraśekhara [Tantra];*[357] the *All-Illuminating Mahākāla;*[358] the *Tantra Purifying Evil Destinies;*[359] and the *King of Tantras, the Universal Secret,*[360] together with its commentaries. In addition, he studied such works as the annotation to the *Sarvatathāgatatattvasaṁgraha* entitled *Awatara,* the approaching and accomplishing text entitled *The Arising of the Vajra,*[361] the *Trailokyavijayā,*[362] and the *Nine Crown Tormas,*[363] along with many other minor texts.

Among the mahāyoga class [tantras], he studied the commentary written by Nāgārjuna and his two spiritual sons [on the *Guhyasamāja Tantra*] entitled *The Illuminating Lamp;*[364] the *Five Stages Mixed with Sūtra;*[365] Āryadeva's *Lamp for Integrating the Practices;*[366] the *Exposition of the Stages of Self-Empowerment;*[367] the *Cittavaranavisodhanamaprakarana;*[368] the spiritual friend Nāgabodhi's[369] classification of sādhana entitled the *Twenty Maṇḍala Rituals;*[370] Candrakīrti's Vajrasattva sādhana; Buddhajñānapada's Samantabhadra *sādhanā* together with its three commentaries;[371] the essential commentary (*don 'grel*) *Dzayanta;* Śraddhākaravarma's Samantabhadra sādhana;[372] the major and minor [33] *Explanations Connected to the Guhyasamāja Tantra Called "A Handful of Flowers";*[373] the root text and commentary of the *Four Hundred and Fifty Maṇḍala Rituals;* the *Wealth of the Teachings* sādhana[374] composed by Mikyö Dorjé,[375] its great commentary composed by Sö Nyompa,[376] and the summary of its meaning entitled *Kahika;* the well-known middling commentary on the *Mañjuśrī Tantra* composed by Gekpé Dorjé[377] and the commentary upon that tantra written by Dasang Pal;[378] and the commentary entitled *Conceptuality of Bliss.*[379] He received teachings upon all these aforementioned commentaries along with their minor supplementary texts.

In the matter of philosophy (*mtshan nyid*), he received teachings on the four treatises of Maitreya except for the *Ornament of Clear Realization,*[380] as well as the *Compendium of Training,*[381] the *Introduction to the*

Bodhisattva's Way of Life,[382] and the *Compendium of Sūtras*,[383] along with many minor teachings on practice (*sbyong*). He understood the meaning of everything he heard.

After that, his elders convened to further discuss his education. They told him, "It would be best for you to seek out the Dharma lineage of your father. Though Puhrangpa Selnying[384] was knowledgeable in this, he has already passed away. However, it is said that his disciple, Khön Gyichuwa Dralhawar,[385] is knowledgeable in this tradition. Also, that lama is a member of your family lineage (*gdung rus*). He would be the best one for you to study with."

Sachen duly departed and took initiation. During the night of preparation, he dreamed of a vast body of red water named the Ocean of Existence.[386] Three bridges extended over it. Many people gathered along its banks desiring to cross over. They pleaded, "Please rescue me! Please rescue me!" And Sachen did rescue them: three people crossed over the farthest bridge, seven crossed over the middle bridge, and a great many people crossed over the nearest bridge. Feeling a little fatigued, Sachen went to rest a while in the sun. Just then, he awoke. In the morning, Gyichuwa asked the lama about his dreams, [34] to which Sachen reported all the above. Lama Gyichuwa famously joked with him, saying, "Based on your ability, you cannot liberate more than three people!"

After that, he received teachings on the three extensive Hevajra tantras together with the *Kumuti* commentary, their detailed supplementary texts, and oral instruction, all of which he had received long ago from his father; the Hevajra lineage of the Black Brahmin [Kṛṣṇasamayavajra],[387] together with the *Garland of Preliminary Yoga* commentary[388] and its supplements; and the commentary called *Essence Cycle of the Eighteen Accomplishments*.[389] He also received teachings on the topic of accomplishment and the twenty-five texts about the *Essence Cycle* and their supplementary texts ornamented by extremely profound quintessential instructions; the two commentaries of Lama Drokmi's teaching lineage entitled *Mahāmāyā* with their branch commentaries; the *Candraguhyatilaka Tantra*;[390] and the *Buddhakapāla Tantra*[391] along with its commentaries and supplements. From the commentary tradition of Marpa Lotsāwa,[392] he received four further teachings on Gur Mahākāla, [the Two] Part [*Hevajra Tantra*],[393] the *Vajracatuhpitha*, and the single *Mahāmāyā Tantra*[394] along with the four explanations and quintessential instructions. He also received further teachings on the three eastern Svātantrika Mādhyamikas, the *Compendium of Training* and the *Introduction to the Bodhisattva's Way of Life* according to the commentary tradition of Lama Ngaripa.[395]

Upon receiving all these teachings, Sachen deeply understood their meaning. At that time, from among the lama's eighteen monk disciples, Sachen most correctly understood the scriptures and their logical meaning. Due to being held tightly in the grasp of Mañjuśrī, he could understand the meaning of a Dharma teaching upon hearing it just once. Lama Gyichuwa would also express how fond he was of this lord.

At that time, Sachen heard that Lama Se[tön Kunrik][396] would travel to a Dharma teaching event (*chos 'khor*) at Doktö.[397] Though the great lama did not much care for festivals, Lama Sé was an excellent teacher and would bestow a Dharma initiation there. [35] As such, he attended in the company of a few young monastic pupils of Gyichuwa. Sachen came into the presence of Lama Setön Künrig, who sat at the head of the row of monks and was teaching. However, he could not hear what the lama was saying. Then Lama Sé asked each of the companions of the Lord of Kharchungpa:[398] "O son of a noble father, where are you from? What do you know? Are you able to teach or are you able to meditate?" He then asked the great lama Sachen Kunga Nyingpo, "O son of a noble father, where are you from?" The great lama replied, "I am from Drom Puk." "And where is your father?" asked Setön Kunrik. "He is in Sakya," Sachen replied. Setön interjected, saying, "Oh, one of my lamas resided there, but he has since passed away. Now I am grieved and do not wish to see anyone from there. I have heard that someone named Bariwa now holds Sakya's monastic seat, so I have no desire to go. Now, what did Khön Könchok Gyalpo leave behind?" The lord Sachen responded, "I am his son." The lama said to him, "O son of a noble father, do not tell such lies! My lama has no son!" Since it was indeed true that Dorjé Chukmo had never borne Könchok Gyalpo a son, the great lama remained silent. His travel companions all interjected to explain the situation on his behalf, "Though Dorjé Chukmo had no sons," they reported, "he was born to another wife named Shangmo." Setön replied, "As long as someone is not yet dead, they have the opportunity to meet another person! And this has surely happened today!"

Holding the great lama Sachen in his lap, he became teary-eyed. "I am old and possess the Dharma," he said. "And I will give it all to you, but you must return quickly to me to receive it. Do not think, 'I will come sometime in the future,' since next year I will die." Sachen [36] stayed with him for one night, during which Lama Setön gave a clear outline of the Lamdré, including various commentaries, their supplementary branches, rituals to expel obstacles, and so forth.

Sachen returned and then thought that he might like to travel to Kharchung.[399] He prepared to do so, and even packed his bags. His companions Tönpa Dorjé Ö and Shangtsün Ratsa[400] told him, "This lama likes you more than any of the monks! In the context of tantric practice, one must consult with one's lama before engaging in any activities. And so you should first ask the lama for permission!" Sachen realized this was true and went off to request permission from Lama Gyichuwa. The lama inquired of him, "Why exactly do you wish to go?" Sachen responded, "I wish to receive some oral instructions." "You are naive!" Lama Gyichuwa retorted. "Though Sé may wag his tongue, he has no oral instructions! After I am finished helping my lama Ngaripa's Dharma activities, then I will give you Dharma." With these words, Gyichuwa did not give Sachen permission and so he was unable to depart. However, he thought to himself, "I can go next year." But in the following year, just as he had predicted, Lama Setön Kunrik passed away before Sachen could visit him. Sachen suffered from profound regret but by then could do nothing about it.

A long time after that, Sachen wished to invite Lama Gyichuwa to Sakya and for him to turn the Wheel of the Dharma there. In preparation, he collected three hundred bushels of barley and other requisites, while also recruiting some other disciples for the task. Just then, Lama Gyichuwa fell ill and requested that the great lama come see him. Sachen went at once, but Lama Gyichuwa passed away before they could have an audience. The lama left a final testament for Sachen: "You must take the novice monastic vows[401] and protect the Khön community!" [37] Lama Gyichuwa's main teaching lineage was then passed on to the great lama Sachen. After all affairs were settled there, he returned to Sakya.

To follow the lama's testament, Sachen desired to ordain as a monk. He duly began to collect monastic robes and so forth. Lama Khaupa heard about this and requested an audience with the great lama. Once Sachen arrived, Lama Khaupa asked him, "Why have you collected monk's robes?" "Because I am going to become a monk!" Sachen replied. But the lama told him, "Do not do that!" The great lama protested, "But I have instructions from Lama Gyichuwa to do just that!" Lama Khaupa retorted, "He and I are lamas of equal rank! Moreover, I am alive and so you should obey my instruction and ignore his final testament! There will be more benefit to the teachings and sentient beings if you stay as a layman." And with this, he would not grant permission for Sachen to ordain.

Though he could not become a monk, Sachen did take over the leadership of the Khön community. After that, the great lama bundled up all the Cakrasaṃvara texts that had belonged to lama Gyichuwa personally, who had been a disciple of Lama Mal Lotsāwa Lodrö Drakpa,[402] and he departed for [the latter's residence in] Nalatsé's Netsar, in Gungthang.[403]

There he received teachings from Lama Mal on such subjects as the Cakrasaṃvara root and exposition tantras, *Vajraḍāka*; the *Abhidhāna*; the *Herukābhyudaya;*[404] *the Yoginīsañcārya;*[405] the *Sambhuta*; the *Caturyoginīsampuṭa Tantra;*[406] the *Ḍākinīabhibhava Tantra;*[407] commentaries on both the *Vajraḍāka* and *Yoginīsañcārya* along with Luipa's detailed supplementary texts and Ghaṇṭāpa's supplementary texts; the six doctrines of Kāṇha[408] and Nāroḍākinī[409] together with detailed oral instructions on the central channel; the three tantras of black Yamāntaka together with their commentaries, and the two teaching traditions of this tantra together with detailed oral instructions; the Gur [Mahākāla] traditions of Nāropa and Tilopa, and the bodhisattva's three commentaries [38] together with its supplementary texts; the three commentaries, sādhanas, and praises of the root tantra of Cakraṃsavara descended from the lineage of Jowo Rinchen Sangpo[410] according to the teaching cycle of Master Kokana Gyalwa Sangpo;[411] the commentary and introduction to the sādhana of the root tantra of Cakrasaṃvara that had passed through Jowo Jé Atiśa; and also teachings upon supplementary texts such as the *Abhıdhana*, *Acala,*[412] *Vajrapāṇi,*[413] and so forth; the sādhana of Tārā together with its branches; the *Śrī Mahāsaṃbarodaya Tantrarāja;*[414] the sādhana composed by the Kaśmīri Rinchen Dorjé[415] together with its many branches; and the root text and detailed commentaries of the [*Six*] *Collected Works of*

Middle Way Reasoning,[416] the *Compendium of the Sūtras,*[417] and the *Collection of Praise to the Middle Way.*[418] He heard teachings upon all these and completely understood their meaning.

In all these transmissions, Lama Sachen mastered each teaching upon hearing it but once. Pretending to be naive, Lama Mal scorned him, "Some need to spend half their lifetime studying, whereas others think they can study a topic but once!" On one occasion when Sachen was absent, Mal and his other disciples were studying the mantra of the *Seven Hundred Essential Concepts.*[419] His disciples could not understand its meaning. The great lama Sachen arrived and told them, "It is not difficult!" and then explained the meaning to them. Lama Mal stood up abruptly and said, "I am delighted if someone develops their understanding, when in fact they do not understand. I am delighted if someone does not understand, when in fact they do understand!" He then departed. Hearing this, Sachen was uncomfortable and wondered to himself why Lama Mal had said this.

Later, they once again gathered [39] to study this mantra. The wind blew a page of the text near the great lama. Sachen picked it up and passed it to Lama Mal, saying, "Here." Lama Mal happily replied, "This is a great auspicious sign that in the future you will turn the Wheel of the Dharma and it will benefit sentient beings."

Later, when Sachen was preparing to take his leave, Lama Mal said, "If someone practices my Dharma, then they will surely achieve enlightenment. As such, in the future someone might give an initiation by drawing an eight-petaled lotus flower atop of an old shield [as a maṇḍala] in a ghost house and simply wrap wool (*bal*) around the neck of a vase of alcohol [for the vase initiation]! You should never do that!" Lama Sachen said, "I will never do such a thing to the Dharma!" and then he left.

At Yeru Nama,[420] Sachen bestowed initiation and gave the bodhisattva vow. In return, he was offered seventeen *sang* (*srang*) of gold. He entrusted this to a *ngakpa* tantric practitioner to pass along as an offering to Lama Mal. Soon after, Lama Mal was presiding over a festival and sitting at the head of a congregation. He was informed: "Someone is here from Sakya who wishes to see you." Mal, however, would not see them, saying, "If they wish for something to eat, then feed them." However, [the attendant] stayed on and wandered about uncomfortably for some time. Lama Mal was once again informed: "The reason that person wishes to see you is because he has an offering for you." Since Lama Mal could sometimes behave facetiously, he went to greet the visitor himself, saying bluntly, "What did you bring me as an offering?" The ngakpa replied, "I have gold!" "How much do you have?" asked Mal. "I have about seventeen *sang*." This made the lama very happy. He took out one *sang* from his own purse and set it atop the seventeen to make eighteen and told the ngakpa, "Now you should go offer this to the monastic assembly!"

After that offering had been made, Lama Mal [40] told the ngakpa messenger, "Sachen upholds his samaya commitments wonderfully! This is something I hadn't before appreciated. Go and request that Sachen come visit me this year. I will then give him the remainder of my Dharma teachings." That [ngakpa] monk then returned and communicated this message. Sachen later came to see Lama Mal and received the following transmissions: *The Purification Tantra*;[421] the *[Concise] Consecration Tantra* together with its seven supplementary texts;[422] the major and minor sādhanas of Vajrasattva; the eight supplementary texts on medical examination; and, especially, the Mahākāla sādhana and permission initiation (*rjes gnang*). As a support for his practice of this latter deity, Lama Mal gifted Sachen a black banner, a nine-pointed iron vajra, and a dance mask of Mahākāla named Sebak Nakpopur.[423] Lama Mal spoke to this mask just as someone would speak to another person. He told it, "I am now old and no longer need you. You should follow the Khön Sakyapa. Act according to the commands of the Sakya and their lineage." Saying this, he gave it away. With the mask in hand, Sachen then took his leave.

At Lhotö,[424] from Puhrang Lochung,[425] Sachen received transmission of the *Cakrasaṃvara Tantra* according to the tradition of the Nepali Bhadanta.[426] In addition, from among the teaching cycles of Śrī Guhyasamāja in the tradition of Hangu,[427] he received three transmissions, such as *Argham* and so forth. He also received sundry transmissions of action class tantras. Sachen completely understood all the teachings he received. In addition, that translator gave the great lama a wish-fulfilling wood Mahākāla statue that had naturally arisen from the charcoal corpse of the brahmin Choksé.[428]

Furthermore, from Dokham[429] he invited A Kyewa of the Drikhung's Kyara [clan][430] to Sakya [41], from whom he received the following teachings: on Guhyasamāja according to the tradition named Lho Dorjé Nyingpo,[431] which follows the intentions of Ārya Nāgārjuna and his sons; on the teaching cycle called Menpa Shap[432] in the lineage of Buddhajñānapāda, including Ārya Mañjuśrī's oral teachings, the seventeen divisions of the Dharma according to Yeshé Shab, and the tantric commentary entitled *Precious Fruit Tree*[433] together with its oral instructions; and the maṇḍala ritual composed by Marmé Dzé Sangpo,[434] including the individual commentaries composed by Menpa Shab and the *Treasury that Gives Rise to Siddhi*,[435] which accords with the intentions of that master. Sachen completely understood everything that he heard.

He also received Bhawapa's commentaries on the *Vajracatuhpitha* together with their supplementary commentaries, the two systems of Mahāmāyā's commentaries together with their supplements, the *Vajra Nectar Tantra*[436] together with its branch commentaries, and the *Eighty [Methods] of Grasping the Mind*.[437] From the Nepali paṇḍita Padmaśrī, Sachen received teachings on *Reciting the Names of Mañjuśrī*[438] and the Kālacakra,[439] together with many quentessential instructions. From the Nepali Jñanavajra, he received many teaching cycles of the Yoginī tantras. From the Indian yogin Bhadrarāhula, he received many oral instructions. From Geshé Ngok,[440] he received teachings on the Prajñapāramitā according to the tradition of Jowo Atiśa, on the root and commentary of the *Illumination of the Twenty-Thousand-Verse Prajñapāramitā Sūtra*,[441] on the root text and commentary of the *Eight-Thousand-Verse Prajñapāramitā Sūtra*, on the root and commentary of the *Ornament of Clear Realization*, on the root text and commentary of *Compendium of Sūtras*, on the root text and commentary of the *Summary of the Meaning of the Eight-Thousand-Verse Prajñapāramitā*,[442] and on a single section of Śāntipa's great scriptural tradition.

He completely understood everything that he heard.

In Particular, How Sachen Received [42] the Oral Instructions [of the Lamdré]

After all this, Sachen wished to receive the oral instructions. He inquired, "Who is superior among the disciples of Sé?" Some told him it was Shama. Others who were more familiar with Shama told him, "He does not possess a complete oral transmission. Shangtön[443] and his brother are the best. While the younger brother has passed away, the older brother is alive still and knowledgeable." Sachen considered visiting him and asked permission from Lama Khau. Lama Khau, however, refused to grant him permission, explaining, "Those great hermit-practitioners may be lying! It is possible that Shangtön possesses no oral instructions. If you have devotion, you meditate upon the sādhana of Guhyasamāja called *Wealth of the Teaching*."[444] Sachen said, "I really believe that he does indeed possess the oral instructions." Lama Khau replied, "In that case, you should go!" With those words, Sachen departed.

Upon arriving in Saktang,[445] [Sachen] encountered a group of weavers (*thags mkhan*). He asked them, "Can you please help me win an audience with hermit Shang?" They replied, "He is right over there!" Sachen looked and spotted him at the center of a large crowd. He wore only a lower garment with his upper body naked other than a goat skin worn inside out. Dressed in this way, he was performing yoga (*yo ga byed*) while babbling incoherently.

Sachen went near to him and began to prostrate. Hermit Shang said, "It seems like you are some important person come here from afar; specifically, a practitioner of the New Translation tradition. Aren't you making a mistake by prostrating to me?" To this, Sachen replied, "I am not making a mistake! I wish to receive the precious oral instructions [on Lamdré] from you." Along with his prostrations, he offered [Lama Shang] some armor (*khrab*). Lama Shang replied, "I am telling you that you are making a mistake! I have no such knowledge. I have never even heard the name of that teaching. I am teaching Dzokchen Tsamunti[446] and the teaching cycle of the brāhmāṇas. You practitioners of the New Translation school suffer from far too many conceptual thoughts! And so, shouldn't you be suspicious of receiving any of my teachings?" Sachen once again made requests, but Lama Shang told him, "I do not hold such instructions!" [43] Then the great lama Sachen thought, "Even though he behaves this way, it seems like he doesn't possess this teaching. I think I have made a mistake." He then departed.

The father of José Öchok[447] then informed Lama Shang, "When I was in Kharchung, [Lama Setön Kunrik] said to a monk from Gyichuwa: 'You are the son of my lama' and then held him in his lap. [That is the same monk who has just visited you!] How can you let him leave?" Lama Shang said, "Oh! In this case, it is possible that I am breaking my samaya commitments! Ask him to return!" Then the lama put detailed questions to Sachen and came to believe that he was in fact the son of Sakya [Könchok Gyalpo]. He told him, "Earlier when I spoke to you, I did not recognize you and lied. In fact, I do possess the instructions you seek. However, I have never taught them before and need some time to prepare. As it happens, at this moment Setön Dorjung[448] is turning the Wheel of the Dharma at Dorka Do[449] for a great many major and minor paṇḍitas, translators, scholars, and masters. I am an old yogi in the area where this teaching is being given. It would thus be unsuitable for me to give any teachings just now. Instead, you should return in the spring and, in the meantime, finish up your current studies." Sachen would later say, "Öchok's father was very kind to me. He pleased me more than if someone had given me a hundred horses!"

In the springtime, Sachen returned. On the evening of his arrival, they engaged in a long Dharma discussion. The Lord Lama [Sachen] was very familiar with the three tantras, and so he could answer any questions Lama Shang put to him. Lama Shang was gladdened and told him, "Many thanks! You are very learned!" He then asked Sachen, "How can one bring the thirty-two channels described in the tantras into one's practice?" Lama Shang asked such questions on the crucial points of the practice. Regarding these queries, Sachen was unable to answer. He realized this lama did indeed possess profound oral instructions [44] and developed enormous trust in him.

Sachen eventually received initiation and the oral instructions [on Lamdré]. Once the preliminary instructions were finished, however, Lama Shang's tongue began to swell and he fell sick. He was unable to continue teaching the Dharma. Lama Shang told Sachen, "It appears that you and I have some broken samaya. You should offer maṇḍalas and recite the hundred-syllable mantra of Vajrasattva." The great lama thought, "There could be no broken samaya other than believing that he did not possess the oral instruction [on Lamdré]. That must be it!" He therefore offered maṇḍalas and recited many hundred-syllable mantras, which repaired the damage.

The lama gave his teachings interrupted by breaks, and so his wife requested that he bestow his teachings to Sachen more quickly. Lama Shang was very strict, however, and he told his wife, "What did you say? You think I should give teachings no matter what happens, like a dog who has seen lungs?"[450] He continued to teach Sachen very slowly and in stages. Sachen remained there for more than four summers and winters while receiving teachings. Because Lama Könchok Gyalpo had been Lama Sé's master, he transmitted the complete Lamdré teaching cycle while keeping the samaya of the entire lineage in mind. In brief, he transmitted the *Nine Cycles of Path and Result,*[451] the *Twenty-Five Essentials,*[452] and its many supplementary commentaries. As a support of the oral instructions (on Lamdré), he received the tradition of very profound commentary on the *Solitary Hevajra Tantra,*[453] the *Union Root Tantra,*[454] the *Root Tantra of Hevajra*, the *Root Tantra of Cakrasaṃvara*, the *Root Tantra of Vajracatuhpitha*, the *Mahāmāyā*, and the teaching tradition of the very profound *Reciting the Names of Mañjuśrī*. Sachen completely understood everything that he heard. [45]

After the transmission of the oral instructions was complete, Lama Shang gave a command-seal of secrecy (*bka' rgyas btab*) to Sachen: "You are forbidden from giving transmissions or teachings [on Lamdré] for eighteen years. You are forbidden from admitting that you know this teaching or even its name! You are likewise prohibited from writing them down. Once that time has passed, you will be the lord of this teaching. You are then permitted to do whatever you like, such as teaching others and composing texts." He then prophesied: "In general, if you principally engage in practice, you will accomplish the supreme siddhi of mahāmudrā in this single life. If you principally engage in teaching, it will benefit countless students. Specifically, there will be three students among your disciples who will achieve the supreme siddhi of mahāmudrā in their lifetime without abandoning their bodies. There will be seven disciples who will achieve the stage of forbearance (*bzod pa*) on the path of preparation. And there will be eighty more who will attain profound realization."

Upon hearing this, Lama Sachen became worried that after eighteen years he would forget the details of the teachings. He vowed that each month he would renew his commitment to eventually teach the complete Lamdré, and that each day he would review six or seven of the *Vajra Verses [of Virūpa]*. He then took his leave from Lama Shang.

As a result, since there were no texts, during the latter half of Sachen's life, the complete Lamdré remained an oral tradition. Once those eighteen years of secrecy had passed, Lama Aseng[455] sought out whether the source of the Lamdré had been cut. He said to Lama Sachen, "You possess the precious oral instructions [on Lamdré]! Why have you never revealed to me whether you even possessed them? Now, you must give me a teaching and record the instructions in writing!" At that time, two conditions had gathered: the period of secrecy was completed and requests had been made. Lama Sachen thought to himself that this was indeed very auspicious. [46] He then bestowed teachings upon Lama Aseng and composed *The Condensed Meaning of the Lamdré*.[456]

After that, over time Sachen composed eleven commentaries on Lamdré according to people's requests, including the *Gathengma*, the *Zhujema*, and the *Lokyama*.[457] At the request of Geshé Nyak,[458] he wrote a specific work on Lamdré. Though only a few verses long, its meaning was profound and it was beautifully written. For these reasons, to this day we use it as our daily text (*phyag dpe*). As for Sachen's commentaries on Lamdré, there are: *The Continuity of the Causal Basis of All*,[459] *The Body Maṇḍala of the Seat, and So Forth*,[460] *Investigating the Signs of Death Together with the Ritual for Ransoming Impending Death*,[461] *Instruction for the Moment of Death*,[462] *The Yoga of the Vital Essence*,[463] *The Characteristics of Mudrā*,[464] *The Instruction on Closing the Door by Means of Syllable*,[465] *The Four Bardos*,[466] *Empowerment for the Time of the Path*,[467] *The Four Nondeceptives*,[468] *The Six Oral Instructions*,[469] *The Five Interdependencies*,[470] *The Vajraḍākinī Fire Pūjā*,[471] *Removing Defilements by Means of the Cleansing Ritual*,[472] *Removing [Defilements] by Means of Tsatsa*,[473] *Protecting the Essential Drop*,[474] *The Method for Reciting the One-Hundred-Syllable Mantra*,[475] *The Oral Explanation of the Seven Prāṇa Practices*,[476] *The Fourteen Syllables of Bhaga*,[477] *Mudrā of the Fourfold Retinue*,[478] and *Clear Realization of the Half of the Thirteenth Bhūmi*.[479]

As for the verse texts that provide the condensed meaning of those commentaries and that elaborate upon their meaning, there is both the root text and the commentary of *The Indivisibility of Saṃsāra and Nirvāṇa,*[480] *Principal Points for the Ritual of the Four Empowerments,*[481] *Text for the Three Supreme Empowerments,*[482] *Instructions for the External Generation Stage,*[483] *Sādhana for Nectar Pills,*[484] *Quintessential Instructions for Removing the Seven Dangerous Defilements,*[485] *The Four Principal Points on Not Giving Away Carelessly,*[486] *Removing Agitated Bodily Elements by Means of Wind and Conduct,*[487] *The Thirty-Two Enlightened Activities,*[488] *The Middling Lamdré,*[489] *The Condensed Lamdré,*[490] *Instructions Precisely as a Textual Tradition,*[491] [47] *Instructions According to the Six Principal Points,*[492] *Instructions According to the Eleven Principal Points,*[493] *Instructions According to Higher, Middling, and Lower Capacities,*[494] *Engagement and Reversal with Path,*[495] *Engagement and Reversal by Means of Mudrā,*[496] *The Seven Oral Instructions that Benefit When Known,*[497] *The Incorruptible Path Along with a Means for Passage,*[498] *The Twelve Outer and Inner Deeds,*[499] *Guru Yoga,*[500] *History of Tibetan Lamas,*[501] *History of Indians,*[502] and *Virūpa's Life Story and His Songs of Realization,*[503] all accompanied by a catalogue of all these texts.

As for the oral instructions on other Lamdré teaching cycles, he received the *Five Inconceivable Pith Instructions of Toktsepa,*[504] *The Life Story of Tsokyé,*[505] *The Nine Profound Teachings of Tsokyé,*[506] the *Four Oral Instructions of Ḍombi,*[507] *Kāṇha's Complete Instructions on the Practice of Inner Fire,*[508] *The Absence of Letters of Ngakwang Drakpa,*[509] *Teachings Obtained by Nāgārjuna Near a Stūpa,*[510] *Instructions for Making the Crooked Straight,*[511] and *The Oral Instructions of Indrabhūti.*[512]

It is uncertain whether Sachen himself composed all these precious teachings cycles on Lamdré together with their commentaries. To make it easier to discover all the Lamdré texts associated with Sachen and his disciples, I have listed them all here regardless.

The Glorious Great Compassionate One, thinking of the continuity of the teachings, himself newly composed the following excellent instructions: *A General Survey and Classification of the Tantras,*[513] *The Concise Meaning of the Two-Part [Hevajra Tantra],*[514] *Commentary upon Difficult Points of the Two-Part [Hevajra Tantra],*[515] *The Condensed Meaning of the Tantra Called "List of Gur [Mahākāla Texts],"*[516] [48] *Nāga's Explanation,*[517] *Clear Realization of the Channels,*[518] *Outline of the Commentaries upon Gur [Mahākāla],*[519]

Commentary upon the Vajra Essence,[520] *Commentary upon Tsokyé's Essential Meaning Sādhana,*[521] *A Chapter-by-Chapter Commentary on the Root Tantra of Cakrasaṃvara,*[522] *Outline of the Root Tantra [of Cakrasaṃvara],*[523] *List of Kāṇha's Cakrasaṃvara Maṇḍala Rituals,*[524] *Maṇḍala Rituals Based upon Painted Cloth,*[525] *The Meaning of the Secret of Suchness Written as Instruction*[526] along with its outline, *The Condensed Meaning of the Olapati,*[527] *Ritual for the Cremation of the Cakrasaṃvara Yogin,*[528] *The Instructions of Olapati* and its outline,[529] *Opening the Condensed Meaning of the Word of the Secret of Suchness,*[530] *Commentary on the Seven Realizations of Yamāntaka,*[531] *The Maṇḍala Rituals of the Seventeen Tārās,*[532] *The Condensed Oral Instructions,*[533] *The Protection Circle of Bhayana,*[534] *Request Letter to Lama Kyara Akyab,*[535] *Oral Instructions for Burying the Treasure Vase,*[536] *Outline of the Tsokyé Sādhana,*[537] *Commentary on the Root Tantra of Cakrasaṃvara Entitled "Pearl Garland,"*[538] *Commentary on the Clear Realization of Cakrasaṃvara According to Lūipa's Tradition Entitled "Pearl Garland,"*[539] and so forth.

In all commentaries composed by this lama, the letters are very clear. Most of them begin with verses of praise and end with a dedication and the name of the author, and so forth, all clearly recorded.

What's more, this great Lama Sachen wrote annotations (*mchan*) and drew diagrams for maṇḍalas, such as for the three Hevajra tantras, the tantra of the cycles of Yamāntaka according to the Kāṇha tradition, the *Vajraḍāka*, the commentary on the *Abhidhāna* entitled *Kumuta*, and diagrams for a few Cakrasaṃvara tantras, the *Sampuṭa Tantra*, and the *Lord of the Feast and the King of the Gods of the Desire Realm.*[540]

The Good Qualities of Sachen's Realizations

Sachen gathered all auspicious signs within himself by perfectly protecting his three vows [49] without even a minor stain upon them, wetting his mindstream with compassion and loving-kindness, not being attached to anything, and pleasing his lama in the matter of devotion and practice. For these reasons, he saw the actual face of the yidam deity and mastered all Dharmas without facing any obstacles to developing clairvoyance and magical powers. As I have mentioned already, on the occasion when he was actually taken under the care of Mañjuśrī, he also beheld the faces of Ārya Acila and Venerable Tārā. By this, all his obstacles were removed.

Furthermore, when he journeyed to Gungthang after the great translator had died and he himself became sick, he recovered because Jomo Tsitsi provided medicine and oral instructions. He later went to Yeru's Drongchung Monastery.[541] There he fell ill for some two months from being poisoned. This caused him to forget all the Dharma teachings he had received, being unable to remember even one of them. He became terribly worried, since he was without a companion to help him in his recollection. Moreover, he worried that even if he were to travel to India to receive those teachings again, he would find no one there to teach him. He then returned to Sakya, undertook a strict meditation retreat at Drangkhang Nyingpa,[542] and made requests to the Lama and Triple Gem. Because of this, he began to recall some of the teachings he had received. Later, the hermit Lord Shang came to him in his dreams. From this, his memory was restored.

From joyfully making strong requests, moreover, one day at dawn he had a vision that Virūpa, Lord of Yogins, appeared to him with legs crossed and displaying the mudrā of teaching the Dharma. [50] He was flanked on the right in the eastern direction by Kārṇha in the posture of legs crossed, holding in his right hand a buffalo-calf horn trumpet and in his left a skull cup full of nectar. To the left was Gayādhara covered by a white shawl and holding a vajra and bell at his heart. Behind was Kotalipa upon his knees in a pose of supplication holding an umbrella. In front was Binasa, or "Forest Dweller," with hands pressed together offering nectar. All five appeared in front of a curtain of white earth. Their seated bodies covered all the land between Upper Möndrok and Lower Beldrok. Virūpa then told him, "This all belongs to me." He truly appeared and revealed his face to Sachen.

For this reason, Sachen developed an unthinkably stable, nonconceptual meditative concentration. When he arose from that meditation, he composed a praise [to Virūpa] entitled *A la la*, or *Marvelous*. He then undertook a strict meditation retreat for one month. During that time, he was regularly visited by either the principal Virūpa or his entourage [Gayādhara and Kāṇha], who gave him transmission of either the seventy-two kinds of unexcelled yoga tantra or the seventy-two kinds of initiations, blessings, and transmissions connected with the unexcelled yoga tantras. He specifically received transmission of the "Four Profound Dharmas Contained within the Iron Fence."[543]

Similarly, once when Sachen was visiting a nomadic area, Geshé Nyak saw that upon the upper part of his neck the mark of the stable *thiklé* had appeared. Geshé Nyak asked him, "Whose student are you?" The great lama replied, "When I was in Tsarkha,[544] I was the student of a lama who taught me over the course of three years." Then, [later,] people asked the older [monks of Sakya], "When did the great lama go to Tsarkha?" They answered, "He never went beyond Gungthang!" Demonstrating [51] his ability in multiple bodily manifestations in such ways, he imparted teachings on some thirty great meditations.

[Sachen] continued to teach the Lamdré at Sakya to fulfill the wishes of the previous lamas. He stayed at Gungthang while attending to Mal and receiving the teaching cycle of Ghaṇṭāpa.[545] In the Drön Lacham Lhakhang[546] at Dringtsam,[547] he built a stainless maṇḍala of Mañjuśrī and performed its consecration. While in the nomadic region of Sangdong,[548] he taught the Lamdré. He turned the wheel of Dharma while in Shabgo Nga.[549] He engaged in all these activities in the same year, in the same month, and on the same day! After he passed into nirvāṇa, all his disciples put this together among themselves; had they not, nobody would have realized! It thereafter became well known that he had simultaneously revealed six bodily manifestations.

How He Manifested Power to Destroy the Poisonous Enemy of the Teachings

The demonic manifestations known as the wicked tāntrika Lhachen Taktsa[550] and the wicked Bönpo Rewa Dzugu[551] were profoundly jealous of anyone upholding the Buddha's teachings. They planned to harm the great compassionate Kunga Nyingpo. They paid gold to Dorjé Gyal,[552] a student of Taktsa hailing from Denma in Kham,[553] to kill the great lama. That Khampa accepted their offer and headed off for Sakya.

At that time, the Great Compassionate One, Kunga Nyingpo, was dwelling at Gorum Simchil Karpo.[554] When the Khampa arrived for an audience, Kunga Nyingpo had him sit right next to him. The Khampa said, "I was born in Kham's Denma. [52] For many years, I traveled about in the upper regions. While doing so, I came to hear of your fame. With great devotion, I have now come into your presence. Please, will you now allow me to abide here with you?" The great lama granted his request. While this Khampa appeared to show only the greatest respect, he thought only about how to kill the lama. While the great lama already knew this, on one occasion, the Jetsun [Drakpa Gyaltsen] and his brother [Sönam Tsemo] played with their father in the great lama's baggy robes. The Khampa saw this and thought, "This is the behavior of an ordinary father, not that of a lama. Forget about him being a Dharma practitioner!" As such egregious wrong views arose, the great lama's clairvoyant mind knew them.

[Sachen] again invited the Khampa to come sit near him and asked, "Do you not have some negative conceptual thoughts?" The Khampa was alarmed and then became nervous. The great lama then said to him, "Holding a wrong view toward the tantric vajra master is a very severe mistake, indeed!" Saying this, he stretched out his two feet. Upon his soles, the maṇḍalas of Hevajra and Cakrasaṃvara appeared more clearly than if someone had drawn them. He showed these to the Khampa, who was gripped by profound regret and confessed his faults. He promised that in the future he would offer his body, speech, and mind to the great lama.

After that, the Khampa returned to Lhachen Taktsa and made up a story that he had killed [52] the great lama. This fooled Lachen Takcha. Dorjé Gyal made him his personal attendant, giving him many instructions, such as "You shouldn't touch my bed or mala; always keep these clean." The Khampa purposefully did such things as mess up his bed, undo the knot of his mala, throw the mala into the toilet, and so on. He also did such things to the wicked Bönpo. As a result, their black mantra magic was thoroughly disturbed.

At that time, the magnificent Lord of Power, the great lama Kunga Nyingpo, submitted a powerful Dharma protector into his service. He then commanded that he do the subjugating activity of direct action. Many wrathful signs arose in the area where both the tāntrika and the Bönpo dwelt. For example, two wild black yaks suddenly appeared rubbing their horns in an area where none had ever lived previously. It is well known that unthinkable manifestations of the Dharma protector then appeared in the form of black birds, black dogs, jackals, and so forth. At the same time, the samaya-holder Khampa Dorjé Gyal conspired for the disciples of the wicked tāntrika and the wicked Bönpo to depart for other regions. Over the next thirteen days, only he was left to offer service to both the tāntrika and the Bönpo. On the eve of the twenty-ninth, just before the thirtieth, he killed both the wicked tāntrika and [54] the wicked Bönpo for the sake of the lama and the Buddha's teachings.[555] He loaded their two corpses atop the wild yaks that were manifestations of the Dharma protector. Then he departed with them for the main seat. It is well known that in a single night, he traveled the equivalent of a six-day journey!

Upon arrival, the Khampa offered the two corpses to the great lama. The great lama was very happy and offered him a large reward. Specifically, he bestowed upon him the essential instructions so that he would be able to achieve enlightenment in a single life and a single body. Dorjé Gyal then returned to Kham. There he meditated and in time became a yogin who impartially showed signs of great accomplishment and who certainly attained the supreme siddhi of mahāmudrā in the bardo.

The great lama then carved out the wicked tāntrika's heart. He set it inside a leper's skull and placed this in a destruction pit (*hom khung*). That, in turn, was kept in front of the mask of great Segön.[556] He commanded that on account of this wrathful activity all his wishes would be fulfilled. In later times, the sun of the Buddha's teachings, the king of mantra holders Ngakwang Künga Rinchen,[557] opened the destruction pit. Therein was a leper's skull inside of which was the heart. [Ngakwang Kunga Rinchen] used visualization to forcefully draw samaya-breaking (*dam nyams*) enemies such as Lha and Né into [the heart]. He then engaged in true speech to the deities, and so forth, and eradicated the samaya breakers. I heard this story many times from my Mañjuśrī Lama and his brothers. It will be necessary in the future to undertake quick action against those among the subjects of Sakyapa who may harm the lineage along with the teachings. At that time, with pure motivation [55] and by following the ritual procedures of the previous lamas, there is no doubt that the signs of success will quickly appear. This is my interpretation.

The great lama himself buried the corpse of the wicked tāntrika at the threshold of the Mahākāla Temple at Gorum.[558] Nowadays, the leather bag containing his corpse is clearly visible to everyone from the circumambulatory path of Utsé.[559] The corpse of the wicked Bönpo Rewa Dzugu[560] was buried near the river at the western gate of Chötri Thangmoché.[561] It was pressed underneath a stūpa, which people intentionally avoid circumambulating. If they do circumambulate, while doing so they recite the root mantra of Mahākāla or the doksé mantra ("reversal and murder")[562] and go about it counterclockwise.

Here, we must note that the direct disciple of the great lama named Khampa Dorgyal and Deshek Khampa Dorgyal[563] have similar names but are not the same person. This is because the name of Phakdru[564] is Dorjé Gyaltsen, while the other is named Dorjé Gyalpo.[565] These stories about the wicked tāntrika and the wicked Bönpo have come to us in the oral tradition of Salo Jampai Dorjé,[566] as these were explained by the king of the holders of mantra, Ngakwang Kunga Rinchen. I, in turn, heard them from the two Mañjuśrī brothers. These are precisely described in brief in the *Description of the Holy Sites of Sakya*[567] written by Jamyang Sönam Wangpo.

Furthermore, as for the way that lama revealed his magical powers: [56] On one occasion, while holding a knife to his breast, a Khampa said to Sachen, "If you refuse to show me signs that you are Avalokiteśvara, I will kill myself!" The lama said, "You needn't stab your heart with a knife. Behold!" He then showed him such things as his palms, upon which were eyes.

If one wonders about the disciples of this lama, among the best of them were Master Palden Tsemo.[568] He was Sachen's spiritual and biological son and gained the first bhūmi. From two bodily manifestations, he went to the pure land Sukhāvati. Also, as the hermit Lord Shang prophesied and as he had once dreamed after receiving the preparatory initiation from Gyichuwa, Sachen had three disciples who achieved mahāmudrā in a single lifetime: one ācārya from the island of Sri Lanka,[569] Jangchup Sempa Tak,[570] and Gompakyi Barwa.[571] He also had seven disciples who attained the forbearance stage on the path of preparation: Jetsun Rinpoché,[572] Shujé,[573] Gatön Dorjé Drak,[574] Nakgom Sönam Gyaltsen,[575] Tsarkhai Naljorpa,[576] Gompa Ödrak,[577] and Mang Chungma.[578] In addition, he had a great many disciples who were knowledgeable, who gained power, and who practiced supreme mental stabilization, but who undertook their unthinkable practice in secret. For the extensive biographies of these disciples, you should consult my text *Ocean of Assembled Elegance: The Great History of the Oral Instructions*.[579]

There were a further eleven spiritual sons who cherished the explanation of the textual tradition, seven spiritual sons who upheld the tradition of explanatory verses, and the four great regional scholar-practitioners. [57]

As it says in the verse and prose praise composed by Shujé:[580]

> The eight males and three females to whom he gave instructions
> were disciples who completely understood the profound meaning.

Those eight male students were: Khampa Aseng,[581] Lhopa Shujé,[582] Lokya José Chödrak,[583] the spiritual son Nyen Phulchungwa,[584] Tsuktor Gyalpo,[585] and Tsengö Sönam Dorjé,[586] along with the manifestations of Avalokiteśvara: Jangsem Dawa Gyaltsen,[587] Sangri Phukpa,[588] Khampa Gatheng,[589] and Nyakshi Darma Wangchuk Gyaltsen.[590] His three female students were his son Kunga Bar's[591] mother, Jocham Phurmo;[592] Jomo Auma from Yalung;[593] and Jomo Mangchungma from Mangkhar.[594] Together, these eleven disciples are well known as the Eleven Who Received Commentary.[595] In reference to these eleven, do not think they are in reference to any others!

Secondly, as for his direct spiritual sons who upheld his teaching tradition, there are: Naro Bandé,[596] Tongom Jangchup Sherab,[597] Minyak Prajña Jala,[598] Shudrak Marba,[599] Yarbu Ba[600] of Uyuk,[601] and Phakmo Drubpa.[602] As for the four regional scholar-adepts, these were: Latöpa Könchok Khar,[603] Khampa Galo,[604] Netsé Baltön,[605] and Shen Dorjé Sangpo.[606]

Furthermore, regarding verses that help us easily learn the names of Sachen's disciples, there is the supplement to Shujé's *Praise of Lord Sachen*[607] written by Paṇchen Minyak Drakdor:[608]

> As for the disciples who Sachen ripened:
> according to Shang Gön Gyichuwa's prophecy, [58]

three are clearly known to have attained mahāmudrā in this life:
the yogi of Singa Ling,[609] Jangsem Tak,[610]
and Gompa Kyiwar.[611]
The seven who attained the path of forebearance were
the Great Jetsun,[612] Shüjé Songdrup,[613]
Nagöm Sögyal,[614] the yogi of Tsarkha,
Gompa Ö Drak,[615] Gatön,[616] and Mangchungma.[617]
And that disciple who remained ever youthful was
Sönam Tsemo, who famously went to Ḍākinī Land.
Additionally, the disciples of the mahātmā
who attained siddhi included
Palchen Galö,[618] who mastered the tantric discipline and accomplished his practice;
the bodhisattva Dawa Gyaltsen;[619]
the glorious and great Phakmo Drubpa;
Gompa Tagen;[620] the yogi Phaktön;[621] and so on.
As for those who were never attached
to the pleasures of the desire realm,
not even in their dreams,
and who practiced the two stages, the essence of tantra, [59]
were countless holy scholar-practitioners
who pervaded across the earth clad in its oceans:
Gyaltsa Talphukpa,[622] born in Tanak;[623]
Yartön Buma Ba,[624] who was born at Uyuk;
Shentön Dor Seng,[625] who appeared in Yortön;[626]
Shentön Gön Karwa,[627] who was born at Yarlung;
Shangtön Sumthokpa,[628] who appeared at Ön;[629]
Drakmar Shu[630] and Shangtön Peimarpa;[631]
Kyura Akyab[632] and his son A seng;
Netsé Baltön, who appeared at Nam;[633]
Lhadrak Kartön[634] and Chakyi Dorjé;[635]
Dzangtön[636] and Dzané,[637] both learned ones from Sangphu;[638]
the excellent spiritual son Sönam Dorjé[639]
("also known as Nyenpül Chungwa"[640]);
Nyaktön Wangyal;[641] Gyagom Tsultrim Drak;[642]

Minyak Tönpa Prajña Jala;
Khampa Gatheng; A Uma;[643] and so forth.
Still more came from among Galö's[644] disciples,
such as Yudrakpa[645] and so forth;
and among Dagyal's[646] disciples,
such as Nyin Phukpa[647] and so forth;
and among Phakdrü's disciples,
such as the three: Dri, Tak, and Ling,[648] and so forth;
and among Gyaltsé's[649] disciples,
such as Rima Chegom[650] and so forth;
and among Aseng's disciples,
Chak, Tsang, and Nyangren,[651] and so forth;
the Lord [Jestun Drakpa Gyaltsen's] student Sakya Paṇchen;
the eight famous ones; and so forth.
All these holy ones who pervaded the eastern edges of the ocean:
these are the succession of that great compassionate one's students.

That great lama held the main seat for forty-eight years, from age twenty to sixty-seven. On the fourteenth day of the waxing phase of the Acvina moon[652] in the Male Earth Tiger Year [1158], he passed into nirvāṇa escorted by dākās and yoginīs at Yeru Kyawo Khadong.[653] At that time, musical sounds, a great cloud of wonderful scents, and an efflorescence of lights and rainbows appeared to the common perception of all people. He displayed the four bodily manifestations: the first departed to the pure land Sukhāvatī, the second to Potala, the third to Oḍḍiyāna, and the fourth to Serdok Chen[654] in the north of the world. This was clearly understood by most of those in his company. The reasons for [these four manifestations] are as follows. Because he possessed the saṃbhogakāya of Avalokiteśvara, he went to Sukhāvatī. Because he possessed the nirmāṇakāya of Avalokiteśvara, he went to Potala. Because the ḍākinī's seal [60] appeared in his tantric volume, he emanated to Oḍḍiyāna, land of Padmasambhava. Because his son had already transmigrated there, he went to Serdok Chen to purify its buddhafield. All this has been explained by Shujé Ngödrup.[655]

While they cremated his body, those in attendance experienced no unhappy feelings and developed meditation experiences. They altogether beheld the four faces of Cakrasaṃvara. Geshé Sangri Phukpa[656] circumambulated the funeral pyre and saw that the principal face turned toward him. Some of those in attendance also saw the eight faces of Hevajra. They threw his ashes into a lake, and the maṇḍala of Cakrasaṃvara clearly appeared upon its surface. Nowadays, they draw the maṇḍala of Cakrasaṃvara at Kubum Namgyal[657] to commemorate this event. Some would claim this maṇḍala formed from the cremation ash.

Allow me to summarize with the following verses:

Sachen was the actual compassionate lord Avalotikeśvara
manifested as the bodhisattva Jinpa Pal,[658]
appearing once again to benefit sentient beings.
Alternatively, he was the powerful lord Virūpa
intentionally taking rebirth.
This is proved by hundreds of thousands of correct reasons.
Concerning all this, those endowed with intellectual skill
see no opportunity to raise even the slightest doubt.
The succession of your sons and lineage holders
left behind an amazing and admirable legacy
in the realms of religion, politics, and the economy.
This transpired in the past and exists still today.
There is no question that it will continue to unfold in the
future.
Concerning that excellent assemblage of causes and legacies,
other than those whose force of compassion is like that of
Avalokiteśvara [61]
or whose power is like that of Virūpa,
who among ordinary beings can bring all this about?
For this reason, your actual biography is inexpressible.
By the compassion of you who possess wisdom and great
kindness,
please bless me and other beings so that we may accomplish
all our wishes!

Recollecting the biography of glorious and compassionate Kunga Nyingpo, I praise and make supplications!

After recalling the life story of the glorious, compassionate Kunga Nyingpo and following the praise and supplication to him, there follows a small expression of praise to Glorious Sakya, which became the primary seat of that great lama.

Like the glorious Gaṇḍavyūha buddhafield,[659]
with an assembly of Victorious Ones endowed with the five certainties,
this is a supreme abode for the many exponents of the Great Secret:
praise to the Great Seat wherein many scholars gather!

[Mount Wangpo,] supreme lord of mountains, encircled by the peaks of the Land of the Snowy Mountains all bowed down with respect,
is spontaneously established as Mount Meru, greatest ruler of mountains.
It is like the king of animals, dwelling among beasts while arrogantly showing off its youthfulness and might.
It subjugates all other mountains without exception, including primarily Jambu, and abides luminous and clear.

All across the area to its right, [water] pools like blue crystal with the nature of the *padmarāga*.
That Great Seat is extensively pervaded by the Lord of Great Bliss and outshines all the Three Realms.
Like Śambhala, the landscape surrounding [Sakya] is beautified by a garland of mountains including Mount Kailash.
As for all this, it is like a well-arranged garland of water lilies, the flower offering [62] of the goddesses of the three times.

Inside is an abundance of various jewels.
This throne of a mountain of riches
is the foundation for the majestic, glorious great Victors
who turn the wheel of the profound and vast Dharma.

Supreme earth, like the face of a lion,
presents itself as if it wished to soon depart to Akaniṣṭha Pure Land.
Its surface is the color of a snow mountain.
This is the foundation for the original Victor's turning of the Dharma wheel.

Because of the great earth being stirred and shaken,
and the King of Asuras having churned up the ocean,
Drachung Gongkha, the lord of mountains to the east,
emerged and sat poised like the Lord of Excellent Ones [Mount Meru].

With an excellent color, fine blue like the vast sky,
sometimes moving swiftly, like a herd of many [beasts],
other times [moving gently, like] the Lord of the Changshé enjoying its food:
The slow flow of Kha'u is a fount of riches.

Blue Wangpo Mountain is like a peacock whose color delights the mind,
who is delighted by gathering clouds,
who flaunts its beautiful tail feathers round while dancing,
and who flies high above the open space of a pond.

Mount Pönpo, the north mountain of the great Dharma college,
abides in a marvelous, excellent state,
[like] a young garuda beautified by feathers,
resplendent amid a flock of ten million birds.

This precious earth wheel[660] is beautified by ornaments, like the gathering of emeralds.
It is like the offering made by the Creator of the World[661] when he requested the turning of the wheel of profound and vast Dharma,

or it is like when [the Buddha] became lord of the four continents and superior to the lord of the earth, Pandu.[662]
It appears like the seven precious objects offered by the Lord of the Higher Realms,[663] [63] such as a wheel and so forth.

Lord of Victors with an exquisite peak,
glorious treasury of beings' desires and a coil of joy,
you are the origin of all auspiciousness and virtuous signs,
and, further, you are the product of the merit of all embodied beings.

There, the beautiful sun is clothed in a dark maroon mist
and the supreme nobility is adorned by flowers and fruit trees.
I respectfully pay homage with pure water flowing continuously
and pleated cords of plucked flower petals.

A crown of gathered gray rain is nothing but a silk turban;
not simply enveloped by sprouting green grass, but a full blue-green cloth robe;
a painting of coiled rainbow-light embellished with jewels:
[other mountains] thus revere its immovable majesty, like ministers toward their leader.

It is said gazing upon supreme unshakeable Mount Wangpo or the supreme earth all about Kha'u,
when the early morning sun hits the peaks of the easterly mountain,
one may hear the profound and vast Dharma proclaimed, and one may clearly see all the many scholars residing at Great Bliss.[664]
The sweet fine light [of its fame] reached even the Heaven of the Thirty-Three.

At that time, He Who Made One Hundred Offerings[665] was amazed [by Sakya] and emanated a thousand eyes by which to behold it.
From this, the goosebumps of his devotion arose and he dedicated the best of his wealth:
he adorned the cloud-driven horse with immeasurable adornments, such as divine clothing and so forth,
and beautified it [64] using an attractive net made from a well-fashioned garland of many varieties of jewels.

Amid the essence of the bouquet of refreshing fragrances of water lilies
in the pool of the nectar of immortality, which beautifies the trunk of [Indra's elephant] Airavata,[666]
the youthful bees of the three times gracefully frolic, making sweet melodious sounds and so forth.
Emanating numberless manifestations of well-arranged oceans of offering clouds,
we offer [all this] to the learned scholars as if we were bearing such clouds!

This precious, rocky mountain, red with the nature of coral,
possessed of qualities unlike any other:
a military commander outfitted with armor of *padmarāga*,
campaigning to conquer hordes of opposing armies.

When touched by the sun's rays, the finest cloth [of snow] of great Mount Meru melts and becomes water; this is just like the clear river flowing along the right [of Sakya].
[Upon the sight of it,] ducks begin to dance excitedly, frolicking about like golden lightning, and one after the other they enter into its ocean of great bliss.
Alternatively, it is beautified as if by a succession of waves of the snouts and feet of youthful crocodiles, together with foam beautiful like a crystal necklace; this is [like] the playful dance of the Daughter of Dzāhu.[667]

Its hanging ornaments making the sound of cymbals ringing, along with the sweet melody of its flowing water, are supreme offerings made respectfully to those practicing asceticism at Great Bliss.

This flowing river of Mañjughoṣa's realizations is not in fact this river; it is the current of Kunga Nyingpo's compassion.
Should one drink from it, all youth and majesty is bestowed, like completing mercury pills.
Should one see it, one's lotus-like mind blossoms, believing the youthful sun has risen. [65]
Should one wash in it, wild thickets of ignorance are burned away, yet still it is the flowing nectar of immortality.

Because the ocean of great bliss[668] beautifies the earth,
it is like the Nāga [King], whose crown is beautified by a wish-fulfilling gem;
who upholds the precious treasure, the Treasury Keeper Lord of Nāgās;
and who provides the collection of glory and abundances that are the fortune of beings' desires.

Here, at the source of the extensive marvels of saṃsāra and nirvāṇa,
Mañjugoṣa, Mañjuśrī, and Vajra Mañjuśrī
gradually appeared in stages over seven periods.
Regents of the Victor, they were in fact just like him.

Lords of the Buddha's teachings and the upholders of the teachings;
refuges of beings for the welfare of beings on behalf of all beings;
sources of liberation by teaching the path to liberation to those who wish for liberation;
bestowers of great bliss with ease and joy: So it is said about them.

[The Khön were] endowed by an intelligent antagonism (*'khon*) to ignorance.
Then the Triple Gem and the earth-protector Emperor
bestowed all virtue and goodness! All virtue and goodness!
Conscientious scholars then arose here in abundance like the dawn.
By this, [Sakya] became the superior among all supreme seats.
Just like the magical city of Kapila,
[Sakya] is the marvelous origin of the abundances of gods and humans.
It was built 3,251 years
after the Lord of Sages had turned the excellent wheel of Dharma,
accompanied by an abundance of auspicious and virtuous signs.

This supreme field possesses the learned, conscientious, and excellent.
If any place possesses the excellent, conscientious, and learned, it is a supreme field.
This is the field of the glorious, powerful, and supreme.
And supreme and powerful fields are glorious.

The Lord of Yogins [Virūpa], emanation [66] of the Victor,
Became overlord of this blessed land.

At the center of the vast expanse[669] of Jambudvīpa,
Is this field whose nature is like the center of a vajra,
Supreme among the entirety of an ocean of buddha fields,
This supreme [land] is Bodhgayā.

Superior among all the oceans of buddha fields,
this superior place is the essence of the earth.
Bestowing joyfulness and magnificence upon all beings,
this is the ground upon which one obtains the essence of enlightenment.

This Vajra Seat [Sakya], in nature like the vajra,
where an ocean of Victors attained enlightenment,
is no different than Maghada,
in nature like the gathering of a great variety of jewels.

The measureless encircling outer iron wall
is marked by many doors, sources of prosperity,
comparable only to the City of Pleasant Sight.
Therefore, its circumference, the nature of the vajra,
subjugates all vicious demons
and completely opposes the collection of harm toward beings.
Great meritorious beings thus have come to rely upon it.

Although there are many places with many varieties of wealth,
as for being a source of knowledge, there is none like this.
Although there are many attractive and fine jewels,
as for wish-fulfilling jewels, there is but one.

This medicinal land (*sman ljongs*), wherein one discovers many kinds of fruit,
is like an excellent pure land wherein all beings are joyful.
Adorned with the eight auspicious symbols,
reddish-yellow light radiating across the expanse of its earth
completely illuminates beautiful flowers,
which emit the aroma of their fragrance into the ten directions.
Atop [those flowers], swarms of young bees laden with honey
dwell while buzzing [67] with joy.
It seems as if they are divine manifestations meant as offerings to Mañjugoṣa.

The Victors, their disciples, and [the disciples'] disciples have thus relied upon this place.
It is a center for all the excellent knowledge of the five sciences.

It is a pleasant grove for those holding the superior saffron robes.
This supreme Great Seat is therefore surely a place for achieving the essence of enlightenment!

This finishes the praise to the Great Dharma College of Glorious Sakya, the primary holy seat of the Great Lama [Kunga Nyingpo], which is taken from *The Power of Sustenance*.[670]

2. The Precious Master, Sönam Tsemo (1142–82)

I WILL NOW DESCRIBE the life story of Sachen Kunga Nyingpo's son, who would come to uphold that Great Compassionate One's teachings and become his regent.

Regarding this, that lama was married to two wives. From among two siblings in the lineage of venerable ones, Sachen was first married to the youngest, who hailed from Rongpa in the Tshamo region.[671] Her name was Jocham Phurmo.[672] Her son, Kunga Bar,[673] was born at Sakya. He would later travel to India to study and became quite knowledgeable in the five fields. However, he fell ill from the heat when he was preparing to return to Tibet. He died at just twenty-two years old in the city of Magadha.

Sachen Kunga Nyingpo later married his first wife's older sister, Machik Ödrön,[674] with whom he had three sons. The eldest of those was the Precious Master, Sönam Tsemo, who was born when his father was fifty-one years old in the year of the Male Water Dog (1142). Upon his birth, ḍākinīs inscribed letters above the gates in Bodhgayā, proclaiming: "An emanation of Mañjuśrī named Khenpo Sönam Tsemo, a sovereign lord presiding over all the Vajrayāna, has been [68] born at Sakya." Following this proclamation, the Kauśāmbī Paṇḍita Dewa Mati searched for him in all directions, finally finding him dwelling in Tibet.

Just after his birth, Sönam Tsemo spoke in Sanskrit and twice announced: "I am done with childish activities!" Thereafter, to everyone's amazement, he always sat with crossed legs. When he was three years old, he directly saw the faces of Mañjuśrī, Hevajra, Tārā, and Acalā, and he recited from his heart five sūtras: [unexcelled yoga] tantras of the three classes,[675] the root tantra of Cakrasaṃvara, and the *Compendium*.[676] He

Fig. 22. Lopön Sönam Tsemo (1142–82)

clearly remembered that he had been reborn eleven times successively as great Indian paṇḍitas, including as Mithup Dawa,[677] who had lived for the benefit of all sentient beings.

He later received Vajrayāna teachings and transmissions from his father, including a commentary on the *Compendium*, sādhanas, maṇḍalas, tantric empowerments, transmission blessings, oral instructions, practical guidance, and reading transmissions. He completely understood all of these. When he was nearly sixteen years old, it is said that he could recite fourteen tantric scriptures entirely from memory. It became well known across Tibet to as far as the Ganges River that he was very knowledgeable in the Vajrayāna teachings.

When he was seventeen years old, he told his younger brother Jetsun Drakpa Gyaltsen, who was then thirteen years old: "I will go to Central Tibet and study the *Prajñāpāramitā*, the texts on logic,[678] and so forth. And then I will return. You should stay here at Sakya and teach the Dharma." In this way, he passed the main seat to his younger brother and left to study at Sangphu Neutok [69] with Chapa Chökyi Sengé.[679] After eleven years of study, he became very knowledgeable. Also, he pleased his teacher Chapa Chökyi Sengé by offering a golden *ganjira*,[680] an extensive *Prajñāpāramitā* text, and many other material offerings.

Master Sengé's disciples became known by being grouped as "The Eight Great Lions," "The Eight Who Are Similar to Lions," and "The Four Noble Sons." The latter group included Khön José Tsemo,[681] Khu José Netso,[682] Ngok José Ramo,[683] and Nyi José Öma.[684] The supreme one from among those four was Khön José Tsemo.

When he was twenty-six years old, in the Female Fire Pig Year (1167), Sönam Tsemo composed the commentary entitled *Entranceway to the Dharma*[685] at the temple of the great holy site of Nala Tsé.[686] Therein, he also provided a faultless elucidation on the practice of astrology. All throughout the night and day, moreover, he continually received teachings on inconceivable Dharma practices directly from his yidam deities and from the glorious Venerable Lord of Yogins Virūpa, which removed all his doubts. As such, he did not forget any field of knowledge whatsoever. It is universally known that by the time he was twenty-seven years old, he had become the supreme life-tree pillar[687] upholding the teachings in this world.

When he was twenty-eight years old, he gave Lamdré teachings at Simkhang Nyingma.[688] On the first day, when it came time to explain the section on philosophical view, three different visions of the lama appeared to the disciples. Jetsun Rinpoché [Drakpa Gyaltsen] saw him as Mañjuśrī appearing in the middle of the sky amid innumerable offering clouds. [70] José Chakyi Dorjé[689] saw him as Virūpa. Most of the others, including Nyak and Moktön Tsuktor Wönpo,[690] saw him as Avalokiteśvara. All of them experienced an extraordinary meditative stabilization.

In particular, while bestowing the initiation on Jetsun Rinpoché [Drakpa Gyaltsen], unthinkable masses of light appeared. Innumerable offerings also appeared, such as the unimaginable sound of heavenly music. Amid all this, Sönam Tsemo truly manifested the maṇḍala and gave the initiation inside it. He delivered a profound teaching and opened the inconceivable door of meditative stabilization. If one wonders how many bhūmis the Venerable Lord of Yogins achieved, Drakpa Gyalsten once said of him:

> In just half a day, he could travel to and from
> Potalaka, Glorious Mountain, Uḍḍiyāna, and more.
> Should he participate in the activities of ḍākinīs and ḍākas,
> many of those manifestations would serve him, rejoice in him,
> and honor him.

As for the meaning of that, Sönam Tsemo attained the ability of multiple manifestations just like that of Kündar and Samantabhadra[691] described in the tantras.

According to the wishes of innumerable groups of disciples, Sönam Tsemo gave Dharma teachings on secret mantra and the sūtras. He was especially knowledgeable about Dharmakīrti's *Ascertainment of Valid Cognition* together with Dharmottara's[692] commentary. During his lifetime, it was well known that among those who wore sleeved clothing,[693] he was unexcelled in his knowledge of scripture and logic and in his skill in debate.

As for the titles of the garland of texts he composed, they included the teaching cycle on the [Lamdré] tradition of oral instruction, such as *Praise to the Great Sakyapa;*[694] *Mixed Prose and Verse Supplication Prayers to the Lamdré Lineage;*[695] [71] *[A Letter] Sent to Gyagom Tsultrim Drak;*[696] *Praise to Master Chapa;*[697] *Classification of the Divisions of Tantra;*[698] *Rays of Sunlight: Explanation upon the Two-Part [Hevajra Tantra],*[699] along with its topical outline; *Classification of the Essentials: Commentary on the Sampuṭa Tantra,*[700] together with its topical outline and a commentary on its second chapter; *Extensive Clear Realization of Glorious Hevajra;*[701] *The Great River of Empowerment;*[702] *The Peaceful Fire Pūja;*[703] *The Six Excellent Consecrations;*[704] and *The List of the Nairātmyā's Initiation.*[705]

As for his writing upon the śāstras, these included *Maṇḍala Ritual in the Dombī Heruka Tradition*[706] and *Commentary on the Fire Pūja Ritual.*[707] As for his writing on the cycle of Tsokyé's teaching lineage, he composed *A Commentary on Tsokyé's Sādhana*[708] and *The Maṇḍala Ritual Entitled Nelingma.*[709] As for his commentaries on the oral instructions, these included *Ghaṇṭāpa's Minor Clear Realization of Cakrasaṃvara,*[710] *Ghaṇṭāpa's Commentary on the Cakrasaṃvara Initiation,*[711] *Luipa's Garland of Offerings to Cakrasaṃvara,*[712] *Commentary on the Tsuktor Namgyal's Tokpa,*[713] *Outline of the Tsuktor Namgyal's Tokpa,*[714] *The Six Doctrines of Dorjé Denpa,*[715] *Praise to the Five Deities of Amoghapāśa,*[716] *History of the Lama Lineage,*[717] *Outline of the Tsuktor Namgyal's Tokpa,*[718] *Precious Garland: Commentary on the Tsuktor Namgyal's Tokpa,*[719] *Water Protector of Blue Acalā,*[720] and so forth. In addition to the above, he composed the *Sādhana Cycle of [Avalokiteśvara's] Lion's Roar,*[721] the *Ritual of the Great Torma,*[722] *Commentary on the Introduction to the Bodhisattva's Way of Life,*[723] *Entranceway to the Dharma,*[724] *Easy Entranceway for Beginners,*[725] and so forth. He composed a great many original, marvelous commentaries such as these. Indeed, all this lama's compositions were excellent and elegantly written.

The annotated commentaries written by this precious master include those for the root tantra of Cakrasaṃvara [72] and for the *Easy Entranceway for Beginners* connected to the *Cakrasaṃvara Tantra*. In sum, through the three scholarly activities,[726] Sönam Tsemo accomplished tremendous activities on behalf of the teachings.

Sönam Tsemo held the main seat for three years and then passed it to his younger brother [Drakpa Gyaltsen]. Thereafter, he mostly dwelled in solitary retreat. When he was forty-one years old, on the eleventh day of the eleventh month of the Male Water Tiger Year (1182), he showed the two bodily displays and departed for Sukhāvatī.

According to the annotation to the supplication prayer entitled *Mournful Melody*[727] by Jetsun Drakpa Gyaltsen, during the night of the tenth day of offerings, the Jetsun, his brother, and others concluded their offering practice. In the morning, the Jetsun left [to visit Sönam Tsemo] and found only his clothing. He had departed for Ḍākinī Land in his own body. Drakpa Gyaltsen then sang a powerful supplication prayer with a mournful melody. Just then, from within the bundle of clothing came the buzzing of a bee delivering a special prophecy. This has also been described in the writing of some other scholars. Another well-known story connected to this is that an old woman from Sakya had a direct vision in which the master himself and a female dog flew higher and higher into the sky from a stone mountain above Chumik Dzingkha.[728] Upon its rocky surface, Master Tsemo and the dog left clearly appearing footprints impressed in the stone. These were left behind for sentient beings as objects for the accumulation of merit. In later times, Ngakchang Chökyi Gyalpo Ngakwang Kunga Rinchen[729] paid homage to this place by installing a back curtain[730] and so on.

According to various biographical accounts, Sönam Tsemo is said to have passed away in diverse places, such as Chumik Dzingka,[731] the Gorum Library,[732] and so on. [73] Some say that he left many holy objects behind, such as ashes from his corpse that were fashioned into a stūpa. As it says in the supplication prayer composed by Jetsun [Drakpa Gyaltsen] upon the master's passing:

> In these ways, you performed a great many activities on
> behalf of sentient beings.
> When you were forty-one years old, in the eleventh month of
> the Water Tiger Year,
> on the tenth day of the waxing moon, O singular venerable
> great lama,
> you became inseparable from Vajradhara's mind.
>
> During meditative equipoise in nonconceptual thought,
> you clasped vajra and bell together in both hands and spoke
> on abandoning all attachments and offering to the spiritual
> master and the Triple Gem;

from this, said you, one progresses from bliss to the Land of
Great of Bliss.

Afterward, when sitting cross-legged in your sleeping
quarters,
by the power of single-pointed concentration with both hands
in equipoise,
the sky became completely filled by sound and light
and you accepted that you would soon depart for Sukhāvatī.

Just then, suddenly the sound of mantras and music
and supreme sweet smells filled the ten directions.
A congregation of millions of ḍākinīs arrived to welcome you,
and then you departed for Sukhāvatī along a pure path.

Since you went to Sukhāvatī, there is no reason for me to be
sad.
Still, when I recall your conduct and practice,
it makes me suffer even more.
Please, O Lord, teach me a method to find peace!

In summary, according to the perception of those with pure karma, [Sönam Tsemo] departed [for Sukhāvatī] without ever abandoning his body. According to the perception of more common disciples, he displayed the manner of passing beyond and departing without impediment for the supreme pure land of Sukhāvatī.

This holy master produced many unrivaled disciples, those who upheld the teachings [74] like his younger brother Jetsun Rinpoché [Drakpa Gyaltsen] and their other siblings, Shujé Ngödrup, and Moktön,[733] and so forth. Together, they beautified the world. Concerning all this, it has been said:

On the broad moon of the maṇḍala of your face
appear your utpala eyes and the clear radiance of your beautiful smile.

When I see or remember your body's appearance,
my mind is powerless and is completely taken by clear faith.

In a single gulp, you completely drank the ocean of sūtra and tantra,
and so the texts you composed encapsulate their essence.
Upon reading them, my mind so desires to know their meaning
that it becomes fixated, like in unmoving, single-pointed concentration.

When I behold the story of your liberated life, it is clear that your mind, O holy one,
is profound and clear and free from any negative action,
and that it is never separate from that nature.
By this, I arouse trusting faith that you are indeed one with Mañjuśrī!

For such reasons, you are Mañjughoṣa appearing as a lay practitioner,
arisen from unmanifested space to marshal the forces of compassion.
Please continually protect me, one who has acquired faith through knowledge,
and all your other disciples!

This prayer of supplication was self-arisen!

3. Jetsun Rinpoché Drakpa Gyaltsen (1147–1216)

Sönam Tsemo's younger brother, Jetsun Rinpoché Drakpa Gyaltsen, was born when their father was fifty-six years old, on the eighteenth day of the eleventh month of the Female Fire Rabbit Year (1147). When illuminating his life story, one must understand it in four parts: how he was born, how he obtained knowledge of the three trainings, how he performed enlightened activity, and how he received prophecies and remembered his former lives.

As for the first, before he was born, [75] he appeared in a dream to his mother in the aspect of a nāga king. He was later born accompanied by auspicious signs. He could speak immediately, took delight in remote places, and enjoyed making effort to acquire knowledge unsullied by any attachment. Such behavior was quite unlike that of any normal child.

As for the second, when he was eight years old, he received the layman's upāsaka vow of pure conduct from the bodhisattva Dawa Gyaltsen.[734] From that time forward, his conduct was more disciplined than any renunciant. He deeply aspired to become a monk. He regularly took part in the monastic confessional ceremony.[735] He would say, "I will serve tea to the monks!" and would carefully observe those serving tea [so as to do so correctly himself]. Due to habitual tendencies from having been a fully ordained monk in his previous lives, while eating food and letting his mind wander, he would think to himself, "I did not return gratitude for the gift of this food!"[736] Whenever he ate, he would take only a small amount. After some time, he began to accept a slightly large portion. Others asked him, "Why are you doing this?" He told them, "I first had a strong desire for barley beer. I even drank it in my dreams! I came to consider this to be the activity of demons and so I stopped.

Fig. 23. Jetsun Drakpa Gyeltsen (1147–1216)

Now I have little desire, so I again drink it." Meat and alcohol but rarely touched his lips.

When he was ten years old, he received transmission of the *Twenty Verses on the Bodhisattva Vow*[737] and the *Tshokyé Sādhana*. When he was eleven years old, he taught these texts. Everyone was amazed and named him Lodrö Chenpo, or "Great Intelligence." When he was twelve years old, he dreamed that he ate the three volumes of the *Hevajra Tantra* and that he then understood the essence of all the Dharma. When Sachen [76] passed away, [Drakpa Gyaltsen] turned the wheel of the Dharma on the *Two-Part Hevajra Tantra* to the assembly of disciples. Everyone was amazed. When he was thirteen years old, his older brother went to [study in] Central Tibet. From then until he was seventeen, he gave tantric teachings.

As for the oral instructions [on Lamdré], Drakpa Gyaltsen's lama gave him the command-seal of secrecy for a period of nine years. Regardless, he kept it for thirteen. During that time, he received teaching from such masters as Lopön Rinpoché, Nyen Tsuktor Gyalpo,[738] Shang Tsultrim Drak,[739] Nyak Wangyal,[740] the Nepali Dzaya Sena,[741] the Lotsāwa Darma Yönten,[742] Sumpa Lotsāwa Pelchok Dangpoi Dorjé,[743] and so forth.

As for the teachings that he received on the unexcelled yoga tantras, these included all of the Hevajra root and explanatory tantras along with their ancillary commentaries and sādhanas according to different exegetical traditions, the Cakrasaṃvara root and explanatory tantras along with their supplements, and the three Guhyasamāja tantras together with their commentaries and branches according to the teaching cycle of Ārya Nāgārjuna. As for the teaching tradition of Jñānapada, he received all quintessential instructions, including those of tantra, Dzayan, and so forth. From within Jñānapada's system, he received Vitapada's[744] tantric commentary together with its quintessential instructions and their branches.

As for the yoga tantras, he received commentaries on the *Assemblage of Suchness* entitled *The Manifestations of Suchness*, as well as the *Vajraśekhara*, the glorious *Supreme*, *The Purification Tantra*[745] together with its branches, the three Yamāntaka tantras together with their supplements, oral instructions on the outer and inner Kālacakra together with its supplements, and commentary upon the *Reciting the Names of Mañjuśrī*[746] together with its supplements. [77]

As for performance tantra, he received the great commentary on [the system of] Acalā,[747] and so on.

In the action tantra class, he received transmission and commentary upon the *General Rituals of All Maṇḍalas, The Tantra of Subāhu's Questions,*[748] and so forth.

He additionally received teachings upon innumerable divisions of the Dharma on topics like the sūtras, chronologies of the teachings, quintessential instructions, and so on.

Whenever people requested that he teach them the Dharma, he would do so immediately. He never adopted the habit of procrastinating. This lord, moreover, once said, "I am not someone who has received a great number of teachings, but I am someone who has studied extensively! There are no texts from the Tripiṭaka that I did not study, other than the scriptures on monastic discipline, which I initially avoided since I planned on ordaining as a monk. Later, I understood that I would not become a monk and then studied this text."

Drakpa Gyaltsen was a strictly disciplined meditator who practiced until the middle of the night. Early in the morning, he would arrange all his clothes. Even if it was winter, he used the water vessel on his belt to perform the showering practice. When it was time to teach the Dharma, he would meditate upon Hevajra while walking to the teaching site. Fully engaged in this meditation, he would take his place upon the [teaching] throne. There he would finish the practices of the chief deity's crown practice. He would substitute the sessional torma with a teaching torma.[749] And he would substitute the recitation of mantra with teaching. When he finished teaching, he would meditate upon Cakrasaṃvara while taking his leave from the teaching site.

In brief, during a single period of day and night, he would meditate upon seventy different maṇḍalas. It is said that nobody ever saw him engaged in any activity other than meditation, reading texts, or teaching the Dharma; no one ever witnessed his body, speech, and mind [78] engaged in any worldly behavior whatsoever.

As for the third, on the topic of his teaching: No matter how difficult a topic or how unfamiliar he was with it, Drakpa Gyaltsen never had to prepare before giving a teaching. He could simply explain it straightaway in such a way that his disciples would understand it easily. In the matter of debate, when he would dispute and pose questions, without second-guessing himself, he would provide answers that made use of scripture and reasoning and were in harmony with the Dharma. By this, he would remove others' wrong views.

Regarding the elegantly composed texts that he composed, they include: *Supplication to the Lamdré Lineage;*[750] *Possessing Purity: Commentary on the Two-Part [Hevajra Tantra];*[751] *The Precious Tree: Clear Realization of the Three Tantras;*[752] *The Tantra in One Hundred and Thirteen Sections;*[753] *Outline of Tongthün;*[754] *Biography of the Venerable Great Sakya Masters;*[755] *Verse Biography of Lopön Rinpoché;*[756] *The Jetsun's Dream Autobiography;*[757] *Catalogue of the 100,000 Tantras [of Hevajra];*[758] *Catalogue of the Teaching Cycle of the Great Lama Mal;*[759] *Catalogue of the Hevajra Teaching Cycle;*[760] *Quintessential Instructions that Transform in the Three Times;*[761] *The Six Limbs of Realization of Hevajra;*[762] *The Bari Lotsāwa Tradition of Solitary Hevajra;*[763] *The Six Limbs of Realization;*[764] *Instructions Given to Gatön Dorjé Drak;*[765] *Hevajra Fire Rituals for the Four Activities;*[766] *The Clear Realization of Vajra Dakmema;*[767] *A Minor Supplication to the Lamdré Lineage;*[768] *The Auspicious [Verse Prayer for] the Hevajra Maṇḍala;*[769] *Ritual for the Time of Death;*[770] *Praise to Hevajra Called Dandaka;*[771] *Praise to Dakmema*[772] and its outline, *Praise to Blue Acalā;*[773] *Outline of the Vajra Tent Tantra;*[774] *Commentary that Is an Ornament to the Vajra Tent;*[775] *Clarifying the Iconography of the Vajra Tent;*[776] [79] *Sādhana of Kurukullā;*[777] *The Six Objects of Glorious Heruka;*[778] *Defining Characteristics of the Vajra and Bell;*[779] *The Three Successes;*[780] *Commentary on the Fifty Verses of Guru Devotion;*[781] *Overcoming Confusion: Commentary on [the Fourteen] Root Downfalls;*[782] *The Origins of Glorious Heruka;*[783] *Cakrasaṃvara Sādhana in the Tradition of Luipa;*[784] *Commentary of the Maṇḍala Ritual of Kāṇha;*[785] the *Maṇḍala Ritual of Kāṇha;*[786] *Outline of Kāṇha's Six Texts;*[787] *Biography and Sādhana of Ghaṇṭāpa;*[788] *How to Make the Offering of the Tenth Day;*[789] *Explanation of the Five Stages of Ghaṇṭāpa;*[790] *Sādhana of Two-Faced Vajravārāhī;*[791] *The Suchness Mantra of the Completion Stage;*[792] *Instructions on the Ten Actions;*[793] *Maitrīpa's Division of the Yoginī Tantra;*[794] the *Yoginī Sādhana of Maitrīpa*[795] and its blessing ritual, the *Yoginī Sādhana of Nāropa;*[796] *Method of Accomplishing the Yoginī by Means of Meditation and Recitation*[797] along with its blessing ritual, concise feast offering, tenth day offering, fire ritual offering, and butter lamp offering ritual; *Instructions for Mirror Divination;*[798] *Instructions for Accomplishing Yakṣiṇī;*[799] *Taking the Essence of Great Medicine;*[800] *Instruction Manual on the Central Channel of the Completion Stage;*[801]

Commentary on the Conduct of the Yoginī[802] and its condensed explanation, *Sādhana of Bright Red Ganesha;*[803] *Sādhana of the Thirty Deities of Dranak;*[804] *Praise to Vajrabhairava;*[805] *Commentary on the Yoga of Dorjé Jungwa;*[806] *Clarifying the Meaning of Consecration;*[807] *The Ārghā Ritual;*[808] *Purification Tantra: General Guidelines for Benefiting Others;*[809] *Outline of the Purification Tantra;*[810] *Rays of Light Benefiting Others: Ritual of the Tantra on the Complete Purification of All Negative Places of Rebirth;*[811] *The Necessity of Benefiting Others;*[812] *Cremation Ritual and Peaceful Fire Offering Ritual;*[813] *General Maṇḍala Ritual for the Lords of the Three Families;*[814] *Tantric Commentary on Accomplishing the Solitary Hero;*[815] *The Wheel of Three Tantras: Praise to Mañjughoṣā;*[816] [80] *How to Chant "Reciting the Names of Mañjuśrī";*[817] *Clear Realization of the Five White Deities of Mañjughoṣā Arapatsana;*[818] *Maṇḍala Ritual of Mañjughoṣā Arapatsana;*[819] *The Ritual of Amoghapāśa;*[820] *Maṇḍala Ritual of Amoghapāśa;*[821] *Praise by Da Jangchup Sempa;*[822] *How to Draw the Yantra Protection Circle;*[823] *Extensive Instructions on Vajrapāṇi's Dhāraṇī;*[824] *Commentary on the Vajravidāraṇa Tantra*[825] and its outline, *Commentary on the Tantra Requested by Subāhu;*[826] *General Sādhana of Tārā;*[827] *Sādhana of the Twenty-One Individual [Tārā] Goddesses;*[828] *The Memorandum Method of Reciting Praise;*[829] *Commentary on the Twenty-One Collective Activities* along with its outline;[830] *The Clear Realization of the Tārā Body Maṇḍala Sent in a Letter to Chim Chöseng;*[831] *Sādhana of Tārā Who Is Peaceful by Day and Wrathful by Night;*[832] *Eliminating Poison;*[833] *Quintessential Advice on the Wealth Deity;*[834] *Condensed Supplication Prayer of the Four Maṇḍalas;*[835] *Extensive [Supplication Prayers] of the Four Maṇḍalas;*[836] *Six Limbs of Tārā According to the Tradition of Nyen;*[837] *Outline of the Praise to Tārā with Twenty-One Verses of Homage*[838] and its commentary entitled *Luminous Clarity;*[839] *Clear Realization of Garuḍa;*[840] *Commentary on the Hundred Sādhanas;*[841] *The Lineage Succession of the Śākya Kings;*[842] *Condensed Royal Succession of the Tibetan Kings;*[843] *How to Categorize Indian and Tibetan Schools;*[844] *Reckoning to Definitively Comprehend a Unit of Time;*[845] *Letter Sent to Garing Gyalpo Requesting Astrological Reading;*[846] *A Precious Garland: A Beginner's Dharma Practice;*[847] *Commentary on the Twenty Verses on Vows;*[848] *Outline of the Introduction to the Bodhisattva's Way of Life;*[849] *Letters about Performing the Nine Homages;*[850] *Many Collections of Spiritual Songs Such as the Great Song of Experience and So Forth;*[851] *Medical Treatments Such as the King's* [81] *Treasure;*[852] and so forth.

As for the commentaries written by this lama, Drakpa Gyaltsen focused most on benefiting others and not primarily on literary style (*sdeb sbyor*). Nonetheless, his compositions are very easy to teach and sweet to the ear. Because of that, scholars are quite taken by them.

On the matter of annotations and maṇḍala iconography, he wrote the *Nyakma*,[853] *Removing Obstacles to Lamdré by Transmission Grounded in the Path of Liberation of the Three Supreme Initiations*,[854] *The Inconceivable Scripture Entitled "Blazing Jewel,"*[855] *The Three Teaching Cycles of Ghaṇṭāpa*,[856] *The Purification Tantra*,[857] *Tantra of Accomplishing Solitary Hero [Hevajra]*,[858] *Clear Realization of the Praise to Tārā with Twenty-One Verses of Homage and the Supplement to the Path Composed by Ravigupta*,[859] *Weapon-Like Introduction to Speech*,[860] and *Examples of the Iconography of Accomplishing Solitary Hero [Hevajra]*.[861]

Furthermore, regarding his attainment of the marvelous signs of meditative accomplishment: he was blessed by his yidam meditation deity; he acquired a clairvoyance that allowed him to know whatever he wished; he could clarify the doubts of any nāga; gods, nāgas, and so forth were obedient whenever he commanded them; if he had difficulty understanding or if he discerned some extraordinary purpose, he would make offerings and requests and the Lord of Yogins [Virūpa] would reveal himself. The lord [Drakpa Gyaltsen] would himself mention this.

As for the respect he showed his lamas, he had no doubt that his master and spiritual sons were truly Vajradhāra. While they were alive, he would please their body, speech, and mind in whatever way he could. Even if his lama made a joking request, he would nonetheless complete it. When the lama passed away, [82] he himself performed a ransom ritual,[862] and so on. Whatever he possessed, he would spend it on behalf of the lama. Since he was unattached to his wealth, he sponsored three extensive Dharma teachings. He continuously made offerings to about a hundred monks. He built a temple known as Utsé Nyingma,[863] a golden chamber for the inner support of Lama Könchok Gyalpo, the [stūpa] of Tashi Gomang[864] for the inner support of Lama Sachen, and a golden image for the inner support of Lopön Rinpoché and his brother. He also established the custom of offering butter lamps all night in front of them. In addition, he made a great many offerings to those great [objects], such as awnings and banners, great canopies, bells, and cloth hangings as beam covers.[865]

He copied most of the Buddhist canon in gold, such as many precious sūtras, tens of thousands of tantras, and so forth. He also extensively recited them. From whatever precious materials he personally received as donations, he used the silver and gold to fabricate more than three hundred copies of *Prajñāpāramitā in One Hundred Thousand Verses.*[866] From among those three hundred, he offered about a hundred to the temple that stood in front of the previous lamas' reliquary stūpas. To further spread the Buddha's teachings, he offered the rest of those scriptures to other temples and put them into the hands of many spiritual masters. Furthermore, one of his students named Chungpawa Gukshi Jobum[867] traveled to the court of Minyak Gyalgö[868] to serve as the court lama.[869] He received many extensive spiritual and material offerings, such as objects made of silver, many extraordinary tantric cloaks, tent canopies adorned with deer, and so forth. All of this and more was offered to Drakpa Gyaltsen. He, in turn, offered it to the Triple Gem and distributed it among the poor. When he departed for Sukhāvatī, he possessed nothing other than his cushion and robes. [83] He would not keep even a sesame-seed-sized piece of gold nor more than a single dré's[870] worth of material wealth.

As for the fourth section, the lord recorded his dreams as follows:

> Nearing the end of my twentieth year, I once took a noonday rest and dreamed that I was reading *Reciting the Names of Mañjuśrī* aloud. When only half finished, I awoke. Another time, near the end of my twenty-first year, I took a noonday rest and dreamed that I read out the entire *Reciting the Names of Mañjuśrī* from having committed it to memory in a previous life. When I had finished, Mañjuśrī explained that he had served as my meditation deity during my previous seven lifetimes.
>
> When I was twenty-two years old, I dreamed [of a previous life in] a place named Bharendra[871] in eastern India, which was surrounded by thick forests. Therein, there was a monastery upon a mountain, inside of which [I] resided, an old tantric paṇḍita-adept. To the north, a king had built a temple and invited the old paṇḍita to consecrate it. [I] replied, "I am old and unable to come to you. I am named Go Thayepai Lodrö.[872]

Inscribe my name upon the temple's door. That will protect against obstacles. In the future, should you still wish for a proper consecration, invite one of my paṇḍita students."

Sometime after [I] passed away, [I was reborn and became] an old monk who was a paṇḍita to the north of Magadha's Vulture Peak.[873] After [I] passed away, there was a monastery on a mountain in northern Oḍḍiyāṇa, below which was a temple housing a group of [my previous life's] disciples. [I was reborn as] a paṇḍita-monk who became their master. After having passed once more, there were still two more lives that followed, but I have forgotten them.

In my life that came after those, [I was reborn] in the Chungpa[874] region of Tibet. [I recall that] its upper reaches are north facing, and its lower reaches [84] are plagued by sandstorms. Looking northward from its eastern valleys, you climb stone steps and arrive at a monastery. To its south is a place called Nakpo Tsang.[875] Further to the north is a temple, inside of which was a gold stūpa and an old tantric practitioner who teaches *Reciting the Names of Mañjuśrī*. At that time, I studied a commentary on that text entitled *Mantra of Meaning*.[876] In its opening pages is written: "'Difficult to obtain along with the continuum' represents the condensed meaning of *Reciting the Names*." That commentary is kept in a chest. Upon its pages, the root text was written using vermillion. I remembered all of this.

In general, I recollected these seven previous lifetimes in my dreams. I then awoke and reported everything to Tönpa Baltön,[877] who was nearby. It is all recorded in the commentary entitled *A Melody of Examples*.[878]

Not too long after Lopön Rinpoché had departed for Sukhāvatī, when I was thirty-seven years old, I dreamed of daybreak after a winter's night. I heard a sound like the buzzing of some great bee coming from Lopön Rinpoché's tomb (*gdung khang*). It told me: "Should you traverse innumerable pure lands to the north of here, you will arrive in the worldly realm of those called 'Golden Ones.'[879] Therein lives a tathāgata named Golden Luster.[880] His disciple is the cakravartin king Sönam

Thayé.[881] You will be reborn as his son, the cakravartin king Yönten Thayé![882]"

Once, when I was forty-nine years old, I went to visit Rutsam.[883] There I dreamed of many people [85] gathered in a large house at the foot of an imposing mountain. Many others had assembled atop its peak. My lama and his spiritual sons dwelled there among the crowd. It occurred to me that I should like to depart. Then my lama and his spiritual sons taught me the four paths and disappeared. To those around me who lived atop that mountain peak, I proclaimed, "If you wish to leave here, you may accompany me! I know the path!" Having said this, I departed directly to the west. Most rose to their feet and followed me. Some rose but only stood in place. The path of our descent cut across sheer cliffs. I faced the north and clung to stairs cut out of the rockface. I said, "Come after me!" About a hundred people followed. Some, like Gungtön,[884] said they wished to go to Gungthang and so departed west. Many others said, "We cannot cross!" and just sat there. They said that from among their ranks a mahāmudrā practitioner had fallen. "Is he not dead?" I asked them. They told me that he was not, and so I said, "In this case, you should now follow after me," and then taught them the four paths.

Then this party and I descended. Moving north, we came across a very craggy hill. Further east, we encountered two paths cutting across a plateau. The Great Lama [Sachen Kunga Nyingpo] had previously sent the bodhisattva Tak[885] along the northerly path. And he had previously sent Shuyé[886] along the easterly path. I told my party, "If you wish to follow the northerly path, then go! I cannot cross it, so I will take the easterly path. If you wish, come along with me." I then climbed the ladder. About thirty-six people followed me. Some thirty others could not make it across, so I taught them the four paths and said, "Now, follow after me!" [86] When we arrived, I was clad in only a single woolen cloth. I recognized five or six people there, including Gatön.[887] They told me, "Behind that mountain is a white and glistening area." I set out to see it, but then awoke.

Reflecting upon the meaning of that dream, I believe that below all those people was the ocean of saṃsāra. Above them were signs that I would have many disciples. That some stood up was a sign that I would bestow initiation. That we went to Gungthang was a sign that they would remain temporarily bound in saṃsāra. Some fell because they had upset me and broken their samaya. They did not die, however, since I restored their samaya and ensured that they would not fall into the lower realms. That some remained on the path indicated that they had engaged in practice. That some remained on both paths indicated that they had achieved some realization. That some thirty people could not cross over indicated that they had achieved a little more realization than others. That some people continued to follow me indicated they had achieved the forbearance level of the path of preparation.

The Jetsun then said:

My disciples will not achieve liberation without first abandoning their body, as Tak did, except for the five or six, like Shuyé, who achieved the path of forebearance.

When I was fifty-six years old, I dreamed that my lama told me: "All the Dharma I have taught you is collected here, including this one:

First, meditate upon suchness;[888]
this is the actual nature of bodhicitta.
Then grasp the wind element in one's hand.
Yogic inner heat will then completely produce warmth.
One's [white and red] bodhicitta will remain in the central channel.
Then, one will control the earth and other elements.
One will draw nearer to the five wisdoms
and attain the immortality [of enlightenment]."

Upon hearing this teaching, I completely understood the interdependence of all external and internal conditions.

Moving along in this marvelous life story, there was once someone in India who attained a high level of realization of the generation stage of Vajrabhairava, [87] but who neither practiced the completion stage nor possessed a pure motivation. As such, when he passed away he was reborn as a malicious demon named Wugui Döwa Ba Gutsek.[889] When the Kāśmīri Mahāpaṇḍita[890] came to Tibet, [this demon] followed after him. Nobody could repel or tame it. Once, when the Mahāpaṇḍita came to Sakya, the Lord [Drakpa Gyaltsen] welcomed him holding a vajra and bell. He knew that some being was hiding and trailing after him. Lifting the vajra and bell, he exorcised [the demon]. The demon was then unable to return to India, so he departed for China. Nowadays, it is the one who wanders after the great wealth of the Chinese.

Another time, when Jetsun [Drakpa Gyaltsen] was practicing meditation in his quarters, the Mahāpaṇḍita asked the Lord of Dharma [Sakya Paṇḍita], "What is your uncle doing?" He replied, "He is meditating." The Mahāpaṇḍita said, "We should go to see him." Sapaṇ responded, "Can I go ahead of you?" The Mahāpaṇḍita said, "No, we should go together!" When they arrived, the Lord [Drakpa Gyaltsen] was finishing the self-generation of Guhyasamāja by doing the offering and praise to the front-generated deities. Drakpa Gyaltsen suddenly rose to prostrate to the Mahāpaṇḍita. He wanted to set his vajra and bell on the table, but in his haste, he left them suspended in the air! The Mahāpaṇḍita exclaimed, "I am unimpressed!" Drakpa Gyaltsen said, "I did not intend to impress you!" Then the Mahāpaṇḍita returned the prostration [offered by Drakpa Gyeltsen]. Some other minor paṇḍitas reprimanded [the Mahāpaṇḍita], "It is inappropriate for you to prostrate to a layperson! We have requested you not to prostate back to him when he prostrates to you, and you promised [88] not to do so!" He replied, "I did, indeed, but he is the actual Mahāvajra!" He further explained that he perceived [Drakpa Gyaltsen] as the actual maṇḍala of Guhyasamāja.

On another occasion at Sakya, the Mahāpaṇḍita made a written prediction that there would soon be a solar eclipse. That Lord [Drakpa Gyaltsen] said, "Please retract your prediction, it will not occur when you say!" The minor paṇḍitas again showed their displeasure. The Mahāpaṇḍita and the Lord of Dharma went together to Shangsekshing.[891] And indeed, the solar eclipse did not occur when he had predicted it would. The Mahāpaṇḍita reflected, "I understand what has happened. To ensure that he is correct, that old layman [Drakpa Gyaltsen] has diverted the solar eclipse!"

Another time, the Lord [Drakpa Gyaltsen] said to the nāga Nakpo Khunshé,[892] "I am going to build a temple here, and so you must move your wealth elsewhere." The nāga searched widely for somewhere to relocate his wealth, eventually finding a modest location along the ocean shore. The nāga reported back, "I have searched everywhere and found only a small locale on the shoreline. Other than that, I could find nowhere else." The Lord said, "How long will it take to move everything there?" The nāga replied, "Just to move the gold will take a thousand years!" "In that case," said the Lord, "stay here and I will give you somewhere to live." Mön Dorjé Rādzā[893] guided him using a lead while the Lord chased behind him. This all happened at what is nowadays the big rock of the eastern labrang [at Sakya Monastery]. The temple known as Utsé Nyingma was later built there.

Another time, Jetsun [Drakpa Gyaltsen] resided to the north in a two-chambered cave. There was a skylight in the middle of its ceiling. On the fifteenth day of the eighth month, many jikdir (*jig dir*) arrived in the lower valley. His attendants then saw that many horsemen were approaching. They eventually came up and into the Lord's cave. The attendants thought [89] they could not squeeze [into the cave] and peered in through the skylight. Within, they saw the group speaking in unfamiliar tongues. An eight-year-old wearing white clothes and turquoise jewelry translated. The guests invited him [to visit their Mongol homeland]. With the benefit of sentient beings in mind, Drakpa Gyaltsen said such things as: "I am now too old and we have no karmic connection, so my coming would be of no benefit to you. My nephew Kunga Gyaltsen has a preexisting karmic connection, so I will send him."

The Lord then emerged from the cave and asked his attendant, "Do you have any alcohol?" His attendant replied, "We have only a little, just a vase full." Drakpa Gyaltsen told him, "It is unsuitable for just anyone to witness this. Do not watch!" He then blessed a skullcup full of alcohol, from which everybody drank until they were drunk. They sang songs and danced the whole night. His attendant witnessed all this. It has been said of those visitors that they were in fact the Mongol deity Namtheu[894] and the Tibetan deity Tsenthang Gyalpo.[895] There was in addition a nāga in attendence, Tsukna Rinchen,[896] decorated with a great many jewels, with his head facing Sakya and his tail facing China. It was auspicious that he positioned himself this way, since Sakya would later become very wealthy.

When he was sixty-one years old, he dreamed that he was seated in tall grass and several blue-colored women invited him to Dākinī Land.[897] The Jetsun replied, "What use is Dākinī Land to me? Even after I am enlightened, there is nothing more important than benefiting sentient beings. For that reason, I refuse to go." Before him was a smooth white stone. They told him, "If you place your feet on this stone, you will go to Dākinī Land," but he refused to stand on it.

When he was sixty-seven [90] years old, during an evening in the yukpa month,[898] Drakpa Gyaltsen dreamed of the great lama [Sakya Kunga Nyingpo] surrounded by eight bodhisattvas. The nine deities of Hevajra were to his right and Śākyamuni surrounded by Koṇḍañña and the other eight arhats to his left. The great lama Sachen then asked him, "If you wished for the novice vows, from whom would you wish to receive them? If you wished for an initiation, who would you wish to bestow it?" He responded, "If I took novice vows or received initiation, only you would serve as my abbot or vajra master!" Sachen approved and replied, "You have understood correctly." He further reported that the great lama Sachen answered his questions and removed all his doubts during the whole of that night.

When he was sixty-eight years old, many divine messengers appeared to invite him to Sukhāvatī.[899] However, he turned them away. When he was sixty-nine years old, many deities approached him. They disparaged this world of endurance[900] and praised Sukhāvatī, and so offered him another invitation. Drakpa Gyaltsen responded, "I have neither aversion to the lower realms nor attraction to the higher realms. From the perspective of the practice of purifying the realm, an impure land is superior to a pure land. I will not go with you, as there are some who rely on me who are without a protector." With that, he turned them away.

When he was seventy years old, they again invited him, saying, "You must come!" In addition, he beheld the landscape of Sukhāvatī while ordinary people experienced such things as earthquakes and sounds and lights issuing from the sky. In his seventieth year, at dusk one day a few of his attendants saw many messenger deities [at his quarters]. It was reported that the Lord of Dharma Sapaṇ, who was staying next to him, also saw this. At dawn, the Lord of Dharma was sitting upright and engaging in prayer, and then he slept a little. [91] He dreamed of many luminous deities arriving from Sukhāvatī and surrounded by a bejeweled net with many offering substances, included an ornamental lion throne. They told [Sapaṇ], "We are here to invite the Lord [Drakpa Gyaltsen]!" However, Sapaṇ requested the deities to not make the invitation, and so they remained silent.

[In his dream, Sapaṇ] also requested the Lord not to depart, but he had decided already. He told Sapaṇ, "Behold the landscape of Sukhāvatī!" while pointing his finger. Sapaṇ then saw its exceedingly beautiful vista, with ground of beryl, precious trees, and so on. Sapaṇ exclaimed, "Is this not a contradiction? Did you not first say you wanted to depart for the Land of the Golden Ones?" [Drakpa Gyaltsen] replied, "I have already made prayers to be reborn in the presence of the Lama and his spiritual sons.[901] By the power of those prayers, I will first go to Sukhāvatī." He then shared more of his life story, but [Sapaṇ] awoke and forgot all the details.

At that time, [Drakpa Gyaltsen] engaged in the preliminary seven-limbed prayers and visualized the maṇḍala and so forth. He then said to the Lord of Dharma [Sapaṇ], "First I will go to Sukhāvatī. I will stay there for but a short time and, as I mentioned earlier, I will then depart for the Land of the Golden Ones. I will appear there as a cakravartin king and purify the land. Then, after three lifetimes without abandoning that body, I hope to achieve the siddhi of mahāmudrā." He then entered a period of strict tantric meditation.

A few succession histories claim that Drakpa Gyaltsen held the primary seat [at Sakya Monastery] for forty-five years, [92] from when he was twenty-six to seventy years old. The *Miraculous Appearance* succession history, however, has it that he took this position when he was just thirteen years old.

In any case, on the twelfth day of the second month of the Male Fire Bird Year (1216), when he was seventy years old, he departed for Sukhāvatī.

Jetsun Rinpoché had innumerable disciples. If I were to try and account for only a few of them here, it would be as follows:

The Mahāpaṇḍita of Sakya, who knew the five major
branches of knowledge,
and the four whose last name was "Drak":
Wangchuk Drak, the monk Shenyen Drak,
the supreme son Śākya Drakpa,
and Rikzin Drak.[902]

In addition, there was Detön Könchok Drak,
Gatön Dordrak, and Setön Lodrö Drak,
and Jikmé Drak,[903] who all together were known as the eight
renowned men.

And there were the four students who received the ornaments
of the *Vajra Canopy Tantra*:[904]
Muchu Jangdrak, Tsangtön Tsöndru Drak,
Lhatok Yönten, and Sherab Rinchen.[905]

And, additionally, those many disciples who were tantric
adepts and renunciants
Such as Tsidül Shön Seng, Kham Kyi Dzitön,
Wöntön Kyer Khang, and José Chakdor.[906]

[Drakpa Gyaltsen] is described in those lines as follows:

Your hair is beautiful like piled-up white lotuses.
Your face has the radiance and brilliance of red coral.
Your body is immovable like a great snow mountain.
Recollecting all this, my devotion and joy increases!

Because your wisdom is vast like the sky,
you explain the definitive, secret meaning of the tantras without relying [upon commentaries].
Never wavering from meditative stabilization,
you always enjoy the company of the seventy maṇḍala deities.

At the end of your life, you traveled in stages to Sukhāvatī.
Presently, you abide in the Vajra Holder bhūmi. [93]
Since you possess wisdom, compassion, and unthinkable magical power,
I faithfully uphold your lineage.

Please powerfully generate realization and scriptural knowledge within me!
Please bestow upon me the unhindered capacity
to greatly increase and preserve
the continuity of the teachings of the Sakyapa!

This supplication arose spontaneously, like a wave moving upon an ocean of devotion.

Fig. 24. Sangdak Palchen Öpo (1150–1203)

4. Palchen Öpo (1150–1203)

The great lama Jetsun's younger brother, Palchen Öpo,[907] wa born on the twenty-fifth day of the ninth month of the Male Iron Horse Year (1150), when his father was fifty-nine years old.

Palchen Öpo was resolute, open-minded, and diligent. He studied the Dharma bequeathed to him by his father and ancestors and came to uphold many of their oral instructions. He specifically used his knowledge about medicine to compassionately benefit many sentient beings. It is well known that he composed a medical text entitled *Rays of Sun: The Minor Eight Branches of Medicine*.[908]

When he was fifty-four years old, on the twenty-first day of the fifth month of the Female Water Pig Year (1203), he departed for Sukhāvatī.

Fig. 25. Sakya Paṇḍita Kunga Gyaltsen (1182–1251)

5. The Lord of Dharma Sakya Paṇḍita Kunga Gyaltsen (1182–1251)

The lama [Drakpa Gyaltsen's] brother-lama [Palchen Öpo] married Machik Garphuma Nyitri Cham,[909] who bore two sons. The eldest became known as the Lord of Dharma Sakya Paṇḍita,[910] whose personal name was Kunga Gyaltsen. He was born when his father was thirty-three years old, on the twenty-sixth day of the second month of the Male Water Tiger Year (1182). When he entered his mother's womb, she dreamed that a nāga king [94] wearing jewelry who was unbearable to behold arrived and asked her to rent him lodging. While he was residing in her womb, she experienced a wonderful meditative stabilization.

After Kunga Gyaltsen's birth, the sky was pervaded by light. As soon as he could crawl, the tendencies from his previous lives began to awaken and he would speak a few words of Sanskrit. His mother asked the Lord [Drakpa Gyaltsen], "Will he become a mute (*gu ba*)? The only words he speaks are gibberish!" The Lord, who knew Sanskrit, assured her: "There is no need to worry that your son will be a mute!" Kunga Gyaltsen would also write out the vowels and consonants (*ā li kā li*) of the Indian alphabets known as Nāgara, Lañja, and so forth. He also revealed that he could read them. Later, so as not to disrespectfully walk over those letters, he erased them with his hand. He understood both the Indian and Tibetan scripts without requiring any study.

As for how he purified his mind by means of study and contemplation, [there are three parts]: (1) how he trained in the object of knowledge at the time of the cause; (2) how he understood the five signs of knowledge at the time of fruition; and (3) how, by means of all this, he became a completely qualified mahāpaṇḍita and, then, how he worked on behalf of the teachings and sentient beings.

Firstly, we may find descriptions from sections of his biographies devoted to records of teachings that he received. An account of his training is also clearly described in his answers to Chak Lotsāwa Chöjé Pal's questions. This will be most easily understood if I put [his answers to Chak Lotsāwa] down in verse.

From Sugataśrī, I heard
the metered text entitled *Candoratnākara*[911]
along with [the sage] Marser's[912] [root text] and Gyalwai Lha's[913] [commentary].
With Saṅghaśrī[914] I studied
poetic treatises, including Daṇḍin's [*Mirror of Poetics*],[915]
Sarasvatī's Necklace,[916] and so forth.
With three scholars I thoroughly studied
treatises on synonyms, [95] such as the *Amarakośaḥ*[917]
and its extensive commentary.
Sugataśrī taught me
Kālidāsa's three poetic plays.
From two mahātmā [Śākyaśrībhadra and Drakpa Gyaltsen]
I heard teachings upon the jātaka tales of the bodhisattva.
From the two mahātmā I heard instructions upon
Ārya [Nāgārjuna's] Guhyasamāja teaching cycle
and Jñānapada's Guhyasamāja commentary along with its supplements.
From the Mañjuśrī of Sakya [Drakpa Gyaltsen], I heard teachings upon
the three tantric commentaries of [Guhyasamāja];
the Cakrasaṃvara root and explanatory tantras;
another seven tantras, including the *Ābhidhāna* supplement;
the three Hevajra tantras
along with Ḍōmbi's commentary on them;
three tantras, such as the *The Unsullied Sovereign Tantra*[918] and so on;
the *Tantra on the Arising of Mahākāla*[919]
together with its commentary, the *Gathering of Suchness*;[920]
the *Vajra Peak Tantra*[921] and the glorious *Supreme*;

the *Tantra of Śaṃvara Who is Equal to Space* [922] and the *King of Tantras, the Universal Secret,*
together with commentaries for them both;
the *Purification Tantra* together with its explanatory tantras;
the *Shorter Tantra for the Practice of the King of Vajra Wrath;*[923]
and also the *Great Secret Tantra,*
the *Tantra of Subāhu's Questions,* the *Great Tantra, Susiddhikara,*[924]
the *General Rituals of All Maṇḍalas,* and so forth;
the four-explanation tradition of *Reciting the Names of Mañjuśrī;*
the commentaries on the Two Part [*Hevajra Tantra*] entitled *The Night Lily,*[925]
the *Pearl Garland Tantra,*[926] *Possessing Lotuses,*[927]
and the *Garland of Jewels Commentary.*[928]
From the two mahātmā,
I again and again heard teachings upon
the *Kālacakra Tantra* together with its explanatory tantras,
the *Two-Section Hevajra Tantra,* and the root tantra of Cakrasaṃvara,
along with Āryas [Nāgārjuna and Āryadeva]'s praise commentaries,
the *Tantra of the Complete Enlightenment of Vairocana,*[929]
and the two exegetical traditions of the *Reciting the Names of Mañjuśrī.* [96]
I heard teachings on these and many other texts.
The following were not yet translated into Tibetan:
the *Sūtra of the Secret Jewel Ornament,*[930]
the *Tantra of Vajrapātāla,*[931] the *Tantra of the Array of Secret Ornaments,*[932]
and the *Ornament of the Vajra Essence Tantra.*[933]
I heard teachings upon them from Sugataśrī.
I then translated and finalized them.

Should you wish to learn more about the record of teachings that Sakya

Paṇḍita received, carefully read the biography composed by the highly realized great master Lhopa Kunkhyen Rinchen Pal.[934]

Secondly, how he came to understand the five signs of knowledge at the time of fruition. This has two parts: first, how he came to know the varieties of conventional objects of knowledge (*shes bya ji snyed pa*); second, how he came to know the ultimate nature of things, just as they are. As for the first, this mahātmā relied upon numerous scholars and realized masters over the course of innumerable previous lifetimes, and he learned all objects of knowledge. As such, from the moment of his birth he was endowed with marvelous, self-arisen wisdom. During his lifetime, Sakya Paṇḍita relied upon a great many scholars, studied well, and was accepted by a yidam personal meditation deity. He possessed unobstructed wisdom with complete understanding. As is described in the text cited above, Sakya Paṇḍita could understand the meaning of an entire text upon hearing it but once, or, if it was very difficult, upon hearing it but twice.

As he himself once put it:

> I am a grammarian, I am a logician, no one overcomes those with wrong views like I do!
> I am learned in composition, I alone am a poet, I am unequaled in synonymics!
> I know astrological junctures, I possess incomparable analysis and intelligence that understands all outer and inner knowledge! [97]
> This scholar is a Sakyapa! All others are merely reflections!

And elsewhere, in reference to the above:

> If someone were to ask me, "O Sakya Paṇḍita, you claim knowledge in subjects widely known to scholars. Is this because of conceited pride, when in fact you know not what you claim? Or is it that you have not considered what you know and what you do not, and therefore you simply accept your stupid words because of selfish desire? Or is this the noble way, such that you recognize your excellent knowledge and, therefore, speak hon-

> estly?" I would answer by saying that such statements about myself were not given without reason, since I undertook correct study, understood the meaning, and can provide answers to others according to the Dharma based upon my own experience. As such, I have said, "I am a grammarian..." and so on.

In addition, [Sakya Paṇḍita] has briefly noted:

> Due to studying in previous lifetimes
> and relying upon many scholars,
> I acquired intelligent wisdom
> and fearlessly realized all objects of knowledge.
> If I were to explain in more detail, the subjects to be known are
> the science of grammar, logic,
> medicine, mechanical arts and crafts, and Buddhist philosophy.

As I have mentioned, these are the five fields of knowledge. The science of grammar includes the commentaries about how to distinguish between terms. The crown jewel of these are the *Kalāpa* and *Cāndra*,[935] together with their supplements, about which [Sakya Paṇḍita] was remarkably knowledgeable. He grasped the elements of grammar without impediment and was thus just like the supreme exponent Candragomin, Gyepa,[936] Nejik,[937] Vālmīki,[938] [98] Norgyé,[939] and so forth.

Sakya Paṇḍita became knowledgeable in the field of logical reasoning (*gtan tshigs*) because he unmistakenly understood its principal treatises: [Dignāga's] *Compendium of Valid Cognition*[940] and [Dharmakīrti's] commentaries upon it, known together as the "group of seven texts on valid cognition."[941] Sapaṇ's Buddhist and non-Buddhist challengers were like elephants whose bodies of natural intelligence were coarse, whose strength of egocentrism were well developed, and whose tusks of pseudo-scripture and reasoning were sharp, such that they could outshine the tenet systems of foolish troops who were ignorant in analysis. Sapaṇ, however, was like a lion possessing the physical strength of unmistaken and complete knowledge; a very weighty mane of the

Well-Gone One's[942] scriptures; sharp fangs and claws of establishing one's own tradition and refuting those of others, by which the brain blood of all unwholesome tenet systems may be drained from their root; and with a fearless bellowing roar of emptiness and selflessness that sounded at all times, just like that of the Lord of Knowledge, glorious Dharmakīrti, and Ārya Nāgārjuna.

He was also knowledgeable in the science of mechanical arts and crafts, for he knew about painting, fabricating statues, and iconography, and was additionally quite skilled in inspecting the virtues and subtle qualities of such images. He was also erudite in the eight types of examination, including surveying landscapes (*sa brtag pa*) and so on. Since many scholars have claimed that mathematics (*rtsi*) should be considered a field in the mechanical arts and crafts, he became familiar with that also. Concerning mathematics, he knew the five subjects mentioned in the *Śrī Kālacakra Tantra*, including numerals, subtraction, addition, [99] division, and multiplication.

He mastered the field of external astrology in topics such as: the five constituents of the calendar; planets, dates, and stars, along with their concurrences and movements; analyses of the fast, slow, straight, and retrograde movements of the five planets; the signs of the zodiac (*khyim*); the passage of the sun, moon, and other celestial bodies through the signs of the zodiac; accounting for their auspiciousness; the face of Rāhu[943] and Kalāgni[944] and how they eclipse the sun and moon; the arising and departure of meteors; and so forth. He also thoroughly mastered the field of internal astrology for attaining perfect enlightenment, such as: the system of inner channel and winds; the sun, moon, planet, and constellations; the junctures (*dus sbyor*); breath (*dpugs*), likṣā (*chu srang*), danda (*dpyugs gu*), prahara (*'pho ba*), sañkrānti (*chu tshod*), and temporal period (*thun tshod*); the cycle of day and night; solar and lunar eclipses; and, based on all these, the waxing and waning of wisdom.

Nowadays, some renowned Tibetan masters who are considered incomparable, to prove the thoroughness of their knowledge of the five fields to their students, write a text in which they simply describe the measurements of the maṇḍala (*gzhal yas khang*) and of statues. In practice, however, they know nothing. They do not even know how to sew clothes or spin wool, yet they nonetheless claim mastery of the five fields to their students! This mahātmā [Sakya Paṇḍita] was completely unlike them. He knew the actual practice of those fields, such that he fabricated the life tree and inner contents [100] for the inner support statue of the venerable Mañjuśrī built by the Jetsun Rinpoché [Drakpa Gyaltsen) and displayed at the Utsé Nyingma Temple. He did all of this himself. (As the Lord of Dharma Lowo Khenchen[945] has described, Sapaṇ even made the back curtain for the statue built by Sangtsa,[946] which is also extraordinary!)

In later times, many qualified foreign artists were brought to Tibet to produce statuary. Their work, however, does not compare to that of Sakya Paṇḍita. He also practiced a style of painting done upon silk which is described in the root tantra. (There are amazing paintings upon silk that Sakya Paṇḍita made by hand and bequeathed to Gyama Pöndrak.[947]) He also painted "the Supreme Vow-Protector" symbol of Mañjuśrī[948] upon the temple wall at glorious Samyé. These days, even the most skilled of artists cannot reproduce it!

Sakya Paṇḍita was erudite in the field of medicine because, as mentioned earlier, he had become completely familiar with medical texts. He knew such topics as healthy daily and seasonal routines;[949] diagnosing symptoms of illness; examining a patient by observation, inquiry, and touch; prescribing disease-subduing medicines[950] and purgatory medicines;[951] as well as the use of other forms of diagnosis, such as the treatment of a single illness, a combination of two illnesses, a trebled illnesses, a single increasing illness, a doubled combination increasing illness, a trebled combination increasing illness, a decreasing illness, a doubled decreasing illness, or a trebled decreasing illness. He not only knew the textual sources but also the actual practice of the five methods of treatment, such as purging through the upper or lower orifices, preventative treatments, reactive treatments, and treatments to stop the recurrence of illness. In the treatment of illnesses caused by the imbalance of the elements, he was like the king of medicine Tsojé Shonu.[952]

Furthermore, as for the internal science of Buddhist philosophy, [Sapaṇ said that] all scriptures of the Sugata contained in the three precious piṭakas are included within the Perfection Vehicle and the Secret Mantra Vehicle. The Perfection Piṭaka includes the Abhidharma Piṭaka, which mainly reveals the training in supreme wisdom; the Vinaya Piṭaka, which mainly reveals the training in excellent discipline; and the Sūtra Piṭaka, which mainly reveals the training in supreme concentration. He learned those many profound textual systems, such as the Perfection of Wisdom and so forth, and many extensive textual systems, including the *Gaṇḍavyūha Sūtra*.[953]

As for the Vajra Vehicle, he learned many root and explanatory tantras of the action tantra class, the performance tantra class, the yoga tantra class, and the unexcelled yoga tantra class. He completely understood the stages of their practice, including the ripening empowerments, the defining characteristics of the path to mental stabilization, the entranceway to the path to liberation, the method of birthing the unborn [wisdom in meditative stabilization], and then, after this birth, of progressing in meditative stabilization, the limits of the path, clearing obstacles upon the path, achieving signs of progress in meditation, the stages of developing wisdom, the quintessential instructions upon the root verses of [Virūpa's] *Vajra Verses* and other Lamdré texts that unmistakably illuminate [102] dependent arising, and the method of traveling the mundane and supramundane grounds and paths by which one may achieve the enlightened state of Vajradhara in a single lifetime. From knowing all this, he was qualified to guide diligent practitioners to achieve the siddhi of mahāmudrā in a single lifetime without abandoning their bodies.

In addition, he thoroughly studied and understood most of the essential teachings attributed to the famous Indian mahāsiddhas, as well as all of the oral instructions well known among Tibetans of generations past, from Shijé, Dzokchen, Mahāmudrā, and so forth to Chöd. In addition, he knew the gradual and nongradual methods by which to enter those paths. He also knew all the important points of mistaken and correct [practice of those traditions].

In the practice of some of those traditions, the visualization techniques merely produce calm abiding. Others cure minor illnesses. Some protect us from the harm of nonhumans. Some help us generate the mind dedicated to helping others. Some generate part of that aspect of realization that is free from conceptual elaboration. Some propel us toward the formless realm. Others help us enter the paths of the hearers[954] and solitary realizers.[955] Some gradually gather together the auspicious conditions to achieve complete enlightenment after three countless eons.

Some others lead us to realize the eight mundane siddhis. A few lead us to the great accomplishment of the supramundane siddhis, the wisdom of the path of seeing. [103] Beyond all of those, some of those practices lead us to achieve the state of great Vajradhara in only a single lifetime.

Because of the kindness of his Lord of Dharma, the Glorious Great Sakyapa [Drakpa Gyaltsen], who is of the nature of the tathāgatas of the three times, Sakya Paṇḍita came to completely understand the differences between all these traditions unfettered by any lingering doubts. For this reason, he proclaimed, "I understand all objects of knowledge in Buddhist philosophy!" By means of his unmistaken ability in logic and examination, he completely understood without difficulty the extremely subtle contradictions between the words and meaning, regardless of whether this was previously well known or not. Those with little intelligence may exert great effort over a long period of time, but they still cannot come to a correct understanding. He, however, could fully understand it all with only little effort. As such, when scholars disputed or questioned on any topic among the well-known five major fields of knowledge, he had the ability, proven by his experience, to answer exactly according to the subject matter. For this reason, he proclaimed, "I possess incomparable analysis and intelligence!"

Based upon the wisdom of his individual analyses and understanding the arrogance of [his opponent's] writing, disputation, and teaching, he proclaimed, "I am incomparable" in the context of this land, this time, and these kinds of people. He is unable to prove or disprove claims made by those in other times, in other places, or in other communities. [104] In this sense, he employed the concepts "comparable and incomparable." Most worldly beings would use these concepts of comparable and incomparable in the same way.

If one were to ask, "Who is knowledgeable in the five major fields of knowledge?" the answer is: "The Sakyapa who dwells in the temple of glorious Sakya, a bhikṣu in the tradition of Śākyamuni named Kunga Gyaltsen Palsangpo." [Opponents] have never even heard of the names or imagined the categories of the fields of knowledge mentioned above, never mind correctly understood their meaning! For that reason, he said, "Other scholars are merely likenesses [of true scholars]!" Like a parrot, they simply repeat some aspect of these fields of knowledge that they only pretend to know well. When asked in debate to expound further upon such subjects as grammar, logic, composition, poetics, figures of speech (*tshig gi rgyan*), grammatical cases, and compounds in accord with the Dharma, they become stupid as sheep. Even so, because of pride they continue to think of themselves as erudite and continue to deprecate all other scholars, saying unkind words about them. Such opponents are but pale reflections, just like the moon reflected in water is only ever a reflection, never able to perform the moon's function (*don byed pa*). Just so, how could scholars with excellent understanding ever be a mere reflection? [105] They are the heart disciples of all the Victors, the teachers of the world along with the gods.

[Sakya Paṇḍita once said,] "As I have described in my biography, only Indian paṇḍitas who know the five fields of knowledge and Tibetan scholars familiar with the textual tradition and its meaning, who are interested in entering discussion about them, and who, over a long period of debate, are familiar with me and are unbiased, will understand. Those foolish ones with narrow understanding, who make examples out of other people's knowledge as if they too were so stunted, who limit their questions to only very specific sections in the scriptures, who debate focused on only a very specific section of a pramāṇa text, and who ask only about some major point in the textual and oral tradition, will find it difficult to appreciate the scope of my knowledge and biography."

As for [Sapaṇ's self-praise] by means of example:

> Kunga Gyaltsen is like Rāhu in the sky,
> moving in the space of objects of knowledge,
> able even to eat the sun and moon of an opposing debater's
> majesty,
> yet remaining unseen to most people.

He did not compose these biographical writings conceitedly to disparage others. Previous great scholars have similarly written about themselves in this way for specific reasons. For example, previous great scholars like Dharmakīrti, Sthiramati, Prajñākaragupta, [106] Sankarānanda, and Vādisiṃhaḥ[956] were not prideful, and yet they composed verses sharing their personal life stories. On that basis, great scholars of the future and students still pursuing their training will become interested in their stories. The young and intelligent will be inspired. They will think, "Wouldn't it be wonderful if I became a scholar just like them?" and then become joyful. It only appears that he composed such words with pride.

It is like what the glorious master Dharmakīrti once said:

> Vālmīki's fable about the monkeys who took hold of a mountain and set it into the ocean
> and the story about Vyāsa and Ārjuna's skill in arrowcraft are all untrue. And yet, still people tell them.
> By contrast, the meaning of the words I have shared are precisely true, as if measured upon a scale.
> And yet, it is as if all beings exercise their throats only to refute them. And so, O renowned one, I pay my respect to you!

And elsewhere, [Dharmakīrti has written]:

> Should the sun of Dharmakīrti's speech ever set,
> the teachings of [the Buddha] will either fall into slumber or die.
> Thereupon, the teachings of those without the Dharma will rise.

Master Sthiramati has said:

> Set my views upon one plate
> and competing views upon another.
> Were it possible to weigh them upon a scale,
> my views would surely be the heavier!

Furthermore, Master Prajñākaragupta [107] has said:

> The sun of Prajñākaragupta's intelligence rises
> embellished by a thousand rays of reasoning's light.
> Unintelligent heretics wandering about in the night

flee from merely the glow of a swarm of fireflies.

He has also said:

Any scholars who did not begin trembling
immediately upon the birth of Prajñākaragupta
were either insentient,
dumb, or evidently an ox or cow!

Once, when the brāhmaṇa Master Sankarānanda was debating the brāhmaṇa paṇḍitas in Vārāṇasi, his skill in reasoning was so profound that it was incomprehensible to his opponents. And so they disgraced him, alleging that he did not understand the system of debate.

The Master then said:

It is well known that a group of fishermen once discovered a priceless jewel.
They all smelled, tasted, and rubbed it repeatedly.
Its smell, taste, and feel, however, frustrated their expectations.
And so, disgusted, they threw it back into the sea.
O jewel! Having fallen into the hands of fools,
you could not be burnt, nor shattered, nor pummeled.
So why not feel happy upon being cast back into your watery home?
Sankarānanda, too, presently faces such a situation.

Likewise, Master Vādisiṃhaḥ once declared:

Repeatedly throwing up both my hands, I say,
"I am propounding in depth upon the nature of things just as they are!"
When I, Vādisiṃhaḥ, am the disputant,
not even Maheśvara would understand a single syllable!

Setting this down in writing upon some long bamboo, I have
rung the bell of victory in the residences of scholars. [108]

Paṇḍita Śrī Ghānaśrīna has likewise said:

An elephant whose bulk is the seven treatises adorned by the
tusks of the *Commentary on Valid Cognition*,
weighted by a mane of the supreme Dharma, with the
extremely sharp claws of grammatical commentary.
He mashes the brains of the heretical oxen, terrifying opponents in debate.
That is [me,] Glorious Majestic, everywhere bellowing the
great roar of the fearless lion.

Written upon a long piece of bamboo, this is known to have
been attached to the door of the king of Kalimka.

Verses like these, which praise one's own good qualities, are part of the biographical tradition of scholars. And so, it is wonderful! Beyond these specific qualities, praising one's worldly riches, such as one's lineage, wealth, retinue, military might, or power, are scorned by the scholarly and are shameful. One should know that previous scholars have not written about themselves in such ways.

Initially, one should learn all fields of knowledge.
Then, in the middle, one should deeply discuss them with
scholars.
At the end, one should meditate upon whatever one
understands.
This is the view and exposition of the Victors of the three
times.

This has been excellently said!

Secondly, how he came to know the ultimate nature of things, just as they are (*ji lta ba*). The Lord of Dharma once said:

> When I was young I requested of the Great Jetsun [Drakpa Gyaltsen] the blessing of guru yoga. He told me, "You see me as your uncle and not as a buddha. As such, you are unable to undertake hardships [109] of body and wealth on behalf of your lama." Saying this, he did not grant me the blessing. Another time, I experienced a fearful sign of impending death and began to feel unwell. Jetsun Rinpoché [Drakpa Gyaltsen] was also not feeling well. I served him day and night, forgetting to even eat or sleep. It seems that my negative karma was a little purified because of this. He then gave me the blessing of guru yoga. When he did, I perceived my lama as a buddha. Specifically, I saw him as Mañjuśrī, the nature of all buddhas. An uncommon devotion to him was born within me. With that, signs of impending death faded and I began to regain my health. I then unerringly understood all difficult points of scripture and realization, and topics such as grammar, logic, composition, literary ornamentation (*tshig gi rgyan*), secret mantra, the perfections, abhidharma, and vinaya. I developed a fearless courage toward the contents of the entire Tripiṭaka. Gods, demons, and humans all began to show kindness to me. Egotistical people, including even the king of India, began to respect me and request teachings. Some slight amount of correct understanding began to arise within me.

Moreover, as is said in the praise [to Sapaṇ]:

> When you were blessed by the profound path,
> you saw your venerable lama as Mañjuśrī,
> and in a single moment understood all dharmas.
> I pay homage to you upon my crown,
> whose mind is liberated!

Moreover, the Great Jetsun [Drakpa Gyaltsen] had been, over many lifetimes, the spiritual master of the mahātmā [Sakya Paṇḍita]. We know this because when he taught the Dharma at Sakya, [110] Sakya Paṇḍita heard a voice sounding from the sky that said: "Over the course of twenty-seven lifetimes, you became a paṇḍita who was very knowledgeable about the *Commentary on Valid Cognition*. During those previous lives, the Jetsun Drakpa Gyaltsen was your spiritual master. Other than him, no one else could train you!" Another time, [Sakya Paṇḍita heard another voice that said]: "This occurred over thirty-seven lifetimes." Once, while he taught the Dharma at Kyao Khadang,[957] he heard a voice bellow from the sky: "Over countless lifetimes, he has been your spiritual master." Sapaṇ said about this, "When I heard that, I was reminded of those other voices as well." I, [Ameshab,] once read the following in a text:

> Sapaṇ himself once said [about Drakpa Gyaltsen]:
> O wisdom body of all the buddhas,
> appearing in the form of a layman
> who cuts through my net of illusions,
> a sound from the sky once told me
> that since long ago you have been my spiritual master.
> I prostrate to you, wonderful teacher (*legs 'doms*)!

The Kadampa master Namkha Bum[958] once asked Sapaṇ, "Without holding anything back, please privately reveal to me whatever qualities of realization you possess. Also, please tell me: if you depart to see the Mongols, is there some reason that leads you to think you can benefit them?" Sapaṇ answered, "I have unmistaken devotion to the teachings of the Buddha. I also have a little understanding of the scriptures. However, I do not have any major realizations. Those Mongols demanded that I come to serve as an object for their patronage (*mchod gnas*). They say that if I do not, they will send an army. Should that happen, Tibet will be harmed and so I intend to go. [111] Though I depart hoping to benefit sentient beings, there is no sure reason to think that I will do so. Regardless, even if it means that I can benefit sentient beings simply by giving up my life and body, I am willing to do so!"

Earlier, the praise said, "I pay homage to you upon my crown, / whose mind is liberated!" According to the author of that praise, "liberated" means liberated from the obscurations to omniscience. In other texts, it is said that one realizes the emptiness of all phenomena when one achieves the first bhūmi on the path of seeing.[959] In addition, being willing to give up one's life for the sake of the Dharma is a sign of the irreversibility of achieving the first bhūmi on the path of seeing. As it says in the *Ornament for Clear Realization*:[960]

> The unobservability of a single particle of phenomena
> abiding in the three bhūmis,
> from being certain of one's own bhūmi
> and giving up one's life for the sake of the Dharma:
> sixteen intervals such as these
> are signs of irreversibility for the intelligent
> who dwell upon the path of seeing.

As for the meaning of that, due to understanding the distinguishing features of generosity and so forth, one engages and then continues to engage in eliminating miserliness, deranged ethical discipline, and so forth. Because all phenomena are the nature of the three gateways [of emptiness], one realizes the unobservability of even a single particle of phenomena. Because one attains clarity and certainty from sudden realization, one abides in one's bhūmi, the nature of the three knowledges. By being well trained [112] in this doctrine and so forth, one is willing to give up one's life for the Dharma. These four are the aspects of the path.

Therefore, because one perfectly obtains the sixteen periods, which are included in the types of patience and knowledge [associated with the path of seeing], as a result one abandons worldly grasping at the subject and object—for example, grasping at form and so on. It is clearly mentioned that these are the signs of irreversibility for a bodhisattva who has attained the path of seeing.

From the perspective of ordinary disciples, it is said that Sakya Paṇḍita is a superior noble one who will take three lifetimes to achieve enlightenment. There was his current lifetime, then he will be a *vidyādhara* knowledge-holder who will reside in the sky, and finally, he will be born as the son of King Nyimai Tophel.[961] In reality, however, he was already the complete and perfect buddha Mañjuśrī. As such, we should understand the good qualities of his learning and realization as magical displays.

Thirdly, [regarding] the manner in which he benefited the teachings and sentient beings, there are two parts: (1) the way he spread the teachings of the Buddha by means of his three scholarly activities and (2) the manner in which he spread the teachings in the northerly land of Mongolia, as prophesied by the Victor. As for the first, there are two parts: (1) how he spread the teachings by means of the three scholarly activities and (2) how he engaged in various enlightened activities for the benefit of others. [113]

The first has three parts: how he increased the lotus garden of prosperity and bliss by means of the sunbeams of his teachings; how this mahātmā unmistakably understood the specific and general characteristics of the Dharma, as mentioned above; and how he already possessed, over countless previous lifetimes, a compassion that could not bear the sufferings of others, like a mother rescuing her only child from a river's currents, directed toward sentient beings whose eyes have been destroyed by the cataract of ignorance and who stumble in regard to what to adopt and what to discard, and so fall from the cliff of misfortune into cyclic existence.

As for his method for freeing [sentient beings] from such suffering, it was to unmistakably instruct them in the fundamental nature of all phenomena. He himself became such a teacher as the fruition of his previous prayers, countless like the number of particles in the ocean. From those, just like [the sun carried aloft by a] wind horse, [his wisdom] was born aloft into the sky of objects of knowledge. Then the limitless light rays of his well-explained teachings shone forth into the ten directions. These then eradicated the darkness of his disciples' ignorance and spread the lotus garden of benefit and happiness in all directions. He was thus the source of a great collection of precious, well-explained teachings. Moreover, when teaching these fields of knowledge to his students, he never forgot to do so according to their capacities.

More specifically, [Sakya Paṇḍita] understood that the root of the suffering of saṃsāra is self-grasping; that its antidote is the wisdom realizing [114] the nonexistence of the self; that the prerequisite for such realization is understanding the textual tradition; that the principal source for such reasoning is the texts of the [Middle Way tradition], free from extremes; and that to understand that tradition, one must rely upon the *Commentary on Valid Cognition.*

The exegetical tradition for the *Commentary on Valid Cognition* was first established by the mahātmā Ngok Loden Sherab,[962] but this lasted only a little while before disappearing. For that tradition to once again flourish, and to extend the legacy of the great Kāśmīri paṇḍita who kindly came to Tibet, Sakya Paṇḍita vowed to offer a teaching on that great text every day. As such, that teaching tradition has continued to spread widely until today.

Furthermore, Sakya Paṇḍita understood that after generating a genuine mind of aspiring bodhicitta, the root of unsurpassable enlightenment, if one never abandons one's dedication for the welfare of others, then even if one commits the five heinous actions of immediate retribution, one will not experience adverse effects and will continue to produce merit equal to the sky. For these reasons, he knew there was great benefit and that it was easy to offer protection. When devoted disciples would extend invitations to this mahātmā, he would travel in any direction whatsoever. Then people would gather, some urged along by their roots of virtue from previous lives, and some intending only to amuse themselves. Though they did not intentionally request that he give teachings, he would extensively or briefly bestow the bodhicitta vow according to the Middle Way tradition. He would reside there a few days and, so that the bodhicitta vow did not decrease and would increase, he would give a teaching on *Clarifying the Sage's Intent.*[963] [115] In the colophon of that text, he wrote, "I have given this teaching to everyone in Ü, Tsang, and Kham. All my students have already received its blessing transmission. Behold this model text (*ma dpe*) and teach it widely!" He thus benefited sentient beings even by teaching them methods to accomplish worldly activities!

All his compositions possessed good qualities, such as being free from being too verbose or repetitive, correctly spelled, melodic, consistent, and so forth. And so all beings became attracted to them. [Drogön Chögyal] Phakpa has written:

In this way, you drew forth your speech,
which was heard by the wise.
Their minds focused single-pointedly upon your words
without wandering elsewhere.
The sweet melody of a celestial musician
and the song of a drunk cuckoo:
neither of these are comparable [to your speech],
so why mention how it outshone other sounds?

Regarding his mental conduct, it was as mentioned above.

By means of wisdom and compassion,
he taught [the Dharma] tirelessly.
His conduct of body, speech, and mind was pure.
In this way, he protected the Dharma: I will practice
devotedly!

As this describes, he possessed all these good qualities of clear knowledge and the intention of benefiting others, exactly the good qualities [of qualified teachers] he described elsewhere. As it says in the *Ornament for the Mahāyāna Sūtras*:[964]

Like this, those with intelligence, tirelessness, and
compassion,
with a good reputation, who know the teaching procedures
well:
this kind of bodhisattva is an excellent Dharma teacher!
When teaching, [116] the core of beings becomes luminous,
like the sun.

And further:

Vast, capable of removing doubt,
revealing the two natures without bias:
such a one as this is a perfect teacher
for bodhisattvas.

[Sakya Paṇḍita] possessed these qualities.

The exegetical traditions upon the magnificent scriptures passed down from this mahātmā include the *Treasury of Logical Reasoning*,[965] [a commentary] on the *Commentary on Valid Cognition* [as well as commentaries upon Vasubandhu's] *Treasury of Abhidharma*[966] and the three Hevajra tantras. He additionally composed a great many texts that are not famous yet are the basis of teaching traditions, including *Vajra Verses*, *Clarifying the Sage's Intent*, and the *Treasury of Aphoristic Jewels*.[967]

Other than these, the remainder of his compositions are no longer extant, including [commentaries on] the rest of Dharmakīrti's seven treatises on valid cognition, [Asanga's] *Compendium of Abhidharma*,[968] Maitreya's treatises, the *Cakrasaṃvara Tantra*, the *Guhjasamāja Tantra*, and their many commentaries. It is certain that these have now disappeared.

However, all the traditions of his exegeses upon the prātimokṣa vows, aspirational and engaged bodhicitta, and countless ripening initiations, blessings for the path to liberation, blessing initiations, and their associated commentaries all connected to the four classes of tantra are still extant today.

Second, how he attracted the attention of scholars by means of the succession of his previous compositions. The ocean-like mind of a scholar in whatsoever circumstances is churned up by the wind of desiring to express [their learning]. By this, a jewel rosary is washed ashore that gives joy to the honest and intelligent captain-like student. [117] The sun maṇḍala of the Lord of Dharma [Sapaṇ] shines to dispel the darkness of ignorance among sentient beings.

> We know a superior horse when it is ridden.
> We know [a superior] elephant in battle.
> We know gold and silver when they are melted.
> We know a scholar when they compose a text.

As this says, to reveal his knowledge to others, [Sapaṇ] composed many stainless treatises.

This has two parts. Firstly, *Treasury of Aphoristic Jewels* was included among the general treatises he wrote in order to teach the path of the holy Dharma. This work condenses the meaning of all the treatises of

Buddhist and non-Buddhist masters. He also composed four treatises on grammar: *Entrance Gate for the Wise, Emanated Wisdom, Entering the Wisdom*, and *Collecting Essential Grammar*.[969] As for treatises on logic, he wrote on the essence of the seven treatises on valid cognition in *Treasury of Valid Cognition*, together with its commentary. He additionally wrote treatises on arts and crafts, on iconography, on surveying land, the precious teachings of astrology, and a summary of the eight branches of medicine.

On Buddhist philosophy (*nang rig pa*), which clarifies the general meaning of the scriptures, he composed *A Supplication to the Buddhas and Bodhisattvas, Differentiating Tenet Systems*, and *The Great Dharma Collection of the General Textual Tradition of the Perfection [Vehicle]*.[970]

As for secret mantra, he wrote a commentary on Jetsun [Drakpa Gyaltsen]'s *Praise to Dakmema*,[971] *Five Letters of Coemergent Dependent Origination: Quintessential Instructions* [118] *on the Vajrayāna, Explanation of the Hidden Path and Guru Yoga, Catalogue of Instructions*, and many others.[972]

On the minor fields of knowledge (*rig pa'i gnas chung*), he wrote *On Composition: A Bouquet of Flowers*, a text that soothes by making use of example; *Entreating the Compassion of the Sugata; On Poetry: Ornament for the Mouth of Scholars; On Synonymics: Treasury of Words; On Drama: Entrance into Abundant Happiness*; and *Treatise on Music*, a teaching on music and related melodies associated with drama.[973]

Beyond all this, anyone in the Land of Snows with doubts about any texts, logical reasoning, or quintessential instructions sought out the Lord of Dharma throughout his lifetime. As such, he also composed texts that answered the questions of a great many tantric practitioners, such as Shanglo, Chaklo, and Lowo Lotsāwa,[974] and a great many Kadampa masters, such as bhikṣu Dorjé Sengé,[975] and a great many accomplished meditators, like Nyemo Gomchen.[976] He also composed many praise texts, including those directed at the Buddha, Mañjuśrī, and so forth.

All his writing flowed effortlessly. With just a few words, he provided the extensive meaning. Even the foolish found his compositions easy to understand and their meaning clear. Because of their excellent literary qualities (*tshig gi rgyan*), his texts were attractive to the minds of scholars. They illuminate profound meanings that otherwise remain inscrutable, even when gathered into a single place for the minds of even a hundred of those pretending to be learned. [Drogön Chögyal] Phakpa has said:

Sapaṇ composed very quickly,
faster even than lightning,
flowing from him effortlessly,
like a swan landing upon seeing a lake. [119]
His works reveal an abundance of meaning
for the best minds among those pretending to be learned;
none among them had ever analyzed in this way before.
Your analysis, O Learned One,
clarifies the mind [of a disciple] like rays of sun striking
the peak of a snow mountain.
[Your compositions] completely produce joy,
Like the experience of the bliss of concentration.

Other than *The Easy Entranceway for Beginners*, *Praise of the Wheel of the Three Tantras*, and a few more, this mahātmā did not compose commentaries upon others' texts. He never composed a word-by-word commentary for any tantra.

Other than sādhanas of Mañjuśrī, Vajravidarana in the tradition of Virūpa, and the short sādhana of wrathful Metsek, he did not compose many sādhanas for the great maṇḍalas nor any of their associated rituals and so forth. The reason is that he did not wish to diminish the tradition of the previous lords [of the Sakya], who were inseparable from Vajradhara.

Though I have already briefly given the names of all these texts, now I will go into more detail. As for grammar, he composed: *Emanated Wisdom*, *Entrance to Grammar*,[977] *Condensed Meaning of the Gateway of Speech*,[978] the *Commentary on the Easy Entranceway for Beginners*,[979] *Letter Composition*,[980] and *Collection of Essential Grammar*.[981] As for logic, he composed the root text and commentary on the *Treasury of Valid Cognition*. As for poetry, he composed *Ornament for the Mouth of Scholars* and *Entreating the Compassion of the Sugata*. As for composition, he wrote *On Composition: A Bouquet of Flowers*. As for synonymics, he wrote *Treasury of Words*. As for drama, he composed the *Entrance into Abundant Happiness* and *Treatise on Music*. On arts and crafts, he composed *Treatise on Statue Iconography*[982] and *Land Surveying*.[983] On medicine, he composed *Summary of the Eight Branches*.[984] [120]

Furthermore, on the topic of Buddhist philosophy, he composed praises such as *Praise to the Buddha, Praise to the Sage, The Two Praises to Avalokiteśvara, Praise to the Sword Symbol of Mañjuśrī, Praise to Samyé, The Holy Place of Spontaneous Accomplishment*, and *Detailed Explanation of the Praise to Mañjuśrī*.[985]

On the topic of the common vehicle, he composed *Differentiating Tenet Systems, Clarifying the Sage's Intent, Clear Differentiation of the Three Vows, Great Bodhicitta Together with Its Textual Sources, Stages of Dharma Practice, The Ten Dharma Practices, Parting from the Four Attachments, Brief Presentation of the Mahāyāna Path*, and *Explanation of the Benefits of Dedication*.[986]

As for texts meant for general use, he composed *Entranceway for the Wise* and *Excellent Analysis of the Textual Tradition*.[987] As for the treatise tradition, he composed *Elegant Sayings*.[988] As for miscellany, he composed *Verses Composed After Defeating Trakjé Kawo, Verses Drawn from the Lines of the Bagora, Verses Posing Questions to Intelligent Disciples*, and the root text and commentary of *The "Eight I" Autobiography*.[989] As for letters and question-and-answer texts, he composed *Supplication Letter to the Buddhas and Bodhisattvas of the Ten Directions, Letters to the Holy Beings, Letter to Gods Who Find Joy in the Teachings, Letter to the Monks Living in Shingkun, Letter to Nyima, Letter to Lo Lotsāwa, Instructions to Zhang Lotsāwa, Letter to the Geshé of Öjowa, Letter to the Great Meditator Nyemo*, [121] *Answers to the Questions of Dogorwa*, and *Answers to the Questions of Chak Lotsāwa*.[990]

As for the uncommon vehicle, he composed *Illuminating the Mañjuśrī Sādhana, Tārā Sādhana, Offering Ritual for Grahamātṛkā, Sādhana of Grahamātṛkā in the Lineage of Śāntarakṣita, Clarifying the Union of the Maṇḍala Ritual, The Meaning of Meditation upon Amitābha*, and *Oral Instructions for the Time of Death*.[991]

As for unexcelled yoga tantra, he composed *Two Praises of the Lama; Praise to Lord of Yogins [Virūpa]; Praise to the Cakrasaṃvara Lineage; The Great Guru Yoga; Outer, Inner, and Secret Maṇḍala; Catalogue of the Lamdré Instructions; Instructions for Practice; Completing the Path by Means of the Five Interdependencies; The Root Text of "Explanation of the Hidden Path" Along with Its Branches; The Ten Great Siddhas Along with the Eight Minor Siddhas; Explanation of the Foundations of Aśṭa; Verses on the Feast Assembly; Commentary on the Praise of Dakmema; Meaning of the Names of the Six Families and Explanation of the Combined Wisdom; The Blessing of Innate*

Saṃvara; Explanation of Vajravidāraṇa According to the Tradition of Virūpa; Sambhuṭa; Vajravidāraṇa Tantra; Clear Differentiation of the Three Vows; and so forth.[992] He composed many stainless treatises such as these. In this way, he elucidated the Buddha's teachings.

Third, how he destroyed the rocky mountain of wrong view by means of the power of vajra debate. He became a great lord of reasoning and the white light of his fame radiated [122] around the entire earth to the shores of the oceans. During this period, six heretical non-Buddhist teachers, such as Harinanda[993] and so forth, who were followers of the great sage Kapilā,[994] the sage Vyāsa,[995] and the Ascetic,[996] and so forth, who adhered to the traditions of the Sāṅkhya,[997] the Cārvāka,[998] and Nyāya, who greatly worshiped Īśvara, Brahmā, Nyinmo Longwa,[999] the son of the wealth deity,[1000] the fire deity,[1001] and so forth, who practiced and wandered about in the southern regions, pledged: "We will depart for the Land of Snows. We will destroy that being living there who claims to be a bhikṣu in the lineage of Gautama but who has taken up the conduct of a woman[1002] and is attached to unwholesome view and conduct." With that, they departed.

Our lion-like guru presses down the crown of the head of unwholesome debaters. While residing at the market of Kyirong of the Avalokiteśvara Temple, sixty *yojana*[1003] to the north of Bodhgayā, the seat of enlightenment, the aforementioned six heretical teachers arrived. Without making prostrations to the Lord of Dharma or to the image of the Sugata, they uttered a few auspicious verses and small greetings and took their seats.

They then proudly said, "Our entire lineage from the time of the Guru Brahmā until now has never relied upon the teachings of Gautama. We have never taken refuge in the Triple Gem, so we are the only pure lineage of the Sage."

At that time, the Lord of Dharma said, "Do you not agree that, although Brahmā deeply respected the Teacher [Gautama], [123] he was deeply ignorant and became overwhelmed by sleep?" Just so:

> Supreme One [Brahmā] with four arms and sixteen half-faces,
> Brahmā who knows the recitations and definitive rituals,
> born from a stainless lotus; even he was overwhelmed by
> sleep.

And also:

> My teacher, who possessed the ten powers, awoke in all regards at daybreak long ago.

[The six teachers] could not bear this and became displeased. They began debating [Sapaṇ's statements]. One by one, [Sapaṇ] silenced all those deficient disputants by debating and refuting [their views]. Once more, he cleared away all their haughty wrong views, cut off their locks of hair, ordained them as novice monks, and enriched them with the jewels of renunciation. Sapaṇ then thought to himself that if anyone with bad intentions were to harm the victor Śākyamuni's teachings, he would tame them as [he had these six]. He then uttered the following verses:

> Mahādeva, clothed in the ocean with this great earth abutting its shores,
> the subduer sage Karka, and so on, those servants and devotees of Harinanda,
> who are followers of Vyāsa, Vālmīki, Ascetic, Akṣapāda,[1004] and Kapilā,
> with topknots, clothes made of tree bark and leaves, covered in dust, and holding sticks and kuśa grass,
> bearing locks of matted hair, covered by muñja [grass], wearing upper garments of deer hide,
> devoted to [Brahmā] whose forehead is adorned by three lines, wearing a brahmā thread from shoulder to armpit,
> who study all the Vedas, are very knowledgeable in its [124] recitation, are experts in [Sanskrit] grammar and composition,
> and who uphold the self-grasping view, perform austerities, and are haughty.
> [I] have thus confounded these drunk elephant-like heretics.
> [I am a] glorious lion-like exponent with the fangs of an incisive and powerful intelligence,
> with mature limbs of the grammar treatises and haloed by a mane of the Sugata's teachings;

I bellow the laughing roar of Sanskrit and stare while refuting
with logical reason.
Such a king of animals as this
now dwells upon the snow mountain of glorious Sakya,
protecting all intelligent beasts
and overcoming the pack of foxes of inferior disputants.
In the future, too, may all heretics
be defeated by the Dharma.
May he who is named Kunga Gyaltsen
uphold the correct teaching of the Sugata!

The matted hair belonging to those [heretics] may still be found in the Utsé Nyingma Temple of Glorious Sakya Monastery. In this way, a Tibetan paṇḍita defeated non-Buddhist heretical disputants. He was the only Lord of Dharma to have ever done so.

Secondly, how he benefited other sentient beings by means of his various enlightened activities. Overall, Sakya Paṇḍita's was an inconceivable, marvelous story of a liberated life. Here I will provide but a brief summary. When this mahātmā was eighteen years old, he dreamed that he was at Achi Bumpa,[1005] part of glorious Sakya Monastery. From a paṇḍita with a sky-blue, well-proportioned body named Master Vasubandhu,[1006] the second Buddha, he received teachings on the *Treasury of Abhidharma* for about one month. When he awoke, he had complete knowledge of the words [125] and meaning of the *Treasury of Abhidharma*. He later recalled that when he received teachings on this topic from the Kāśmīri mahāpaṇḍita [Śākyaśrībhadra], it was not so different from what he had heard while dreaming. For this reason, Jampaiyang Sherab Gyatso[1007] wrote in his *Record of Teachings Received* that he had received the oral transmission of the *Treasury of Abhidharma* in a lineage descended from Master Vasubandhu and Lord of Dharma Sakya Paṇḍita.

Among his other amazing dreams, once, before the Kāśmīri mahapaṇḍita came to Tibet, Sakya Paṇḍita dreamed that he heard one of [Śākyaśrībhadra's] profound teachings given as a vajra song. When he awoke, he remembered its words and the meaning. Later, when Śākyaśrībhadra came to Tibet, Sakya Paṇḍita inquired about this. It is well known that Śākyaśrībhadra replied, "That night, I had a similar dream!" This is similarly described [in the praise of Sakya Paṇḍita]:

> Understanding the Abhidharma without study,
> completing all learning in his youth,
> praised among the assembly of many scholars:
> I pay homage to you upon my crown, O Intelligent One!

And furthermore:

> Based upon thorough study over many lifetimes,
> even in your dreams, spiritual masters
> taught you all the divisions of the Dharma:
> I pay homage to you upon my crown, O Unmistaken One!

Additionally, on another evening he dreamed that the mahātmā was informed that he would be enthroned at the primary seat of the great master glorious Dignāga.[1008] "Please come!" they requested of him. There was a place called Dignāga's Cave, with a wooden door. The walls of the cave were lined with many volumes of text. In his dream, they passed [Sapaṇ] the key for that cave. He said that, after that dream, he could understand texts on logic and epistemology effortlessly.

Another time, while traveling [126] to Kyirong, he dreamed that he was offering praise to its Jowo statue:

> Actually combining the wisdom and compassion
> of all the buddhas of the three times,
> and whose actual name is Great Compassionate One:
> I pay homage to you, Avalokiteśvara!

He offered such praise as this. When he awoke, however, he could only remember the first four verses.

On another occasion, he dreamed that he was giving teachings in Sanskrit on the verses of homage from the *Commentary on Valid Cognition* to a great monastic assembly. As a result, a sun and moon arose simultaneously from his two shoulders. He later reported this to the great Jetsun

[Drakpa Gyaltsen], who responded, "It is difficult for this to occur!" Sapaṇ then prepared a community tea offering to an assembly of five thousand monks.

Another time, a king invited him to the spontaneously arisen temple of glorious Samyé to turn the wheel of the Dharma. He accepted, and after he had finished teaching on chapter five of the second section of the *Hevajra Tantra* and on most of the Lamdré, Sinpo Ripa[1009] invited him to head a monastic festival. On the evening before his departure, many people requested him to bestow instructions about visualization (*gmigs pa*), to give them blessings, and to answer their questions. Unquieted by all this, he was unable to fall asleep until the break of dawn. He then fell asleep for a while. He dreamed that a young layman appeared and made prostrations and offerings to him. He asked the Lord of Dharma, "Do you not think that all sentient beings suffer from the great river of birth, aging, sickness, and death?" Sapaṇ answered, "Yes, indeed, they do suffer from this!" The layman then asked, "I request that you please compose a supplication prayer that will help liberate us." He replied:

> I understand the meaning of birth and birthlessness, [127]
> and yet I am still bound to the mud of birth.
> In all my lifetimes I have been reborn as [saṃsāric] beings.
> Please protect me in all my unfortunate rebirths!

Sapaṇ told him to pray and recite in this way. The young man then asked him, "May I substitute the three others [old age, sickness, and death for birth]?" "Yes, you may," Sapaṇ replied. The young man then made prostrations in thanks. That was his dream. It has been said that once Sapaṇ awoke, he related that this young man was in fact the kingly Dharma protector of that temple.

Sapaṇ additionally revealed his actual form as Mañjuśrī to benefit a few disciples with completely pure minds. The author of his praise text recorded that Bodong Rinpoché Tsöndru Dorjé[1010] was one of the disciples who witnessed this:

> A few pure-minded disciples
> saw you as Mañjuśrī with their own eyes.

This became known, even in the Land of Noble Ones![1011]

According to the biography of Tsang Nakphukpa Jamyang Sherab Öser,[1012] he once realized he was dreaming and flew eastward through the sky and arrived at China's Wutaishan. A beautiful palace appeared, nestled in an idyllic, grassy mountain. He thought, "This is surely the palace of Mañjuśrī!" and proceeded to circumambulate while reciting prayers. It took him some time to locate the door. He eventually found it along the eastern wall and entered. Inside was a beautiful temple. [128] In the center of that temple was a jewel throne. The Lama Lord of Dharma of the Sakyapa sat atop it facing north. Jamyang Sherab Öser thought to himself, "This is Mañjuśrī!" and made prostrations, circumambulations, and prayers. Sakya Paṇḍita did not speak. He did, however, give him a single volume wrapped abundantly in silk. Opening it, he found that it was an edition of *Reciting the Names of Mañjuśrī* printed in gold. That was his dream. For a long time afterward, during the daytime his understanding of emptiness improved, and at night he was beset by magnificent dreams. This was a wondrous magical display.

On another occasion, the Lord of Dharma was invited to Central Tibet to turn the wheel of the Dharma. While there, Geshé Yakdé Sönam Sangpo[1013] was engaged in meditation practice to the south of his residence. At dusk, Sönam Sangpo had a vision of the assembly of his personal Hevajra maṇḍala deities. He later wondered what had happened. At daybreak, he left to ask the Lord of Dharma [Sapaṇ]. He arrived in his presence while the Lord of Dharma was making torma offerings. After making prostrations, the Lord said to him, "Are you the geshé who has come here?" Sönam Sangpo replied, "Yes, I am the one who has come here." "Why," Sapaṇ asked, "have you come here?" Sönam Sangpo said, "I have to ask you a question." Sapaṇ asked, "Is it about last night? King Pekar[1014] was making a magical display. Now you have met me, and nothing too unfortunate has happened. Still, it may be possible that you are suffering from some serious illness." And indeed, that year, Yakdepa suffered from a severe malady that almost killed him. When he recovered, his meditation experiences and his merit increased. [129] It is well known that Yakdepa said, "I have unshakable faith that this Lord of Dharma is actually a buddha."

Nyentö Dulwa Sengé[1015] compiled the biographies of the lamas of the Lamdré lineage. His text describes how others among Sapaṇ's direct disciples came to strongly believe that he was actually Mañjuśrī. Umapa Sherab Bum[1016] once received the precious Lamdré teachings. While meditating upon them, he would often become drowsy. He went to see the Lord of Dharma about this. He requested, "I am suffering from drowsiness. Please help remove this obstacle!" [Sapaṇ] said only, "If you possess wisdom, you will not be drowsy." Umapa Sherab Bum thought carefully about the meaning [of what Sapaṇ had said], and a supreme meditative stabilization arose within his mind. This is all recorded in his life story.

This is all part of the marvelous story of [Sakya Paṇḍita's] life, which illuminates the ways he benefited sentient beings.

It is additionally said that the detailed signs of impending death as described in the Lamdré teachings happen to only a few people. Should they arise, then imminent death is certain. Such signs once appeared for Sharpa Sherab Jungné;[1017] he then practiced only guru yoga and made prayers [to Sapaṇ]. By this, he was freed from death's specific signs and lived a long life. This is described in his biography.

Moreover, wherever Sapaṇ dwelled, epidemics created by elemental spirits (*gdon*), foreign or domestic battles, [130] and crop failures always ceased. If they occured, they would quickly disappear because of his power. Furthermore, all locals would develop an attitude of loving-kindness toward each other. Because of that, during his life, wars with foreign peoples such as the Mongols, domestic conflicts, and so forth would never occur in his vicinity.

As for his increasing activity,[1018] which caused incalculable abundances of Dharma and worldly wealth to arise, the lotus grove of his teachings and practice spread extensively. This cultivated countless disciples, who acquired the good qualities of learning and [meditative] accomplishment. It is said that during his life, even the most famous of scholars held his lotus feet respectfully atop their crowns and made offerings.

For example, Nyelshik Jampal Dorjé[1019] was one of the most famous scholars and teachers during Sapaṇ's time. Jampal Dorjé could not bear the fame of the Lord of Dharma. Among his disciples, Uyukpa Rikpai Sengé[1020] was the most intelligent. He was sent to debate the Lord of Dharma. For the first few days, he attended [Sapaṇ's] teachings and waited for any contradiction. He could not, however, find any. Not only was he unable to debate Sakya Paṇḍita, he developed unshakable faith in him. For a long time thereafter, while sat at his lotus feet, he relied upon Sapaṇ's instructions and became one of his foremost disciples. The number of his supreme students will be briefly explained later. For a more detailed account, consult Sakya Paṇḍita's extensive biographies.

On one occasion, Sapaṇ went to Samyé Monastery in Central Tibet upon the invitation of King Shakya Gön.[1021] At that site, [131] he drew Ārya Mañjuśrī's hand symbol on the middling circumambulatory route. Among other topics, he composed verses in praise of the Dharma kings and bodhisattvas of old and extensively turned the wheel of the Dharma. The Dharma king [Phakpa] wrote a few aphoristic verses recollecting all this:

> Due to being endowed with the two eyes of language and
> logic,
> you possess the intelligence of the view of the fullness of
> objects of knowledge.
> With extensive hearing and thorough study,
> glorious translator of the Sakyapa,
> you clearly explain the jewel lamp of the holy Dharma
> to sentient beings equal to the reaches of space
> so that they may obtain the state of the omniscient Victor
> and for the sake of pleasing that guru of sentient beings!
>
> Lama of beings and treasury of precious good qualities,
> the fragrance of your renown pervades in all directions!
> For the sake of illuminating the teachings in this world,
> the glorious Sakyapa, upholder of the Tripiṭaka,
> taught the profound and vast Dharma
> here at the spontaneously arisen, great holy site of Samyé.
> Whatever roots of virtues arise from all this,
> may all sentient beings be freed from the ocean of saṃsāra!
>
> Hare-holder possessing cooling light rays,
> you illuminate the earth and sky at night,

outshining the moving stars of the minds of those with wrong views
and causing kundalini flowers to blossom.

Regarding these verses, the [Dharma] King [Phakpa] was overjoyed when the great lama, the Lord of Dharma Sakya Paṇḍita, sat upon the lion throne of that crown jewel of scholars, the great master Kamalaśīla, at the spontaneously arisen [132] great temple of Samyé and turned the wheel of the profound and vast Dharma instructions, wiping clean the precious teachings and benefiting a great many sentient beings.

[Lama Phakpa] also recollected the biographies of the previous holy ones and clearly understood their holy activities. Given the changing nature of his times, many beings in his day grew hateful. With this realization, he became rather despondent. He wished that in the future the Dharma would help produce happiness and joy among all the beings of this world. He then wrote down the above verses upon whatever surface at suitable spots he could find along Samyé's circumambulatory route. He extended his precious right hand and wrote down all these poetic lines. He drew the "Supreme Vow-Protector" symbol by hand. All this was inscribed upon the wall. May the mind of whoever sees and reads these gain the exalted wisdom and behold its creator, [Sapaṇ]! All this was described by the bhikṣu Phakpa, and written elegantly upon this wall.

Secondly, [regarding] how he worked for the benefit of the teachings in northerly Mongolia. After this mahātmā had already extensively served the Sage's teachings here in the land of Tibet, he observed that those who are called "Mongols" [133] were malicious beings, more ignorant of what is to be adopted and accepted than animals, less compassionate than the Lord of Death, with greater physical prowess than yakṣas, who were as numerous as the armies of the demigods, and who inspired terror. They had first conquered China, then conquered all northerly peoples, such as the Tanguts,[1022] and so forth. Without differentiating between the laity and monastics, they forced all those they conquered to serve in the ranks of their armies, to become taxpaying subjects, and to be engaged as laborers. The Mongols thus effaced even the name of the teachings. They had brought themselves and others to ruin.

With unbearable compassion toward them, Sapaṇ had previously prayed that the minds of the Mongols would be brought into the Dharma and that they would be tamed. He now perceived that the time had come to act upon his prayers. When Sapaṇ's abbot, the mahāpaṇḍita Śākyaśrībhadra, was journeying to Siṅghala,[1023] the god Namtheu Karpo[1024] invited him to come to Mongolia. Śākyaśrībhadra prayed to Tārā, who prophesied: "Even if you were to go there, it would be of no benefit. However, if one of your disciples who currently stays in Tibet were to go, that would be of benefit." The mahāpaṇḍita passed along this prophecy to Sakya Paṇḍita. Furthermore, before the great lama Jetsun [Drakpa Gyaltsen] passed away, he prophesied [to Sapaṇ]: "Later in your life, the Mongols will extend an invitation to you. If you go, it will greatly benefit the teachings and sentient beings. You must go!" For all these reasons, when the Lord of Dharma was sixty-one years old, he made extensive preparations to undertake this journey.

When he was sixty years old, Köden Ejen,[1025] [134] the son of Ögedei Qaγan,[1026] who was in turn the son of the turner of the wheel of power, Činggis Qan, sent an envoy [with a letter for Sakya Paṇḍita]. In it, Köden gave the following invitation:

> Most powerful sky deity who relies upon glorious great merit, this is my command as king: O Sakya Paṇḍita Kunga Gyaltsen Palsangpo, understand my speech!
>
> I need a lama who can show me what to adopt and what to discard to repay the kindness of my parents, heaven (*gnam*), and earth. Upon investigation, that person is you! Because of this, you must come here without considering the difficulty of the journey. If you make excuses, saying "I am old!" consider how many times the Buddha gave his body for the benefit of sentient beings in his previous lives. Wouldn't this contradict the commitments of your Dharma knowledge? Should you still not come I will order my army to harm a great many beings. Are you still not afraid (*me skrag pa e yin*)?
>
> With all this in mind, think about how to benefit the Buddha's teachings and the multitude of sentient beings. Then journey here as quickly as possible!

I will then make you well known to monks from the easterly direction of the rising sun. I will gift you: five *dre* of silver, a silk Dharma robe garnished by 6,200 individual pearls, a long sleeveless monastic shirt made from *lu-hang* together with shoes, two rolls of *khati khatsangma* brocade cloth, two rolls of *thönti khatsangma* brocade cloth, and twenty rolls of the five types of silk.

This message has been dispatched [135] with Dorsi Gön and Önjo Darma.[1027] It was written on the day of the auspicious new moon during the eighth month of the Dragon Year.

Though he was by then quite old, with these reasons in mind [Sakya Paṇḍita] set out to journey [to the Mongols] without regard for his life.

When he was sixty-three years old, he arrived in the northerly territory of the Tanguts. At that time, the teacher from Domé Lodrö Rabsel[1028] asked him some Dharma questions. Sapaṇ gave an answer that elucidated the meaning of the scriptural system (*gzhung lugs*). His actual answer was as follows:

The teacher Lodrö Rabsel
has posed questions accompanied by a scarf and offerings,
which I have now received in hand.
I am gladdened by this.
As for your first question,
it says in *The Treasury of Knowledge*:

> Whatever exists will disintegrate, like a pot.
> Sound also exists, which is evidence of its identical essence.

So you have said.
And from *Clear Differentiation of the Three Vows:*

> Additionally, the dharmadhātu is nonexistent,
> for, as Dharmakīrti has explained so clearly,
> the existent is pervaded by impermanence.

Are we to take the meaning of these passages literally?

[Sapaṇ's answer:]

As Dharmakīrti has said in the *Commentary on Valid Cognition*:

[Any phenomenon that] can perform a function
is ultimately to be taken as an ultimate existent (*don dam yod pa*).
All the rest are to be taken as conventional existents (*kun rdzob yod pa*).
Those are the definitive characteristics of all ultimate (*rang*) and conventional (*spyi*) phenomena.

As this says, any phenomenon that can perform a function (*don byed nus pa*) is ultimately existent, while any phenomenon that does not have such capacity is conventionally existent. Furthermore [according to Dharmakīrti]:

As for disintegration: result and existent.

This means that, to prove that sound disintegrates, a result is posited as a reason (*rtags su bkod pa*) and an existent is posited as a reason.

Here, this tenet school accepts that any acts of accepting and refuting
do not, in fact, rely [136] upon a nonfunctioning object
nor an external object.
They rely instead upon the referent of a term (*sgra don*).

Moreover, from the usage of a term alone,
we accept the term "existent."

So it says. Simply because [it is a referent term], it is not nonexistent. To say so using the referent of a term uses the terminology "existent."

Alternatively,

> Here, we say "existent" because something can be seen as an object
> [of a valid cognizer]. Nothing exists other than what is seen to exist.

[Dharmakīrti] is here explaining that anything that can be observed by a valid cognizer is the definitive characteristic of existence (*yod pa'i mtshan nyid*). As for what is included in this category:

> There are two types of existents:
> actual existents and nominal existents.
> Actual existents can perform a function.
> Nominal existents perform the function of rejecting and accepting.

As for your second question:
"Is the dharmadhātu not an object of knowledge?"
The answer is as follows:
the *Diamond Cutter Sūtra*[1029] says:

> The dharmakāya of all the buddhas:
> all [spiritual] guides view it as the dharmadhātu.
> The dharmadhātu is not an object of knowledge.
> This is beyond understanding.

And as it says in the *Introduction to the Bodhisattva's Way of Life*:

> Ultimate [truth] is not an object of mind.
> It is asserted that objects of mind are conventional [truths].

As for the meaning of this, from its own side the dharmadhātu is beyond any object of knowledge or expression. In terms of elimination of the other (*gzhan sel*), however, it is designated as an object of knowledge.

As it says in the *Sublime Continuation*:[1030]

If there were no buddha nature,
there would be no remorse over suffering.
There would be no longing after nirvāṇa,
nor striving and aspiration toward this aim.

And further, as it says in *Distinguishing the Middle from the Extremes*:[1031]

The synonyms of the dharmadhātu:
suchness, limit of reality,
absence of marks, the ultimate.
The meaning of the synonyms:
not other, nondeceptive,
cessation, the object of a noble being's [137] sphere of experience,
the cause of a noble being's qualities.

So it is said. And from the *Treasury of Abhidharma*:

[Buddha nature is] the expanse of beginningless time,
the ground of all phenomena;
because it exists, all beings
can obtain nirvāṇa.

The meanings of those verses are as follows:

Ultimate [truth] is free from the elaboration of the four extremes,
cutting off the mutual contradictories, such as
conventional [truth], existence, nonexistence, and so forth.
It is not existent, and it is said to be nonexistent.
Furthermore, from the *Commentary on Valid Cognition*:

Other than accept (*sgrub*) and refute (*dgag pa*),
No other terminology arises from sound.
Also, [the object of] refutation is a non-entity (*dngos po med pa*)
So nothing much can be said about it.

As for your third question:
"Is the truth of cessation unproduced virtue?"
[Sapaṇ's answer:]
Although the truth of cessation is unproduced,
it is not accepted that this is authentic virtue (*dge ba mtshan nyid*).
As Āryā Nāgārjuna said in *The Fundamental Verses on the Middle Way*:[1032]

Were an action uncreated,
one would be fearful of encountering the uncreated.
There would also follow
the fault of not abiding in pure moral conduct.
All conventions, without a doubt,
would then be contradicted,
and any differentiation between virtue and nonvirtue
would then be inadmissible.
Whatever might then ripen,
would do so again and again.

One should know that [Nāgārjuna] rejected the existence of uncreated authentic virtue and nonvirtue.

I, bearing the name Kunga, like an omniscient one have [answered]
all the questions the intelligent one
appropriately posed [138] to me using his intelligence.
Examine all these excellent distinctions carefully!

Biji Rinchendrak[1033] transcribed these answers to the Domé teacher Lodrö Rabsel's questions in the garden.

Later in Domé, along his journey [to the Mongol court], Sapaṇ answered questions from the yogi Trumapa.[1034] As for this [it has been said]:

> When the manifestation of Lord Mañjuśrī, the Lord of Dharma Sakya Paṇḍita, was riding across Domé on his journey to Mongolia, the great meditator named Yogi Trumapa offered outer and inner robes to the Lord of Dharma. He then asked the Lord of Dharma, "It is said in your treatise *Distinguishing What Is True from What Is False* [i.e., *Clear Differentiation of the Three Vows*]:
>
> > It is taught that the foolish meditating upon mahāmudrā
> > is mostly a cause for rebirth as an animal
> > or as rebirth in the formless realm,
> > or else a cause to fall into the cessations of a hearer.
> > However, when [mahāmudrā] meditation is of an excellent quality,
> > it is nothing other than meditation upon the Middle Way.
> > Meditation upon the Middle Way, while very good in itself,
> > is nonetheless extremely difficult to accomplish.
>
> "What is the meaning of this?" [Yogi Trumapa asked.]
>
> The Lord of Dharma replied as follows: "'Śamatha[1035] meditation that merely blocks conceptual thought…': This refers to forcing the mind to go blank, and to remain for a long time in this vacuity while becoming sleepy and foggy-minded.
>
> "'And vipaśyanā meditation that merely produces blank [thought]….' [In reference to this,] King Indrabhūti[1036] once said:
>
> > As for the meditation of the deluded:
> > On the basis of delusions, they will accomplish delusions!
>
> "Ārya Nāgārjuna has similarly said:
>
> > By misperceiving emptiness,
> > a person of little wisdom is ruined!

"Without scrutinizing using the wisdom of individual analysis, one may believe that nothing exists simply by fixating upon the phenomena of perception, and then believe that whatever one sees and experiences is empty. [139] Both are great causes of falling into the lower realms. They must both be abandoned by those who wish for excellence.

"'Śamatha meditation that is unclear because of stupor...': [In reference to this,] a stupefied mind is unclear and naturally fixates upon the object of awareness.

"'And vipaśyanā meditation that rejects visual forms...': This means that, without study of the Abhidharma and so forth, one identifies and experiences all phenomena as being like the sky, and the mind as nothing whatsoever, as neither cognizant nor noncognizant.

"'...are together a great cause for rebirth in the formless realm. They should be abandoned by those wishing for liberation.': This refers to the accumulation of the nontransferring karma (*mi g.yo ba'i las*) for being reborn in the formless realms.

"'Sāmanta meditation with neither recollection nor feeling...': This refers to abiding in thoughtlessness for a long while during one's practice of meditative stabilization.

"'And vipaśyanā meditation that rejects the six aggregates...": This refers to indistinct action of the six aggregates of consciousness, such as the eye and so forth.

"'Both are partially in accord with the cessation of a hearer...': This refers to the arising of an experience that is like the meditative absorption of cessation. This should be abandoned by those wishing for the supreme [cessation].

"'Śamatha meditation that possesses the bliss of pliancy...': As for the meaning of this, it is said in the *Ornament of the Mahāyāna Sūtras*:[1037]

> After that, [the bodhisattva] will accomplish
> the great pliancy of body and mind.

They will be known as possessing the [eleven] mental
contemplations.

"'Vipaśyanā meditation that completely pacifies all elaborations…': [Regarding this] Āryadeva has said:

Neither existence, nor nonexistence, nor nonduality,
nor the nature of not nonduality;
This is the supreme meaning, free from the four extremes.
This is the tradition of Madhyamaka.

["And furthermore:]

Both are, together, the great path of the Perfection Vehicle.
It would be good for the children of the Victor to practice
this.

Other than the ordinary continuum of all-absorbing
concepts,
there is not another bond of saṃsāra.
Whatsoever mind that quarrels with that
Shall not become entangled with the all-absorbing
concepts.

"The *White Lotus of Compassion Sūtra*[1038] says:

Beyond the quality of the subtle particles,
like the aspect of a mirror diviner,
endowed with all the supreme aspects,
mahāmudrā is the bliss of immutability.

"Thus it was said.

"Sāmanta meditation that completely pacifies conceptual thoughts…': [Regarding this] Sangyé Yeshé Shab said:

There are no saṃsāric bonds
other than the activity of an ordinary being's conceptual
thought.
Any mind that opposes those
has no conceptual thought.

"'Thoroughly subsided śamatha [140] and vipaśyanā meditation, which is the union of bliss and emptiness…': [Regarding this], the *White Lotus of Compassion Sūtra* says:

Mahāmudrā is the bliss of immutability,
beyond even the nature of the subtle particles,
in aspect like the mirror diviner,
and endowed with all supreme qualities.

"This is the supreme path of secret mantra mahāmudrā.

"It would be good for those wishing to be emancipated in this life."

Sakya Paṇḍita has said: "If one correctly understands the meaning of those five verses, one will understand whether one's practice of mahāmudrā is authentic or not. As such, one should analyze them carefully." These five verses of instruction to the yogi Trumapa were recorded just by Biji at Lingka in lower Dokham.[1039] These three questions and their answers have not previously been well known. Dorjechang Kunga Wangchuk[1040] collected them and I have written them down here.

It is said that these annotations were recorded by Biji just as they were spoken by the Lord of Dharma. Later, as Sakya Paṇḍita traveled across Domé, a person offered him a black cloth decorated by many gold circles. Sapaṇ gave this to the doctor Biji, telling him, "You should keep this! Soon our Sakyapa teachings will shine like the stars in a clear sky." Some people say that the Sakyapa reject relics (*ring bsrel*). However, [as Sapaṇ wrote in *Clear Differentiation of the Three Vows*]:

Most relics are made by evil spirits (*gdon*).
It is possible that a few are manifested by virtuous gods.
It is also possible they are created by the four elements.
As for the relics of the three kinds of noble beings,
they appear from the force of virtue
and are like jewels arisen from the source.
One cannot count their number.
Such relics do not decrease; they increase.

[141] Regarding this, Sapaṇ said to Biji, "If such a support were to arise from me, they would be innumerable. You should keep them. Use this black cloth to wrap them." But then [Sapaṇ] said, "I am only joking with you! Do not tell others what I have said, since it would become a cause for accumulating wrong deeds!"

The protector of beings, the Dharma king Phakpa Rinpoché, gradually entered into a patron-patronized relationship with the Dharma king Sachen Qan [Qubilai Qaγan].[1041] Subjects speaking many different languages from across the dominion of Qubilai Qaγan, including even in areas where the words "Triple Gem" had never before appeared, developed devotion and adopted and abandoned conduct in relation to the law of karma and its results. Even the Mongols received teachings upon Mahāyāna bodhicitta, received [tantric] initiations, made offerings to the Triple Gem, worked on behalf of the benefit of sentient beings, abandoned some of their evil nonvirtuous actions, and then entered into the excellent path.

Under Qubilai Qaγan's reign, knowledgeable people like monks and tantric yogis from among the Tibetans, the Uyghur, the Tanguts, the Mentsé,[1042] and so forth were exempted from serving in the military, paying taxes, or doing forced labor. Again and again, Qubilai made countless excellent offerings to them of food, drink, clothing, gold and silver, silk, and so forth. He also bestowed upon them the excellent title of "Imperial Preceptor,"[1043] and served them greatly. The precious teachings of the Victor were respected and honored, and they endured for a long time.

Furthermore, [the Mongol court] was suspicious there would be an uprising because their empire [142] was extremely large with a very fickle (*shes pa 'char*) population. And so, each year they killed all males over the age of nine. But even that was not enough. They would herd them together and march them into the outer oceans! Phakpa had great compassion for them, and he asked the qaγan insistently [to stop this]. The qaγan provided [the cessation of such killing] to [Phakpa] as an offering after receiving a tantric initiation. It is well known that from then on, that [killing] practice was discontinued.

For these reasons, if nowadays there is even a little happiness and joy in the north of the world, this is due to the uncommon kindness of the Lord of Dharma [Sapaṇ] and his nephews. Nowadays ordinary beings have no idea about any of this. Even very knowledgeable geshés—especially those among them with clear knowledge about what is right and wrong, and who are renowned to have taken responsibility for the Buddha's teachings and sentient beings—do not recognize this. They would all either prefer not to believe it, or else their minds are biased.

Because of all this, in reality uncle and nephew acted for the benefit of sentient beings in ways that no previous Tibetan geshé had done before. Some say that it was because the Sakyapa were originally led by the Mara of the Divine Son[1044] that they later had relations with the Mongols. But this claim is unreasonable. It is true that, though they were monks, they took on some of the aspects and conduct of the Mongols. However, if they had not done so, the Mongols would not have entered the Dharma. Even the Sage [Buddha] himself acted in conformity with the world so that others would enter the Dharma. Had those Mongols not entered the Dharma, then all the problems described above would have continued to occur. In this case, the purpose was simply more consequential than the object of negation.

This is the marvelous biography of the bodhisattva mahāsattva [Sakya Paṇḍita]. Its details are difficult to fathom for those of lesser intelligence.

When the Lord of Dharma [Sapaṇ] passed away, he explained the intended meaning [of his life story] as follows:

> According to the thorough explanations
> of the supreme scriptures of you protectors,
> I diligently practiced whatever I could
> and I became liberated from impediments.

I put into practice
whatever was taught in those scriptures,
just as it was explained.
I take refuge in you, O Speaker of Truth!

For these reasons, some biographies that adopt the perception of ordinary beings claim that [Sakya Paṇḍita] was uninterested in traveling to the north. However, the reality is that he certainly understood the great benefit that would accrue for other sentient beings and so went there gladly. This is described in *Questions and Answers*:

By the power of my previous actions,
I have caused the sun of the teachings to rise in the east.
By the wish-fulfilling jewels of learning, contemplation, and meditation,
may I quickly complete the wishes of all the faithful of Ü and Tsang!

Just as these lines describe, when he was sixty-five years old, in the eighth month of the Male Fire Horse Year [1246], he departed for northerly Liangzhou.[1045] At that time, King Köden[1046] was returning from Mongolia, where he had gone to enthrone Güyüg Qaγan.[1047] They met in the first month of the [Fire] Sheep Year [1247]. The king was extremely happy, and they held extensive discussions about the Dharma and politics (*chos srid*). The king had previously held audiences with Tibetan monks, but until then he had not yet personally cultivated any of the specific good qualities described in the Buddha's teachings. [144]

During prayer assemblies and during oath-taking rituals (*dbang bar khas len pa*) [at Köden's court], Akawun[1048] and Mongolian oracles were seated ahead of the Buddhist monks. Later, the king and the lama, Lord of Dharma, held many discussions about the Dharma. Whenever they could not understand one another, many scholarly Uyghur spiritual friends translated for them and helped the king completely understand the meaning of the Dharma. The king became immensely happy and declared: "From this day on, do not sit Akawun and the oracles ahead of the monks! During the prayer assemblies, the lama, Lord of Dharma, must sit ahead of everyone. And during prayers, the monks must be the first to make recitations." In such ways, Köden glorified Buddhist monks in the kingdom of the Mongols.

Later, King Köden began to suffer from a skin disease. As a healing ritual, Sapaṇ made many Mañjuśrī water torma offerings (*chab gtor 'jam dpal ma*). At dawn on the eleventh day of the third month of the Sheep Year, Sapaṇ dreamed that a being with crooked legs and a crippled body covered by wounds and abscesses appeared to him. Sapaṇ asked, "Who are you?" The being replied, "I have a leader who told me, 'I am being called forth by the Sakyapa. You should go on my behalf and hear what he has to say. I am too ill to go myself.' That is the reason that I have come." Sapaṇ explained to him, "Köden sent a gold-letter bearer to invite me here from my distant homeland. Now I must help him. What is causing his illness? What method should I use to heal him?"

The being replied, "Long ago, all these lands were unowned and retained by my leader. [145] At that time, Köden was reborn a king who accumulated merit by serving the Buddha Śākyamuni. He later passed away and was reborn as a Tangut king. He built a palace right over the top of our abode. That Tangut king then ordered his monks, 'I will build a palace, so perform the earth pacification rituals (*sa gzhi slong*)!' Those monks sang some melodies, used some instruments, and offered some tormas, but they did not know how to perform the actual earth ritual. And so, we never gave them permission to build. Regardless, that king built his palace right on top of us. My ruler and we subjects felt as if we were being pressed down by a mountain! Since we could not compete with the merit of those humans, we departed for this northerly land and came rightfully to occupy it. However, later that king came even here! He started fires on top of us, dug into the earth, and harmed us in many other ways! We could not continue to live here. My leader became very upset. He summoned all the local gods and demons and told them, 'That king has twice robbed me of my land! I wish to harm him, and you must help me!' The gods and demons replied, 'Because this king accumulated merit in the presence of Buddha Śākyamuni, you cannot compete with his merit. And so, you should leave this dry place [146] and go live instead in [some aquatic] place replete with springs and muddy waters.'

"My ruler [and his subjects] went to live [in this watery region]. At that time, this [Tangut] king began to examine the historical record of what previous kings had offered to monks. He exclaimed, 'They offered too much!' and so began to offer the monks less in his court. He also decided, 'I want to examine whether this statue of Śākyamuni is made of gold, wood, or stone!' and then cut into its feet using a chisel!

"When this occurred, the gods and demons recognized: 'Now some portion of this king's merit has decreased. It is now the time to attack him!' All the gods and demons gathered for the effort but, since this king was very fortunate, no one could defeat him. They schemed instead: 'We should cause a schism between the king and the entourage of his ministers.' They did so, and the ministers subsequently murdered the king. Just before he died, the king prayed, 'In my next life, may I be reborn as a prince. And then, may I turn all of you into my servants!' He was duly reborn as the grandson (*tsha ba*) of Činggis Qan. This was Köden.

"Later, Köden came to this northerly region. Right on top of our watery and muddy abode, he held horse races and even killed horses! Wherever the horse blood pooled, some of us fell sick and others died. The frogs and tadpoles on my body nearly died. It was only because of the heat of my body that they did not!"

Then he showed Sakya Paṇḍita the half-dried and nearly dead frogs and tadpoles clinging to his body. The being said, "Previously, monks made prayers on behalf of Köden, but it did not benefit us nāgas. Now, you, Sakyapa, have offered us good medicine and good food. This helps us. Before, I couldn't travel anywhere, but because I am now so nourished, I can come here to see you. My leader is nearly dead. Should he die, know that Köden will also die! Should he survive, know that Köden, too, will survive! A simple healing ritual is not enough to help or heal him. And so you must make great effort to ensure the survival of my leader and of Köden! If my leader survives, [147] Köden too will survive! If they survive, you will become exalted!" Listening to this, the Lord of Dharma thought to himself, "What healing method should I use?" Just then, a small obstacle arose. The being disappeared [and Sapaṇ] awoke.

Sapaṇ then performed the ritual of Noble Siṃhanāda[1049] on behalf of the ailing king. By this, the king recovered from his illness and became very devoted to Sapaṇ. Köden received many transmissions of the vast and profound Dharma on topics like Mahāyāna bodhicitta and so forth. He came to honor Sapaṇ as the highest object of veneration. From then on, Sapaṇ helped those disciples who spoke various languages and who previously had no faith in the Dharma to develop faith. For those with faith already, Sapaṇ helped lead them into the Mahāyāna path.

In summary, Sakya Paṇḍita ripened and liberated countless disciples. He helped the teachings of the Buddha spread extensively and flourish.

Sapaṇ also visited China's Wutaishan. There he met a resident engaged in recitation named Tokden Gyenpo.[1050] In order to liberate his mind, as a preliminary ritual Sakya Paṇḍita bestowed the full initiation of Bhagavatī Hevajra according to the lineage of Ḍombī [Heruka], then the blessing empowerment of the sindhura maṇḍala of Jetsun Dakmema. He then bestowed the inconceivable, quintessential instructions, such as those describing the profound completion stage. He then gave the profound pointing-out instructions in order [for him] to realize the wisdom of mahāmudrā.

It has been said that when the emanation of the venerable Mañjuśrī, the Lord of Dharma Sakya Paṇḍita, traveled to China's Wutaishan and resided there, there was a great meditator named Tokden Gyenpo. He circumambulated and [148] prostrated to the Lord of Dharma. The Lord of Dharma then said to him: "It is wonderful that you, Tokden, make circumambulations and prostrations to me. You dwell here in this holy place, so it is important that you should rely upon the profound teachings and meditate."

Tokden considered this carefully. He then retrieved a white cloth from his dwelling and offered it to the Lord of Dharma and asked: "Do you, O Lord of Dharma, accept that the view of mahāmudrā amounts to meditation upon all vehicles? What is mahāmudrā? Why is it called 'mahāmudrā'? How might we use this method to traverse the grounds and paths? Please give me the profound instructions of mahāmudrā!"

This caused the Lord of Dharma to become very happy. He gave the Hevajra initiation according to the Ḍombī tradition. He then gave Tokden the instruction on the generation of coemergent mahāmudrā, followed by the complete instructions of Doktsepa.[1051]

[Sapaṇ] then told him, "This is my way of teaching mahāmudrā: Avoid all egotistical pursuit of siddhi and rely instead upon single-pointed meditation. These instructions will not deceive you! Keep in mind the summaries of the following answers to your questions.

"In general, the vehicle of the transcendental perfections is sealed by the four seals of the view of the marks [of existence]. The tradition of the three lower classes of tantras, moreover, is sealed by the nonduality of the profound and manifest. In all this, there is no mention of the terminology of mahāmudrā. According to these traditions, there is mention of the 'supreme siddhi,' but not the 'supreme siddhi of mahāmudrā.' And so, it is unacceptable to meditate upon the actual view of mahāmudrā [according to these traditions]. [149] In those traditions, while the object of profound emptiness is explained, there is no explanation about the subject of profound method. So, we cannot accept that [their meditative traditions] include the actual qualified mahāmudrā. For example, although the tradition of the hearers describes generosity, ethics, and so on, there is no mention of extraordinary method and wisdom, and so it does not include the perfection of generosity and so forth. The foolish might misname people 'oxen and cows.' Similarly, someone may meditate upon their view and call it 'mahāmudrā,' but I refuse to simply debate mere names!

The natural state of mahāmudrā
is the unchanging bliss of mahāmudrā.
That is the purity of the apprehended object, the apprehending subject, and shape.
All this is free from conceptuality and expression.

It is like the city of gandharvas.[1052]
The yogi, with skillful method and wisdom,
understands like a mirror divination:
I pay homage to the letters *evam*!

Beyond the qualities of the subtle particles of phenomena,
like the aspect of a mirror divination,
and endowed with all supreme qualities:
I pay homage to the state of mahāmudrā!

"As these verses describe, the object of realization is the 'natural state.' It is emptiness endowed with all supreme qualities. As for the manner of realizing [that object], it must be understood as beyond words, thought, and expression, much like a mirror divination.

"The nature of the object is called 'the yoga of the union of wisdom.' It possesses many synonyms, such as the union of experience and emptiness, the union of awareness and emptiness, the union of bliss and emptiness, the union of great bliss and emptiness, coemergent wisdom, self-arisen wisdom, self-cognizant wisdom, the wisdom of discriminating awareness, and so forth. [150]

"The method to understand all this is described in the *Garland of Vajras Tantra*:[1053]

> Properly please the lama
> and correctly receive the authentic initiation;
> then one will understand the meaning of [mahāmudrā].

"So it is said. From the *Two-Part* [*Hevajra Tantra*]: 'Later, one will understand it.' As this says, [the mind realizing mahāmudrā] will arise based upon receiving an authentic initiation and properly meditating upon the liberating two stages together with their branches.

"Ārya Nāgārjuna has said:

> All the teaching of the buddhas
> are completely based upon the two stages:
> one is the development stage,
> the other is the completion stage.

"This is the main point: All methods for bringing about the wisdom of the unexcelled secret mantra are included within the two stages.

"As for the etymology of the term *chakya chenpo* [i.e., Skt. *mahāmudrā*; Tib. *phyag rgya chen po*], someone unlearned in Sanskrit will claim that *chak* (*phyag*) means the wisdom of emptiness and that *gya* (*rgya*) means liberation from the net of saṃsāra. As proof, they will cite the *Guhyagarbha Tantra*,[1054] the *Drop of of Mahāmudrā*,[1055] and so forth. This is all a mistake. In Sanskrit, *chakya chenpo* is called 'mahāmudrā.' In Tibetan, *mahā* means great (*chenpo*) and *mudrā* (*chakya*) means seal, sign, mark, *guk kyé*,[1056] and so forth. Here, it is to be translated as 'seal.' As for its meaning, the *Avadhūtipa* says:

> Due to being sealed, it is called 'seal.'
> Since the three cycles of existence are of one taste, it is called 'the great seal.'

"As this says, one views all the phenomena of saṃsāra and nirvāṇa as sealed within the union of bliss and emptiness, and then one engages in practice. Because of that, this view is called [151] 'mahāmudrā.'

"As for the stages of the manner of generating the view of mahāmudrā: When receiving the descending wisdom initiation, some fortunate disciples realize the authentic wisdom of mahāmudrā. But most must rely upon methods like meditation and so forth. At first, one generates an artificial mahāmudrā, and later one realizes authentic mahāmudrā. There are two kinds of 'artificial' mahāmudrā: (1) similar [or] poisonous [mahāmudrā] and (2) solitary [or] faulty [mahāmudrā]. Regarding 'poisonous,' though one has not yet dispelled knowledge arising from hearing, contemplating, or the waves of conceptual thought within one's meditation, still, an experience associated with union is born. As for 'solitary,' there are various kinds: only dwelling; only individually investigating; only appearance; only emptiness; of the body, blissful heat or levitation; of speech, unspecified utterances; of mind, unspecified varieties of meditative experience. These become the single experience of the three doors. Fainting, inactive six consciousnesses, and so on all become 'partial mahāmudrā.'

"As for how to traverse the grounds and paths: In general all Buddhist schools accept that first generating the mind of enlightenment and taking the ripening empowerment, up to achieving the imperfect experience, is called the 'path of accumulation.'[1057] The *Two-Part [Hevajra Tantra]* says, 'Similar to omniscient wisdom.' Just so, though one has produced the genuine wisdom of the union of bliss and emptiness [152] in one's mind-stream and the experience of nonconceptuality arises continually, still, subtle tendencies toward conceptual thought remain. Like the sun rising at dawn, symbolic wisdom (*dpe'i ye shes*) is thus generated in one's mind stream. This is called the 'path of preparation.'

"It is said in *Reciting the Names of Mañjuśrī*:

> [It is] beyond the nature of consciousness,
> wisdom, bearer of the means of nonduality,
> without conceptual thought, spontaneously accomplished.

"Like this, the authentic nonconceptual exalted wisdom that directly realizes the emptiness endowed with all supreme aspects is the actual wisdom of mahāmudrā. When this first arises, it is known as achieving the 'path of seeing.'

"From there, continually familiarizing oneself and progressing [along the path] until the achievement of the twelfth bhūmi is known as the 'path of meditation.' From there, when one attains the thirteenth bhūmi, one achieves an ocean of good qualities, such as the four kāyas, the five wisdoms, and so forth. This is known as attaining the 'path of no more learning.'

"Furthermore, according to the general Buddhist schools, first one achieves the path of preparation. According to the uncommon Buddhist schools, first one generates the authentic symbolic wisdom of mahāmudrā. Then one achieves the authentic true wisdom (*don gyi ye shes*). Should one aspire to achieve the state of the unity of Vajradhara in this single lifetime, if one properly practices the conduct, secondary causes (*nye rgyu*), and so forth as explained in the tantras, one will surely achieve realization on the example of the Indian siddhas. It has been taught that if the authentic symbolic wisdom has been born in one's mindstream, but one does not complete the practice, one will accomplish [the authentic true wisdom] at the moment of death or upon receiving instructions in the intermediate state.

"Some say: [153]

> It is wrong to count the grounds and paths
> of the all-sufficient mahāmudrā.

"But this is mistaken. *Reciting the Names of Mañjuśrī* says, "[He is] the guardian, the powerful lord of the ten grounds of mind..." And according to the *Abhidhāna*:

The thirteen bhūmis are:
The Joyous and the Stainless,
likewise, the Radiant, the Brilliant,
the Very Difficult to Overcome, the Realized,
the Far Gone, the Immovable,
the Good Intellect, the Dharma Cloud,
the Without Example, the Great Wisdom,
and the Vajra Holder.

"And so forth. This is all according to the extensive explanation of the grounds and paths in the tantras and by master adepts.

"From *Reciting the Names of Mañjuśrī*: 'Completely enlightened in an instant.' This indicates that at the end of traversing the grounds and paths, one achieves complete enlightenment. From the *Wisdom at the Moment of Death Sūtra*: 'You should contemplate that if you understand the mind, you will become enlightened. You do not need to search for enlightenment elsewhere!' Regarding this, Saraha has said:

Only the mind is the seed for everything.
It radiates saṃsāra and nirvāṇa.
It gives rise to whatever one desires.
I pay homage to the mind, which is like a wish-fulfilling
 jewel!

"As this says, one becomes enlightened by understanding the appearance (*kun rdzob*) and natural mode (*don dam pa'i gnas tshul*) of the all-ground consciousness (*sems kun gzhi'i rnam par shes pa*). As has been said:

Other than the precious mind,
there are no buddhas and no sentient beings.
The nature of consciousness [154]
exists neither internally nor externally.

"And further:

> There is not even the slightest difference between
> completely pure wisdom and
> conceptual thought within cyclical existence.

"Just so, this is because all appearances of saṃsāra and nirvāṇa are one taste of mind. O Tokden, keep this in mind and undertake the practice! You will derive great benefit!'"

[Sakya Paṇḍita] taught this specific instruction to Tokden [at Wutaishan]. This was recorded as *Medical Implements for Removing Cataracts with Mahāmudrā: Instruction for Tokden Gyenpo.*[1058] It was recorded at Wutaishan by Biji, who carefully examined the words of the Lord of Dharma.

It is well known that, on another occasion, while the Lord of Dharma resided at [Köden's] Liangzhou Palace and taught the Dharma, elsewhere a large group was preparing to depart for Wutaishan to pay homage. As they did so, they all dreamed that Mañjuśrī was not then residing at Wutaishan but at the Liangzhou Palace teaching the Dharma. When they awoke, they had no doubts and departed for Liangzhou. At that time, the Lord of Dharma was indeed teaching on the generation of bodhicitta. They came into his presence and received those teachings.

Another time, the Lord of Dharma and Köden, the king of Mongolia, were holding long discussions. Their conversation turned to a passage from the *Sūtra of Sublime Golden Light*[1059] that describes the unlikely figure of a turtle with hair.[1060] In order to disprove that claim [i.e., that a turtle with hair exists, as given in the sūtra], King Köden presented a fathom of animal hide with long, rainbow-colored hair to the Lord of Dharma. The mahatma [Sapaṇ] said, "This is not the skin of a turtle! [155] The scriptures speak of a bodhisattva who once manifested in a form like a turtle to benefit water-bound sentient beings. This hide belongs to that bodhisattva, not a turtle. If someone can reveal this situation, and if it is seen by those able to see, the image of a thousand buddhas and the eight bodhisattvas will appear clearly upon the surface of this hide." Sapaṇ then revealed all these. Everyone gathered about him was amazed.

The king was somewhat embarrassed and decided that he'd like to provide some kind of rebuttal. He held discussions with his ministers, and then the king's magicians used various substances and mantras to conjure a beautiful landscape. Therein, they created such things as a splendid temple and a monastery. The king then said to the Lord of Dharma, "I invite you as the object of my patronage. You are knowledgeable and I see many of your great qualities. I am now overjoyed. I have an excellent monastery in a quiet place that I would like to offer to you. We should go there!" The mahātmā and his disciples, along with the king and his retinue, then departed. The moment the Lord of Dharma set eyes upon that landscape, he knew it had been conjured by magicians. [Sakya Paṇḍita] gave a command to the many terrifying gatekeepers and threw flowers upon the senior monks as a consecration. As a result, the magicians were unable to dissolve their illusion. That temple has remained there until today. It is well known by the name "Emanated [Temple]." [156]

By means of these many excellent deeds, he caused the Dharma to spread and flourish extensively in China. Eventually, the Lord of Dharma understood that it would be of most benefit for the teachings if he continued to reside in the northerly lands and not return to Tibet. He thereafter resided there contentedly. He sent many gifts and offerings to monks and disciples in Tibet. As a gift of the Dharma, he sent *Clarifying the Sage's Intent*, which describes the stages for entering the bodhisattva path. In an accompanying note, he wrote, "I have sent *The Dharma for the Assembly*.[1061] I have explained this teaching across Ü, Tsang, and Kham, and so all my disciples have already received the transmission of this text. As such, look at it and teach it to others! You should practice according to this text."

Along with this letter, he also sent along the following written order (*bka' shog*):

> *Oṃ svasti siddhaṃ!*
>
> I prostrate to the lama and to the protector Mañjughoṣā! This is a letter from glorious Sakya Paṇḍita to the spiritual masters, patrons, and patronized of Ü, Tsang, and Ngari.
>
> I came to Mongolia intending to benefit the Buddha's teach-

ings and all beings, especially those who speak Tibetan. The wonderful benefactor who invited me was greatly pleased. He said, "Out of consideration for me, you brought Phakpa and his brother, despite their youth, and have come here along with the rest of your retinue. You have surrendered using your head, while others have surrendered with only their feet. I invited you, while the others came here out of fear. How could I not have recognized that? [157] Phakpa and his brother already know the Dharma of Tibet. Phakpa should still study the Tibetan Dharma. Chakna Dorjé should study the Mongolian literary and spoken languages. If I protect all beings according to the worldly dharma (*mi chos*) and you do so according to the supramundane Dharma (*lha chos*), then would the teachings of Śākyamuni not then spread and pervade to the shores of the outer oceans?"

In general, this bodhisattva king [Köden] greatly respects the teaching of the Buddha, and especially the precious Triple Gem. With good laws and discipline, he takes care of all his subjects. In particular, he has shown special regard for me, even more than for others. He has told me personally, "You should teach the Dharma with a peaceful mind. I will provide you with whatever you require. I know how to make you famous! Whether I do such great things, only heaven knows." His care for Phakpa and his brother is especially great. If you voluntarily follow his system of laws (*khrims lugs*), his admirable intention is to benefit all the subjects of his kingdom. In particular, he told me, "You should correctly explain the imperial laws to your people, the Tibetans. I know how to help them abide contentedly." As such, I urge all ritual specialists (*rim gro ba*) to offer prayers for the long life of the king and his descendants.

Here is the vital point: Mongolia's troops are innumerable. It seems as if he now has sovereignty over the entire world. For those who are in accord with him, their happiness and suffering [158] are identical with his.

It is his character that, if you do not sincerely listen to what he says, surrendering in name only will be insufficient. In the end, you will be destroyed. Before crushing it, the Mongols favored the Uyghur kingdom. Now, they have taken possession over their population and wealth, and have appointed their own scribes, treasurers, and religious authorities (*bu dga'*). The Chinese, Tanguts, Sokpo, and so forth were all previously considered allies of the Mongols. And yet, they would not obey the orders they received. As such, they were crushed and, in the end, with nowhere to go, they had to surrender. Nevertheless, they eventually began to obey Mongol commands, and nowadays they appoint leaders, religious authorities, treasurers, military commanders, and scribes from among their own ranks.

Since our Tibetan people are insolent and stubborn, they might think they can escape using various means. Or they might think that because of the distance, the Mongols will not come, or that they can outfight the Mongols, or that they can prevail using deceit, subterfuge, and cunningness. There are many who have now surrendered to the king. Because our people are so insolent and stubborn, I can see us becoming only serfs and servants, with not more than a few out of every hundred appointed as leaders. Although many Tibetans have submitted already to the Mongols, [Mongol] officials are dissatisfied with the paltry tributes.

I have submitted in the company of Biji. This was done in an excellent manner, and, as such, now the people of Tö, Ngari, Ü, and Tsang have all submitted to the Mongols as well. I told Köden that the other regions in Biri would surrender, too. Because of that, his troops have not yet invaded. [159] The population of Tö is not yet aware of this. Though they also submitted, nowadays they do not correctly pay their tribute, and so the Mongolian army has attacked their untrustworthy people. You have surely heard that all their people and wealth were destroyed. All those who were attacked were once hopeful they could resist due to inhabiting impenetrable lands, their courageous heroes, their many soldiers, their good weaponry and armor, and their skill in archery. And still, they were destroyed.

People have assumed that the Mongolians are inferior in terms of compulsory postal service[1062] and military tax, and that others are superior. The Mongolians are superior. Others are, by comparison, far inferior.

Moreover, if you listen to what you are told, the Mongols will appoint leaders for your territories and communities from among your own people. You must invite the gold- and silver-letter bearers of Sakya. Then report to them who is suitable to serve as your leaders.[1063] Send capable messengers back and forth. Then, make three [copies of a] clear record with the names of the leaders, the community population, and the amount of tribute to be offered. Send one copy to me. Deposit one at Sakya. The other copy must be retained by your leaders. Once again, make clear who is surrendering and who is resisting. There is otherwise the possibility that those who have surrendered will be destroyed along with those who resist.

O gold-letter bearers of the Sakyapa, go and confer with the regional leaders! For the benefit of all beings, do not abuse your power. The regional leaders must, in turn, [160] not abuse their own power without consulting the gold-letter bearers of the Sakyapa. It is against Mongolian law to do so. It will be very difficult for me to advocate here if you have made a mistake there. You simply must agree to all this.

By strictly adhering to Mongol law, good things will arise. You should appropriately welcome, send off, and serve the gold-letter bearers. Before asking any other questions, the Mongols will inquire upon the safe passage of the gold-letter bearers. Did they flee? Did they resist? Did they appropriately respect the golden letters? Did they pay their compulsory service? Have those who previously said they would surrender actually done so? If the gold-letter bearers are displeased, they will file a report that will surely bring harm to you. If you please them, it will be of great benefit to you.

Should you ignore the speech of the gold-letter bearers,

I foresee that it will be difficult for you. Noble families and those who come bearing tribute (*'thab nor*) are treated very well here. Thinking of good treatment for ourselves, all my officials should come bearing tribute on behalf of the people of Sakya. Please discuss an appropriate tribute amount among yourselves. I will also do so here. From all this, the Mongols will come to our land and benefit will come to all, including ourselves and others.

In general, over the past year, I have been sending dispatches and advising that it will be good for us to do this. However, you have not all followed what I told you to do. Do you all wish to listen to whatever they have to say before you are destroyed? It seems that you do not understand me. In the future, please do not complain that you have not benefited from the visit [161] of the Sakyapa to Mongolia.

With others in the forefront of my mind, I have come to the Mongols to benefit all Tibetan speakers. It will benefit you to listen to what I have to say. You have not seen the situation here. It is hard for you to believe what you are hearing. For this reason, you still delude yourselves that you can be victorious. However, I suspect that, just like a ghost may smother a sleeping man, the Mongols will capture all the men and boys of Ü and Tsang. As for me, good or bad, whatever happens, I have no regrets. With the blessings and kindness of the lama and the Triple Gem, it is still possible that things will work out well for us. You too should pray to the Triple Gem.

The king cherishes me unlike anyone else. As such, the scholars and nobility of China, Tibet, Uyghur, Tangut, all these different places, are amazed and come to hear the Dharma and pay great homage to me. There is no need to worry about how the Mongols will treat me and my party. They all hold us in high regard and we are well. As such, do not worry. Tributes of gold; silver; elephant tusk; large pearls; vermillion; antelope hide; horses for military generals; solidified elephant bile (*gi wang*); the hides of tigers, leopards, caracals, and otters; Tibetan wool; fine blankets from Ü: these are all much appreciated [among the Mongols] here. Generally, even if some treasure is not highly valued here, it is acceptable to come bearing whatever fine product comes from your region. [162] Know that if you have gold, whatever you wish for will be granted.

May the teaching of the Buddha spread widely to all directions!

All the people of Ü and Tsang, such as the monks, disciples, patrons, and so forth were overjoyed and set at ease upon receiving this letter.

That lama [Sapaṇ], the second omniscient one of the age of strife, taught the Buddhadharma and ripened and liberated countless sentient beings until his seventieth year. If I were to explain how, in the end, he dissolved the arrangement of his form body, it is as follows [drawn from the written record of the physician Biji, who was in the company of Sapaṇ].

During the Male Iron Pig Year, he departed for the benefit of other sentient beings [i.e., passed away]. In the month of Acvina (*tha skar gyi zla ba*), eighteen great signs appeared. A great earthquake occurred on the eighth day of the Acvina month. I, the physician Biji, inquired about the reason for this. [Sapaṇ] told me, "This is the sign that a great bodhisattva will soon depart on behalf of all sentient beings. It seems that we are also following along!"

At midnight on the twenty-ninth day [of that month], King Sounding the Inexhaustible Melody[1064] appeared as the saṃbhogakāya. His body was white, with one face and two arms. [Sapaṇ] asked that I offer incense, which I did. At dawn, he had a vision that Eleven-Faced Avalokiteśvara appeared and granted blessings. [Sapaṇ] asked me to offer incense, which I did. [163]

On the sixth day of the waxing moon during the tenth month, we heard a variety of sounds. I was near [Sapaṇ] and asked, "Are people doing the victorious offering ceremony (*rnam rgyal mchod pa*) in the temple?" Sapaṇ replied, "You should go inside and see." When I did so, those in the temple reported also hearing the sounds and asked me to return to [Sapaṇ] to inquire. When I did so, he said, "Many welcome-party gods are making offerings. Now I must go and benefit other sentient beings."

Also, flowers rained down but would not touch the earth. A great many remained suspended in the sky. On the thirteenth day, while he reposed beneath an umbrella, the sun was shining, and a fine white cloth appeared. He pointed to the sky and smiled, asking, "Do you see it?" I responded, "I do not see it, but I feel very happy." [Sapaṇ] said, "It appears you have some small negativity. Still, negativity is just like dirt. You should purify!"

[On another occasion,] he had a vision of the Buddha Bhagavan sitting atop a lion throne surrounded by hearers. He asked me to offer incense, which I did. In the afternoon of the fourteenth day, he sat below an umbrella. In the sky, just as before, clouds appeared. He clearly beheld the maṇḍala of glorious Hevajra. He asked me to offer incense, which I did.

In the morning of the fifteenth day, while he rested outside, the clouds once again appeared as before. He thrice beheld Mañjuśrī. I made incense offerings at his behest. [164] After the third time offering incense, he looked at me and smiled. I asked him why. He said, "Mañjuśrī and Maitreya are holding a discussion." He even reported their words, but I cannot recall them. The next day, while he did circumambulation, Chokjin Pal[1065] went ahead holding a small seat and table and a very soft cushion. I supported Sapaṇ's left shoulder and helped him go around. When he arrived at the temple hall, he sat atop the throne. He then said, "Chokjin Pal, go and prepare tea!" He told me, "Go and retrieve the incense and return here." When I did so, he said, "*A yu tā ra.*" He must have been beholding the face of Tārā at that time.

At midnight on the seventeenth day, I was sitting next to him, when he suddenly stood up and asked, "Didn't you see anything? Did you hear any songs, melodies, or musical cymbals?" At that time, many people were assembled, including myself and Lopön Joden.[1066] We reported that we heard cymbals but never saw anything. He looked at me and said, "I experienced visions of thirteen maṇḍalas, of which Cakrasaṃvara was the principal one. All the ḍākas and ḍākinīs sang songs and danced." He then recited many verses, but I do not remember them. It seems that Lopön Joden remembered many of those words, but I haven't written them down here.

[Sapaṇ] said, "Do not report this to others. That would become a source for producing negative karma."

At Jugur Memar,[1067] a geshé named Dorang[1068] had fallen sick. [165] I sent my disciple Rinchen Gyaltsen to go visit him. He had soiled his blankets and was without anyone to care for him. He suffered greatly. After this was reported to the Lord of Dharma, he said, "All the buddhas and bodhisattvas also know of this, and they look [upon him] with compassion."

At dawn of the following day, Lama Jetsun [Drakpa Gyaltsen], Master Virūpa, and Kṛṣṇācārya all appeared, and [Drakpa Gyaltsen] said, "You should not be disappointed. This defiled body suffers from the four great rivers of birth, aging, sickness, and death." Virūpa smiled and said, "That is true." Virūpa dipped his ring finger into nectar from a skullcup and said, "Stick out your tongue." He then dabbed the nectar upon his tongue. At that moment, he had an experience of bliss, clarity, and nonthought beyond the extremes of conceptual and nonconceptual thought. He thought to himself, "Even the Buddha's mind does not have a better experience than this!"

After that, Lama Jetsun said [to Sapaṇ], "When you depart on behalf of other sentient beings, traverse eastward across many realms of this world and you will reside beyond in space as a vidyādhara knowledge-holder. Then you will please many tathāgatas, and you will completely purify a buddhafield. You will thoroughly ripen many sentient beings and cross most grounds and paths. By this, in your third future lifetime, you will be reborn to the southeast of India in this world, in a land called Mumuni. You will be reborn as the son of King Nyimai Tophal.[1069] In your youth, you will compose texts and give many commentaries. [166] You will behold all the world by means of your higher perception (*mngon par shes pa*). You will liberate many hundreds of thousands of devoted disciples. At that time, everyone to whom you bestow initiation and who has a Dharma connection with you will become your disciple."

(However I forgot the exact words and the details of [Sapaṇ's future] lives.)

"...After passing beyond that life, you will be reborn as a buddha named Drima Mepai Pal. You will work on behalf of sentient beings." The Jetsun then turned to Virūpa and asked, "Is this true?" The Master [Virūpa] said, "That is true." Nakpapo also supported this prediction and said, "This is true."

Then Sapaṇ asked me to prepare offerings, which I arranged. Then, by the power of diligently practicing the profound path, his secret part became invisible, an uṣṇīṣa clearly arose atop his head, and a hair coil between the eyes curled like a conch shell.[1070] He developed bodily marks such as these.

On the seventh day of the waxing period of the eleventh month, many musical instruments sounded in the manifested temple, which were heard by all those assembled. They asked, "What is the reason for this?" [Sapaṇ] said, "All of you make effort in supplication (*gsol ba 'debs pa*). Compared with giving one's head, feet, and wealth according to the system of the path of the perfections, there is more merit in showing respect and serving the lama from whom one receives the supreme initiation for even one moment."

Whatever I had once possessed had already been offered to the lama. And so I had nothing then to offer. [167] I fixed an elder's feet, and for my fee he offered a new, handmade red hat. I then offered the first opportunity to wear it to Sapaṇ. The Lord of Dharma then wore it. I then thought that I should offer it to Sapaṇ to keep. Having considered my offering, Sapaṇ smiled at me and said, "You don't have to make this offering, for you have already offered it to me before. When I achieve enlightenment, I will see all the service you disciples have done for me as clearly as *arura* medicine held in the palm of my hand! The lives of all those sentient beings who have taken initiation, cultivated the awakened mind, and served me, as well as those who see me, who remember me, who touch me, and who spoke with me, and all those who developed a connection with me, will not become meaningless. They will be liberated from the suffering of the lower realms. You have offered me great service, Biji. You should be very happy!"

One night, from dusk until dawn, I supported Sapaṇ at his back and sometimes at his side. He said, "Dulwa Gyaltshan,[1071] come here!" When he did, Sapaṇ told him to bring the chamtsé (*phyam tshe*), which had been offered by the female leader (*dpon mo*) Sorγaγtani.[1072] He then told me, "You should wear this. We both have many connections from our previous lives. First, you were my tea maker. Then, [I sent you] to Jobum Gukshrī at Minyak Ga.[1073] There, you were chased by Mongols but survived. And now you have so greatly served me. There is no doubt that you will be reborn near to me in the next life."

At dawn of the fourteenth day of the waxing period of the eleventh month, accompanied by a variety of victory banners, [168] the sound of musical cymbals, many entoned offerings, and earthquakes, he passed into nirvāṇa.

On the twenty-fifth day, they performed the cremation. All the smoke took the form of a rainbow. The sound of musical cymbals was heard by all those assembled. Most of his corpse transformed into self-arisen relics and statues. This is truly inconceivable!

As for how these later acted for the benefit of sentient beings, this is described in the praise biography by Yarlung Drakpa Gyaltsen as follows:[1074]

Hevajra and a stainless statue of Mañjuśrī clearly appeared
at the center of the supreme uṣṇīṣa;
the assembly of Cakrasaṃvara at the center of the forehead;
the Buddha Bhagavan at the back of the neck;
Khasarpaṇi atop the shoulder bone;
Avalokitśvara inside the marrow;

the four secret mothers on the back;
Tārā and Acalā atop the two knees;
and Maitreya displaying the turning of the wheel of Dharma mudrā
atop of the nāga tree fingers of his right hand.[1075]
These ten manifestations appeared as the bodily supports.
The melodious speech of Brahmā sounding the lion's roar of emptiness;
an elongated syllable *ah* revealing the meaning of unborn reality;
a victory stūpa (*rnam rgyal mchod rten*) atop each ear;
the center of the samayavajra is adorned by the letter *hūṃ*;
his pure intention appearing as the naturally arisen dharmakāya;
In addition, unthinkable varieties of other relics also appeared.

Among the mahātmā's major, middling, and minor monastic seats, the most major are Glorious Sakya and, [169] to the north, Lingchu Tserkhab.[1076] The middling are Samyé, Nyangtö Kyangthur, and Shangsek Shing.[1077] The minor seats include the many monasteries he administered across Kham, Tsang, and Ü.

In general, the Lord of Dharma sustained the teaching tradition of the sūtras and tantras, and especially the dialectical tradition (*mtshan nyid*) of the *Commentary on Valid Cognition*. It was this Lord of Dharma alone who upheld this excellent tradition. During his lifetime, Sapaṇ appointed Uyukpa Rikpai Sengé[1078] as the head of the assembly of dialecticians, Shangtsun Dorjé Pal[1079] as the leader of the assembly of tantric practitioners, and Geshé Shākya Sangpo as the leader of the major seat. He then departed for Mongolia. It is well known that, at that time, there were eighty pairs of degree holders.

As for the many monasteries that upheld the dialectics of the sūtra tenet tradition and so forth, following the passing of the Lord of Dharma, they included a great many that helped it flourish, such as Nālendra, Serdokchen, Kyitsal, Thupten Namgyal, Thupten Yangchen, Utsé Thang, Jang Ngamring, Pal Sakyai Thupten Lhachen, and so forth.[1080] Furthermore, as for those that upheld the tantric tenet tradition, there were a great many large and small monasteries that caused it to increase.

This is a story of a liberated life that, when compared to others, is truly marvelous!

6. Sangtsa Sönam Gyaltsen (1184–1239)

As for that lama's [Sakya Paṇḍita's] younger brother, Sönam Gyaltsen,[1081] he was born in the Male Wood Dragon Year at Kyao Khadang[1082] [171] when their father was thirty-five years old and his mother twenty-three. He thoroughly studied the Dharma of his forefathers and focused his practice principally upon Hevajra and Vajrakīlaya. He subdued the Dharma protector Chamdral[1083] along with his retinue and turned them into his servants. He built Utsé Nyingma and erected a fence enclosure around the monastery. It is said that at that time, he declared his intention to also build a fence encircling [the towns of] Möndrok and Baldrok, as well as the territory of Sakarlok.[1084] He also intended to produce a back curtain [for a temple]. Upon the advice of his elders, however, he instead built a fence at Shingmoché and then at Dagyang Khang.[1085]

He established marketplaces at Sithang[1086] and elsewhere, and built a town for the local population. He laid the foundation for Dromtö, Dromé, Takthok, Mangkhar Drilchen, Tsangwarphuk, Shabtomé, Tanak, and so forth.[1087] He settled a great many nomad groups at Jangchung, Khabso, Komdré, Garphuk, and so forth.[1088] He established horse herds at Rasa[1089] and so forth. Having relied upon many holders of the teachings, he furnished them with necessities and provisions. He built supports of the holy body, speech, and mind. He continually made offerings. He established an ongoing tradition of holding annual memorial ceremonies for the lamas of previous ages. He pursued these and countless other such activities.

He possessed a higher perception (*mngon shes*) and beheld his future lives. At the time of his passing, he said, "In my next life, I think I will

Fig. 26. Sangtsa Sönam Gyaltsen (1184–1239)

bestow initiation to a few followers in a southerly region near the foot of a great grassy hill. I will be a secret yogi who practices the profound path." There is also an oral tradition [172] that claims he [was a manifestation] of Nasadrak Phukpa.[1090]

When he was fifty-six years old, on the twentieth day of the twelfth month of the Female Earth Pig Year, this lama had many pure visions. He realized the inseparability of the lama and yidam. "The Lord of Dharma [Sapaṇ] is the actual Buddha," he said. "Devote yourself to him without any lingering doubt!" He then passed away at Palri at Doktoro, in Latojang.[1091]

When he passed, he instructed his disciples: "You should burn my bones atop the far slopes [of Palri]. There are auspicious signs that the family lineage of my sons and grandsons will submit the entire country under their power." They did just as he predicted.

Some claim that Sangtsa Sönam Gyaltsen's mother hailed from Tarerong, that she was a member of the Sangwa lineage, and that her father was known as the José of Sang.[1092] She gave birth to Sangtsa Sönam Gyaltsen's younger brother. It is a mistake, however, to say that he shared the same mother with [Sönam Gyaltsen], since the Lord of Dharma's mother was not Sangtsa. The letter sent by Jetsun [Drakpa Gyaltsen] to the ruler of Garing,[1093] moreover, does not mention that they had different mothers. And so, it is true that they had the same mother.

Fig. 27. Guoshi Drogön Chögyal Phakpa Lodrö Gyaltsen (1235–80)

7. Guoshi Drogön Chögyal Phakpa Lodrö Gyaltsen (1235–80)

That lama [Sönam Gyaltsen] had five consorts. The first of them hailed from Dokgi Tsanaidap.[1094] Her father was named Gyatso of Surkhang and her uncle Gyalwa Pal.[1095] She was named Machik Kunkyi.[1096] The eldest of her sons was Protector of Sentient Beings, Lord of Dharma [Drogön Chögyal] Phakpa.[1097] On the sixth day of the third month of the Female Wood Sheep Year [1235], when his father was fifty-two years old, he was born at the nāga residence (*klu khang*) of Yeru Ngamring.[1098] Auspicious signs accompanied his conception and birth. When he was very young, he understood a few among the five fields of knowledge without ever having been taught, including writing [173] and reading. He grew competent in other fields with but the slightest effort.

He also possessed a higher perception that made him capable of remembering his previous lives. It is said he had previously been born as Satön Ripa,[1099] [a holy being] who held discussions with Avalokiteśvara. It was two of Satön's former disciples who went to see [Phakpa] and investigate whether he was the true incarnation. Upon their arrival, the lama [Phakpa] was playing with other children. When he saw the two monks approaching, he said to them, "Have you come here?" They both asked, "Do you recognize us?" and he replied, "Yes. You are my disciples, such and such…" They then developed devotion to him and made full prostrations.

As for why they had come, previously his father, Sangtsa, was attempting to realize the state of Ganeśa. Ganeśa appeared and carried him with his tusks and shepherded him to the peak of Mount Meru. There he told him, "Gaze down below!" Sangtsa, however, was afraid and unable to look. Eventually, he brought himself to peer down and Tibetan regions like Ü, Tsang, and Kham, each the size of sesame seeds, appeared laid out before him. Ganeśa told him, "You will one day reign over wherever it is that you behold. You have seen the three provinces of Ü, Tsang, and Kham, and so your son or male descendents shall rule over them. However, since you did not look immediately, they will lack the karmic potency to rule on their own."

For a long time after that, Sangtsa could not bear a son. Sorely disappointed, he made special praises to Ganeśa. On one such occasion, Ganeśa appeared to Satön Ripa in Gungthang and announced, "Sangtsa is persistently invoking me. He says that he wishes to rule over the three provinces of Ü, Tsang, and Kham, [174] but that he does not possess the karmic connection to do so himself. For someone to be born as his son, they must already be a bodhisattva taking their last rebirth in saṃsāra and who has previously made prayers to submit this vast world under their power. You, Satön Ripa, possess all these qualities! Should you take rebirth as the son of Sangtsa, you would rule most of Tibet, including Ü, Tsang, and Kham. You must accept and intentionally take this rebirth!" Satön Ripa then did as was requested.

It is well known that on one occasion, Chögyal Phakpa traveled to Kyirong as an attendant for the Lord of Dharma [Sapaṇ]. There, many of Langripa's[1100] monastic disciples came to have an audience with Sapaṇ. Among them was one senior monk; Chögyal Phakpa called out, "My disciple, Tashi Döndrup,[1101] has appeared!" With that, Tashi Döndrup recognized his lama. He immediately threw himself before Chögyal Phakpa, grasping at his feet and shedding tears.

When he was three years old, Chögyal Phakpa could recite from memory such texts as the elaborate Hevajra sādhana known as *Sādhana of the Lotus Born*.[1102] Everyone was astonished and would remark, "There is certainly no doubt that he is an authentic noble one!"[1103] From then on, he became widely known by the name "Phakpa."

When he was eight years old, Chögyal Phakpa could recite the jātaka stories by heart.[1104] When he was nine, while the Lord of Dharma was teaching the preliminary practices, Chögyal Phakpa recited the *Two-Part Hevajra Tantra* from memory. He also gave a profound public teaching at a Dharma gathering, which amazed everyone. He shattered the pride of the many scholars who were present and so became widely known.

When he was ten years old, Chögyal Phakpa journeyed north as the attendant of the Lord of Dharma. Along the journey, while still in Central Tibet, he received novice ordination vows. The Lord of Dharma served as the abbot. Nasa Tresöl[1105] [175] of Sulphu[1106] served as the master. He received instructions about the novice vows from Khenpo Sherab Sengé[1107] of Kyormo Lungpa.[1108]

By the time Chögyal Phakpa was seventeen, he had received all of the Lord of Dharma's teachings. As such, the Lord of Dharma was very pleased with him. He understood that Chögyal Phakpa had developed the capacity to carry forward his teaching activities, and so he gave him his Dharma conch shell, begging bowl, and so on. He also appointed Phakpa to lead a group of his disciples, saying: "Now is the time for you to benefit many sentient beings. You must recall your promise from previous lives!" With these words, Sakya Pandita passed along his teaching responsibilities to Chögyal Phakpa.

After that, in the Ox Year [1253], the emperor [Qubilai] Sečen Qaγan invited Chögyal Phakpa to his palace. He posed many questions to Phakpa that had confounded others in his court. Chögyal Phakpa answered them all using logic and reasoning, and so the emperor was greatly pleased. Qubilai Qaγan asked, "Tell me, who were the eminent people of Tibet?" The precious Phakpa replied, "The greatest in my Tibetan homeland were the three ancestral Dharma kings."[1109] "Why do you claim they are the greatest?" the emperor inquired. Chögyal Phakpa replied, "Because Songtsen Gampo was an emanation of Avalokiteśvara, Trisong Detsen was an emanation of Mañjuśrī, and Tri Ralpachen was an emanation of Vajrapāṇi.[1110] As such, I consider them the three greatest Tibetans." Qubilai Qaγan inquired further, "And who has been the most courageous (*pho rgod*) among the Tibetans?" Chögyal Phakpa replied, "It is said that the most courageous was Milarepa,[1111] because early in his life he violently subjugated his enemies, but he later practiced the Dharma and gained realization." The emperor further inquired, "Who has been the most learned to appear in your lands?" Chögyal Phakpa replied, "The most learned person to have appeared is my lama, the Lord of the Sakyapa." "What knowledge did your lama, the Lord of Dharma, possess?" asked the emperor. "How much did you learn from him?" Chögyal Phakpa replied, "The knowledge of my lama, the Lord of Dharma, was like an ocean, from which I received only a handful of water."

Sometime after, the emperor proclaimed that he would require mandatory military service from the Tibetans and that he would impose taxes upon them. The precious Phakpa repeatedly entreated the emperor: "Tibet is but a small borderland territory. It has little wealth and is unable to supply soldiers." The emperor, however, would not listen. Phakpa grew discontented and requested, "In this case, I am a Tibetan monk who has come here, but there is no longer any reason for me to remain. May I now return to my homeland?" The emperor said, "Very well. Go if you wish!" The consort Čabui[1112] intervened, saying, "Such a monk as this is rare indeed. None of the other old monks who have journeyed here, such as Tsalpa[1113] and the others, possessed even a fraction of this monk's qualities. Nor did they have any of his stories about the past. Do not send him off to Tibet! You should instead hold Dharma discussions with him."

The emperor agreed. Then patron and patronized (*mchod yon*) held many discussions. On one such occasion, Chögyal Phakpa acted pridefully. Qubilai Qaγan admonished him, "Why are you so arrogant? What qualities do you have?" Chögyal Phakpa replied, "I have only a little knowledge. Since ancient times, however, we Sakyapa have been appointed as lama officiants (*bla mchod*) for the kings of China, the Tanguts, India, the Mön, and so forth. For that reason, I suppose I do have some pride."

The emperor interjected, "Do not speak such lies, monk! When did Tibet ever have a king? [177] And who among them ever paid homage to [you Sakyapa] or take initiation?" "The Tibetan kings once fought against China and captured two-thirds of the world's territory," Chögyal Phakpa replied. "After that, the rulers of Tibet and China became kin [through intermarriage]." He then recounted the story of the Chinese princess Kongjo[1114] and how the [statue of the] divine Jowo had come to Tibet. "If all that is true," Qubilai Qaγan replied, "there should be imperial records. Check this!" The emperor was informed that everything Chögyal Phakpa had reported was indeed chronicled in Chinese historical records, and he was greatly pleased.

"Not only that," Phakpa continued, "ten million years ago a torrential rain of blood fell upon the earth over the course of seven days." The emperor also had this verified and discovered that it, too, was reported in the Chinese records. He then developed a deep trust in Phakpa. Chögyal Phakpa continued, "A Tangut king once offered my forefathers a silk brocade canopy together with deer horns." With that, the emperor sent envoys to Sakya Monastery and did indeed discover the brocade and horns there. Upon being informed of this, Qubilai Qaγan and his heirs developed a deep devotion to Phakpa.

Later, the consort Čabui said to the emperor, "It was excellent that we did not permit Chögyal Phakpa to leave for Tibet! I have heard it said that the Sakyapa possess a profound secret mantra empowerment unknown to other schools. We should request that he bestow it upon us!" The emperor replied, "You should receive it first. If it is worthwhile, I will then take it." The consort received the Hevajra empowerment and became very devoted to Chögyal Phakpa. She asked him, "What special offering should I make for receiving this initiation?" Chögyal Phakpa [178] replied, "You should offer your physical body, material goods, and other possessions, and especially anything to which you are strongly attached and consider most valuable." "When I married my husband," she replied, "my family gave me these earrings. They are decorated along their top by pearls and were the most valuable part of my dowry." She then removed a large pearl from an earring and offered it to Chögyal Phakpa. He later sold it to a Mongolian for a large *dré* measure of gold and one thousand large *dré* measures of silver. [When Phakpa eventually returned to Tibet, he used this wealth to fund] the installation of a large Dharma wheel at Tsang Chumik[1115] and the framing for the golden roof at Sakya.

After [the consort received the Hevajra empowerment], she reported to the emperor, "Phakpa possesses a Dharma tradition unlike any other. You should certainly request to receive empowerment as well!" The emperor agreed and made his requests to the lama. [Chögyal Phakpa replied,] "You would in general be unable to guard the samaya commitments associated with receiving this empowerment. Additionally, I do not have a knowledgeable translator with me at this time, so I will bestow this empowerment upon you in the future." "What kind of samaya commitment will I be expected to keep?" the emperor inquired. "Upon receiving an empowerment," Chögyal Phakpa told him, "you must seat the lama upon a throne higher than your own. You must prostrate to him with your body. You must listen to whatever instructions he gives you. And using your mind, you must never go against your lama's intent. You will thereafter be unable to act in such a way."

The consort suggested the following solutions: when the emperor received Dharma transmissions and when he was among only a small gathering, his lama should sit upon a throne higher than his own, but when the emperor was among his wider imperial family, his sons-in-law, eminent persons, and in public gatherings, he would sit upon the higher throne in order to administer his sovereignty over his subjects. In the matter of imperial affairs in Tibet, the emperor would follow whatever the lama instructs and would not assert his own orders. In other major or minor matters, decisions would be made by the emperor in consultation with the lama since he possessed great compassion. Since some might take advantage of the lama's compassion, however, the emperor might have trouble controlling the empire. And so, the lama would confer [179] on all decisions with the emperor.

Lama Phakpa then told the emperor, "According to your Mongolian tradition, you ought not to send someone into a great battle before he has received considerable training. Likewise, according to our [Dharma] tradition, the teacher must undertake a close retreat[1116] before bestowing a higher empowerment. I must therefore make the appropriate preparations for the empowerment." While Phakpa entered retreat, the emperor dispatched gold-letter bearers to summon a qualified translator to the palace.

Phakpa later bestowed the complete Śrī Hevajra empowerment upon principally the emperor and twenty-four of his retinue. He did so three times, according to the unique tradition of the Sakya school. In this way, the Vajrayāna was first established in the kingdom of Mongolia.

It is said that, in appreciation for receiving the first round of empowerment, the emperor offered the thirteen myriarchies of Tibet to Chögyal Phakpa.[1117] Each myriarchy, moreover, consisted of four thousand monastics and six thousand laypeople.

After the middle round of empowerment, the emperor principally offered The White Dharma Conch [that Sounds] from Afar.[1118] He further offered the entire monastic and lay population of the three provinces of

Tibet.[1119] It is said that the three provinces together made up one *zhing*. They included the territory starting from the three Ngari regions of western Tibet up to the Pale Gray Pass[1120] in Sok territory, which altogether are known as the "Holy Dharma Province"; the territory extending from the Pale Gray Pass in Sok down to the Mekong River, which altogether is known as the "Province of the Humans";[1121] and the territory extending from the Mekong River to the White Stūpa of China, which is altogether known as the "Province of Horses."[1122]

As for the technical meaning of *zhing*, [it is a unit made up of] a six-pillared house with six [household members], including a husband and wife, a son and daughter, and a male and female servant, as well as livestock such as horses, donkeys, cows, ox, goats, and sheep, and fields able to yield twelve loads of grain. Altogether this is called a "small Mongol household." [180] Twenty-five of those make up a single "great household." Two great households were together called a "horse head." Two horse heads were known as a single "circle of a hundred." Ten of those were together known as one "circle of a thousand." Ten of those were together known as a "circle of ten thousand." Ten of those were known as one "nāga." Ten of those were together known as a single "*zhing*."

The Mongol Sečen Qaγan had sovereignty over eleven *zhing*. The three provinces did not in fact make up even a single *zhing*, but since it was his lama's homeland, and since it was a place where Dharma had become so widespread, it was counted as one *zhing* and offered to [Lama Phakpa].

As an offering after receiving the final empowerment, Qubilai Qaγan offered Phakpa the Gyami Yur Chenmo [Drum][1123] in accord with his lama's instructions. Lama Phakpa was delighted and composed the followed dedication prayer:

> The sky element, red-colored like blood,
> and the outer oceans brimming with the corpses of the flat-footed:
> by the virtue accrued from ceasing such [violent] behavior,
> may the intentions of the Lord of Wisdom be fulfilled!
> May the doctrine, source of happiness and bliss, greatly increase!
> And may the Lord of Humans enjoy a long life!

The History of "The White Dharma Conch [that Sounds] from Afar," which Qubilai Qaγan Offered after Receiving the First [Hevajra] Empowerment

Poetic Power of Lake Nyer: Exaltation of Glorious Sakya says:[1124]

> The White Conch Shell sounding Brahmā's melody from afar
> was taken from among the treasure of the nāga king,
> then offered by Indra to the Lord of Sages when he taught the Dharma.
> Later, it arrived here.

Just so, if one were to ask in regard to this flawless white conch shell, majestically brilliant with blessings, [offered] when the perfect and fully enlightened Buddha first turned the wheel of the Dharma: If it came into the hands of the Sakyapa from China long ago [181], what was the history of its arrival in China?

During the reigns of the Indian king Dharmapāla and the Chinese king known as Devarāja, while they never came into each other's presence, they became friends. During the reign of the Indian king Dharmapāla, heretical armies devastated Śrī Nālandā Monastery,[1125] along with much of the Buddha's teachings. As such, King Dharmapāla entreated the Chinese king to send support. The latter replied, "Though I cannot direct any troops, I will send abundant material support. With this, you will be able to defeat the heretics. Do not allow the Buddha's teachings to diminish!"

The Chinese king sent a seamless robe made of *lu-hang* with many designs and thin cloth. No weapons or piercing instruments (*gzong*) could penetrate it. Upon its chest area was a bejeweled endless knot. King Devarāja twice sent such material support. Principal among his gifts was [this robe]. He also shared plenty of helpful strategies and advice. Considering this, King Dharmapāla could gather the auspicious circumstances together to prevail against the heretical forces and to reestablish the Buddhist doctrine as clear as sunshine. In gratitude, the jubilant Indian king and his ministers wrote to the Chinese king, "This wonderful turn of events for the Buddha's teachings is due to your advice and support. Please tell us, what we might send you in thanks."

The Chinese king replied in a letter, "If you truly wish to send me a gift, I would like to request a statue depicting the Buddha when he was eight years old; the Buddha's conch shell; as well as the following texts: *The River Sūtra*, *The Dense Array Adornment Sūtra*, the *Commentary on the Vinaya*, and *The Designed Jewel Chest Sūtra*.[1126] [182] I also request that you send four diligent bhikṣus." King Dharmapāla replied, "I can hardly fathom actualy sending you [the statue] of my meditation deity Śākyamuni and the rest. However, you have been so kind. You should, therefore, take all these from me and use them as a foundation to benefit many sentient beings!" [Accompanying these gifts,] extensive welcoming and receiving ceremonies were performed using many varieties of offering substances. In this way, the Jowo statue, the white conch shell, and so forth made their way to China.

As for the manner in which [the white conch shell] arrived into the hands of the Sakyapa from China, the best-known version of events describes the mighty Qubilai Qaγan offering it to Chögyal Phakpa, as described above. There is, however, another tradition that claims that Köden Ejen offered the conch to the Lord of Dharma Sakya Paṇḍita, and that Sapaṇ later gave it to Lama Phakpa. In either case, the conch should be known as "Sapaṇ's White Dharma Conch Shell," since Sapaṇ turned the wheel of the Dharma in unthinkable ways, such that the teachings of the Buddha spread into the many lands of the Mongols and among populations speaking different languages.

In this way, Drogön Chögyal Phakpa brought this exceptional Dharma conch shell, which had belonged to the perfectly and fully enlightened Buddha, to glorious Sakya upon his return from China. It remains there still as a refuge and protector for all sentient beings without exception. Though it is impossible to provide a detailed explanation of the good qualities of this Dharma conch shell here, in brief: when disciples who are suitable vessels behold this shell, [183] they observe numerous naturally arisen designs upon its surface, such as the mantra of Kālacakra. Whosoever hears the bellowing of that shell will purify obstacles and hindrances accumulated over eons, will close the door to rebirth in the lower realms, and will be established in the states of higher rebirth and liberation. Additionally, stores of different kinds of grain, the source of the happiness of sentient beings, are destroyed by the eight malevolent spirits who bring hail and so on. Upon hearing the sounding of this conch, these spirits immediately cease doing harm. The soil becomes more fertile and yields an abundance of happiness and joy for sentient beings.

During the lifetime of the mantra holder Ngakwang Kunga Rinchen,[1127] King of the Dharma; the enemy of the Buddha's teachings, Lhasa Dzongpa;[1128] and so forth, those demonic emanations swindled many offering objects from the great temple [of Sakya], including this Dharma conch shell. The [shell identified] its new abode as a place of evil conduct and an unsuitable residence. It wished to return to the Great Seat [of Sakya], which had been blessed by the Lord of Yogins [Virūpa]. Though it had been stored among other offering substances, the inside of the conch shell became filled with insects. It still made sounds, even though no one blew into it. Because of this and other displays of inauspicious signs, Lhasa Dzongpa immediately returned it to the Great Seat and offered his apologies.

For these reasons, this Dharma conch shell is no different than a wish-fulfilling [184] jewel. This is because whosoever makes prayers in its presence will without any obstacle have their wishes granted for either temporary or ultimate goals. This has been proven by experience many times.

The Performance of Miracles

Sometime after Chögyal Phakpa Rinpoché was appointed imperial preceptor (Ch. dishi 帝師) to the great Qaγan, the supreme being Karma Pakshi began to display fantastic magical displays [at the Mongol court].[1129] At one point, in front of the consort, ministers, and their entourage, the emperor professed: "Both of our great lamas are the tathāgata Amtitābha appearing in human form, and in terms of their magical ability there is no difference between them. However, from the perspective of ordinary beings, the thick-bearded one [Karma Pakshi] appears superior in terms of his magical ability and realization." However, the consort Čabui had unshakeable devotion in her lama and especially in the Sakya teachings. She visited Phakpa Rinpoché and reported recent events. She requested of him: "If you, O lama, do not make magical displays to shift the basis of the emperor's devotion, and by this fulfill his wishes, it is quite possible that he might change his mind [and patronize Karma Pakshi]!"

Chögyal Phakpa replied, "It is in general the appropriate time for Pakshi to make such magical displays. And, more specifically, his magical abilities are indeed authentic. However, it would be incorrect for me to deny the wishes of the devoted and samaya-holding emperor. Vajrayāna texts describe such behavior as a major [185] fault. I thus accept your request and will show such magical displays. Please fetch me a razor-sharp blade." She fetched a knife and offered it to him. "I am blessing all my limbs to become the five buddha families," Phakpa said. "O kings and ministers, make prayers to be reborn in the pure land of whichever of the five buddha families you desire! So that you may believe it for yourself, I have left my entire body laid out upon my bed. Go and see for yourself!"

He then blessed his head to transform into Vairocana and both his hands and feet into the other four buddha families.[1130] The emperor, empress, ministers, and their entourages used their bodies to make prostrations and circumambulations. Using their minds, they made fervent prayers. Upon beholding [Phakpa's] vase-like body laid out upon the bed, they saw that his blood had wetted the floor. Beholding this, the emperor and ministers were unable to bear it and made loud requests. Phakpa, however, did not dissolve his magical display for quite some time. Later, the consort Čabui requested, "O Lord of the World, please arise from this illusory spectacle! If you do not, the emperor will suffer a heart attack and die!" With this, Phakpa finally suspended his magical display.

It is well known that after these events, even though many great scholars and adepts came to perform marvels in front of the emperor, even if they performed the greatest of feats, the emperor would think to himself, "Though these are amazing demonstrations that may benefit sentient beings, not one of them exceeds [186] the good qualities of abandonment and realization possessed by my lama!"

Early in the Female Water Ox Year (1253), when Chögyal Phakpa was nineteen years old, Qubilai Qaγan received empowerment. As his principal offering of thanks, Qubilai appointed [Phakpa] as the *dishi*, or imperial preceptor,[1131] and offered an ornamental, bejeweled jade stamp inscribed with the letter *sa*. He also offered a golden, pearl-adorned monk's raiment (*snam sbyar*); an outer robe (*sku chos*); a *chamtsé* monk's cape; a hat; shoes; a cushion; a golden throne; a canopy; cup and plates; and so forth, as well as camels and mules with gold-covered saddles. Principally, he offered Phakpa the myriarchies, the conch shell, and so on as described above.

In the following Year of the Tiger (1254), the emperor issued a decree in the Tibetan language entitled "Edict to Increase the Power of Monks."[1132] He offered Chögyal Phakpa fifty-six large *dré* measures of silver, two hundred bricks of tea, eighty bolts of brocade, and 1,100 bolts of silk. Chögyal Phakpa commanded that the gold-letter bearers never stay the night[1133] in monastic residences, nor should they demand compulsory labor or tax from monks. [Qubilai Qaγan] accepted this.

The qaγan, moreover, ordered that all the monks of the western regions conduct themselves according to the Sakya tradition.[1134] Furthermore, the qaγan said, "I plan to order that no tradition other than Sakya may be practiced anywhere in Tibet." However, Chögyal Phakpa replied, "Whoever now practices their own Dharma tradition must by all means [187] be allowed to continue to do so! Any edicts from the patron and patronized should instead encourage all to exert themselves in their own Dharma tradition. In this way, both patron and patronized shall wield their power appropriately (*dbang spurs bzang*) and show exceptional compassion." By such immeasurable kindness as this, the precious one, Chögyal Phakpa, inaugurated a golden age of happiness in the north of the world.

To understand his kindness more fully, I now provide both the well-known "Pearl Edict"[1135] and the "Edict to Increase the Power of Monks," otherwise known as the "The Tibetan Language Edict,"[1136] which were issued by the Mongol [emperor]. To wit, it is said in the "Pearl Edict":

> On the authority of the long-life deity and by relying upon the glory of great merit, I, the emperor, address the great many communities of Saṅgha and laity.
>
> All the abundances of this world arise from following the law of Činggis Qan.[1137] To benefit the next life, however, we must rely upon the Dharma system. To that end, we must care-

fully investigate and determine for ourselves that the path of the Buddha Śākyamuni is perfect.

Master Phakpa, moreover, is exceedingly knowledgeable [in the Buddha's path] and teaches unmistakably. For these reasons, I have taken initiation from him. I have offered him the position of the *guoshi* state preceptor (Ch. *guoshi* 國師). I have appointed him as head of all Buddhist saṅghas. The Master shall in general work splendidly on behalf [188] of the teaching of the Buddha; serve as chief of the Saṅgha; and lead in the affairs of teaching, studying, and meditating.

The Saṅgha, moreover, shall never contradict any of the Master's commands. He who knows the Dharma system very well is obliged to teach, since this is the very root of the Buddha's system. The young with stable minds must study. Those who already know the meaning of the Dharma very well, or those who are unable to explain or listen to the teachings, must correctly engage in meditation. Acting thusly is likewise the foundation for the Buddha's teaching. At the same time, I, the patron, shall complete the accumulation of merit and serve the Triple Gem.

If you, members of the Saṅgha, incorrectly teach, study, or meditate, what can be considered correct activity [according to] the Buddha? The Buddha has said in the sūtras, "My teaching is like the lion, king of animals. Unless it is harmed from within its body, nothing from without may ever injure it." Should you follow the vast path, heed my orders, and deeply recognize the Dharma, I will venerate you excellently and serve [as ruler] impartially.

O military leaders, soldiers, garrison leaders (*mkhar dpon*), appointed leaders,[1138] and gold-letter bearers: you are forbidden from treating the possessions of any Saṅgha member who is acting according [to this edict] like "wealth [found] on a mountain."[1139] Never enlist such a Saṅgha member into the army, nor tax them, nor compel them into any other involuntary activity. Never contradict the tradition of Śākyamuni. Let [monks] abide [unbothered] so they may offer to Tngri[1140] [189] and perform prayers on my behalf.

I issue this edict from here so that you may keep it with you! The gold-letter bearers must not stay the night in the temples or residences of the Saṅgha. Appoint servants to provide food for them. Do not take anything belonging to the temples, such as land, water, water mills, and so forth. Gold-letter bearers must not act unlawfully. The Saṅgha, however, must never contradict the system of Śākyamuni while saying, "We possess an edict!"

I have written this at Shongtho,[1141] on the first day of the middle summer month of the Bird Year according to my calendar system.

Piloting the Dharma boat of the Sugata's teaching,
one quickly crosses the ocean of saṃsāra.
Relying upon the skillful captain named "Phakpa,"
I have written this for the benefit of others.

Access the jewel island of the Buddha's good qualities,
perfect the light of enlightened activity, and be pleased by virtue.
By this, may all the darkness of mind be removed!

This is Sečen Qaγan's "Pearl Rosary Edict."

Thus ends the "Pearl Rosary Edict." I now provide the contents of the "The Tibetan Language Edict," otherwise known as the "Edict to Increase the Power of Monks." To wit:

Oṃ svasti siddhaṃ!
I prostrate to the Triple Gem, the source of all auspiciousness and prosperity, protectors of the entire world including even the gods!
Your body is established by the jewel of merit, a fully expanded wisdom maṇḍala, and completely blazing with all [190] the major and minor marks.

By the wind of compassion, you thoroughly traveled across the sky of the dharmadhātu, fully radiating ten million rays of elegant speech.
Outshining the constellation of the hordes of demons, you cleared away the darkness of their deficient scriptural traditions, teaching a variety of [topics], and perfectly caused the lotus of wisdom to bloom.
On behalf of all the world's disciples: I pay homage to the perfect Buddha, lamp for all living beings!

His elegant speech is completely pure, clear, and unsullied,
like cooling rays that completely clear the suffering of saṃsāra,
destroying the clouded vision of conceptual thought,
free from elaboration; everyone everywhere pays homage to the moon of the holy Dharma!

The seed of superior intention and an ocean of devotion [fallen] upon the soil of the all-ground [consciousness];
sprouted by the speech rays of the sun-like Buddha, endowed with the leaves of virtue and goodness;
unsullied by the blemish of mud, the fully developed essence of wisdom;
possessing the taste of honey from benefiting others: may the lotus grove of the Saṅgha flourish!

Though you had already achieved the supreme nirmāṇakāya, still, on behalf of limitless disciples,
you incarnated in an ordinary body, and when you were twelve years old
you beheld the face of Mañjuśrī, who revealed to you all the Dharmas of wisdom and compassion.
A hundred gods pay homage by placing the feet of the one named "Nyingpo" atop their crowns!

Clouds of compassion gathering in the sky of the pure dharmadhātu,
garlands of wisdom lightning and sweet rolling thunder,
rain of elegant speech ripening the fruit of complete liberation:
Please, Luwang Drakpa,[1142] be seated as an adornment upon the crown of sentient beings! [191]

With the good qualities of the turquoise mane of the three trainings perched atop a snow mountain of merit,
possessing the skill of wisdom, sounding the roar of selflessness and emptiness,
and terrifying opposing beasts with the fangs of wisdom and compassion:
I pay homage upon my crown to the feet of the lion among men!

(The above verses of praise were composed by Phakpa Rinpoché himself.)

Chief son, born from the heart-mind of the lama and Buddha,
renowned across the entire world as supreme,
because of the great force of merit, he was born from the womb
with marvelous lineage, form, and wealth, and power comparable to Indra.

It is said that in his previous life, he was born again and again
as a paṇḍita who strenuously studied
the teachings of the Victors and their children.
At that time, you, O Glorious One, were venerated by all the glorious.

Later, to liberate beings from saṃsāra, when you were just three or four years old,

you taught on Tārā and Mañjuśrī to those who called you "my disciple"
with self-grasping, although they had realized selflessness.

When you were eight years old, you taught on tantra and the *Jātakas*
to 1,800 upholders of the Tripiṭaka
with unhindered courage like the four faces of Brahmā.
I prostrate to you, an inconceivable manifestation!

The Lord of Dharma [Sapaṇ] predicted: "When you turn twelve years old,
you will become like the Great Lama Rinchen and the Great Jetsun.
When you are seventeen, you will perfect all good qualities."
When the time came, your enlightened activities were indeed equivalent.

Upon hearing or perceiving that the suffering of the ocean of saṃsāra
is bottomless, [192] your face became wetted with tears, and you were anguished.
You thus made requests to the Victors and their children of the ten directions.
Endowed with such great compassion, you are the lord Avalokiteśvara!

You completely understood the great Sage's teaching upon hearing it but once.
Even now, you manifest magnetizing activities and enlightened deeds;
there is no question that you will benefit sentient beings when you become an enlightened buddha!
Endowed with incomparable wisdom, I prostrate to you, Mañjuśrī!

(The above verses of praise were composed by a disciple of Lama Phakpa.)

Due to accumulating inconceivable merit during your previous lives,
you gained the marvelous abundances of lineage, form, and wealth,
and you were appointed lord of humans by the king of the gods:
Činggis Qan, that splendid illumination who was like the sun for all beings!

The supreme son [Ögedei Qaγan], born from the merit of that lord of men [Činggis Qan],
he who the best among men respected like an ornament upon their crown,
who, by means of both destruction and care, excellently protected all beings:
this earthly lord was victorious in all directions!

Ögedei's brother [Köden Ejen],[1143] who possessed boundless merit and the mind of compassion,
who pleased that praiseworthy qaγan with deference and service,
and who, to benefit other beings, made effort in various methods:
that intelligent one was a supreme friend and relative to all sentient beings!

His principal heir [Qubilai Qaγan], resplendent with the glory of merit,
endowed always with the mind of compassion for all sentient beings like a mother for her only son,
whose activity arose spontaneously and who was honored to the shores of the ocean:

you were the qaγan of the Mongols who appeared as the
glory of the entire world.

(The above verses of praise were also composed by Lama Phakpa.)

In this way, by the blessing of the Lama and the Supreme
Gems, [193]
may the merit of the heavenly appointed Činggis Qan
and that of all other rulers of the Uyghurs and Mongols
further benefit the Buddha's teaching. This is the speech of
Qubilai.

The perfect and complete Buddha Śākyamuni, with inalienable wisdom and unobservable compassion, has completed the accumulations of merit and wisdom like the full moon, and has destroyed the darkness of ignorance and its residue like the sphere of the sun. Just as the king of animals is the lion, [the Buddha] is victorious over all demons and heretics. By the power of my [i.e., Qubilai Qaγan] and Čabui's conviction in [the Buddha's] good qualities, activities, and teachings, earlier we patronized the lord of the teachings and the Saṅgha. We now possess still more devotion in Lord of the Sakya Dharma [Sapaṇ] and Master Phakpa, and we trust in the Dharma. Later, in the Female Water Ox Year, we received initiation and numerous teachings. And in particular, I now have developed a strong intention to become patron to the teachings and the Saṅgha.

For that reason, we have issued an edict to protect the supports of the Triple Gem and the divisions of the Saṅgha in the kingdom of Tsang as an offering of thanks to Lama Phakpa. Furthermore, we offered a monk's raiment decorated with gold and pearl, a cloak adorned by jewels, a Dharma robe, a bejeweled hat, shoes, a cushion, and so forth as clothing for the master. As other necessities for him, we offered a golden umbrella, a small golden throne, a golden cup, a silver teapot, a knife with a bejeweled handle, [194] and so forth. As wealth, moreover, we offered a large *dré* of gold, four large *dré* of silver, a young camel mount, a mule, a golden saddle, a cushion, and a bridle. Furthermore, in the Tiger Year, as material supports we offered fifty-six great *dré* of silver, two hundred *sik* bamboo boxes[1144] of tea from Wutaishan, and 110 rolls of brocade.

In conclusion, this edict and all these material offerings were made in thanks for receiving the Dharma. All you monks of Tsang, know this! Otherwise, why have we sent this edict? You monks must not quarrel or debate over leadership. Having many leaders is hardly desirable. Those who have received an edict may not thereafter simply act however they wish toward others. You monks must not wage war or come into conflict. According to the system of Śākyamuni, those who know the Dharma should teach. Those who do not know the Dharma should listen. You should put effort into writing, reading, and meditating upon the Dharma. Pay homage to the [Tngri of the] sky and make prayers on my behalf!

Some claim that study is unnecessary and that one may simply pursue practice. However, without study, what should one practice? Only after cultivating understanding should one meditate. Older monks must give advice and teach the Dharma to younger monks. Younger monks should listen to what their elder monks have to say. Do you Saṅgha not recognize that, due to the kindness of the Lama and Triple Gem, you are free from military service, tax, and forced labor? If you do not conform to the tradition of Śākyamuni, Mongols will ask, "Is this the tradition of Śākyamuni?" and will then criticize you. Do not think that [we] Mongols are without any knowledge! It is possible that we may not understand a first or even a second time, but then we shall know! You Saṅgha must not misbehave. Do not embarrass me in front of others! You should act according to the Dharma. Worship the [Tngri of the] sky and pray [195] on my behalf. I will act as your patron. This is the actual edict of the Qaγan.

Son of the Victor, Qubilai:
by the power of merit, you possess lineage, form, and wealth.
Your mind is devoted, intelligent, and compassionate.
Without bias, you protect the earth and are a supreme friend of the teachings.

Queen Čabui[1145] together with her son:
your merits fashioned you into a jewel-like woman.
You possess a beautiful form with a smiling countenance.
You are ornamented by glory and possess a mind of loving-kindness.

Whatever merit I have collected from making
numerous collections of billions of
immeasurable actual and visualized offerings
to an ocean of Thus-Gone Victors of the three times,
and the collection of riches and supreme mounts,
varieties of clothing ornamented by multiple colors, and
tea that vanquishes the suffering of thirst and bestows supreme hope:
I respectfully offer all these for the sake of the Dharma!

So that the teachings may flourish,
this edict bestows fearlessness upon
[those of] the Saṅgha who uphold the holy Dharma.

By the merit from this and from whatever other source,
may Qubilai, lord of men, qaγan of the Mongols,
along with his son and queen, be healthy and long-lived!
May there be joy and happiness in the kingdom and harmony within the Saṅgha,
and may the Buddha's teachings spread in the ten directions!

By this merit, in all my future lives,
may I gain the freedoms and endowments, lineage, form, and wealth!
May I come to behold the Buddha [196] and listen to the holy Dharma!
May I be of benefit to sentient beings!

May I liberate the embodied who are drowning
in the ocean of saṃsāra's suffering!
May I quickly achieve the state of a perfectly enlightened buddha
who knows all phenomena directly, without exception!

The lord among men has requested devotedly
that his excellent edict, made on behalf of the teachings,
opens with praises for the praiseworthy
and ends with full dedications.

These praises to the Triple Gem and to the Qaγan
have been penned to achieve all that is exalted in saṃsāra and nirvāṇa!
My words about the nature of the Buddha and the good qualities of the lama
do not contradict the meaning of scripture or reasoning.

I have composed these verses of dedication
following the pure Mahāyāna scriptural tradition.
This was written in an easterly valley along the Chinese-Tibetan frontiers
on the ninth day of mid-summer during the Male Wood Tiger Year (1254).

This is widely known as the "Edict in Tibetan Writing" given by the Mongol Qaγan. Until now, it has remained at the Great Seat of Sakya. I have copied it down directly here.

Just so, the lord of Dharma, glorious Phakpa, a holy being who brought benefit and peace to many parts of the world in general and to Ü, Tsang, and Kham in particular, clarified Dharma terminology and concepts to the many who spoke a different language. In a prophecy given by Master Padmasambhava to King Trisong Detsen, it was said:

> You, Kawa Paltsek[1146] [197] the translator,
> will one day benefit the beings of India and China.
> Then, at Urgyen Gana,[1147]
> in consultation with me, Padma,
> you will be reborn in the Khön family during the Sheep Year
> in the Drompa region[1148] of Tsang.
> You will uphold the Tripiṭaka and the doctrine.
> With the name "Phakpa," you will protect the Mantrayāna.
> You will subdue the beings of the borderlands!

This all came to pass, just as was predicted.

The following year, the qaγan waged battle in the Jang kingdom.[1149] While this was occurring, Chögyal Phakpa traveled north. There he consecrated the *kumbum*[1150] of the Lord of Dharma [Sapaṇ]. He then planned to depart for Ü-Tsang where, according to the Lord of Dharma's previous instructions, he would take full monastic ordination and receive further teachings from Uyukpa.[1151] While journeying through Dokham, however, he learned from other travelers that Uyukpa had died in the Ox Year (1253). Phakpa then reversed his journey and returned [to the Mongol court]. The emperor was then also making his return to court, and so together they returned to the lands of China.[1152]

At Utho, on the banks of the great river that runs through a region called Thélé along the borderlands of Mongolia and China, [Phakpa] turned twenty-one years old on the fifteenth day of the fifth month of the Female Wood Rabbit Year (1255). Requests were made to the abbot of Nyethang Monastery[1153] named Drakpa Sengé.[1154] He duly bestowed the vows of a fully ordained monk [upon Phakpa]. At that time, Phakpa himself wrote the following letter inviting the lord Drakpa Sengé [to the Mongol court]:

Oṃ svasti siddhaṃ!

Prostrations to the lama and Mañjughoṣa! I respectfully prostrate at the feet of the Lord of Dharma, the holy lama whose true mind is indistinguishable from the wisdom of all the tathāgatas of the three times! I write this letter with a genuine motivation.

Great master, you were born with an excellent body endowed with the seven unique qualities of higher rebirth, which are the fruit of an excellent accumulation of merit and wisdom. By the force of having accomplished prayers made in your previous lives, you completed the entirety of the three trainings. You thus abide as a captain of diligence sailing a boat of inexhaustible intelligence upon the ocean of learned lamas who are well accomplished in the three trainings and who, through detailed analysis, discover extraordinary riches. Because of the bejeweled ornaments of your precious qualities, you outshine all other scholars and attract all beings. I send this letter to Drakpa Sengé, the teacher of all the world, including the gods. I, a novice monk in the lineage of Śākya[muni], the vajra holder Lodrö Gyaltsen Palsangpo, manifest the pride of conceit and submit the following request.

In this place, the lama Lord of Dharma, who possessed unobservable compassion and the highest wisdom, beheld the great benefit to be had for sentient beings in foreign lands. He then vowed he would become perfectly enlightened as a tathāgata named Drima Mepa Pal.[1155] He thus passed into mahāparinirvāṇa accompanied by unthinkable displays of his magical power.

Before passing, however, the Lord of Dharma predicted [to Qubilai]: "You will be considered excellent under any circumstances!" And the qaγan [199] did indeed remain healthy and the kingdom at peace. Meanwhile, the qaγan accepted [Lama Phakpa's request]. He decreed, "All ritualists such as monks, Bönpo priests, and so forth may from now on abide contentedly, for they are exempted from military conscription and taxation. Let the leaders of those communities and all monks know that the Sakyapa are their leaders!"

I send this letter and gifts with [the messenger] Druk[1156] to invite you, O master. When the Lord of Dharma [Sapaṇ] was still alive, he was required to repeatedly travel to meet Prince [Köden]. He was so preoccupied with his meritorious activities that he did not have time to satisfy me in the bestowal of Dharma teachings. As such, I had little opportunity to be contented by the Dharma. For this reason, we discussed [the possibility of] receiving many Dharma transmissions from you and receiving the vows of a fully ordained monk, with you serving as either the abbot or the master [during the ordination ceremony]. I suggested this to the Lord of Dharma Sakya Paṇḍita. He agreed and sent you a letter of request. I also sent you insistent letters, but still, you never came. Had you accepted our invitation when the Lord of Dharma was alive, you would have made him very happy. Even if he had passed while you were here, he would have been happy to know that you remained on here. Still, you never came. We are left wondering why. I am feeling somewhat disheartened.

Nowadays, the Lord of Dharma no longer abides here, and there are no other masters. Still, I hold on to the hope that you will one day come! I wish to receive many transmissions from you on such topics as vinaya, the perfections, logic and epistemology, and so forth. Just before the Lord of Dharma passed away, he said, "I have just one concern, which is that you have not yet received full ordination. Other than that, I have no worries." We [200] close disciples pleaded with him, "Please do not leave us! Remain here longer in our company!" But he said, "That would be very difficult!" and refused our request. I then asked him, "In this case, if you cannot stay here and serve on my account, from whom should I request [full ordination]?" He replied, "Nowadays, there are none so learned and righteous in all of Ü, Tsang, and Kham as Master Drakpa Sengé. He is the equal of Ṣāntipa."

You were thus the Lord of Dharma's hope! To fulfill his wishes, please come! Should you refuse, I see no one who is a suitable candidate to serve as my abbot, and so I will remain without full ordination for the remainder of my life. Also, I will not receive any more Dharma transmissions. Everything now relies upon you! Nowadays, the Lord of Dharma is no longer alive and so my hope is in you. Please keep this in mind. If you come here, my devotion to you will be no different than to the Lord of Dharma. Please consider this samaya pledge: If even a single word of what I have written is untrue or fake, may Vajrapāṇi's vajra smash my heart into hundreds of pieces! May the lama who possesses the wisdom eyes of the Buddha please remain as a witness!

I now set my other requests into verse and send them to you.

My guru has passed into nirvāṇa.
The maṇḍala of his emanation has vanished into space.
The sun of wisdom has set.
The clouds of compassion have dispersed.

The continuity [201] of the rain of samaya has ceased.
Kye ma! Alas! I am indeed unfortunate.
Because of my misfortune, this has happened.
For this reason, I make requests to you!

If you refuse to look upon me with compassion,
Whom shall I request to be my teacher?
For this reason, as I compose this letter
I recollect the good qualities of the lama.

Alas, you live such a vast distance away;
recalling this obstacle, I shed tears!

By the power of my lama's kindness
and your compassion,

and by the power of my appeals,
may these requests be fulfilled!

Should you not even consider my request,
what is shame? What is embarrassment?
What is samaya? What is compassion?

Should one make requests,
calling out someone's name while crying,
then they would help you,
even if they otherwise did not know you.
And so, why will you not consider me with your
compassion?

Upon reading this letter,
your supreme coarse body
will be compelled to come here,
forced along by the whip of compassion
and driven forward by the wind of diligence!

I wish dearly to travel to [Tibet], make prostrations at Sakya Monastery, and then receive full ordination vows from you. Our objectives in this land must be accomplished, however, and so I have not yet come. Please consider my situation. The journey here will be easy for you since the empire is peaceful and stable. The people of Dokham [through which you will pass] are all our subjects. Please, keep this in mind. I have already assigned Kamchuwa[1157] to escort you during your travels. He will serve you [202] in whatever circumstance.

I offer fifty-three large *dré* measures of silver from the qaγan along with this letter to fund your travel. This is not too arduous. I pray that in the future, when you have come here, we may all faultlessly gather an abundance of Dharma and material wealth and that all will be auspicious!

I have written this letter at the temple of Lingchutsé[1158] on the third day of the waxing moon period of the middle month of spring in the Male Water Mouse Year (1252). May it be auspicious!

This letter was dispatched with a messenger. The lord of Dharma Drakpa Sengé was thus invited [to the Mongol court].

The lord of Dharma [accepted the invitation, and, during Phakpa's ordination] served as the abbot. Jodan Jangpa Sönam Gyaltsen[1159] served as the master. Yarlungpa Jangchup Gyaltsen[1160] served as the interviewer master (gsang ste ba). Amid a quorum of twenty fully ordained monks—including the lord of Dharma Ugen,[1161] the abbot of Mangrawa [Monastery] named Tro,[1162] Nampharwa Tsulrin,[1163] and so forth—Phakpa received the bhikṣu ordination. The abbot then taught upon the *Ornament for Clear Realization* and the *Clear Words* [commentary].[1164] He received teachings from the master on the *Prātimokṣa Sūtra*,[1165] the *Aphorisms on Monastic Discipline*,[1166] and so forth. The interviewer master taught on [Dharmakirtī's] seven treatises on valid cognition. Phakpa completely mastered all of these.

When he was twenty-three years old, Lama Phakpa journeyed to Wutaishan upon the invitation of Dong.[1167] There he received commentaries on tantras such as the *Four Signs of Yamāntaka*,[1168] *Mahāmāyā*, the *Vajradhātu*,[1169] and commentary on the *Kālacakra Tantra* and its ancillary tantras. He also received many transmissions from [Nāgārjuna's] Collection of Middle Way Reasoning[1170] and Collection of Praises,[1171] the Abhidharma, and so forth.

In the evening of the thirteenth day of the fourth month of that year, the Lord of Dharma [Sapaṇ] clearly appeared to [Phakpa] in a vision. [203] He prophesied and encouraged: "After 101,000 years, you will achieve the supreme siddhi of mahāmudrā!" It is said that Lama Phakpa composed the following verses of praise soon after:

> Exhausted by experiencing the copious sufferings
> of existence over a long period of time,
> I am now encouraged by these elegant words.
> Lord of Compassion, chief among scholars,
> to the Lord of Dharma, I prostrate!

It is well known that he composed *The Ocean of Study*[1172] at this time. After that, [Chögyal Phakpa] invented a script for the Mongols, who previously possessed none. In appreciation, the qaγan offered the "Edict to Increase the Power of Monks." Phakpa then departed for the royal palace. While he turned the wheel of Dharma there, the qaγan saw that the many [Daoist] monks from Sinshing who followed [the master] named Heshang Lagyin and who were attached to wrong view were harming themselves and others. Following the qaγan's command, Lama Phakpa defeated in debate seventeen teachers from Singshing who were deeply learned and completely knew their textual systems.[1173] He set them into the right view and ordained them as [Buddhist] monks.

After that, when he was twenty-eight years old, Chögyal Phakpa sent much wealth to Sakya Monastery. He instructed the Pönchen of Sakya, Shākya Sangpo,[1174] to construct a golden roof on the west side of Utsé Nyingma [Temple].

Then, when he was thirty-one years old, in the Female Wood Ox Year (1265), he returned to glorious Sakya. At Serthok Chenmo,[1175] he offered remarkable jewels to the Tashi Gomang Stūpa,[1176] which houses many deities of the Vajradhātu. He offered umbrellas to the outer supports of the previous Jetsun's [204] seven kumbums. He built a Dharma wheel made of gold and copper, and, mainly, a golden roof for the kumbum. He produced more than two hundred golden volumes of the Victor's teachings, including sūtras, tantras, and Perfection of Wisdom scriptures. He extensively turned the wheel of the Dharma and set many sentient beings upon the path to ripening and liberation.

Although this mahātmā had completed his education and was already a Lord of Dharma, he possessed no conceit and thus relied on many spiritual masters for the sake of the Dharma. These included: the great Kāśmīri paṇḍita Śrī Tathāgatabhadra; the lama vajra holder and translator hailing from Lo, Sherab Rinchen;[1177] the abbot of Narthang Monastery, Chimnam Khadrak;[1178] Ösung Gönpo from Sangwa Nyen;[1179] the great siddha known as Cherepa;[1180] the master Yönten Pal;[1181] Tsokgom Kunga Pal from Gyerbu;[1182] Dorjé Öser from Shang shung;[1183] Rinpoché Kyobpa Pal;[1184] Rangwen Marpa, the Lord of Yogins [named] Ralo;[1185] the nephew of Chak Lotsāwa named Nyima Pal;[1186] Rinchen Dorjé from Epa Shangngon;[1187] the spiritual master from Drakpuk named Bumpa Öser;[1188]

the upholder of the Vinaya from Doklo named Shākya Jangchup;[1189] the upholder of the Abhidharma Wangjuk Tsöndru,[1190] who had been a disciple of the Dharma Lord; the practitioner of secret mantra from Rongri Lungphuk named Chökyi Gönpo;[1191] the geshé from Dzilbuwa named Taktön Sherab [205] Öser;[1192] Master Sangyé Bum from Ü;[1193] the Drekhüpa geshé;[1194] the physician (*lha rje*) Darma Sengé;[1195] and so forth.

Chögyal Phakpa learned the Hinayāna from a few of them; from others, the Mahāyāna; and from still others, the Secret Mantra. In short, he learned nearly all the teachings that existed then in Tibet, including the five major fields of knowledge, the Tripiṭaka, the four classes of tantra and their commentaries, the sūtras and tantras, initiations, blessings, and the oral instructions together with their supplements. In this way, he worked with great diligence to listen to the holy Dharma, motivated only for the growth of the Buddha's teachings and to work on behalf of the benefit of all sentient beings.

When he was thirty-three years old, in the Female Fire Rabbit Year (1267), gold-letter bearers arrived to summon Chögyal Phakpa back to the court of the great qaγan. He organized the thirteen categories of retainers (*las tshan bcu gsum*) and departed. At that time, Chomden Raldri[1196] was promoting the following criticism [of Phakpa]:

> The teachings of the Buddha have been obscured by the clouds of the Ka[dampa] and Chak[chenpa].
> The happiness and well-being of sentient beings have been lost to the hands of human overlords.
> A monk of the degenerate age now appears with the accoutrement of a secular leader.
> You do not recognize these three facts, and so I realize you are no supreme being!

The Lord of Dharma [Chögyal Phakpa] wrote this reply:

> That the teachings would thrive and decline was taught by the Victor.
> The happiness and well-being of sentient beings depends upon their karma.

[One may take] whatsoever appearance and activity to tame sentient beings.
You do not recognize these three facts, and so I realize you are no scholar! [206]

As for the "thirteen categories of retainers," it says in the *The Ornament Adorning the Mouths of the Noble succession history*:[1197]

As for this ancillary topic,
These are the outer and inner [attendants]:
three comprising chamber staff, food servers, and shrine masters;
three comprising appointment keepers, scribes, and treasurers;
three comprising cooks, household staff, and a throne manager;
and four comprising grooms, animal tenders, special assistants, and small pet minders:
these are the thirteen sorts of retainers suitable for an important person.
These categories of retainers were established during the time
of the glorious Lord of Dharma, Chögyal Phakpa.

Just so, these are together known as the "three sets of three" and the "two sets of two." Here, it is well known that the "three sets of three" refers to the chamber staff, food servers, and shrine masters; to the appointment keepers, scribes, and treasurers; and to the cooks, household staff, and throne manager. And it is well known that the "two sets of two" refers to the groom and animal tender, and to the special assistants and small pet minders. Nowadays, people are inventive and will enumerate these in whichsoever way. My presentation here, by contrast, is based on trustworthy texts.

When Phakpa was thirty-three years old, in the Rabbit Year (1267), he departed on his return journey to Mongolia. Along the way, he met the Kadampa master Namkha Bum, who was then sixty-one years old. [Namkha Bum] posed many questions about the Dharma to the Lord of

Dharma [Phakpa]. The Kadampa lord of Dharma developed unshakable devotion in [Phakpa]. Namkha Bum then composed a two-part biography that chronicled some of the marvelous activities of Chögyal Phakpa Rinpoché. In the first part we read:

> *Oṃ svasti* [207] *siddhaṃ*! *Namo guru Mañjughoṣāya*!
>
> Lord of Dharma, Source of the Dharma, Sovereign of the Dharma, Intelligence of the Dharma, Victory Banner of the Dharma, Glorious Protector of the Dharma, Reliable Source of the Dharma: to the Dharma King Phakpa, I pay homage with my three doors!
>
> Were I to describe this supreme being, as a sign of having accumulated merit and studying the Dharma over the course of uncountable previous lifetimes, when he was seven years old he could remember five or six of his previous lifetimes and provide descriptions about them without any difficulty. The Lord of Dharma [Sakya Paṇḍita] told him to stop doing this, and thereafter he never again shared these stories. At that time, everyone agreed that he was no ordinary being, rather a noble being. It is well known that for this reason, he aquired the name "Phakpa." I heard this story directly from the mouth of that noble one's disciples.
>
> He later received the novice vow when he was thirteen years old. He received the vows of a fully ordained monk when he was twenty years old. When he was eighteen years old, the Lord of Dharma passed into nirvāṇa, and [Phakpa] assumed responsibility for his disciples. When he was thirty years old, he returned to Ü-Tsang. In the Sheep Year (1259), when he was thirty-three years old—but when, according to the astrological system of the Sakyapa the year had not yet ended—on the fifth day of the tenth month of the Fire Female Rabbit Year, he went to Dam.[1198] On the twenty-sixth day, he journeyed onward from Dam. At that time, I, Namkha Bum of the Rabbit Year, was sixty-one years old.
>
> Based on my understanding and using the Kadampa system of reckoning, it had then been 229 years since the Jowo [Atiśa Dīmpaṃkaraśrījñāna][1199] had passed into nirvāṇa.

It had then been 219 years since Dromtönpa[1200] had passed. It had been ninety-five years since Potowa[1201] [208] had passed into nirvāṇa. It had been 129 years since Sharawa[1202] had passed into nirvāṇa, and ninety-six years since Tapkawa.[1203] It had been eighty-three years since Shangtön[1204] had passed, and thirty-nine years for the master Gönchenpo.[1205] These lamas are known collectively as the "Single Succession Tradition of the Jowo and his Spiritual Sons."[1206] Two hundred forty-seven years had passed since the Jowo arrived in Tibet. It had been 228 years since the foundation had been laid at Radreng Monastery.[1207] Beyond [dating] these former Kadampa masters and teachers and so forth, I could go into more detail and describe more thoroughly the Kadampa reckoning systems, but I see no reason to do so and will stop here. These are taken from among the ancillary topics.

Returning to my primary topic, the lama Dharma King [Phakpa] stayed in Dam for eleven days. I had audiences with him on seven of those days. When he first arrived, I went to see him, but there were large crowds also wishing to see him. I therefore waited to have an audience with the lama but could not. At nighttime, the flow of people in and out concluded. I wrote a long letter explaining why I wished to have an audience and sent it off with Jamser.[1208] [Lama Phakpa] saw my letter and said, "All those wishing to see me do so motivated by self-interest. He is the only one who wishes to see me on behalf of the Dharma!"

Lama Phakpa later told Jamser, "Tomorrow morning you should go see him and bring him two texts: *Illumination of the Mahāyāna*[1209] and *Summary of the Scriptures*.[1210] [You should make sure] everything is well with him, including his sleeping arrangements." In the morning, [209] Jamser the scribe did indeed come to see me. He said, "Lama is especially pleased with you!" We then held a long discussion. The evening following his arrival, Lama sent Jamser to fetch me for an audience. My two attendants and I went to him. We came into his presence and presented him with gifts. He then offered us tea and we had a long discussion.

After that, he said, "What do you wish to receive tonight?" I replied, "I wish to receive the profound bodhisattva vow, since it is the essential teaching of the Kadampa tradition. I have been able to safely keep the samaya of the Mantrayāna, but I have not yet received tantric teachings. Could you check whether I am qualified to enter the doorway of the Mantrayāna or not? If I am, then I wish to request tantric teachings." He replied, "It is perfectly acceptable for you not to take tantric teachings. [However,] you should enter the door of the Mantrayāna, since it is the essential teaching of my tradition." Then Lama Phakpa said, "Tonight I will give you the bodhisattva vow." He also asked his attendant to prepare excellent offerings. Then Lama said, "Come close to me!" Lama poured water over the top of a large mirror maṇḍala. While Lama was holding my hands, we completed the contemplation, meditation, and recitation. He then told me, "It is very important to complete all the maṇḍala rituals," after which he did so himself.

He even passed the offering substances one by one into my hands and asked me to do all the visualizations and chanting. [210] He then likewise gave me a detailed explanation on all the seven branches and their rituals. As he bestowed upon me [the bodhisattva vow], he said, "This is drawn from the *Bejeweled Lamp*.[1211] This sūtra is not yet translated into the Tibetan language." He then thrice performed the elaborate bodhisattva vow ritual written by the Lord of Dharma [Sakya Paṇḍita].

He said, "This can be found in Nāgārjuna's commentary on bodhicitta." And then [he] thrice recited "Whatsoever Buddha Bhagavan..." and so on. He then said, "This may be found in Śāntideva's *Introduction to the Bodhisattva's Way of Life.*" And then he thrice repeated, "Just like the previous sugatas..." and so on. He then said to me, "In case you think that this represents the fault of repetition, there is a quote from a sādhana that says according to certain tenet systems, [repeating three times] is not a fault of repetition." He then performed an extensive concluding ritual, after which he gave many oral instructions. He then taught on the recitation of the sādhana and the method for reciting the *Three Heaps Sūtra*,[1212] the yoga of Amitābha for the time of death, the *Arapacana* sādhana along with its sleep yoga practice and its method for increasing intelligence, together with *Reciting the Names of Mañjuśrī* and the method for chanting it. [Once all this was done,] it was well past midnight.

After that, on the evening of the seventeenth, he called upon me for another audience. I arrived at a large felt tent, wherein a great fire was blazing. He offered me copious amounts of tea and asked detailed questions [211] about the conduct, life stories, good qualities, time of death, name, birth lineage, number of disciples, and so forth of the previous masters of the Kadampa tradition, such as the Jowo and his spiritual sons, the three brother yogins, as well as Langthangpa, Sharpa, Nesurwa, Chayulwa, Tölungpa, and so on.[1213] Since I possessed detailed knowledge about all this, he was very pleased. He wrote down most of their names.

I then [told Lama Phakpa] that I had sent letters with questions [to him] via Tönpa Könchok Sengé[1214] and had been disappointed to never receive a reply. "Even if you have no time to answer my questions now," I asked, "after you return to the Mongolian court could you reply and send your answers to me? Or, alternatively, could you send my questions on to Sakya [Monastery] along with an introduction letter, where someone might be qualified enough to provide answers?"

[Lama Phakpa] replied, "I would indeed be happy if someone at Sakya could answer your questions, but unfortunately there is no one there who is qualified. But I have kept all your letters." He then retrieved my question letters from the sack of his personal belongings. Lama himself then read them out by the light of a butter lamp. He inquired about each of them, "What did you mean by that?" He then gave verbal answers to each until well after midnight. After reading through my questions, he told Jamser, "Using textual evidence and logic that will be very pleasing to him, I will provide detailed answers to all this once we are back at the Mongol court. Then I will send it back to him." He then passed all the letters of questions over to

[Jamser]. He also gave me many instructions on performing the mudrās to expel obstacles related to the bodhisattva vows that he had bestowed upon me the night before. He then offered me morning tea and we once again picked up our discussions from the previous evening.

Then, on the morning of the eighteenth day, Lama sent Jamser to me bearing this message: "You should make offering maṇḍalas and prayers today and tomorrow. Do you [212] wish to receive the initiation alone, like Ghaṇṭāpa?[1215] Otherwise, yesterday evening many outstanding geshés arrived and requested the two evening empowerments of Mahāmāyā.[1216] You should choose whether [to be initiated] with these excellent companions or else alone. I will follow whichever you prefer."

I confessed to Jamser, "I do not know what to do. Which is better?" He replied, "Nowadays, Lama is very busy. If he bestows initiation upon you alone, Lama will become tired. If you join that group of geshés, however, it will be easier on him. You ought to proceed with whatever your heart desires!" "You are right," I replied. "It would indeed be unfortunate to cause Lama to be fatigued. Since these are good Dharma companions, I will join with them." I then instructed: "All of you—Tönshön, Geling,[1217] and the rest—proceed to the initiation manager (*dbang gnyer*) to decide what I should offer." This was all reported to Lama, and he became greatly pleased.

That evening, Lama bestowed the initiation upon many people, including the chieftain of Taklung. On the evening of the nineteenth, all the geshés and leaders of Mardro[1218] gathered and served Lama. Lama gave them detailed advice on proper conduct, such as on eating correctly, and so on. He also explained to the geshés how to progress through the stages of initiation, including keeping the many precepts.

After that, on the evening of the twentieth day, he performed the preparatory initiation of Mahāmāyā. On the evening of the twenty-first, he bestowed the main initiation. To do so, Lama sat upon a raised golden throne. To his right were displayed various supports [such as statues, images, and so on]. [213] In front of him were displayed hosts of delightful offerings. From the left of the throne to the right, near the offerings, twenty-four disciples sat in a circle of geshés and important people, at the head of which was [Geshé] Ngönpawa.[1219]

Behind them were many attendants displaying the initiation materials (*dbang gtad pa*). In the inner circle were the close disciples and attendants of the shrine assistant (*mchod g.yog pa*). Amid all this was Lama's throne. Nearby was a fine cushion. For each of the initiation rituals, Lama performed them first for me and for longer than for the others. Lama placed the conch shell, Dharma wheel, and the bow and arrow into my hands. He did this himself, not one his attendants. For the rest of the attendees, it was his attendants who placed these items into their hands. From time to time, when an instruction was given and needed to be repeated, Lama looked at me and it seemed as though he were teaching me alone.

After completing the concluding rituals, [Lama said,] "Come here again tomorrow after the noon meal. Meet outside this tent." He then departed. After lunch on the twenty-second day, everyone dutifully gathered. At that time, Lama was giving Dharma teachings to the leaders of the Taklungpa. Then Lama emerged from the tent. Behind the tent, the purificatory water attendant Tönshön was distributing water. [214] I went there hoping for a mouthful. Lama said, "Charuwa,[1220] is my Chekawa[1221] here yet? "I am here!" I exclaimed, running toward him to receive a mouthful of blessed water. However, I was on the far side of the great crowd assembled there, and so I could not reach Lama quickly. Lama said, "Make way so he can pass through!" Lama then let me sit near his throne.

Lama said, "This Kadampa master does not have time to receive the elaborate transmission of the tantra, and so I will instead give a short transmission of the text and sādhana." He first gave me the reading transmission of the tantra and a complete commentary. This was followed by [transmissions and explanations] of the sādhana and supplementary texts. After, some requested that he give the transmission of *The Jewel Garland*.[1222] He called upon me and asked, "Do you have this text?" I replied that indeed I did. Lama then instructed a disciple, "Fetch me a copy and I will teach it." He gave the transmission by the light of a butter lamp, focusing especially on the chapter describing worldly existence. After the assembly had dispersed, Chögyal Phakpa and I held a long discussion.

Later, on the evening of the twenty-third day, Lama continued to teach the *Jewel Garland*. When he had finished, he asked me directly if I had understood the meaning of this text. I replied that I had. He even offered me a careful explanation of this tantra. After the assembly had dispersed, I told Lama that I needed the reading transmissions of *The Two Purifications of Rebirth in the Lower Realms*,[1223] the four deities of the Kadampa, Medicine Buddha,[1224] Gaṇapati,[1225] Dharma protectors, the hundred-syllable mantra [of Vajrasattva], and the one-syllable mantra. "I have already received the transmissions and do these practices," I beseeched, "but I request that you bestow the reading transmissions upon me one more time [215] so that I may quickly achieve the results of these practices!" After I made requests for all these transmissions, Lama bestowed them.

Later, on the evening of the twenty-fourth day, a great snowstorm fell in the lower valley. Everyone and their horses thus journeyed from the upper valley. Lama gave teachings at Radreng Monastery. It is said that some [of his entourage] requested a rest for a few more days [before departing]. Lama declined, for he had to urgently visit two people who were gravely ill.

On the evening of the twenty-fifth day, Lama took a meal with local leaders and told them in detail about his story as well as my own. He then bestowed an excellent edict (*'ja' sa*) upon me. Lama said, "We ought to give an ounce of gold to the scribe. You are a Dharma practitioner, however, so I will not permit them to accept any offering from you!" That evening, Lama called on me to visit. I arrived at twilight while he was teaching an assembly of Kadampa masters and some two hundred nobility (*mi chen*) in a large text. He gave teachings about the unfolding of the general vehicles[1226] and detailed teachings about the philosophical positions of the individual tenet systems. He emphasized that the essence of the teachings is the Mantrayāna. He gave detailed instructions upon the six perfections within the context of the Mantrayāna system. He taught that if one has a correct understanding, there is in fact no difference between the six perfections, the three natures, the two truths, and the two stages of the path. He explained that during the age of degeneration, Mantrayāna is superior, and that all the Indian [216] siddhas achieved their realization by practicing this vehicle. [Lama's] teaching continued on, extoling the superiority of the Mantrayāna. When he had finished, everyone dispersed.

I had earlier requested that [Lama] bestow upon me the transmission of guru yoga. He now instructed me to sit. [His entourage] permitted me to do so atop a cushion near Lama's throne. They prepared a fine display of offering substances. Lama said [to two others who were present], "This Kadampa master wishes to receive the teachings on guru yoga. I will permit you both to also join." Instructing them to sit before him, he clarified for me, "These two are geshés from Neuthok."[1227] Lama asked me to sit upon the higher cushion. He explained, "During this teaching, you must repeat after me. There are brief, middling, and extensive guru yogas. Today, I will give the extensive version." And then he gave a detailed explanation. When this was finished, with my hands pressed together, I showed my deep respect for Lama. While I did so, he removed his outer robe and told me, "Wear this and it will improve your practice of guru yoga." He then kidded with the other two attendees, "You may wonder why you are not receiving such gifts, but you have not yet practiced sufficiently!"

At that point, Tönpa Chögön[1228] arrived and chastised me, saying, "You are participating in this assembly, but did the Kadampa not use to say that fraternizing in crowds is poison?" I replied, "I do not at all consider this poison. [217] I have come here to meet Lama and receive initiation from him. I am an imperfect teacher with the opportunity to see a great lama, and so I have of course joined this crowd. As Master Potowa would say, 'I am old and gray-haired, but with a sturdy horse, sufficient supplies, good companions, and a noble aim, even a long journey grows more pleasurable with time.'" [Chögyal Phakpa] heard me and was delighted. He asked me to repeat what I had said. I did and then explained its detailed meaning.

After that, he entrusted me to one of his attendants and said, "Because this text belongs to Joden,[1229] I cannot send it along with you." [And to his attendant:] "Take him to my tent. There you will find ink and paper. Let him copy this prayer text using the light of a butter lamp." He then declared, "I must now journey to meet the great emperor," and departed. I was then taken to the tent by one of the attendants, where I copied most of the text. At around midnight, Lama suddenly returned. He said "Kadampa, do you want to come to my tent?" I said "Yes, I do!" Lama later said the following to five of us [who had gathered in his tent]—Ngönpowa, the two hailing from Neuthok, Dulzin Chögön,[1230] and me—"You are all very important. If I do not do the following, then all the masters and students will be unable to bear the separation." Saying this, he hosted an extensive feast offering. That feast itself included many rituals and instructions, during which he held many discussions. He then told me, "You should sleep here." They set up a curtain in the lama's tent, and I slept there. Because the holy supports and the lama were so near to me, I felt like I was tied up and I did not sleep!

At sunrise, [218] I went to wash. When I returned, the lama was wearing a new Dharma robe. He said, "You are a pure offering object. Last night I offered you a Dharma robe, and now this morning someone offered me this Dharma robe!" They then offered Lama breakfast and he told them to offer it to me at his side. They took about a third of the lama's food and gave it to me. There were eleven others in the tent, to whom they then offered a piece of bread and a piece of meat. Then the lama departed. As he did so, people made countless offerings of silk scarves to him.

At that time, the lama said, "Invite him and offer him a horse!" He then directed his attendants to offer me a fine horse. I passed my horse along to my disciple-attendant. Others departed ahead of me, but Tönshön was waiting for me. Then I went inside [his tent] and asked him for a nectar pill. While he gave one to me, he also offered me one *zhor* of gold and said, "You should always do rituals on my behalf." He gave me a long blessing and then stared at me for a long time. I thus left his tent feeling it unbearable to separate from him. I could not contain my tears.

While I was staying [in the presence of the lama], sometimes people like Jamser, Kunga Drak, and Chöngön would request to form a Dharma connection with me and asked many questions. I provided answers to all queries, and many people reported becoming very happy. I, too, became very happy.

I have written all this based roughly on whatever I can remember. I am aware that were I to record events in more detail, then possibly I would fill up the lines with falsehoods and superimpositions (*sgro btags*). It is said that while Lama remained in Tokgong, he taught the root text of the *Treasury of Abhidharma* to the people of Chumik in morning sessions, and so forth. He also taught [Sapaṇ's] *The Entranceway for the Wise* to many people. [219] He occasionally bestowed the bodhisattva vows and gave personal teachings based upon whatever was requested of him.

In conclusion, day and night he continually engaged in Dharma activities, held Dharma discussions, and thought about how he could help. He thought only of how he could directly and indirectly benefit other sentient beings. Other than this, he held no conceptual thoughts related to this life, such as self-interested desires or the eight worldly dharmas. He was a holy person whose mind was thoroughly mixed with the Dharma. I continuously felt that whosoever enjoyed a connection with this being possessed a meaningful life and was liberated. Were I to list all the reasons why, they would be too many!

Just as in this life, may I please the lama and be born next to him in all my future lifetimes! May I become first among his disciples! May I fully understand the lama's liberated life story! Based upon that understanding, may I set all sentient beings on the path to perfect enlightenment!

This concludes the first of the two sections on the amazing life story of the Dharma King Phakpa's life story composed by the Kadampa Namkha Bum.

Now I will expound upon a section of the liberated life story of the Dharma king written by the same author, [Namkha Bum]. As it is said there:

With the deep devotion [220] I prostrate to the Guru and
Mañjugoṣa with my body, speech, and mind!

I pay homage to the renowned retinue of the Sakyapa;
those who dispute (*'khon*) negative deeds and obscurations
are like the ground (*sa*) from which all positive qualities arise,
and like the dawn light (*skya*) that eliminates grasping.

I take refuge in the holy body of Chögyal Phakpa,
who through wisdom and compassion developed a supreme intellect,
who raised the victory banner of the Dharma on behalf of beings,
and who by means of excellent activities accomplished the welfare of others.

I praise and make offerings to your clan (*rus*),
your dwelling place (*gnas*), and your names!
I request that I, Namkha Bum, may be protected!
And that I, [a follower of] Chekawa, may be accepted by your compassionate mind!

Because of my previous actions and prayers,
I have met you and, over seven days,

with gifts of the Dharma and material objects,
you have cared for me compassionately, like a mother
reunited with her son.

As such, I was encouraged (*spobs*) and emboldened (*bskyang*),
and I became fearless to engage you in question and answer.
Such questions and answers
came to feel as if I were speaking with an ordinary person.

He was also gladdened by this
and ignored all esteemed persons surrounding us.
While showing a smile and gazing upon me,
he answered my questions from the depths of his heart:

Q: Regarding the end of the bodhisattva's vow, in his explanation on its benefits, the Lord of Dharma [Sakya Paṇḍita] taught: "Although an individual may abandon bodhicitta, bodhicitta will not abandon the individual." In northern Uru[1231] they distorted these words, writing instead: "According to the Sakya tradition, whatever you may do, you will not lose your bodhicitta." Most people thus misunderstand and accumulate negative karma. [221] What is the intended meaning of [Sapaṇ's words]?[1232]

A: Any individual who has received the bodhicitta vow from a qualified Dharma master, such as the Lord of Dharma Sapaṇ, and who strictly follows its instructions will certainly achieve enlightenment. However, if one does not strictly follow the instructions and does not abandon negative actions, then that means such an individual has abandoned their bodhicitta. Because of the ripening result, such a person will be reborn in the lower realms. Such a person will depart from the lower realms, and the seed tendencies of bodhicitta that were imprinted earlier upon the all-ground consciousness then become the cause for further developing their bodhicitta. [Sapaṇ] thus said: "Bodhicitta will not abandon the individual."

This is why the Mahāyāna is supreme in terms of blessings, abundance, and auspicious interdependence. A second reason is that Mañjuśrī once encouraged some demons to take the bodhicitta vow. There were two types of demons: those who delighted in virtue and those who did not. Whatever Mañjuśrī said, the demons would not listen to him. Mañjuśrī then snapped his fingers and all the demons became old, enfeebled, and marked by every sign of ugliness. The demons then discussed who among them could discover how to escape their plight. One of them suggested two options: to make requests to either the Buddha Śākyamuni or Mañjuśrī. Following a long discussion, they all agreed that, indeed, no one else other than Śākyamuni or Mañjuśrī could liberate them. "Mañjuśrī is our adversary, and so we cannot ask him," they determined. So they requested [222] Śākyamuni to free them from their trouble.

Buddha Śākyamuni, however, refused. "Even as many tathāgatas like me as there are grains of sand in the Ganges River cannot liberate those bound by Mañjuśrī!" With this, the demons who delighted in virtue decided: "Should we remain in this state, it will be a tremendous loss. We must therefore ask Mañjuśrī to liberate us!" The demons who delighted in nonvirtue, however, said, "Even if we must lose our lives, we will never request help from Mañjuśrī. For if we do, he will simply ask us to take the bodhisattva vow." One particularly deceitful demon then said, "I have a plan. Let us request help from Mañjuśrī. He will then release us. When he asks us to take the bodhisattva vow, we can do so merely by repeating the words. We can then disregard keeping our vows!"

All the demons agreed and so they made requests to Mañjuśrī to release them. Mañjuśrī replied, "Should I agree to release you from bondage, will you all agree to take the bodhisattva vow?" They promised, "Yes, we will!" Mañjuśrī snapped his fingers once again and their bodies became even more beautiful and more marvelous than before. Mañjuśrī then bestowed the bodhisattva vow. All the demons repeated [the words of the ceremony] after him, but as they did so, they thought, "Secretly I will abandon this bodhisattva vow." Because bodhicitta is formless, however, it merged with their minds and the demons could not in fact abandon it. [223] On this basis, over time they ceased wishing to abandon their bodhisattva vow. All of them guarded their vows and eventually achieved liberation. This is [another reason] why it is said that bodhicitta will not abandon the individual. This is the textual source for [Sapaṇ's explanation].

Q: What is the difference between a newly planted seed and a previously planted seed?

A: There are two kinds of persons. There is the one who receives the bodhisattva vow who has never received it before and is called a "newly planted seed." The person who has previously received the bodhisattva vow is called a "previously planted seed."

Q: Why do some practitioners achieve clairvoyance relatively quickly and others relatively slowly?

A: It is said: "By achieving the mind of stable mental engagement (*rnam gnas*), one attains the power and accomplishment of the yidam meditational deity." Here, "stable mental engagement" refers to calm abiding.[1233] "Power" is in reference to clairvoyance. Without calm abiding, there can be no clairvoyance. A clairvoyance that arises from a powerful calm abiding is slower to develop. That which arises in tandem is faster.

Q: How do we distinguish between aspiration and engagement?[1234]

A: [Chögyal Phakpa] gave a detailed explanation on the view of the Lord of Dharma [Sapaṇ], who had taught that there are six types. There are three kinds of aspiration: the mind of aspiration, aspirational bodhicitta, and enhanced bodhicitta. Engagement also has three: the mind of engagement, engaged bodhicitta, and enhanced engagement.

Q: There is agreement that a meditation session devoted to aspirational bodhicitta should be one-third of a day and night. But there is disagreement about whether sessions devoted to engaged bodhicitta should be equal to that or longer.

A: In general, sessions devoted to engaged bodhicitta should be longer. To clarify, [224] the sessions should last an entire day and night. This is because if one does not make three offerings to the Triple Gem, one is committing a fault (*nyes pa bya ba*). But if one does not make even a single offering during one's daily practices, that produces a fault (*nyes pa bskyed*). This is the reason for specifying the duration of that session.

Q: If one is motivated by anger and directs vulgar language toward the object of a bodhisattva, what level must the bodhisattva be [for such behavior to produce heavy negative karma]? And how strong must the anger be? And how foul the language?

A: Regarding a bodhisattva who has for the first time [received his vows] from the bodhicitta ritual, regardless of whether he still possesses the vow or not, or whether he is alive or dead, if you understand him to possess the bodhisattva vow, then this is the object. Regarding the required measure of anger, your mind itself must be motivated by negative emotions such as being uncomfortable with a person or jealous of them. But if you are joking or simply repeating negativity you have heard secondhand about them, then the actual fault will not arise. To produce a fault, one's words must be associated with the four types of decline. Telling a person that they are dumb or ugly creates a fault. This does not, however, create a major fault.

Q: Regarding taking refuge in the Triple Gem, Kharuwa[1235] accepts that we ought to limit the number of sessions devoted to this subject. Potowa disagrees. How should we correctly measure the number of sessions to devote to this topic?

A: If performing common refuge, then we need not count the sessions. If we are performing extraordinary refuge, however, we ought to count the sessions.

Q: Beyond these [common and extraordinary manners of going for refuge], are there any other categories of going for refuge?

A: The Lord of Dharma accepted four divisions within "mundane" and "supramundane." Mundane [in turn has two subdivisions]: ordinary and supreme. [225] Supramundane [has two also]: common and extraordinary. Mundane ordinary refuge is the refuge taken only by an ordinary being. Mundane supreme refuge is the refuge of beings who, although they have some fear, take refuge motivated by desire. Supramundane common refuge is a refuge possessing both [fear and desire], which is taken by a being who is motivated by devotion. Although extraordinary refuge possesses all three—fear, desire, and devotion—such a being takes refuge only motivated by compassion.

Q: Everyone belonging to the Mahāyāna takes refuge in the Triple Gem. This is the same as [the refuge taken by those belonging to other Buddhist schools]. Do adherents of different schools take refuge principally in any one [of the objects of refuge] more than another?

A: Yes, they do. Bodhisattvas take refuge in the Triple Gem, but principally in the Buddha. Solitary realizers take refuge in the Triple Gem, but principally in the Dharma. Hearers take refuge in the Triple Gem, but principally in the Saṅgha. Chögyal

Phakpa then gave the textual sources for each of these claims. He also correctly explained how each of these take refuge.

Q: The three manners of going for refuge are the essential teaching for the Kadampa. Long ago, the Kadampa were renowned as the "Refuge-taker Tradition." I am among the followers of this tradition, and so how should one contemplate (*bsam*) and meditate (*bsgom*) upon refuge?

A: In general, all practices of the Mahāyāna [include] preparations motivated by bodhicitta, actual practices recognizing nonapprehension, and a conclusion dedicated to the welfare of all sentient beings [226]. Specifically, after taking refuge in the Buddha, one should meditate that the entirety of the form realm is not inherently existent. After one takes refuge in the Dharma, one should meditate that the entirety of the formless realm is not inherently existent. After one take refuge in the Saṅgha, one should meditate that all of those [form and formless realms] have lacked inherent existence since the beginning and permanently.

Q: I personally only delight in my daily recitation. Which is better: daily recitations or the recitation of mantra?

A: For one who has not yet received initiation, daily recitations are better.

Q: When doing daily recitations, which is more meritorious: reading the abridged sūtras (*sdud pa*) or reading sādhanas (*mngon rtogs*)?

A: Because of differences in the mental continuums of the buddhas and bodhisattvas, those reading texts composed by each receive different kinds of merit. Also, one gains more merit from reading commentaries written by those whose mental continuums are more cultivated.

Q: When reading abridged sūtras, which kind [of text] produces more merit: those written using precious jewels or those written with ordinary ink?

A: In terms of writing, we may indeed draw distinctions based on its materiality. In terms of reading, we may draw distinctions based on the words. In terms of meditation, we may draw distinctions based on the meaning. Regarding reading, clear pronunciation and quality (*bzang ba*) [recitation] is more meritorious, not the [materiality of the] text. However, if texts are written with jewels and if the binding belt and cloth covering are bejeweled, that is good and excellent, and more respect and care has been shown. The opposite demonstrates less respect and care. It is therefore possible to differentiate between accumulations of merit [based upon reading different kinds of texts].

Q: When reading the abridged sūtras, I cannot recite them all from memory and so I mostly read from the text. To recite it, I have memorized the final section, "Bodhisattvas should always keep giving…in mind." I read some sections and recite others. Is there any fault in mixing the [ten] Dharma activities?

A: There is no fault, since all the ten Dharma activities[1236] are already partially mixed.

Q: In this case, in terms of merit, is there any difference between reading and recitation?

A: Regarding all the ten Dharma activities and all the six perfections, and so on:

> Relying upon the earlier, the later is produced.
> The [earlier] remains lower and [the later] superior.
> The [earlier] is approximate and the [later] more detailed.
> This all shows their relative status.

Just as this says, by relying upon what is earlier, the later arises. Whatever is earlier is lower. Whatever is later is superior. As such, recitation is superior [to reading]. Recitation is better than even teaching the Dharma. Superior to recitation is contemplation (*sems pa*). Superior than that is meditation. From among the ten Dharma activities, there are only two that are superior to recitation: concentration and meditation. Your interest in recitation thus possesses greater merit [than reading]!

Q: In this case, what is the difference in merit between reciting *Reciting the Names of Mañjūśrī* and the abridged sūtras?

A: There is no difference in the merit accumulated. You will acquire more merit through whichever is of more interest to you.

Q: Regarding the purification of negative actions, is it not [228] best to apply the power of the antidote?[1237]

A: That is correct. The power of applying the antidote has four types. (1) Every Dharma practice is, in general, an example of applying the force of the antidote. (2) Specifically, applying an antidote to whatever negative actions one has committed is called the "power of the antidote." (3) From among Dharma [practices], one undertakes whichever is said to be the most meritorious. That is an antidote. And (4) engaging in whatsoever purificatory practice is of interest is an antidote.

Q: Which among those four kinds of antidote is the most important?

A: To purify negative actions, all four powers must be present. Regarding whichever negative action one is purifying, it is most important to cease engaging in it any longer. [Lama Phakpa then] gave many further reasons why this is most important.

Q: How should we differentiate among the three: Dharma relatives, vajra relatives, and close relatives?

A: "Dharma relatives" include everyone who practices the Buddha's teachings, from those who have just taken refuge up to those holding Vajrayāna commitments. Those who are called "vajra relatives" include all those who have received empowerments from their different lamas, into different maṇḍalas, in the company of different groups of disciples. Those called "close relatives" have together received empowerment from a single lama, into a single maṇḍala, in the company of various disciples.

Q: All Kadampa masters study and cite the *Fifty Verses on the Guru*.[1238] Which tantra was the basis for this composition?

A: It is based on the commentary in fifteen verses upon the first four lines of the first among the fourteen root downfalls, which begins "Therefore, for Vajradhara..." [229]

Q: It is sometimes said that after one dies, for three days one's consciousness remains in a state without senses (*brgyal ba*). It is elsewhere said that during that period, one perceives one's previous lives. Can you expound upon this in more detail?

A: For half a day after one's death, one remains in a state without senses. For the next two and a half days, one perceives one's previous lives. At that point, three and a half days after one's death, one realizes that one is dead.

Q: Can beings remain in the bardo for more than seven days?

A: Those who cling to perceptions and who are bereft of an accumulation of merit may remain in the bardo for a longer period. Those who have accumulated merit may remain in the bardo for but a moment. The majority of beings remain in the bardo for seven times seven days. That is why it is said to be [forty-nine days].

Q: Is it certain or not that a bardo being is the size of a five-year-old child?

A: This is usually the case, but it is not necessarily always so.

Q: Is it true that bardo beings can travel anywhere, without any obstruction from earth, stone, mountain, or craggy hill?

A: Other than a mother's womb and Bodhgayā, a bardo being may pass anywhere unobstructed. There are no obstructions other than these two.

Q: What is the reason for that?

A: This magical ability occurs not through practice but from the force of karma. Because of that, such beings may move in a moment across the Three Thousand-Fold world system.

Q: Which among the three kinds of bardo beings are in the majority?

A: It is said that most beings occupy the bardo of becoming (*srid pa bar do*). As proof, [230] if Mount Meru turned into a heap of flesh, in a matter of days it would become a heap of worms.

Q: Can those who have died experience the ripening of a living being's karma?

A: There are many ways to explain this. There are sources that say both: that the dead can experience the karmic results of the living, and that they cannot. However, these sources do not contradict one another. From the perspective of the empowering condition (*bdag rkyen*), the dead can experience such ripening. From the perspective of the causal condition (*rgyu rkyen*), however, the dead cannot experience any such ripening.

Q: What are the defining characteristics and etymology of "individual beings" (*so so'i skye bo*)?

A: Those called "individual beings" have not yet perceived the true nature of reality (*chos nyid*). Also, those who are reborn individually according to their individual karma are called "individual beings."

Q: What are the defining characteristics and etymology of "noble beings" (Skt. *ārya*; Tib. *'phags pa*)?

A: Those called "noble beings" have directly perceived the true nature of reality. Noble beings have passed far beyond karma and the afflictions, and so they are called "noble beings."

Q: What is the etymology of "samaya" (*dam tshig*)?

A:

Regarding the etymology of samaya:
because it is difficult to escape its bonds, it is called "tight" (*dam*);
because one will burn if one escapes, it is called "burn" (*tshig*);
in this sense, one is protected from crossing beyond.

Q: In general, the ripening of karmic results (*las rnam smin*) and the congruent cause (*rgyu mthun*) are the same. It is possible that as a ripening result, one may become rich, but as a congruent cause, one may become stingy. But also, [it is possible] that as a ripening result, one may be poor early in one's life yet still have no attachment. Please explain.

A: In most cases, the results of these two kinds of karma are similar, but there are cases in which their results are dissimilar. [231] For example, I once explained to my emperor [Qubilai Qaγan]: "In one of your previous lives, early on you were stingy. But later in life you met a bodhisattva, and out of devotion you offered him fine things. As a result, you have now met a lama like me and you have become wealthy. However, since you were once stingy in that previous life, you are now still unable to let go of any of your wealth." This is an example of the mixing of the kinds of ripening karmic results.

Q: Is the Vairocana[1239] who was the great being who emanated the Bhagavan Śākyamuni the same as the one who is counted among the five buddha families?

A: They are not the same. Since these five dhyāni buddhas [i.e., five buddha families] are symbolic buddhas (*brda'i sangs rgyas*), if one is not enlightened, one is not counted among the embodiments of those [five]. However if one is enlightened, then one is counted among these embodiments. The form aspect of that buddha is Vairocana. His voice aspect is Amitābha. His mind aspect is Vajrasattva. The aspect of his qualities is Ratnasambhava. The aspect of his activities is Amoghasiddhi. To benefit sentient beings, a buddha will manifest one of these [aspects] more prominently, whichever will be most helpful. It is not possible for any buddha to be bereft of these five aspects. Vairocana Mahāhimasāgara[1240] has said:

> The peace body is clearly manifested as a wish-fulfilling tree.
> Like a wish-fulfilling jewel, it is free from conceptualization.
> Since it remains until all beings are liberated, it is called "permanent."
> This can be perceived by those free of preconceptions.

This quality appears only to a bodhisattva who has advanced to the tenth [232] bhūmi.

Q: To perceive a nirmāṇakāya buddha like Śākyamuni, one must have already achieved the path of accumulation. Does this entail that all those who saw the Buddha during his lifetime had already achieved the path of accumulation? Or was it the case that only those who perceived the Buddha after he passed into parinirvāṇa had achieved the path of accumulation?

A: There are two ways to perceive the Buddha: either based on the power of others or based on one's own power. As for seeing by means of the power of others, imagine if someone wished to see my emperor and then the emperor traveled to Ü-Tsang; such a person could see him with little effort. If such a person had eyes, they could see him. Similarly, it was unnecessary to have already achieved the path of accumulation to have perceived the Buddha during his lifetime. Even ordinary beings could have seen him. Seeing based upon one's own power thus means that one must go to see him, such as traveling a great distance and undertaking great hardship to see the emperor. Upon arriving, you can see him. Likewise, to see the face of the nirmāṇakāya after the Buddha had passed into parinirvāṇa, one must have already achieved the path of accumulation.

Q: It has happened that someone who achieved the path of accumulation then took rebirth in the lower realms. To be reborn in the lower realms, one must have accumulated powerful negative karma. To have achieved the path of accumulation, one must have accumulated powerful virtuous karma. For a being who has achieved the path of accumulation, is it that the negative karma for lower rebirth [233] already existed in their mental continuum [prior to their realization], or that they newly accumulated negative karma and became worse and worse?

A: In general, the majority of those who achieve the path of accumulation are never again reborn in the lower realms. It is possible, however, that some of them still retain unexhausted seeds of negative tendencies in their mindstreams. On that basis, they might newly accumulate negative karma, which then becomes a cause to take lower rebirth. The seed alone does not lead to lower rebirth. Without that seed, however, there is no basis for accumulating negative karma. As such, both must be present together.

Q: Well then, abandoning the Mahāyāna is considered a cause for taking lower rebirth. However, the traditions of both hearers and solitary realizers abandon the Mahāyāna. And yet, their practitioners are not reborn at all. How is this so?

A: To abandon the Mahāyāna and be reborn in the lower realms entails that one [first] understands that the Mahāyāna is the [true] Dharma, later develops negative emotions, then develops nonvirtuous afflicted emotions, then follows a nonvirtuous spiritual master, on that basis develops wrong views, and then completely abandons the entirety of the Mahāyāna teachings. In such a case, one will be reborn in the lower realms. Proponents of the traditions of the hearers and solitary realizers criticize the Mahāyāna tradition to strengthen and further establish their tenet system. Even in the Mahāyāna tradition, proponents of the Mind Only school[1241] criticize proponents of the Middle Way,[1242] for example, and vice versa. To stabilize and establish their own tradition, proponents of higher and lower schools criticize each other. But this does not entail rebirth in the lower realms. Hearers always accompany the Buddha [234] without being separated for even a moment. Such beings have listened to all the Buddha's Mahāyāna teachings without missing even a word. However, they only remember praise for their own school and its good qualities.

Q: In regard to the lama, is it best to first visualize him as the Buddha without any prior examination? Or is it better to first investigate whether it would be suitable to do so, and then to visualize him as the Buddha?

A: One who visualizes [the lama] as the Buddha without any prior investigation is known as a "faithful devotee" (*dad pa'i rjes 'brang*). This is not excellent. One needs wisdom derived from investigation. If one resides near a lama who knows the Tripiṭaka and is without bias, who is without any faults even when you look for them, then, even if you do not contemplate him as the Buddha, this mind [of devotion] will arise. And then, naturally, you will receive blessings and develop good qualities.

Q: Regarding developing good qualities, which among these two is most powerful: the blessings of the lama or the devotion of the disciple?

A: In terms of the common good qualities, sometimes the devotion of the disciple is more powerful. In terms of the supreme good qualities, the power of the lama, disciple, and instructions must all be gathered. For example, to make a fire, one needs a functioning fire stone, a fire iron, and tinder. Similarly, a lama who is not cut off from a continuous lineage of blessings, a disciple with the unmistaken auspicious arising of devotion, and instructions uncontaminated by invented words: if these three are gathered, then good qualities will arise [235] without effort. It is very difficult to gather those three together without committing any fault.

Q: Again, the abridged sūtras say:

> The buddhas of the past, future, and those now residing in
> the ten directions
> take the perfections as their path and nothing more.

And in *Reciting the Names of Mañjuśrī*:

> This mantra was spoken by the buddhas of the past
> and it will also be spoken by the buddhas of the future,
> just as it is spoken by the present perfect buddhas.

How might we determine the intended meaning of these two teachings?

A: These are explanations according to the various vehicles. According to the vehicle of the perfections [i.e., the Mahāyāna], all the buddhas of the three times achieved enlightenment based on their practice of the perfections. One thousand two buddhas will achieve enlightenment in this fortunate age. Other than Śākyamuni and Chungmopa,[1243] the other thousand buddhas were enlightened based on the perfections. [During their lifetimes,] even the sound of mantra was entirely unheard anywhere in the entire universe. They understood "entering the easy path" in reference to the perfections [and not secret mantra], and so they say, "...buddhas of the past, future..." and so on.

From the perspective of mantra, the perfections are considered the causal path, while mantra is considered the resultant path. The perfections have no more than ten bhūmis. In addition, it is said that in mantra one must traverse the three bhūmis of the vajra holder. Even a bodhisattva who has achieved the tenth bhūmi of the perfections still requires the empowerment of great light rays bestowed by the tathāgatas [236] of the ten directions. Until they receive that initiation, they will not actually realize the dharmakāya. As such, it is said that all buddhas of the past and future must rely upon mantra or, in other words, initiation. A great many textual sources describe this.

Alternatively, the aforementioned abridged sūtras say: "Their path is the perfections and no others..." Here, "no others" refers to the paths of the śrāvakas and pratyekabuddhas. There are a great many explanations of the six perfections. In the mantra vehicle, there are even careful word-by-word explanations given for "wisdom" (*shes rab*), "beyond" (*pha rol*), and "gone" (*phyin pa*). Therefore, textual sources are as malleable as stakes driven into the mud!

Now then, there are also a great many comparable explanations of the six perfections in the Mantrayāna. There are also many given in the divisions of the sūtras and [scriptures of the] Perfection [Vehicle]. Most commentaries—such as those by Maitreya, [Śāntideva's] *Compendium of Training* and *Introduction to the Bodhisattva's Way of Life*, the *Jātakas*, and so forth—exclusively describe the six perfections. What is the reason they are restricted to six [perfections] so definitively?

A: Compassion toward the stingy, compassion toward the pernicious, compassion toward the agitated, compassion toward the careless, compassion toward those distracted by the power of objects (*yul gyi gzhang dbang*), and compassion toward those attracted to wrong views. [I have compassion for] sentient beings have these six wrong views. The six perfections are antidotes for them. Additionally, sentient beings possess three faults (*skyon*) or errors (*nyes pa*). It is said that each fault requires as an antidote two of the perfections [which makes six]. The first fault is the mind being unable to renounce (*'phags pa*) saṃsāra. The second fault is even though one has renounced, one then turns back. The third is the fault of squandering (*chud 'dza' ba*), [237] even if there's no turning back. As for the first, being unable to renounce saṃsāra: this is due to attachment to one's outer material enjoyments. As an antidote to this, the perfection of generosity was taught. As an antidote to attachment to [enjoyments] within one's mind, the perfection of morality was taught.

Just so, the mind renounces and enters the Mahāyāna teaching. But upon hearing teachings that one must then give away one's head, which is the most important bodily limb and one's eyes, which are the most important of one's faculties, one may say, "I am unable to do this," and it is possible that one will turn away from the path. Patience was taught as an antidote to this. Hearing that one must accumulate merit over three countless eons, one might think, "I cannot possibly do this," and so it is possible one will turn back. As an antidote for this, effort was taught.

Even if they do not turn away, there are two kinds of squandering. As an antidote to squandering caused by a wandering mind, concentration was taught. As an antidote for the squandering caused by deficient wisdom, wisdom was taught.

Because of that, sentient beings have no more than six faults. And so, one does not need more than six perfections. It would be insufficient if there were any fewer, and so the definite number is six.

Q: On this point, we also come across passages describing the ten [perfections]. Why is this?

A: In these cases, [the perfection of] wisdom has been divided into four. These internal subdivisions, however, do not contradict the definite number [of six perfections].

Q: The Kadampa possess an oral tradition that holds there is no difference in the amount of time [required to achieve enlightenment] between the Mantra and Perfection Vehicles. If one practices scrupulously, moreover, the Perfection Vehicle is said to be the swifter path. Proof [238] for this claim comes from the story of the bodhisattva Ever-Weeping,[1244] who in just eight years realized the four paths. There is a tradition in the Mantra Vehicle that a disciple will achieve the realization of mahāmudrā within twelve years, should master and disciple meet auspiciously. Can you please explain this discrepancy?

A: Those Kadampas are making ignorant statements! The Mantra Vehicle offers certainly a shorter path than the Perfection Vehicle. According to the general Dharma teachings, the Perfection Vehicle provides what is considered the longer path. The maṇḍala is the easy path. Mantra is swifter. If one is an expert in its methods, the Mantra Vehicle offers the easier path.

"Maṇḍala" is the maṇḍala of the Mantra Vehicle. "Swifter" is the swifter Mantra Vehicle. As for the textual sources and reasons for this position, even if I had an eon I could not enumerate them in time!

The Mantra Vehicle describes the timeline [until enlightenment] for those of middling and lower capacities. As for those of the highest capacity, [practitioners of the Mantra Vehicle] achieve in a single moment what practitioners of the Perfection Vehicle achieve by practicing asceticism over the course of innumerable lifetimes.

> Practicing the perfections for a thousand eons
> and accumulating merit by giving away one's head, feet,
> legs, and so on,
> can be cut in an instant by means of this guru path.

For a practitioner of secret mantra of the highest capacity, nobody can measure the auspiciousness of the guru and disciple coming together. The bodhisattva Ever-Weeping had already achieved a great many qualities when he cut flesh from his thighs and broke his own bones. As such, we cannot measure beings just by words.

[By examining] the lineage of your Kadampa tradition, you will see that the father and son [Jowo Atiśa and Dromtönpa], along with their brothers who achieved the highest siddhi [239], were always bestowing initiations. The contemporary must follow the path of their elders. A unique feature of the followers of Buddhadharma is that results arise from similar causes. Nonetheless, a tradition has arisen and spreads today of those uninterested in the cause of receiving initiation, yet who practice generation and completion stage meditation and recite mantras. How has this come about?

If one is uninterested in receiving empowerments and practicing the Mantra Vehicle, there is another path for achieving enlightenment. One may produce aspirational and engaged bodhicitta, or practice the three trainings, or the six perfections, or the ten Dharma activities. On that basis, one may then gradually achieve enlightenment stage by stage. This is also a joyful path that is pleasant to embark upon. Furthermore, there are those who practice many rituals that depend on the Mantra Vehicle. If you are interested in such rituals, it is important that you receive empowerment! If you do not, then your behavior is simply contradictory.[1245] It is very important that the Buddha's teachings remain pure, unmistaken, and complete.

Moreover, some think that nowadays there are no qualified gurus or disciples, and so it is best not to bestow empowerments. But in the matter of bodhicitta, such persons bestow the bodhicitta vows even though it is very difficult to find qualified teachers and students [lit. "vessel and contents"]! Likewise, today it is difficult to find anyone with the defining characteristics of a qualified abbot and disciple according to the standards of the Śrāvakayāna, and it is likewise rare that a disciple may develop a truly renounced mind. And yet, they still bestow monastic ordination.

[Namkha Bum:] While continuing to pile up a great many scriptural citations and logical reasons, he gazed directly at me, wide-eyed and wrathful.

Q: On this point, [240] we find a few lines of mantra given in [Śāntideva's] *Compendium of Training*. [If I recite these,] am I committing the fault of revealing the Secret Mantra Vehicle?

A: Doing so does not constitute a fault. These are called the "dhāraṇī of the knowledge mantra." However, when you teach this text, you do not need to read this dhāraṇī aloud. Instead, you can explain its meaning.

Q: The *Lamp for the Path to Enlightenment*[1246] contains a phrase (*tshig*) that constitutes bestowing the secret wisdom empowerment (*gsang shes rab kyi dbang*). Does it count as committing the fault of disclosing secrets [if that word is read aloud]?

A: There is consensus among all previous masters of the Sakyapa that it does constitute such a fault. That said, [the phrase] is most likely a mistranslation or a misspelling. This is because the Jowo [Atiśa] was a mahāpaṇḍita of the Mantra Vehicle and so would never disclose this. It is forbidden for even the name "secret wisdom" to be heard by those without the empowerment. It is more appropriate to say that there is an empowerment that is unsuitable for those who follow a celibate discipline (*tshang par spyod pa*).

Q: On this point, it is my understanding that our Geshé Potowa taught many texts for which he never received transmission. Did he commit a downfall?

A: There are circumstances in which doing so does not commit a downfall, such as having no doubts in one's mind or even if one does have doubt, making requests to one's yidam or clarifying one's doubts in a dream. You should not say that because he taught without receiving transmission, this creates a bad example for others. Because it is the period of transmission, it is most important to rely upon them.

Q: Geshé Chekawa told [Geshé] Sharawa, "Enjoy whatever is translated into Tibetan." Does this qualify as a transmission?

A: That is known as an "approximate transmission" (*'jam lung*). It does not qualify as a transmission but is better than nothing. [241] "In this case," I [i.e., Namkha Bum] said, "I wish to receive such a transmission from you!" "You may do just as they did," he [i.e., Lama Phakpa] told me. But I replied, "Such permission is not enough. Please say to me, 'You may enjoy at your pleasure everything that is translated into Tibetan, such as sādhana and quintessential instructions and so on!'" He then said to me, "You may practice everything already translated into Tibetan, including sādhanas and quintessential instructions, other than what has been supplied by demons or transmitted by those with broken samaya commitments."

Q: Well then, before the buddhas were enlightened, when they were still sentient beings, they lived in different times and places and engaged in different practices. After their enlightenment, did they continue to abide separately, or did they come to abide united in a single dharmakāya?

A:

> The uncontaminated realm of the buddhas
> is like space, since it is bodyless.
> It will follow the previous body.
> The buddhas are neither individual nor manifold.

There are four possibilities here: the buddhas are neither individuals nor manifold, or else they are singular or manifold.

Q: Earlier Kadampa masters declared that the bodily remains of some deceased persons are suitable [for being inserted in a stūpa] and others are not. If it is suitable, they make *tsatsa*[1247] with the remains and pile them inside stūpas, and so forth. Nowadays, such things are done for whosoever has great attachment or wealth. Is there any appropriate measure for determining who is suitable for such practices and who is not?

A: Bones that have been purified by mantra and maṇḍala practice, which are later crushed up and mixed with earth, whose materials have been blessed, [242] and which are then made into tsatsa [are suitable]. If all the dhāraṇī are correct side up, they should be placed inside a stūpa with the tsatsa. There is great benefit in doing this, even if there are some small mistakes made. If one places only bones inside a stūpa vase or a copper stūpa, they must have belonged to someone who achieved a virtuous state. This can be explained in a great many ways. Nowadays, not knowing how to make these kinds of differentiations, the wealthy and those with attachment collect donations to build large supports [such as stūpas]. By doing so, they transform all offering places into charnel grounds! This attracts inauspicious ill omens everywhere in Tibet.

Q: Regarding dedicating merit on behalf of the dead and engaging in weekly funerary rituals, is there a way to determine who is qualified and who is unqualified to perform such rituals?

A: Whosoever engages in the weekly funerary rituals, consecrations, fire offerings, and the "collection of activity" rituals (*las tshogs*) must have already received empowerment. After having heard a tantra, one must then complete at least one close retreat in order to protect one's samaya. [Then one becomes qualified.]

Why is it that nowadays all the practices of the Kadampas and so forth are contradictory and mistaken? When dedicating [on behalf of the dead], rely upon someone with an unbroken lineage, pure ethics, and the motivation to benefit others. That said, if someone without all these qualities wants to do this, since it is prayer, there is likely still some kind of benefit. The most important thing is that they possess the mind of bodhicitta.

Q: Again, Geshé Tonglungpa[1248] once said that if we do funerary rituals for any of the lamas who are unqualified to receive a funerary ritual, we harm them, [243] and whosoever performs the ritual incurs a major fault. Can you explain this in more detail?

A: There are two kinds of offerings. One offering is made in order to request siddhi, the other made to accumulate merit. To perform a funerary ritual to request siddhi, that [deceased] lama must be highly qualified. When performing a funerary ritual in order to accumulate merit, it is not necessary that the [deceased] lama be highly qualified. Even if you are performing such a funeral for your father or mother, there is still benefit.

Q: [Nāgārjuna's] *Friendly Letter*[1249] says:

> The wise venerate images of the Sugata,
> regardless of the material, even those made from wood.

Can you provide a word-by-word commentary on [the meaning of] "Regardless of the material..."?

A: These words advise us not to look down upon any kind of support [such as images, statues, and so forth]. Specifically, this verse emphasizes the basest kind of material, [wood]. And so, the wise must worship images that are well made or not, of good quality or not, and which have been consecrated or not. These verses say explicitly that the wise must pay homage [to the Sugata's image], regardless. And they say implicitly that those who avoid doing so are to be left out of the ranks of the wise.

Q: On this point, it is said:

> If one makes prostrations and offerings to images
> that have not been consecrated, one receives no results.

Can you please explain?

A: This explanation was given for those with inferior minds. It is not the definitive meaning.

Q: Moving along, the six desire realm gods[1250] possess an obstructed physical form. Why is it that when they die, they do not leave a corpse?

A: On this point, these days if somebody has a very strong and vigorous human body but is beset by a terrible illness [244] for a year, then they will no longer possess even the smell of their previous body. They will feel like their stomach has been burned away on a stove. Similarly, for seven days, each god experiences the signs of impending death, and they are beset by terrible suffering. Their bodies then become insubstantial.

Q: Is there ever an end to saṃsāra?

A: Throughout history, about half of Dharma practitioners have claimed that there is an end to saṃsāra, while the other half has claimed that there is not. They have debated this topic until their tongues were exhausted. There are textual sources that support both positions. But in reality, there is no end.

Q: On this point, it is said that all sentient beings possess buddha nature.[1251] If that is true, can there be any doubt that they will all become enlightened? Additionally, no new sentient beings will appear, and in every moment every buddha and bodhisattva liberates countless beings from among those still caught in saṃsāra. And so there is no moment when some sentient being is not achieving enlightenment. If this is true, does it not appear that saṃsāra will one day end?

A: If it is true that sentient beings are of a limited number, then what you say is correct. If a single buddha can benefit a single sentient being, then there is no question that they will do so. "Just as the nature of the sky is limitlessness, so too is the number of sentient beings." This is a correct scriptural source.

Regarding this, I wish to tell you a story. Long ago, there was a great logician named Gangpa Sheu.[1252] He claimed that saṃsāra was unending, while some other logicians held that it would end. He stretched his arms wide and asked them, "Which is wider, the sky in front of me or the sky behind?" Those before him replied, "They are similar." He asked again, "Are they the same?" And they replied, "Yes, they are the same." He then jumped forward five or six steps and asked, "Is the sky now wider in front of me or behind?" No one had anything to say in response. He then said, "If you have a reason for the first claim, then why do you not accept that, as I take five steps forward, the sky behind me becomes bigger and in front of me becomes smaller?" With that, all the scholars were satisfied by his reasoning. Moreover, imagine that the three-thousand-fold world system was filled with sesame seeds and that a mighty person filled up the bottom fold of his *chupa*[1253] with all those sesame seeds. Imagine, further, that he then began walking across all the world and dropped a sesame seed from his chupa down upon the ground with each step. He would exhaust his sesame seeds before filling even just the easterly expanse of even a relatively small world system. Doing more would be inconceivable. The same outcome would be true of doing this in any other direction.

[Lama Phakpa] then said that the deeds of the tathāgatas are without end. And so, if sentient beings in saṃsāra are with end, then that would entail that the deeds of the tathāgatas would end. Since their deeds are unending, in general saṃsāra is without end.

Q: Who was the actual guru of Master Śāntideva, and who were his actual disciples? [246]

A: Master Śāntideva did not have an ordinary guru. Mañjuśrī taught him the Dharma in his dreams. With devotion, [Śāntideva] made requests, and Mañjuśrī appeared and taught him the Dharma. As such, Mañjuśrī was his guru. Later, he relied upon the teaching of the Buddha while meditating and composed the *Compendium of Training*. As a commentary to that, he taught the *Introduction to the Bodhisattva's Way of Life* in a single breath. [Those in attendance heard] three versions of the *Introduction to the Bodhisattva's Way of Life*: one in seven hundred verses, one in a thousand verses, and one in fourteen hundred verses. When he was later asked, Śāntideva confirmed that the version in one thousand verses is the correct one. They then asked, "Where is the *Compendium of Training*?" He replied, "In my monk's cell, I wrote it out on long sheafs of paper," but he did not give them a more elaborate title for this text. In summary, these two texts are like the actual teaching of Mañjuśrī. Because Master [Śāntideva] possessed supreme bodhicitta, he greatly benefited sentient beings and his teachings widely spread. Lord of Dharma [Sakya Paṇḍita] greatly revered these texts.

Q: To which of the three sections of the Tripiṭaka [247] does secret mantra belong?

A: Secret mantra completes the final taming of the minds of sentient beings, and so it is included in the Vinaya. Since every tantra and quintessential instruction reveals methods for realization, they may also be counted among the Abhidharma. In the tantras, one finds statements like "If one listens to this sūtra...," and so they may also be counted among the Sūtrapiṭaka.

Smiling, [Lama Phakpa explained that] because secret mantra is the highest of the vehicles, there is a competition to count them among each three of the piṭakas! However, it was the Lord of Dharma's position that they be included in the Sūtrapiṭaka.

Q: How are we to distinguish between the old and new tantras?

A: By the period in which they were translated.

Q: How are we to translate the six-syllable [mantra] into Tibetan?

A: *Oṃ* means body. *Maṇi* means method. *Padme* means wisdom. *Hūṃ* means mind. And so, the mantra means: "Body, method, wisdom, and mind."

Q: How many years have passed since the Buddha's mahāparinirvāṇa?[1254]

A: Under [Lama Phakpa's] cushion was a small yak-hair blanket, which he raised to scratch some calculations into the earth. He then said, "Three thousand four hundred years have passed."

Q: How many years have passed since the Jowo Śākyamuni statue came to Tibet? How long will it remain? When it departs, where will it go? How exactly will it depart?

A: It will travel to the land of the nāgas. Its manner of travel will be by water. As for the year when this occurs, I will give it to you privately.

At this point, I [Namkha Buṁ] went outside and filtered some water. Then I returned inside. Observing me, [Lama Phakpa] inquired, "Your body appears a little stooped. Is this due to some illness? Or have you remained bedridden for a long time?" I replied, "I have never been sick, but because I was in retreat for so long, I am now unable to stand up straight." Lama Phakpa asked, "Before I met you, I imagined that your face would be suntanned with white hair. But when I met you, I discovered that both your face and hair were white. And you? Did your image of me match [248] my appearance?" I replied, "You are more striking and resplendent than I imagined!"

He then asked me, "Have you ever served as an abbot or a master?" I replied, "I could have taken on these roles, but previous masters of my [tradition] never did, and so I never had the experience of doing so myself. I do not know why the previous Kadampa masters never served as abbots or masters, but for some reason they never did." Then Lama suggested a few reasons why they may have never served in those roles.

Then he asked me, "What virtuous Dharma practices have you committed yourself to in long retreat?" I replied:

Rising early in the morning,
I go for refuge and generate the mind of enlightenment.

Then I engage in the correctly ordered sequence of practice,
sealed by preliminaries, then the main practice and
conclusion.
These are my activities during the day and the night.

To purify the faults of my body,
I make two hundred prostrations and circumambulations.

To purify the faults of my speech,
I first focus on the practice of confession (*ltung bshags*)
and then do fourteen recitations of the long dhāraṇī of Amoghapāśa,[1255]
recite the dhāraṇī of Palden Ngensong,[1256]
do twenty-one recitations of the *Immaculate Essence*,[1257]
and recite *Reciting the Names of Mañjuśrī* and five other sūtras.
I then recite the *Essence of the Tathāgata*[1258]
and one hundred recitations each
of the [mantras of the] Dharma protectors and four special deities.
I again go for refuge to purify all additions and omissions.

To purify my mind,
I do all this motivated by bodhicitta.
I perform all actions without attachment, seeing all perceptions as illusory.
I engage in the practice of the stages of the path
without missing a session.
I read sūtras, tantras, and commentaries,
and between sessions I make torma offerings.
In general, the periodic and daily torma offerings
purify faults of the body, speech, and mind. [249]
I also engage in minor practices that I need not mention here,
such as the seven-limbed prayer and so forth.
Each evening, to purify any additions, omissions, or mistakes,
I recite the one-hundred-syllable mantra [of Vajrasattva].
I spend my days and nights,
months and years in this way.
I am committed to this
until I draw my last breath.

[Lama Phakpa said,] "Jampel Serpo [i.e., Jamser], most of our lives are now behind us and we have not accomplished this much! Write down all that he has said!" Then he asked, "What can you tell me about Langri Thangpa's[1259] *Eight Verses of Thought Transformation*?"[1260] I carefully recited these eight verses to him from memory and [Phakpa] exclaimed, "That is wonderful! Write those down!"

[Phakpa] then asked, "Please tell me more about the stages of the path practiced by you Kadampas. What is its textual basis?" I replied, "Our Kadampa stages of the path illuminates the freedoms and endowments, so difficult to find; death and impermanence; karmic cause and result; the shortfalls of saṃsāra; love and compassion; the two aspects of selflessness; and the dharmakāya together with its enlightened activity. Because this is the sleeping site for the youthful ox,[1261] whoever teaches it to you must be considered your root guru. To clarify the view, we rely upon the *Short Truth of the Middle Way*.[1262] To clarify meditation, we rely upon the *Quintessential Instructions on the Middle Way*.[1263] To clarify conduct, we rely upon the *Lamp for the Path to Enlightenment*. These three texts thus support the stages of the path." "Your [lineage] is wonderful!" Lama Phakpa exclaimed. "I once asked Rinchen Gangpa[1264] about the textual foundation of this stages of the path, [250] but he only referenced some texts in general. I also asked Chilphuwa,[1265] and he told me it was organized around the beings of three capacities." Like this, [Lama Phakpa] had much to say on [the stages of the path].

Q: I also asked him, "Lama, when did your Khön ancestor Lui Wangpo Sungpa live? During which king's reign?"

A: Among the nine translators of King Trisong Detsen, he was the most knowledgeable. [That king] was an emanation of Mañjuśrī, and [Lui Wangpo Sungpa] lived at the same time.

Q: How many generations have passed from his time to ours?

A: [Lama Phakpa] told me about fifteen or sixteen have passed.

Q: On this topic, there is a letter that says that after the Lord of Dharma [Sakya Paṇḍita] passed away, he would take rebirth as the son of King Nyimai Tophel in Mumuné[1266] in eastern India. Did the Lord of Dharma ever talk about this with you?

A: Firstly, he never said this to me. He reported this to his physician, Biji. I later asked him about it, and he admitted that it was true. He planned to first take a few other rebirths over several years [before being reborn as the son of King Nyimai Tophel]. A few years have now passed since he took that rebirth.

Q: In general, some come to know about the lama's good qualities from receiving many teachings, investigating the meaning of all their words, and then realizing their meaning. Others become familiar with the lama's good qualities by spending a long period of time together and coming to understand his behavior. I have no opportunity to receive many teachings from you, nor to spend a long time together. [251] Please, reveal your good qualities to me!

A: Smiling, Lama said: "What kind of good qualities do I have? My good qualities are that wherever I reside, I accumulate great wealth due to practicing generosity in my previous lives. As a result of protecting my moral discipline in previous lives, I have acquired a pure human body. As a result of practicing patience, I have a fine and handsome body. Moreover, because of the virtue from practicing the remaining [perfections...]" and so forth.

Then, Chögyal revealed many more extraordinary stories about his life. Whatever he taught, such as detailed or condensed teachings on the common vehicle or the profound and vast uncommon vehicle, it appeared that he had studied it by himself but that he could give elaborate teachings upon its meaning! The Tripiṭaka holder lord of Dharma was himself wearing a Dharma robe, which he took off and gave to me. "This will help you accomplish guru yoga," he told me.

When I recall our discussions,
my body hair stands on end.
When I behold the Dharma robe you gave me,
tears fall from my eyes.

Whosoever makes a connection by seeing or hearing your
teachings,
their life then becomes meaningful,
in lifetime after lifetime;
so be joyful that this is the result!

When I and the others who rely upon you
commit the fault of displeasing you,
like smoke from an extinguished fire,
may it become clear like the sky! [252]

By the virtue that sticks to us like dew
from your ocean-like qualities,
may I and the six types of sentient beings
be born at the feet of the lama!

In your presence, may we then please you
and completely learn your holy life story.
Then, may we liberate all beings of the three realms
who are as yet without a refuge or protector!

This written record of these questions and answers was roughly recorded by Namkha Bum, a fully ordained monk and follower of Śākyamuni, when he was sixty-one years old. During the Sheep Year of the King of the Dharma, who was then thirty-one years old, which according to the Sakya astrological system was the Female Fire Rabbit Year, he arrived in Dam in the evening of the fifteenth day of the Mindruk month.

I met him in the evening of the sixteenth. Over the course of seven evenings, I put the above questions to him and received from him principally bodhicitta vows, teachings on guru yoga, and so forth, as well as other unthinkable Dharma teachings such as on various sādhanas. Whatever teaching I could name, he taught me. In the early morning of the twenty-sixth, we departed together. In the evening of the thirtieth, I returned to Chekar. On the first day of the Go month, I wrote this text so that I would remember all I heard from him.

Moreover, as it says in the biography of Ārya Maṇibhadra, by always contemplating the virtues of the spiritual master one accomplishes all benefits. Further, it is recorded in the *Perfection of Wisdom Sūtra [in Eight Thousand Lines]* that once the bodhisattva Ever-Weeping had met his guru Dharmodgata,[1267] he constantly recalled him and the teachings of the perfections. From this, all good qualities of the path arose in his mind. It is also said in Potowa's [253] *Instructions* that the root of all quintessential instructions is never to become separated from one's spiritual master. One should be devoted to him, for he is a treasury from which one will acquire all good qualities, such as bodhicitta and so forth.

In summary, I have heard many reasons proving that all mundane and supramundane good qualities arise from relying upon the spiritual master. With these in mind, I have composed this text. May this remain unseen by those who are unsuitable vessels! Though it should remain hidden, if it is then revealed to those who are critical, may their nonvirtue ripen upon me! For those who read these words and develop devotion, may their virtue ripen upon them! This text is thus sealed and should never be shown to just anyone.

Since you possess no faults and have completed all good qualities, I and other spiritual masters take refuge in you.

Should I explain the senses in which you possess every
good quality,

My words would not penetrate the ears of most peoples in
the slightest.
For this reason, I shall keep quiet.
It is better that I put these words down secretly as prayer.

The above was composed by the lord of Dharma, the Kadampa Namkha Bum. This concludes the second section of the life story of the king of Dharma [Lama Phakpa].

To review, the great emperor [Qubilai Qaγan] urgently summoned the mahātmā glorious Phakpa using a golden letter. With compassionate eyes for the uncountable sentient beings of the eastern direction, [254] [Lama Phakpa] once again departed for Mongolia. Along the way, he met the spiritual master Namkha Bum. They held a great many Dharma discussions. This great Kadampa spiritual friend discerned that this lama's holy activities were no different than a bodhisattva realized in the higher bhūmis. He developed very stable devotion to him. He then received many vast and profound teachings from him, such as on bodhicitta and so forth. This great Kadampa master later composed the marvelous, liberated life story of this mahātmā [included above].

During the rest of his journey to meet the emperor, this lama similarly ripened countless other fortunate disciples. He traveled in stages to the imperial court [255] of the lord of the earth [Qubilai Qaγan], located more than a hundred *yojana* from Tibet. He did so by undertaking very difficult travel, having to cross many rivers, valleys, mountain ranges, bridges, and narrow footpaths (*'phrang*). Upon his arrival at the court, the mahātmā was encircled by a vast retinue of disciples like a sun enclosed by a halo of light, or like the cooling moon encircled by a constellation of stars, or like a tathāgata surrounded by an assembly of hearers.

Chögyal Phakpa's is the liberated life story of a bodhisattva. It is exactly as described by the Bhagavan, who once said in a sūtra that a bodhisattva would travel a hundred *yojana* to teach the holy Dharma to sentient beings. When [Lama Phakpa] arrived [at Qubilai's court], the principal holy heir of the great emperor named Čingkim,[1268] along with the emperor's consort and a group of ministers, welcomed him with many great offerings, such as a throne adorned with Indian elephants and a jewel net, along with offering banners and the sounds of many musical instruments. After they invited him into the great imperial palace, he bestowed many vast and profound teachings upon them. He clarified the Buddha's teachings like rays of moonlight striking a grove of *kumudu* lotuses.[1269]

A year after [Phakpa's] departure [for the Mongol court], the distinguished minister Shākya Sangpo[1270] laid the foundations for the great temple [at Sakya]. All the thirteen myriarchies were encouraged to support that building project. In coordination with the great minister Kunga Sangpo,[1271] the construction was completed. They additionally built Rinchen Labrang, Lhakhang Labrang, and Düchö Labrang.[1272]

That great lama then arrived at court. In the Male Iron Horse Year (1270), when he was thirty-six years old, the emperor once again received empowerment. In thanks, the emperor offered him the Lingdruk Crystal Seal,[1273] which was a modification of the Tangut king Gyagö's[1274] crystal seal, as well as a special edict [256] that bestowed upon Phakpa the official title "Son of the Indian Gods under the Sky and above the Earth, Buddha's Emanation, Script Creator, Pacifier of the Kingdom, Paṇḍita of the Five Kinds of Knowledge, the Noble Imperial Preceptor."[1275] As material offerings of thanks, [Qubilai] offered one thousand large *dré* measures of silver, 59,000 silk brocades, and so forth. Whenever they held an audience together, [the emperor] made prostrations, made a scarf offering, always offered one *dré* measure of silver, and so forth. When taken all together, the emperor's offerings famously amounted to more than a hundred *dré* measures of gold, about one thousand *dré* measures of silver, many thousands of silk brocades, and so forth.

In these ways, Lama Phakpa set all Mongolian people upon the path of the Mahāyāna. Like the sun, he greatly illuminated the jewel-like teaching of the Tathāgata. He again promised to return to Tibet and began to prepare for the journey. He informed the emperor and his entourage that he would soon depart. The emperor, Lord of Men, was worried that Lama Phakpa would soon depart [this life] to benefit sentient beings, and that there were signs that the object of offering [Phakpa] and patron [Qubilai] would never again see each other. As such, they both resisted separating. [Lama Phakpa's departure] was thus delayed from days to months, and from months to years.

They traveled together to a Tibetan region in the foothills of Magura[1276] near Mount Bomra Lha[1277] in the vicinity of the Machu River.[1278] Like the sun and the moon, [257] the object of offering and patron resided there a while in each other's company. The imperial retinue of four army divisions and over a hundred thousand civilian servants offered cloud-like material offerings that covered the earth like summer pasture. They greatly venerated the object of offering and patron.

At that time, the entire sky and earth were pervaded by wondrous signs. From east and west, a cloud appeared in the shape of a great elephant's tusk. Upon this cloud appeared Venerable Lord of Yogins Virūpa and Lord Great Sakyapa Kunga Nyingpo, surrounded by Indian and Tibetan lineage gurus, buddhas, and bodhisattvas. All those fortunate beings gathered there actually witnessed this. Innumerable other magical manifestations then appeared in one billion worlds to benefit sentient beings.

In summary, relying upon the blessings of the body, speech, and mind of the refuge of beings, Chögyal Phakpa Lodrö Gyaltsen Palsangpo, most of the Mongolian emperor's subjects thoroughly established the foundation of virtue in their mindstreams by developing pure aspirations and the three-fold faith in the Dharma. They thus planted the seeds to soon achieve unsurpassable liberation.

This mahātmā then established all beings of China and Mongolia upon the path to liberation. After that, he once again compassionately beheld the sentient beings of the Land of Snows. [258] With loving-kindness, he gradually made his return to the Great Seat [of Sakya] with his entourage of disciples. Upon the path, many beings of the human and nonhuman realms offered him unthinkable forms of welcome, accompaniment, offerings, and respect. They built bridges for him to use to cross dangerous rivers. The body hair of whosoever saw or heard him stood on end and tears fell from their eyes. Many inconceivable, marvelous signs also appeared. He ripened and liberated each of them by extensively teaching the holy Dharma according to their individual interest, realm, and latent tendencies. In the Mouse Year, when he was forty-one years old, he arrived at the Great Seat.

Immediately upon his arrival, the spiritual masters of Ü and Tsang who were interested in the holy Dharma and the great lords of men upon the earth [i.e., regional rulers and nobility] all gathered. Additionally, those who had heard of his fame along with paṇḍitas from the Land of Noble Ones [India] and Kāśmīra also congregated. They all offered whatever they could and paid homage. With strong devotion, they requested [Lama Phakpa] to teach the holy Dharma. This mahātmā told them, "Nowadays, I hold every sūtra and tantra doctrine known in Tibet, whether large or small. As such, please request me to teach upon whatever Dharma topic is of interest [259] to you!" He subsequently bestowed countless individual teachings on the vast and profound Dharma, [for the breadth] of which we lack an illustrative example. He additionally bequeathed extensive material gifts. [Lama Phakpa] spent his nights and days in such activity at the Great Seat. He set many sentient beings upon the path to ripening and liberation.

After that, in the first month of spring (*dpyid zla ra ba*) of the Female Fire Ox Year (1277), emperor Čingkim[1279] sponsored [Lama Phakpa] to extensively turn the wheel of the Dharma at Chumik Ringmo[1280] in Tsang. At that time, the mahātmā offered sumptuous food to some 70,000 monks. He offered each monk one *zho* of gold and woolen cloth. He extensively turned the wheel of the vast and profound Dharma. Some 100,000 beings gathered there, including 70,000 monks, many thousands of spiritual friends who were exponents of various textual traditions, and many ordinary beings. He bestowed upon them the vows of supreme Mahāyāna bodhicitta, the great path over which all previous buddhas have passed. In this way, it became certain that they would all ripen the experience of unsurpassed enlightenment.

At the conclusion of a chronology of the teachings (*bstan pa'i rtsis*) that he had written, it says: "I, the fully ordained monk and vajra volder Phakpa, bestowed the vows of supreme bodhicitta upon a gathering that, including ordinary beings, amounted to some 100,000 people. On that day, I also wrote this chronology." Like this, [260] the mahātmā turned the wheel of the Dharma for fourteen days. A few days into the teachings, there arose a great wind that blew away all dust and dirt. A rain then began to fall so fiercely that it was impossible to know whether it was a rain of flowers or of ordinary water. The ground became shiny and unblemished. Everyone smelled a fragrant odor unlike anything they had previously experienced. In the early morning, rainbows appeared in the sky. Sometimes these had two circles, and other times three, four, or five circles.

They also witnessed many offering substances in the sky. Inside the tent, the buddhas of the ten directions along with bodhisattvas appeared emitting light. They remained there, filling up the sky. This was witnessed by all those who had purified their negative karma, principally eleven tutors (*yongs 'dzin*) with pure vision, Chancellor Yöntri[1281] and twelve other chancellors,[1282] and several others. At the same time, a variety of actual offerings appeared above the courtyard of Chumik. A brocade imprinted by feet, head, and hands was laid out for Phakpa. He prostrated while making clouds of mentally generated offerings, just like Samantabhadra. He then made requests to the buddhas of the ten directions.

A few days later, in the evening after the sun had set, the great lama [261] was in his inestimable mansion while the twelve chancellors and other fortunate beings sat nearby. They smelled a *sur* offering (*gsur*), but it was unlike anything they had smelled before. It became stronger, and the chancellors were no longer able to bear it. They began to vomit everywhere. Yöntri asked [Lama Phakpa] "What is this?" "Eighteen *vidhyādhara* knowledge-holders[1283]have arrived in the sky," he replied; "the ḍākas and ḍākinīs who remain in their primary abodes and those abiding in dispersed areas (*gnas dang yul*) have made offerings to them. It is smoke from human fat burning in the eight charnel grounds. It is certainly true that the faculties of you ordinary beings are unable to bear it!" From a kapāla containing the inner offering, [Phakpa] then took drops of nectar and placed them upon their tongues. From that, they developed a supremely clear awareness.

At that time, in the sky appeared principally Nāgārjuna and the Lord of Yogins [Virūpa] to the right and the eighteen knowledge-holders, such as Padmavajra, to the left, surrounded by an assembly of ḍākas and ḍākinīs. They placed their hands upon Phakpa Rinpoché and they clearly revealed instructions, prophecy, supreme investment (*mchog tu mnga' gsol ba*), and the announcement of auspiciousness.

On the fourteenth day of teaching the Dharma, Lama Phakpa explained the benefit of making offerings and reciting words that dedicate the roots of virtue. Early in the morning, the sky and earth were everywhere pervaded by amazing signs. [262] In general, it is well known that while the king of the Dharma resided there, rainbows and rain of flowers would regularly appear.

As I have described already, while that lord of scholars named Chom[den] Ral[dri] resided at Narthang, he was under the power of scholarly pride. As such, he did not at first come to see the lord of Dharma. On the fourteenth day [of Lama Phakpa's teachings], that incomparable scholar thought to himself, "That Phakpa has assembled all the gods and humans of the three realms. If I were to allow him to depart without first examining him, I would be guilty of ignorance. I must therefore go and investigate." On that very day, he changed his clothes and set off.

Chomden Raldri waited to depart until most of the assembly had already been seated. Along the way, while passing through a valley between two mountains southwest of Narthang, he heard some chatter. Upon investigation, he discovered sixteen *sthavira*-elders in a cave wearing tattered Dharma robes. He thought to himself, "This Phakpa is utterly unlike any other master. Elders such as these journey from far away to see him!" With these thoughts, he arrived in Chumik. [He beheld] that the Lama King of the Dharma sat in the center of an ocean of laity and ordained Saṅgha. His body was radiant with the major and minor marks. [263] His speech thunderously proclaimed the vast and profound Dharma combining unborn sound and emptiness. His mind remained fixed in stabilizing meditation upon the union bliss and emptiness.

Seeing this, his mind became absorbed entirely upon Phakpa. He was unable to focus on any other activity. Soon after, the King of Dharma extensively explained the benefits of offering and of dedicating the roots of virtue. Phakpa later sat upon the rooftop of the temple. An ocean-like assembly sat [below him] in their individual seats. At that time, Chomden Raldri detected an excellent aroma unlike anything he had experienced before. He peaked through the curtain onto the Chinese roof were Phakpa Rinpoché was seated. Inside the celestial mansion, he saw that there were sixteen cushions of variegated colors and five layers, as well as immeasurable offering substances. He then remembered the arhats he had earlier encountered in the mountain valley. He thought regretfully, "I have previously been under the power of a rigid mind. I have now come here to investigate." Thinking this way, the tremendous smell grew stronger. He could then perceive the sixteen arhats sitting upon the cushions making the seven-limb offering. Beset by regret, he offered countless prostrations and confessions.

His [265] mind was then made peaceful and gentle. He later composed verses of great devotion to the Lama King of Dharma, entitled *Dragon Thunder of Brahmā*.[1284] Later, the great emperor Lord of Men [Qubilai] invested Chomden Raldri with the title "mahāpaṇḍita" and offered him many gifts, which were sent along to the Great Seat. Additionally, it is well known that the master Bingbing Kausi[1285] and his attendants then transferred those offerings to Narthang.

[Phakpa] thus showed such unthinkable magical displays. Furthermore, at Gang in Dokham,[1286] he produced 115 volumes [written in] golden [ink]. At Tagthok Shimoché,[1287] he sponsored the printing of many sūtras, of which fourteen were done in gold. Moreover, at the Great Seat [of Sakya], he built the golden Gomang [Stūpa][1288] as an inner support for the Lord of Dharma [Sapaṇ]. He also installed a great golden roof on the temple where this stūpa was installed.

In summary, whatever donations he received, even those the size of a sesame seed, he never used toward his own interest. He used them instead to make offerings to the Triple Gem and to give to the poverty-stricken, offering them whatever they wished for. As a result of this, he came to possess unthinkable wealth. In all, he principally produced six complete Kangyurs, out of which about 2,157 volumes were printed with gold ink, along with many other countless imprints of scripture. Of all the material offerings he received, famously it was the emperor Qubilai who principally offered him about two thousand [266] great *dré* measures of silver. In summary, it is well known that he received unthinkable offerings.

In addition, he benefited many sentient beings by preserving the training in ethical discipline. In total, he acted as abbot for 1,425 bhikṣu, bhikṣunī, śrāmaṇera, and śrāmaṇerikā ordination ceremonies.[1289] Additionally, in a single year his personal disciple, Dülzin Chökyi Gönpo,[1290] acted as abbot for some 947 ordination ceremonies for fully ordained and novice Chinese monks and nuns. With their ordination lineage, they increased the number of novices in every direction.

Furthermore, he also [emphasized] the good qualities of training in concentration. Though he outwardly engaged continuously in scholarly activity, inwardly he never wavered for even a moment from single-pointed concentration. As such, he beheld the face of his yidam meditation deity, abided continuously in clear light, and so on. He was thus endowed with unthinkable good qualities, such as unobstructed clairvoyance, and so on. Furthermore, when he went to the town of Kyirong to visit the Jowo statue there, he dreamed that he beheld the face of Avalokiteśvara, who then praised him.

Furthermore, when the Lord of Dharma [Sapaṇ] was traveling to the land of the Mongols, his party encountered Jé Yangönpa,[1291] one of [Sapaṇ's] direct students. He said, "Now the Lama departs for Mongolia ... We, your disciples, need a representative who is qualified to receive our prostrations, veneration, [267] and devotion. Is your nephew suitable?" The Lord of Dharma replied, "Yes, he is." Lama Phakpa was then sleeping upon a soft cushion off to the side, though with his eyes open. Gesturing to him, the Lord of Dharma said, "That is a sign of someone who can recognize clear light. In general, everyone among my pure family lineage can recognize clear light to some degree."

On another occasion, the Indian paṇḍita Gotambhidra had a dream one evening. Due to his clairvoyance, the mahātmā [Phakpa] observed the dream. In the morning, he recounted the dream exactly for the paṇḍita. The paṇḍita was amazed. He exclaimed, "Incredible! This mahāguru has clairvoyance!" and became very devoted. These events are well known.

Moreover, once while Lama was journeying to see the emperor, he stayed over at Uyuk.[1292] A tax collection was then underway in this region. A *joden* official[1293] from Shangtabu[1294] went to report [to Lama Phakpa]. He saw that surrounding [Phakpa's] tent were many Mongols harming sentient beings. [Inside,] he saw Lama [Phakpa] sitting upon a throne (*'ja' li*). To his right was a scribe who made a record of whatever [texts] the lama composed. To his left was a clerk (*'dri mkhan*) who recorded any of his edicts. Before him was an arrangement of daily tormas and water offerings. The joden thought to himself, "What kind of lama is this? He is surrounded by Mongols harming sentient beings. To his left he issues edicts [268] that order others around, just as I do! To his right he composes texts through his scribe, for what? He does not hold the Dharma in his mind! And why is he offering tormas without offering a single word of dedication? This is no lama!" [As he thought this,] the mahātmā was staring directly at the joden. He then said, "If there is merit to be gained by preparing tormas, it will go to the person who arranged them. If there is merit to be gained by the practice of visualization, I will keep it. If there is merit to be gained by dedication, I will give it to you!"

The joden became utterly terrified and thought to himself, "This lama possesses unobstructed clairvoyance, and I have had wicked thoughts that are critical of him. This is terrible!" With this in mind, he made full body prostrations to the lama, made confessions, and became truly astounded [by Lama Phakpa]. He later widely offered words of praise [to Lama Phakpa], wherever he went. He understood that the lama's conduct was to tame beings according to their need. He developed extraordinary certainty that it was due to an individual's karma if they were killed or wounded, taxed (*khral 'u lag*), pressed into compulsory service, and so forth.

For these and many other reasons, it is widely known among the realized that [Lama Phakpa] possessed a capacious form of clairvoyance. That is why that holy being possessed such great qualities, such as an expansive vision, being unhindered in his activities, composing commentaries, and so on. His biography is thus like those of previous great masters like Āryā Nāgārjuna. [269] He composed eloquent texts to benefit beings directly and indirectly. The lines of these works are easy to read, and their meaning clear. He also penned innumerable letters and instructions.

As for the texts he composed on praise and requests, these include: *Requests to the Lamdré Lineage Gurus;*[1295] *Requests to the Tantric Lineage Gurus;*[1296] *Requests to the [Vajra]bhairava Lineage Gurus;*[1297] *Requests to the Lineage of Bari [Lotsāwa];*[1298] *The Hundred Thousand Names of Lamas;*[1299] *Large and Small Compositions on Holy Bodily Conduct;*[1300] *A Flower Garland: A General Praise to Lamas;*[1301] *Great Wisdom: Requests to the Lord of Dharma;*[1302] yet another *Praises and Requests to the Lord of Dharma;*[1303] *Praise to the Lama Composed at Wutaishan;*[1304] once again, *An Ocean of Songs of Praise; Praise to the Lord of Dharma;*[1305] *Praise to the King of the Śākyas;*[1306] *Praise to Mañjuśrī Based upon the Meaning of His Names;*[1307] *Praise to Wutaishan;*[1308] *Praise to "Wheel of the Teachings";*[1309] again, *Two Praises to Mañjuśrī;*[1310] *Praise to Avalokiteśvara;*[1311] *Praise to Maitreya;*[1312] *Praise to the Sixteen Arhats;*[1313] *Praise to the Triple Gem;*[1314] *Praise to the Eight Supreme [Bodhisattvas];*[1315] *Praise to the Fifteen Nairātmyā Goddesses;*[1316] *Praise and Exhortation of the Ten Wrathful*

Deities;[1317] *Praise to the Maṇḍala of [Cakra]saṃvara;*[1318] *Praise to Amitāyus;*[1319] *Praise to Parnashabarī;*[1320] *Praise to the [Goddess] Endowed with Light Rays;*[1321] *Praise to Kāmadeva;*[1322] *Praise to the Deities of the Five Protectors;*[1323] *Praise to the Deities of the Protectors' Maṇḍalas;*[1324] [269] *Praise of Acalā;*[1325] *Praise of [Mahākāla] Panjarnata and Chamdrel;*[1326] *Praise of Four-Faced [Mahākāla];*[1327] yet another *Garland of Flowers: Praise of the Lama;*[1328] *Garland of Lineages;*[1329] *Word Commentary on the Prayer of Uncommon Requests;*[1330] and *Requests to the Lamas of the Ten Directions and Three Times.*[1331]

As for texts he composed on the uncommon quintessential instructions, these include: *Guru Yoga;*[1332] *Maṇḍala Offering Rituals to the Lama;*[1333] *Textual Commentary on Lamdré;*[1334] *Some Words about Phowa;*[1335] *Commentary on the Three Purities;*[1336] *The Five Stages of the Ghaṇṭāpa [Tradition];*[1337] *The Meaning of Meditation upon Amitābha;*[1338] *Illuminating the Profound;*[1339] *Quintessential Instructions for Meditating upon Mahāmudrā;*[1340] and *The Seven-Branch Mahāmudrā.*[1341]

As for the texts he composed on the topic of unexcelled yoga tantra, these include: *The Condensed Meaning of the Hevajra [Tantra];*[1342] *Dak chung;*[1343] *Jön chung;*[1344] *Annotated Commentary on the Two-Part Hevajra Tantra;*[1345] *Chapter-by-Chapter Commentary on the [Vajra] Tent [Tantra];*[1346] *Outline of the Sambhūta;*[1347] *Vajrasattva Meditation and Recitation;*[1348] *The Wish-Fulfilling Jewel: Solitary Hero Together with Protection Circle;*[1349] *The Six-Limbed One;*[1350] *The Self-Initiation of Jimgyima and Paljungma;*[1351] *A Catalogue of Empowerments that Rely on Self-Initiation;*[1352] *The Empowerment for the Time of the Path;*[1353] *Words on the Three Foremost Ones;*[1354] *Body Maṇḍala;*[1355] *Nectar Vase: Gaṇacakra Feast Gathering [Ritual];*[1356] *Consecration; Gaṇacakra Feast Gathering [Ritual] Composed for the Benefit of Lashü;*[1357] *Sādhana for Nectar Pills;*[1358] *Sādhana of Nairātmyā;*[1359] and *Sādhana of the Heart Wheel of Kālacakra.*[1360]

As for his compositions on Cakrasaṃvara, these include: in the Kṛṣṇācārya[1361] tradition, a summary of initiations, a self-initiation, [270] a sādhana, the *Garland of Offerings,*[1362] a summary of fire offerings, and [the ritual for] fire offering; in the Luīpa tradition, *The Sādhana Clarifying the Stages,*[1363] yet another single sādhana, *The Stages of Method: The Thirteenth Accumulation of Merit,*[1364] *[A Ritual for the] Sixteen Wisdom Consorts,*[1365] and *Exhortations to the Ten Messenger [Ḍākinīs];*[1366] and in the Ghaṇṭāpa tradition, the *Clear Realization,*[1367] a self-initiation, *Sādhana of the Five*

Deities,[1368] *The Coemergence of the Tenth Yoga,*[1369] *Composition for the Benefit of Prince Pakchu,*[1370] *Fire Pūja for the Cannibal Demoness Vajraḍākinī,*[1371] and *The Auspiciousness of Cakrasaṃvara.*[1372]

On the subject of [Vajra]yoginī, [he composed] *Visualization of Vajravārāhī Abhibhava,*[1373] *Major and Minor Sādhanas of Nāropa's Ḍākinī [Tradition],*[1374] a self-initiation, and a gaṇacakra feast [ritual].

On the subject of the *Mahāmāyā [Tantra]*: the maṇḍala ritual, the brief and extensive visualizations, and the gaṇacakra feast [ritual].

On the subject of Tārā: the *Sādhana of the Seventeen Deities;*[1375] the maṇḍala ritual; *Vajra Tārā*; a Tārā body maṇḍala practice; the individual sādhanas of Oḍḍiyāna Tārā,[1376] Tārā who Rescues from the Eight Fears,[1377] and Six-Armed Tārā;[1378] and the maṇḍala ritual together with the method for recitation.

His compositions on Guhyasamāja include: *The Acalā Maṇḍala Ritual,*[1379] *The Meaning of the Summary Visualization of Vajra Mañjuśrī,*[1380] the *Biography of Jñānapāda,*[1381] and the *Sādhana of the Nineteen Deities.*[1382]

As for his works on Yamāntaka, these include: *The Sādhana of the Sworn Enemy,*[1383] a maṇḍala ritual of Bharaiva in the tradition of Ra [Lotsāwa], a sādhana, a ritual for Six-Armed [Yamāntaka] together with a gaṇacakra feast offering, and yet another sādhana of Six-Armed [Yamāntaka], a sādhana of Two-Armed [Yamāntaka], a fire offering ritual, [271] sādhanas of peaceful and wrathful Mañjuśrī according to the Kyo (*Skyo*) tradition, a sādhana of the thirteen Red Bharaivas, a sādhana of the five deities, *The Fearless Play Sādhana,*[1384] and *Coemergences.*[1385]

[As for his compositions on the practice of the general Mantrayāna,[1386]] these include: *The Concise Meaning of the Fifty [Verses on Devotion to the] Guru*[1387] and *Clarifying Samaya: A Commentary on the Root Downfalls,*[1388] both of which are vital [for the shared practice of Mantrayāna].

As for compositions upon the yoga tantras, these include *Amitābha as Described in the Action Tantras*[1389] and the *Fire Pūja of Akṣobhya.*[1390] As for his compositions on action and performance tantras, these include a sādhana of Vajrapāṇi; a sādhana of [Vajra]vidāraṇa;[1391] a sādhana of Accomplishing Hero Mañjuśrī;[1392] a sādhana of Arapacana [Mañjuśrī]; three sādhanas of the Four-Armed Great Compassionate One [Avalokiteśvara]; a sādhana of Lion's Roar[1393] [Avalokiteśvara]; a sādhana of Hayagrīva with Garuda Wings;[1394] individual sādhanas for

Maitreya, Acalā, Four-Armed Acalā, and All-Victorious Sitātapatrā;[1395] two sādhanas of the goddess Ritröma;[1396] individual sādhanas of the [goddesses] Tsünda and Possessing Light Rays; a sādhana of [the goddess] Without Suffering Possessing Light Rays; a fire pūja; the sādhana of Locanā;[1397] and a sādhana of the Sa Mother.[1398]

As for his compositions upon the Five Dra (Gra lnga), these include *Two Verses on the Sixteen Wisdom Consorts;*[1399] the *Conduct of the Boundary;*[1400] two sādhanas of the five protectors; directional torma offerings; *Supplication Prayers to the Planets and Constellations;*[1401] rituals for removing misfortune, extracting poison, accomplishing victory, and [taking and keeping] vows; mantras for bestowing initiation; and sādhanas of Yellow Mañjuśrī.

In the genre of catalogues, he composed *Catalogue of the Divisions of Tantra*[1402] and *Catalogue of the Dharma that I Myself* [272] *Received.*[1403]

On the topic of Dharma protectors, he composed a sādhana of Mahākāla Panjarnata, works on how to make offerings and how to make offering tormas, and a confession ritual.

On the topic of tormas, he composed rituals for the daily torma offerings, torma offering for nāgas, water tormas, and the torma offering for the four directions.

As for philosophy (*mtshan nyid*), he composed such texts as: *Increasing the Ten Dharma Activities;*[1404] *The Tenth Dharma Activity;*[1405] *Bodhicitta Composed on Behalf of the Great Masters;*[1406] a work on refuge and bodhicitta; a work on refuge composed for the benefit of regional protectors and related advice; liturgies for [taking and keeping] the prātimokṣa vow; a ritual for the one-day precepts (*bsnyes gnas*); *Clarifying the Supreme Vehicle*[1407] and a summary of its meaning; *Illuminating the Knowable; The Mirror that Clarifies Actions and their Effects;*[1408] *Definitively Ascertaining the Two Truths;*[1409] *Quintessential Instructions on the Mahāyāna;*[1410] *Summary of the Meaning of the Sūtra Requested by Bumo Rinchen;*[1411] *Summary of the Five Profound Sūtras;*[1412] *Summary of the Meaning of [Maitreya's] Sublime Continuum;*[1413] *Distinguishing the Vehicles;*[1414] *Essence of the Path;*[1415] *The Manner of Practicing the Profound;*[1416] and *The Correct: A Commentary Clarifying the Mahāyāna.*[1417]

His miscellaneous verses include: the *Drop of Nectar Advice;*[1418] *Discourse on the Seven Limbs;*[1419] the *Supreme Seven Paths for Agelessness and*

Deathlessness;[1420] *Discourse on Sorrow;*[1421] *Discourse on Degeneration;*[1422] *Promoting the Alphabet;*[1423] yet another two collections of miscellaneous writings; *Praise to Gönyak;*[1424] *Verses for Taming Zinshing;*[1425] *Tsangkhama;*[1426] and *Praise to Mentsé Ngotepa.*[1427]

His answers to queries and his letters include: *Answers to Yak Depa's Questions;*[1428] [273] *Definitive Answers to Questions;*[1429] *Answers to Drakrin's Questions;*[1430] *Answers to Tönpa Tsöndrü's Questions;*[1431] *Answers to the Chieftain Lodrö Sengé's Questions;*[1432] *Advice to the Emperor*[1433] and its summary; *Garland of Jewels: Advice to Čingkim Temür;*[1434] *Auspicious Rosary: Advice to Mangala;*[1435] *Letter to Prince Nomuqan;*[1436] *Advice to Hogo;*[1437] *Advice to Degubhoga;*[1438] *Advice to Themu Ogala;*[1439] *Advice to the Chieftainess Pundarīka;*[1440] *Three Instructions for Emperor Čingkim;*[1441] *Advice to Atsara;*[1442] *[A Letter] Sent to the Seat of Lama Dong;*[1443] *[A Letter] Sent to Drakzang;*[1444] *[A Letter] Sent to the General Monastic Population of Tibet;*[1445] *[A Letter] Sent to Tsarongpa;*[1446] *[A Letter] Sent to Jibik;*[1447] *The Ninth Dharma Discourse Sent to Princes;*[1448] letters sent to Alago, Śrī Rinchen Pal, Paṇḍita Laksikara, and Shong Lotsāwa; *[A Letter] Sent to Rawön;*[1449] *A Letter to Raldri;*[1450] *[A Letter] Sent to Chiwo Lhepa;*[1451] *[A Letter] Sent to Trophuwa;*[1452] *[A Letter] Sent to Chak Lotsāwa;*[1453] *A Letter Sent to the Dialecticians of Central [Tibet] During the Later Period of the Turning of the Wheel of the Dharma;*[1454] *[A Letter] Sent to the General Kadampas of Ü;*[1455] *[A Letter] Sent to Taklungpa;*[1456] *[A Letter] Sent to the Great Meditators of Ü;*[1457] *A Letter to Prince Jibik;*[1458] *A Letter to Drakzang;*[1459] and *[A Letter] Sent to Tönshön.*[1460]

As for verses he composed for the afterword of texts, these include those in the afterword of scriptures [sponsored] by Prince Čingkim and also for the *Garland Sūtra;*[1461] those in scriptures [sponsored] by [274] Mangala;[1462] verses for scriptures [sponsored] by Prince Jibik; verses for scriptures [sponsored] by Arokché;[1463] verses for scriptures [sponsored] by Esena; and verses for the *Perfection of Wisdom in Eight Thousand Verses* [sponsored] by Lotsāwa Rinchen Pal.

As for the dedications and [verses of] auspiciousness he wrote, these include: the expression of homage and lines of dedication penned while making the offering of 5,940 bolts of cloth and silk; the expression of auspiciousness for Chieftainess Durgen Durmi;[1464] the expression of auspiciousness for Prince Čingkim; the expression of auspiciousness for the *Garland of Auspiciousness* and three verses of auspiciousness [composed] for Noko; one four-line verse and also four verses [composed] for Mangala and his consort; one four-line verse composed for Prince Čingkim and his consort; and three four-line verses and also a single verse of auspiciousness [composed] for the great Chieftainess.

All of [Lama Phakpa's] compositions are easy to read, possess a coherent (*don 'bral chags pa*) internal meaning, are sweet to the ears of others, and are quickly taken to heart. They have flourished all the way to today.

The Manner in which [Lama Phakpa] Produced Disciples Who Upheld and Clarified the Sugata's Teachings by Means of His Immense Activities, Such as Explaining, Composing, and Debating the Holy Dharma

Although in general the disciples of this mahātmā were innumerable, like particles of dust blanketing this vast earth, principal among them were upholders of his commentarial tradition such as the three great ones, Shar, Nub, and Gung, as well as their disciples who became supremely knowledgeable, like Lama Drakpa [275] Öser,[1465] Lama Tashi Pal,[1466] and Malo.

As for those who upheld his practice tradition, although in general there were many who received quintessential instructions from this lama, synthesized (*dril*) these as their essential practice, and, in this way, came to uphold the victory banner of accomplishment, it is well known that from among them two individuals completely received his teachings like a vase filled to the brim. These were the great lama Shang Könpal[1467] and the monk Kunlo.[1468] In addition, he produced a great many champions of the teachings who were sure to sustain his lineage, including Laruwa, Nyenchenpa, Sulungpa, Salawa Öserbum, and Üpa Sangbum.[1469] [Phakpa] thus greatly clarified the general and particular teachings of the Sugata comparable to when the Tathāgata himself was alive!

In such ways he worked unfathomably on behalf of the teachings and sentient beings with his marvelous activities. By means of his clairvoyance, this mahātmā eventually understood that he had already ripened and liberated all disciples of that lifetime. He also understood that the time had come for him to greatly benefit other sentient beings by means of different manifestations. He then shared the life stories of the great Sakyapa lamas and others with the great master

Dharmāpalarakṣita, saying, "In such ways, those holy lamas possessed heaps of good qualities and worked on behalf of the teachings. I, too, have done whatever I could in my teaching activities and work for sentient beings. [276] Understand that I must now follow the others [and depart this life]!"

One time, when this lama was very young, he dreamed that he had been given a walking stick made of wood from a *ba* (*sba*) tree. It was inscribed with eighty verses, of which the forty-sixth was slightly crooked. In the morning, he shared his dream with Sapaṇ. [Sapaṇ told him,] "This number of verses symbolizes your lifespan. The forty-sixth is a little crooked. When you reach that age, you will face some danger. You will have to be careful."

According to that prophecy, deities who delighted in the teachings recognized that Lama Phakpa was approaching the time to display the great passing beyond sorrow. They said among themselves, "If such a holy being departs, who will then uphold the Buddha's teaching?" With unhappy minds and tortured by suffering, they began to cry. Their tears washed over the entire earth. Even the birds began to sing unsweet songs, display unusual (*phyin ci log pa*) colors, and so forth. The sun became obscured. The solar pathway and constellations now progressed in the wrong direction. The minds of sentient beings became disturbed and agitated. They could no longer distinguish between right and wrong conduct, just like being bewildered at a crossroads. The minds of renunciant meditators grew apathetic (*yed yed pa*), and they could no longer rest in single-pointed concentration. Those engaged in study lost interest in listening or teaching and became distracted by other positive and negative kinds of conduct. The Earth God became discontented, and the harvest [277] refused to grow.

In this way, darkness came even before the sun and its netting of light set over the peaks of the western mountains. Indeed, all such signs suddenly appeared when Mahātmā had barely begun to consider departing for the pure lands. It is, moreover, quite normal for such signs to appear whenever a holy being considers departing for the pure lands. Because the happiness of each sentient being depends upon such holy beings, when they begin to have such considerations, even though all sentient beings experience such negative signs, the Mahātmā himself experiences visions of the tathāgata Amitābha shining resplendent like a mountain of lotus rāka in Sukhāvatī, of many gathered bodhisattvas making great clouds of offerings like Samantabhadra, and so forth, as well as beholding the arrangement of many other pure lands.

In this case, on the evening of the third day of the twelfth month of the Dragon Year, Lama Phakpa dreamed of the great ācārya Nāgārjuna sitting near a bodhi tree upon the slopes of Mount Śrī Parvata,[1470] a mountain whose width and height are beyond measure. He listened to teachings from Nāgārjuna upon such topics as the Collection of Middle Way Reasoning. Many sons of the gods made unfathomable offerings in the sky. He also dreamed that Maja Chenmo, the queen of knowledge,[1471] appeared before him. [278] He spent his days and nights in such wondrous ways.

On the first day of the tenth month, Lama Phakpa began the memorial rituals (*dus kyi mchod*) for the lama Lord of Dharma [Sakya Paṇḍita]. [On this occasion, Lama Phakpa] made more extensive offerings than usual to [Sapaṇ's] reliquary stūpa (*thugs dam*). Those around him inquired, "Aren't the anniversary rituals for Sakya Paṇḍita usually held in the eleventh month?" "That is true," he replied, "but I vowed to myself that I would pay homage to the lama Lord of Dharma for approximately a month [each year]. I worry that if I wait until the eleventh month of this year, I will not have time to finish the maṇḍala offerings and so forth. For this reason, I have begun earlier." Every day until the eighteenth, he joined the prayer assembly and also gave Dharma teachings. However, on the nineteenth, twentieth, and twenty-first, he remained in his residence.

Then, in the early morning of the twenty-second day of that month, he asked for an extensive offering to be arranged. He then grasped a vajra and a bell. To eliminate the mistaken view of grasping at permanence among the ignorant and to encourage diligence among the lazy, as well as to further tame sentient beings by his activities, a great many wondrous signs came from the sky, such as sounds, lights, and a rain of flowers. Then, in his forty-sixth year, during the Male Iron Dragon Year, he made the appearance of mahāparinirvāṇa at Lhakhang Labrang.

At that moment, the great earth stretching to its distant ocean [279] shores shook six times. The gods were joyful and pervaded the world with offering substances. The sounds of many musical instruments resounded from the sky. Extraordinary incense wafted about, unlike anything experienced before. A great shower of flowers rained down. They then cremated his body. This lama had indeed been very rich, for he built a great many temples, traveled regularly between China and Tibet, collected an enormous amount of tax and compulsory service while protecting the two systems, and so forth. There were, therefore, unfortunate ones without faith in him who incurred small faults in their samaya. As such, his skeletal remains turned mostly black.

At that time, Master Drakpa Shönu,[1472] known as [an incarnation of] Blue Mañjuśrī,[1473] approached the chamber containing the corpse even though it had not yet been officially unsealed. As he did so, he struck his head against some plaster, which caused him to utter some blameful prayers. Just then, from a crevice in the corpse chamber, a single piece of charcoal fell out. Scratching away at it, he discovered that it was a thumb bone. He beheld the five buddha families the size of a needle upon its surface. He again made prayers, and the face, hands, and ornaments [of the five buddha families] clearly appeared. It is well known that this thumb bone is housed inside the statue of the Buddha that remains today as the holy object of Master Drakpa Shönu at the temple of Rinchen Dzö Monastery[1474] at Shangdrü.[1475]

According to a version of events recorded in a different history, later somebody [280] opened that statue and nowadays that thumb bone is the possession of Gyatsowa.[1476] [In reality], however, the statue of the King of Subduers, wherein that marvelous thumb bone (*gdung rus*) is housed, is as valuable as the world. It was crafted authentically according to tradition and stands about a foot high. It once wandered about in the possession of Lhasa Dzongpa.[1477] It later came into the possession of Jetsun Dampa Kunga Drölchok[1478] and remained a while at Möndro.[1479] Later, it spontaneously passed into the hands of the Sakyapa Ngakchang Ngakwang Kunga Sönam.[1480]

At some later time, [the rest of Phakpa's] skeletal remains turned black. People were fearful that the emperor of China would punish whoever delivered news to him that the lama had passed away. For that reason, no one wished to travel [to the court]. [In the meantime, Lama Phakpa's] skeletal remains were mixed with crushed ivory. Because he had been the great lama [Phakpa's] offering master (*mchod dpon*), Dishi Drakpa Öser[1481] declared, "Even if I am to be punished, since it is for the sake of my lama, I will go!" He thus departed, while continuously performing the cleansing ritual (*khrus gsol*) for [Phakpa's] bodily remains. When he arrived in the vicinity of the emperor, he remained and undertook practice exactly as Lama Phakpa had done. The emperor heard about this and said, "Who is practicing exactly like my lama? Go there and find out!" The emperor's envoys arrived and discovered who it was, and then reported this to the emperor. "Invite him here!" commanded the emperor.

[Dishi Drakpa Öser arrived] and explained exactly how Lama [Phakpa] had passed away. They also held many Dharma discussions. The emperor became devoted to him and received many teachings. In this way, he became the emperor's master. [281] The emperor's attendants helped place the bodily remains upon his crown. While doing so, the emperor then made extensive prayers. With this, the bodily remains developed pearl relics. Saying, "This is not part of my lama's body," the emperor later discarded all the crushed ivory. It is well known that he set aside a portion of the relics and gifted them back to Tibet.

We might summarize all these events with the following verses:

Long ago, you were the emanated translator Paltsek Sung.[1482]
In a later life, it is well known that you were the bodhisattva Satönri.[1483]
You returned once more to protect the north of Jambudvīpa;
named "Glorious"[1484] and "Noble,"[1485] you are indeed suitable for praise!

Because of your marvelous, liberated life story, just after you were born
everyone affirmed that you were "Phakpa," a supreme being.
You became a treasury of Dharma for authoritative scholars and practitioners.
But were you not also a lord for all other beings, without exception?

To work on behalf of countless sentient beings,
you were a nirmanakāya who intentionally took birth
into the family lineage of the Sakya, so worthy of everyone's reverence.
As such, reality came to match the name Phakpa.

If there is someone who can compete with you
in the matter of guiding sentient beings, reveal them!
Someone may indeed be enriched by the wealth of the Dharma,
but in terms of worldly wealth, they have only enough to survive.

Although an earth-protecting emperor acquires power and wealth,
it is like a star in daytime should he also acquire the power of the Dharma.
This is like the worldly wealth of a cakravartin emperor
and the Dharmic wealth of the son of Śuddodana.[1486]

A single person such as you, who completely
possesses such amazing, marvelous forms of wealth,
has never existed before nor [282] will ever exist again.
This is proved by direct valid cognition, and so I am devoted to you from my heart.

From your kindness, the activity of glorious Sakya
has come to spread across the entire earth.
Since then, who lives in Ü, Tsang, or Kham,
that has not become a subject of Sakya? Tell me!

This concludes the biography of Chögyal Phakpa Lodrö Gyaltsen.

8. Drogön Chakna Dorjé (1239–67)

As mentioned above, that great lama Phakpa had the same mother as his younger brother, Drogön Chakna Dorjé.[1487] He was already born when his father passed away at fifty-six years old during the Female Earth Pig Year (1232), at Gelo in Yarudok.[1488] His mother was from Doktötsen[1489] and was named Machik Kunkyi.[1490]

When he was six years old, he accompanied the Lord of Dharma Sapaṇ to the land of the Mongols. Even while he was still very young, he was capable of undertaking [the Vajrayāna practices of] union and liberation. From his uncle, the Lord of Dharma, and from his older brother [Phakpa Lama], [Chakna Dorjé] received many initiations and quintessential advice. His mindstream was further enriched by prodigious learning. From practicing extraordinary activity, he subjugated all manner of malevolent forces. He could hang the three kinds of weapons[1491] upon sun rays. From the pockmarked earth into which he shot arrows, water bubbled forth. That place is still well known today as Water Achieved by Arrow.[1492] It is superior to other water and the local population makes good use of it, due to its special qualities. In these ways and many others, [Chakna Dorjé] displayed a great many unthinkable signs of accomplishment.

In conclusion, from among those manifestations of the lords of the three families arriving in the world, it is well known that he was the incarnation of Vajrapāṇi, Lord of Secrets, endowed with the largess of power and magical display.

The Mongol emperor Sečen Qaγan [i.e., Qubilai] appointed him lord of Salen,[1493] and bequeathed to him the Thongchi [283] Golden Stamp[1494] and the Right and Left Court of Justice.[1495] Furthermore, for his wife, the

Fig. 28. Drogön Chakna Dorjé (1239–67)

emperor gifted his daughter Mekhadun.[1496] [The emperor] had him wear Mongolian clothing and appointed him as chief justice (*khrims bdag*) of the three regions of Tibet (*chol kha gsum*). It is well known that the history of Tibetans acquiring the title of imperial preceptor and other leadership positions [in the Mongolian and Chinese imperial courts] began with these two brothers. As such, they greatly benefited Tibet.

[Chakna Dorjé] resided in those northerly reaches for some eighteen years. When he was twenty-five years old, he returned to the great seat of Chökor.[1497] Over the course of more than three years, he set a great many beings upon the path of ripening and liberation by means of his extraordinary activity (*grub pa'i spyod pa*). When he was twenty-nine years old, upon the first day of the waxing moon period during the seventh month named Drozhin (Gro bzhin) of the Female Fire Rabbit Year (1267), he showed the manner of passing into nirvāṇa at the Gorum Library.[1498]

9. Dishi Rinchen Gyaltsen (1238–79)

The second wife of Sangtsa [Sönam Gyaltsen][1499] hailed from the Chudowa[1500] region of Sakya. Her father was named Jetsé.[1501] She was named Machik Jodro.[1502] She bore two children, a boy and a girl. The elder boy's name was Master Rinchen Gyaltsen.[1503] He was born at the Great Seat when his father was fifty-five years old, in the Male Earth Dog Year (1238). He studied with his uncle, the Lord of Dharma [Sapaṇ] and brother [Lama Phakpa], as well as Lama Uyukpa. He became well versed in many tantras and oral traditions. He composed texts on secret mantra maṇḍala rituals and other topics. He benefited the Buddha's teachings in many ways, such as by teaching and listening. When Phakpa Rinpoché departed for Mongol lands, [Master Rinchen Gyaltsen] served as the Sakya Trizin [at Sakya Monastery]. He also journeyed [to Mongol lands] and served as the emperor's lama officiant (*bla mchod*). He established a monastic community near the royal palace. [284] He thus immensely benefited the Buddha's teaching. He passed away into peace at Metok Rawa[1504] when he was forty-two years old, on the third day of the third month of the Male Earth Rabbit Year (1279).

Alternatively, other sources claim that when Phakpa returned to Ü-Tsang, this master was appointed Seat Holder at China's Shingkun[1505] and Metok Rawa. This version of events had it that he passed away at Shingkun. In still other sources, it is said that he passed away on the nineteenth day of the Takar month (*Tha skar*). We must further investigate these alternative accounts.

His mother had two children. His younger sister was Master Dodé.[1506] She journeyed to Müsugo,[1507] where it is widely documented that she excellently bore a son named Müchen Gyaltsen Palsang.[1508] Both the

Fig. 29. Dishi Rinchen Gyeltsen (1238–79)

Ornament Adorning the Mouths of the Noble and *The Tsang Jampa Succession History* claim that the mother of these two siblings hailed from Chudo[1509] in the Sakya area. Alternatively, the succession histories written by Taktsang and Nyidé each claim that her name was Shabjo Droma[1510] and that she hailed from the region of Shab.

The third wife of Lama Sangtsa, moreover, hailed from the area of Ngari Güngthang.[1511] Her father was a Gungthang chieftain. She was named Lhachik Dzema.[1512] She bore two children, a boy and a girl. The eldest became well known as Master Sönam Bum.[1513] He would later build Jomo Ling[1514] and establish an assembly of nuns there. After having widely taught and studied, he passed away accompanied by [285] amazing signs. It is recorded that his inner support, a statue of Tārā, remained at Düchö [Labrang]. However, nowadays it is no longer to be found there. Additionally, his younger sister Nyima Bum[1515] would later leave to serve as the wife of the Ngari chieftain Tashi Tsekpa Pal.[1516]

The fourth wife of Sangtsa, moreover, hailed from Yalung. Her name was Jocham Hormo, or, alternatively, Jomo Horcham.[1517] She bore a daughter named Master Rinchen Jungné.[1518] She would later journey to Chumik in Tsang. There, she bore a son who became known as Gyatso Pöndrung.[1519]

Fig. 30. Yeshé Jungné (1238–74)

10. Master Yeshé Jungné (1238–74)

The fifth wife of Lama Sangtsa was Lhachik Dzema,[1520] a daughter of a Gungthang chieftain from Ngari. Her attendant (*nye gnas ma*), known as Dorjé Den,[1521] bore a child who became known as Master Yeshé Jungné.[1522] He was born at Samling at glorious Sakya when his father was fifty-five years old, in the Male Earth Dog Year (1238). He studied, listened, and practiced the holy Dharma with both Sharpa Sherab Jungné and Sharpa Dorjé Öser.[1523] The great master Shākya Sangpo built Shar Ling as a residence for this lama. For the benefit of sentient beings, moreover, he traveled across Kham. He became the lama officiant for a ruler named Hukarché.[1524] It is recorded in several major and minor succession histories, [286] such as those written by Tsang Jampa and Sherab Dorjé, who had been a direct disciple of the holy lama, that [Master Yeshé Jungné] passed away at Jangyul[1525] when he was thirty-seven years old, on the fourteenth day of the eleventh month of the Male Wood Dog Year (1274).

Alternatively, according to the succession history written by Taktsang Lotsāwa Sherab Rinchen, he passed away when he was thirty-six years old on the tenth day of the third month of the Female Water Bird Year (1273), at Sernang[1526] in Dokham. The *Succession History of Nyidé* agrees on the location and his age at death, but has the date as the eleventh day of the Gyal month (*Rgyal*), and so on; the early succession histories do not agree on a great many topics.

Fig. 31. Dishi Dharmapālarakṣita (1268–87)

11. The Dishi Dharmapālarakṣita (1268–87)

Drogön Chakna Dorjé had three wives. From among them, neither king [*sic.*] Köden [Ejen]'s daughter Mangala[1527] nor Machik Dentsa Chöbum[1528] bore him any sons. His third wife, named Khandro Büm,[1529] hailed from Shalu. Her father was an inner minister for the Mongolian emperor Kushang Ngadra.[1530] She bore a son named Mahātmā Dharmapālarakṣita. He was born at Nedruk Lhakang[1531] in the south of Rinchen Gang, six months after his father passed away in the first month of the Male Earth Dragon Year (1268), just as the great temple was being constructed.

Those around him cherished him very deeply and worried that he would be injured in an earthquake. As such, they built a wooden labrang especially for him. When he was nine years old, Lama Phakpa returned from China, and [Dharmapālarakṣita] received many initiations, tantric commentaries, and oral instructions. He completely understood them all. As such, when he was just eleven years old, he gave a teaching on the *Two-Part Hevajra Tantra*. While teaching, he declared his care for the teachings to the monastic assembly. [287] Everyone was amazed. When he was thirteen years old, he was entrusted with the Great Seat. After Phakpa Rinpoché passed into peace, [Dharmapālarakṣita] prayed that he would be able to complete all [Phakpa Rinpoché's] wishes and, to everyone's astonishment, he proceeded to teach the great Dharma assembly. Everyone was truly amazed. In addition, as an inner support he commissioned the construction of an image of Mahā Śrī Heruka,[1532] and as outer supports, a copy of the *Perfection of Wisdom in Eight Thousand Lines* printed in gold, wall paintings for the temple, many images for individual labrangs, and many statues thirteen measures in size.[1533]

He undertook extensive activities, such as establishing a tradition of continuously performing memorial offering ceremonies. At the same time, he continually studied with Lama Yeshé Rinchenpa.[1534] When he was fourteen years old, he departed to have an audience with the emperor. He met Qubilai Qaγan and they held long Dharma discussions. The emperor was delighted and became devoted to him. He then built a great crystal stūpa, in which he installed the relics of the great Lama Phakpa. Over the course of five years, he resided at Metok Rawa. He constructed a large temple to house the crystal stūpa. He greatly benefited the teachings in that region before returning to Tibet. Along the way, he journeyed through Dokham. There, when he was twenty years old, he made the appearance of passing away in a place called Tré Mandal,[1535] on the eighteenth day of the Melpo month (*Smal po*) of the Male Fire Pig Year (1287).

12. The Kinsman Ratnabhadra (ca. late thirteenth century)

That lama's wife, the daughter of emperor Čingkim Temür named Palden, did not bear any sons. In response to constant requests [288] that he take a second wife for the sake of the continuity of the precious succession lineage, he made Jomo Tak Büm[1536] his wife, and she bore him a son named Ratnabhadra.[1537] That child, however, passed away when he was five years old.

Fig. 32. Dungsé Ratnabhadra (ca. late thirteenth cent.)

Fig. 33. Guoshi Mahātmā Sangpo Pal (1262–1324)

13. Guoshi Mahātmā Sangpo Pal (1262–1324)

During the period [of Sangpo Pal's life], it appears that there was not a widely agreed upon succession lineage. In that context, Sharpa Jamyang Rinchen Gyaltsen[1538] installed roof brocades (*gnam rgyan*) and shrine objects (*mchod cha*) at Sakya's Sheldak, Serthok, Yuthok, and the Great Temple.[1539] He also made innumerable yoga tantra maṇḍalas in the Thik Khang.[1540] By the time the mahātmā [Sangpo Pal] completed his studies, it was well known that he would be then required to serve as lama to the emperor.

Sangtsa Sönam Gyaltsen, moreover, took five wives with whom he had eight children. From among them, Drogön Chakna [Dorjé]'s son was Dharmapāla. His son was Ratnabhadra. From then on, there were no further sons in this lineage. The great Master Yeshé Jungné was the younger brother of Phakpa, Lord of Dharma, but they did not share a mother. He married a woman named Machik Khabmema, otherwise known as Jomo Bumé.[1541] Their son, who became known as the mahātmā Sangpo Pal,[1542] was born at Bodonger[1543] when his father was twenty-five years old, in the Male Water Dog Year (1262). This is recorded in both *The Succession History of Taktsang* and *The Succession History of Nyidé*. *The Succession History of Tsang Jampa* claims that he was born at Khabmé.[1544] [289]

In any case, sixteen years after Sangpo Pal was born, Phakpa Rinpoché returned from the land of the Mongols and they met. He received many Dharma teachings, such as initiations, transmissions, oral instructions, and so forth. While this was happening, Phakpa Rinpoché stared at him for a long time. He then said, "It is possible that the time will come when we will 'run out of the human body and work down to the knees.'[1545] As such, you should put effort into your studies." On another occasion,

Lama Phakpa told him, "I dreamed that there were only two members in Chakna's family lineage, but there were many in the lineage of Ye[shé] Jung[né]."

When this mahātmā was nineteen years old, Phakpa Rinpoché passed into nirvāṇa. At that time, even though he was older than Chakna's son Dharmapāla, because Chakna had long been responsible for increasing the succession lineage and was more popular, his son Dharmapāla was enthroned at the Great Seat. Sangpo Pal thereafter lived as an ordinary person. He extensively turned the wheel of the Dharma during the funerary rituals [of Phakpa Rinpoché]. Just after that, when he was twenty-one years old, in response to the invitation of the empress Abu, he departed for the [Mongolian] imperial court. This version of events is based on the [historical] tradition that claims he did indeed take this journey. Based on some reports, the emperor said, "I need to spend some time investigating [your lineage qualifications]. While I do so, go stay at Mentsé."[1546] Sangpo Pal dutifully resided in Mentsé in a large [290] residence known as Suzhou[1547] located on a tributary river twenty great *jel-lam*[1548] from the great outer ocean. He later stayed at another large residence called Hangzhou[1549] seven *jel-lam* away. It is said that another ten-*jel-lam* journey beyond that was Mount Potala.

Sangpo Pal resided [at Hangzhou] as a secret yogic practitioner. In time, he had a son with a Chinese woman. He was served by a Khampa devotee who was a chieftain (*dpon chen*) named Kunga Öser.[1550] Worrying that the emperor would issue an imperial command to him, Sangpo Pal fervently prayed to Tārā. One morning as the sun was rising, atop a lotus flower on the surface of the ocean, Tārā revealed her face to him. Using the mudrā of granting protection, she touched him upon his crown and said:

> Whosoever desires a son will be granted a son.
> Whosoever desires wealth will be granted wealth.
> One will gain whatever one desires.
> There will be no obstacles and one will overcome individual
> [obstructions].

Upon hearing this prophecy, all his worries were relieved.

When this mahātmā was twenty-seven years old, Dharmapāla passed away. Sharpa Jamyang Chenpo[1551] then held the Great Seat. It is said that he undertook innumerable and unthinkable activities on behalf of other beings, such as teaching, listening, contemplation, and accomplishment. Specifically, at the Great Seat he directed [291] the construction of Serthok, Yuthok, and so forth to house the outer supports [i.e., reliquary stūpas, etc.] of both Lama Phakpa Rinpoché and Mahātmā Dharmapāla. The great chieftain Shākya Sangpo laid the foundation of the great temple [Sakya]. Kunga Sangpo subsequently completed the construction. Later, during the tenure of this lama [Sharpa Jamyang Chenpo], it is well known that the chieftain Akleng[1552] sponsored the renovation of the interior of this temple by installing floor brocades, canopies, shrine objects, wall paintings, and so forth. It is well known that in the Female Wood Sheep Year he also sponsored the construction of the large wall enclosing the great temple.

Additionally, to inaugurate and beautify the great maṇḍala house,[1553] this lama [Sharpa Jamyang Chenmo] directed the creation of maṇḍalas belonging to the lower [tantra systems] up to yoga tantra. He appointed Lama Lochen and Nur Yeshé Gyaltsen[1554] as close advisors for this project. One hundred forty-eight great maṇḍalas were eventually made, each of them containing many more small, detailed maṇḍalas, totalling altogether 639. They were made by following the tradition of previous masters and of this specific lama. This project was started in the fifth month of the Female Wood Snake Year and finished in the eighth month, including the consecration.

In addition to all this, [Sharpa Jamyang Chenpo] offered other kinds of great service to the Great Seat as well. In conclusion, over the course of eighteen years, from the passing of Dharmapāla and the time the great mahātmā [Sangpo Pal] began to reside at the imperial court to when he returned to pursue his studies at the Great Seat, he who was famed under the name Sharpa Jamyang Rinchen Gyaltsen undertook enlightened activities that were no different from those of the stainless venerable succession lineage. He carried the responsibility for the Great Seat. [292]

In this way, the Great Seat had been passed to a chief disciple [i.e., Sharpa Jamyang]. Chakna's son Dharmapāla had passed away. Ye[shé]

Jung[né]'s Mahātmā son was away living in China. The Great Seat [of Sakya] appeared no longer to be held by a member of the actual [Khön] succession lineage, which had apparently become enfeebled. Akleng, the chieftain of Yardrok,[1555] could not bear this. He worked very hard [to amend this situation]. Wönak[1556] from Kham became his ally. They held discussions with the leadership of Sakya and sent a letter to the imperial preceptor, Drakpa Öser, who was then installed at the Mongol court. The gukśrī[1557] from Nyidé named Sherab Pal and the nobleman Obu[1558] supported [Drakpa Öser] and helped relay regular reports to the emperor.

It was for this reason that Dharmapāla's bones turned into relics and were offered to the emperor. [The emperor] was amazed. "Even if this was merely my lama's nephew," he exclaimed, "that is good enough for me! Alas, there is now not even a nephew left!" Thereupon, he wept. The great lama Drakpa Öser, Dampa Hepo,[1559] and others clarified: "The mahātmā [Sangpo Pal] is [another of] your lama's nephews!" The emperor's mood ameliorated. "In this case, summon him here from Mentsé!" he commanded. This is recorded in *The Succession History of Tsang Jampa.*

An alternative version of events is found in *The Succession History of the Taktsang Lotsāwa*, which states: The great lama Drak[pa] Ö[ser], the gukśrī of Nyidé Sherab Pal, and the nobleman Obu sent a letter from the Great Seat to the dishi Drakpa Öser. He, in turn, passed along the news that Dharmapāla had [293] passed away to the emperor, that the mahātmā [Sangpo Pal] resided in Mentsé, and that, currently, the Great Seat had been passed to a great disciple of Lama Phakpa. Furthermore, a noblewoman (*lcam*) of Sakya was traveling at that time in Mongolia. Along her journey, she fell off a precipice and died. Marvelous signs accompanied her death, including the appearance of rainbow relics. The emperor was amazed. He said, "These [woman's relics] are a part of my lama's bone lineage and are good enough for me!" Thus inspired, he issued an order to search for Sangpo Pal. [And this mahātmā] duly returned from Mentsé.

In any case, at that time the powerful lord Ga Anyen Dampa[1560] entrusted a Dharma protector to act on his behalf. An iron bird the size of a mountain descended upon the roof of the emperor's palace. If it moved even one of its feathers, the ground shook in every direction. A great variety of other magical displays also appeared, such as *khau* (*kha'u*) stones raining down from the sky. All this helped [convince the emperor to allow the mahātmā Sangpo Pal to return to Sakya].

When [Sangpo Pal] was thirty-five years old, he was summoned from Mentsé. Along the way, he passed by the fortress of the previous emperor Bongnachen;[1561] the site where Kongjo's[1562] father, the king lord nobleman [emperor] Taizong,[1563] had once invited the sixteen arhats to spend the rainy season retreat; the great palace of Kyinchang Hau[1564] that once housed the lower garment (*sku yol*) of the Lhasa Jowo [statue]; and Pöden City,[1565] which in Chinese is Shintuhu, where the bodhisattva Dharmodgata[1566] had once taught the perfection of wisdom to [the bodhisattva] Ever-Weeping.

When he was thirty-six years old, the emperor [294] made abundant gifts to him, saying, "Because you are the nephew of the imperial preceptor Phakpa, you must increase the lineage and hold the seat of Sakya!" He made this order accompanied by an elegant edict. Upon receiving the emperor's command, he quickly took his leave.

When he was thirty-seven years old, in the Male Earth Dog Year (1298), he arrived back at the Great Seat. At that time, Sharpa Jamyang Chenpo lived in Shithok Labrang.[1567] He passed the Great Seat to the mahātmā. However, because the latter wished to engage in his studies full time and because he was slightly uncomfortable with taking over the Great Seat immediately, even though the emperor had ordered that he propagate the lineage and hold the Great Seat, he temporarily resided in the Lhakhang Labrang. There he pursued teaching, study, and so forth, and did not immediately take responsibility of the Great Seat. Sharpa Jamyang Rinchen Gyal thus continued to hold the Great Seat until the mahātmā was forty-five years old.

Dharmapāla passed away when the mahātmā was twenty-seven years old. From then until he was forty-five years old, for a total of eighteen years, the Great Seat was held by Sharpa [Jamyang Rinchen Gyal]. Until a later age, [because of this history,] the official seat holders of Sharpa [Monastery] were permitted to sit upon the great throne of the mahātmā Sakya Paṇḍita during monastic assemblies at Sakya. This is well known.

This lama mahātmā eventually came to completely understand the Dharma of his forefathers. When he was forty-five years old, he took on the heavy responsibility of the Great Seat. He then moved to Shithok

Labrang and acted excellently in service of the teachings by such activities as teaching, learning, meditation, and accomplishment, leading memorial offering rituals, [295] serving the Triple Gem, and focusing upon the needs of his disciples and the general monastic and lay community. He also brought about peace across the [Mongol] empire (*rgyal khams chen po*) in line with the Dharma. At the Great Seat, during the lifetime of this mahātmā and Sharpa Rinchen Gyaltsen, the foundations were laid for Serthok and Yuthok, which housed the outer supports of Lama Phakpa and Dharmapāla, as well as for the fence of the Lhakhang, and so forth.

In conclusion, from when he was forty-five years old until he passed away, he upheld, preserved, and spread the tradition of the Great Seat according to the two systems. It is famously for this reason that during this period the Great Seat vastly increased its wealth.

He thus held the Great Seat exactly according to the prophecy he had received from Ārya Tārā. He produced a great many children in the [succession] lineage. They were all born before he was fifty-one. He also constructed many supports of the [enlightened] body, speech, and mind. This lama mahātmā is thus famous for producing both humans and images of the deities! When he was fifty-two years old, he was ordained as a monk and took the name Amoghadhāśrīpa.[1568] In all these ways, he pursued far-reaching activity [on behalf the Sakya tradition]. When he was sixty-three years old, in the Male Wood Mouse Year (1324), he passed into bliss in his sleeping quarters at Shithok [Labrang]. This is recorded in many major and minor succession histories, such as *The Succession History of Taktsang Lotsāwa*, *The Succession History of Tsang Jampa*, *The Succession History Composed by the Direct Disciple of the Great Lama Sherab Dorjé*, and so on.

Alternatively, [296] *The Succession History of Nyidé* claims that he passed into peace when he was sixty-one years old at the end of the Drozhin month (Gro bzhin) during the Male Water Dog Year (1322), after Phakpa Kun[ga] Lo[drö Gyaltsen][1569] had already begun to turn the great wheel of the Dharma. We must, however, investigate this claim further. This specific son of the Mahātmā became known as the [Fifth] Dishi Kunga Lodrö Gyaltsen. He was born when his father was forty-eight years old. Later, when he was eight years old, he taught the *Two-Part Hevajra Tantra*.

All this was recorded by Nyidé. Other succession histories claim that he was nine years old when he gave this teaching.

When [Kunga Lodrö Gyaltsen] was eleven years old, he set off for the court of the [Mongol] emperor. On this, both Tsang Jampa and Nyidé agree. However, Sherab Dorjé, the direct disciple of the holy lama, has it that he departed when he was sixteen years old. Other than his birth and death years, there is no clarity about the exact chronology of his life. Sherab Dorjé writes that he returned [to Sakya] from the Mongolian court when he was twenty-five years old to receive the vows to become a fully ordained monk. Musé,[1570] by contrast, has it that he returned when he was twenty-four years old. Nyidé's succession history agrees. After receiving full ordination, when he was twenty-four years old, he extensively turned the wheel of the Dharma. Although there is no clarity about the years that followed, sometime after that time his mahātmā [297] father passed away, as is recorded in the *Succession History of Nyidé*.

For that reason, we must accept that his father lived at least one year more than when [Kunga Lodrö Gyaltsen] first turned the wheel of the Dharma. According to other succession histories, because he was twenty-six years old when his father passed away, his father must have lived for two years after he first turned the wheel of the Dharma. We must accept that this is true! Even if it is not and he lived but one year more, the mahātmā must have lived for twenty-six years after Kunga Lodrö was born. That is unquestionably established as true. Even if he passed away when [Kunga Lodrö] was twenty-four years old and turning the wheel of the Dharma, there is simply no doubt that he lived twenty-four years after his son was born.

In this case, Nyidé must accept that after Dishi Kunga Lodrö's birth, his mahātmā father lived only twenty-three more years. This is because Nyidé himself claims that the son born to the mahātmā when he was thirty-eight years old was Dishi Kunga Lodrö and that the mahātmā passed when he was sixty-one years old. As such, Dishi Kunga Lodrö was twenty-three years old when his father passed away. But this cannot be true; he was twenty-four years old when he received full ordination. Only after that did he turn the wheel of the Dharma, and only after that did his father pass away. This is according to Nyidé himself and agrees with many other succession histories. This is obvious to the eyes of the intelligent. Because of that, the claim in *The Succession History of Nyidé* that the mahātmā was sixty-one years old when he passed is likely a typographical error. If it is not, there is an inner contradiction in the dating proposed by the text. This is something we should investigate further. [298]

In any case, during the lifetime of this lama mahātmā, the sun of his body rose here in the Land of Snows. From this, the lotus flower of the Victor's teachings completely blossomed, which provided a wealth of nectar to a great swarm of bees of fortunate ones. His activity specifically produced those who, even by just holding the virtuous and good name of the precious succession lineage of the stainless glorious Sakyapa, could clarify the precious teachings, and who gained the status of scholars and practitioners. Like a constellation of stars shining in the clear sky, such beings have emerged continuously up through our present time. They clarify the teaching of the Buddha like the sun rising at dawn. We must know that all this has happened only due to the kindness of that great being [Sangpo Pal], he who held the title of "mahātmā."

From the history of the succession lineage of those who possessed the three supreme names of the celestial lineage of the Khön Sakyapa, this has been the story of the precious succession lineage of those who upheld the general Sakya tradition. In summary:

> The kindest is he who first opened the
> gate for the billions among the emanated succession lineage
> to protect against the loss
> of the worthy tradition of the Sakyapa, those regents of the Sage in Tibet.
>
> The one named Sangpo was the supreme glorious protector of beings.
> From the ocean of his stainless lineage,
> tributary rivers of scholars and practitioners
> have continuously emerged. How amazing!

Thus concludes the intermediary verse.

Notes

1. Throughout this book, foreign terms in parentheses are Tibetan unless otherwise noted as Sanskrit (Skt.), Mongolian (Mong.), and so forth.
2. Gtsang sde srid karma bstan skyong dbang po, 1606–42.
3. For relevant surveys of these seventeenth-century transitions in Inner Asian religion, politics, and economy beyond what is possible to summarize here, see: Bryan J. Cuevas and Kurtis R. Schaeffer, eds., *Power, Politics, and the Reinvention of Tradition: Tibet in the Seventeenth and Eighteenth Centuries*: PIATS 2003, Brill's Tibetan Studies Library (Leiden: Brill, 2006); Karl Debreczeny and Gary Tuttle, eds., *The Tenth Karmapa and Tibet's Turbulent Seventeenth Century* (Chicago: Serindia Publications, 2016); Cyben Žamzaranovič Žamcarano and Rudolf Loewenthal, *The Mongol Chronicles of the Seventeenth Century* (Wiesbaden: Harrassowitz, 1955); Zahiruddin Ahmad, *Sino-Tibetan Relations in the Seventeenth Century* (Roma: Istituto italiano per il Medio ed Estremo Oriente, 1970); Françoise Pommaret, *Lhasa in the Seventeenth Century: The Capital of the Dalai Lamas*, Brill's Tibetan Studies Library (Leiden: Brill, 2003).
4. Ronald M. Davidson, *Tibetan Renaissance: Tantric Buddhism in the Rebirth of Tibetan Culture* (New York: Columbia University Press, 2005).
5. Some of the most impactful histories of these later Mongolian Buddhist historians are now in English translation, and readers may be interested to consult them to see how the Sakya school and, in particular, Sakya Paṇḍita and Phakpa Lodrö Gyaltsen are quite central to Buddhist identity and historical conceptualizing in Mongol Inner Asia. For example: Sagang Sechen, *The Precious Summary: A History of the Mongols from Chinggis Khan to the Qing Dynasty*, trans. Johan Elverskog (New York: Columbia University Press, 2023); Thuken Losang Chökyi Nyima, *The Crystal Mirror of Philosophical Systems: A Tibetan Study of Asian Religious Thought*, trans. Geshé Lhundub Sopa, vol. 25, The Library of Tibetan Classics (Boston: Wisdom Publications, 2009); Dharmatāla, *Dharmatala's Annals of Buddhism*, Śta-Pitaka Series: Indo-Asian Literatures (New Delhi: Sharada Rani, 1975); Matthew King, *Ocean of Milk, Ocean of Blood: A Mongolian Monk in the Ruins of the Qing Empire* (New York: Columbia University Press, 2019).
6. See: E. Gene Smith, "The Early History of the 'Khon Family and the Sa skya

School," in *Among Tibetan Texts: History and Literature of the Himalayan Plateau*, ed. E. Gene Smith (Boston: Wisdom, 2001).

7. Namri Songtsen was purportedly the thirty-second ruler of the Yarlung dynasty, but one of the first to appear in the historical record while expanding Tibetan sovereignty across and then outside the Tibetan plateau. Namri Songtsen's successor, Songtsen Gampo (Srong btsan sgam po, 618–649), begins the recorded (though, of course, still widely reimagined) history of Tibetan courtly patronage of Buddhism. The Sakya Khön family memorializes its ancestors as having been ministers and advisers in these early courts. On the Tibetan empire, including its prehistory, see: Christopher I. Beckwith, *The Tibetan Empire in Central Asia: A History of the Struggle for Great Power among Tibetans, Turks, Arabs, and Chinese during the Early Middle Ages*, first paperback edition (Princeton, NJ: Princeton University Press, 1993); Christopher Irving Beckwith, "A Study of the Early Medieval Chinese, Latin and Tibetan Historical Sources on Pre-Imperial Tibet" (PhD Diss., Bloomington, IN: Indiana University, 1978).
8. These include especially the expansionist seventh-century reign of King Songtsen Gampo (Srong btsan sgam po, r. 618–650) and in the eighth century the reign of King Trisong Detsen (Khri srong lde brtsan, r. 755–797/804).
9. Rnam gnon ngang tshul.
10. Na len dra.
11. Bi ru pa, Bir wa pa; *alias* Mthu stobs dbang phyug.
12. Bdag med ma.
13. Ronald Davidson has reconstructed with great liveliness the ways in which the transformative feudalization of post-Gupta Indian society became the framework for the rise of esoteric tantric Buddhism and how the Hevajra system specifically was emblematic of this transformation (the fragmentation of political authority and patronage, the decline of female participation, the rise of massive monasteries, the rise of formalized Buddhist scholasticism, and the regional patronage of tantrism as a structure by which to authorize new regional power). Interested readers should consult: Ronald M. Davidson, *Indian Esoteric Buddhism: A Social History of the Tantric Movement* (New York: Columbia University Press, 2002).
14. Tib. *Kye rdo rje'i rgyud;* Ch. *Dabei kongzhi jingang dajiao wang yigui jing* 大悲空智金剛大教王儀軌經.
15. For a wonderful survey and introduction well beyond what is possible here, see: Cyrus Stearns, *Taking the Result as the Path: Core Teachings of the Sakya Lamdré Tradition*, Library of Tibetan Classics (Boston: Wisdom Publications, 2006).
16. For a thorough survey, see: Jan-Ulrich Sobisch, *Hevajra and Lam 'bras Literature of India and Tibet as Seen through the Eyes of A-Mes-Zhabs*, Contributions to Tibetan Studies (Wiesbaden: Reichert, 2008).
17. For wonderful overviews of the Lamdré and the Sakya tradition, see: Cyrus Stearns, *Luminous Lives: The Story of the Early Masters of the Lam 'bras Tradition in Tibet* (Boston: Wisdom Publications, 2001); and Cyrus Stearns, *Taking the Result as the Path: Core Teachings of the Sakya Lamdré Tradition* (Boston: Wisdom Publications, 2006).

18. An important example of father tantra in the Tibetan systems is the ca. eighth-century *Guhyasamāja Tantra* corpus (*Gsang ba 'dus pa'i rgyud*).
19. For surveys of its history and contents, interested readers might explore: David L. Snellgrove and Kṛṣṇācāryapāda, *The Hevajra Tantra: A Critical Study*, London Oriental Series (London: Oxford University Press, 1976); G. W. Farrow, I. Menon, and Kṛṣṇavajrapāda, *The Concealed Essence of the Hevajra Tantra: With the Commentary Yogaratnamālā*, first ed. (Delhi: Motilal Banarsidass Publishers, 1992); Shashibala, "Hevajra in Buddhist Literature, Imperial Ceremonies and Art," in *Written Treasures of Bhutan: Mirror of the Past and Bridge to the Future*, ed. John A. Ardussi and Sonam Topgay, vol. 1, Proceedings of the First International Conference on the Scriptural Heritage of Bhutan (Thimphu: National Library of Bhutan, 2008), 357–80.
20. We find them in various editions of Kangyur, one next to the other, such as Toh 417–18.
21. Ch. *Dabei kongzhi jingang dajiao wang yigui jing* C (T. 892). See: Charles Willemen, *The Chinese Hevajratantra: The Scriptural Text of the Ritual of the Great King of the Teaching, the Adamantine One with Great Compassion and Knowledge of the Void*, first Indian ed., Buddhist Traditions (Delhi: Motilal Banarsidass Publishers, 2004).
22. Janos Szerb, "Glosses on the Oeuvre of bLa-Ma 'Phags-Pa: III. The Patron-Patronized Relationship," in *Soundings in Tibetan Civilization* (New Delhi, India: Manohar, 1985), 166. Cited in: Sagang Sechen, *The Precious Summary: A History of the Mongols from Chinggis Khan to the Qing Dynasty*, trans. Johan Elverskog, 243n26.
23. Ibid.
24. In large part through such Hevajra-mediated activity, Phakpa and later Sakya hierarchs in the Mongol court extended a model of preceptor-patron sovereignty and relationality (*yon mchod*) earlier developed between Tangut rulers and Tibetan lamas in the previous century.
25. 'Khor lo bde mchog.
26. Mgon po.
27. Rdo rje 'jigs byed.
28. Rdo rje rnal 'byor ma.
29. Yang dag he ru ka.
30. Rdo rje phur pa.
31. The Viśuddhaheruka and Vajrakīlaya systems had been transmitted within the Khön family since the life of their ancestor Lui Wangpo (Klu'i dbang po), one of the original seven Tibetans to take Buddhist monastic ordination in the eighth century. Sachen Kunga Nyingpo married this timeworn family inheritance with the new exoteric and esoteric Buddhist traditions flowing into Tibetan societies.
32. On the imagination of Sakya in its landscape, see: Federica Venturi, "Creating Sacred Space: The Religious Geography of Sa Skya, Tibet's Medieval Capital" (PhD diss., Indiana University, 2013).
33. For a wider survey than is possible here, see: Stearns, *Luminous Lives: The Story of the Early Masters of the Lam 'bras in Tibet*; Stearns, *Taking the Result as the Path*. Readers will also be interested in the remarkable Sakya Kongma

Series, an ever-expanding list of core Sakya literature from the five forefathers translated by Christopher Wilkinson, including: Dragpa Gyaltsan, *The Hermit King*, trans. Christopher Wilkinson, Sakya Kongma Series (Concord: Suvarna Bhasa Publishing, 2014); Sakya Pandita, *Poetic Wisdom*, trans. Christopher Wilkinson, Sakya Kongma Series (Concord: Suvarna Bhasa Publishing, 2014); Sachen Kunga Nyingpo, Jetsun Dragpa Gyaltsan, and Sakya Pandita, *An Overview of Tantra and Related Works*, trans. Christopher Wilkinson, Sakya Kongma Series (Concord: Suvarna Bhasa Publishing, 2014); and Sonam Tsemo, *Admission at Dharma's Gate*, trans. Christopher Wilkinson, Sakya Kongma Series (Concord: Suvarna Bhasa Publishing, 2014).

34. *Rdo rje tshig rkang*.

35. For introductory studies on Sangphu, see: Leonard van der Kuijp, "The Monastery of Gsang-phu ne'u-thog and Its Abbatial Succession from ca. 1073 to 1250," *Berliner indologische Studien* 3 (1987), 103–127; Shunzō Onoda, "The Chronology of the Abbatial Successions of the gSang phu sNe'u thog Monastery," *Wiener Zeitschrift für die Kunde Südasiens* 33 (1989), 203–13.

36. For an introduction to Chapa Sengé, see: Helmut Tauscher, "Remarks on Phya pa Chos kyi seng ge and his Madhyamaka Treatises," *The Tibet Journal* 34.3–4 and 35.1–2 (2009–10), 1–35.

37. Skt. *Pramāṇaviniścaya*; Tib. *Tshad ma rnam nges*.

38. Tib. *Tshad ma sde 'dun*. These include the *Commentary on Valid Cognition* (Skt. *Pramāṇavārttika*; Tib. *Tshad ma rnam 'grel*), the *Ascertainment of Valid Cognition* (Skt. *Pramāṇaviniścaya*; Tib. *Tshad ma rnam par nges pa*), the *Drops of Reasoning* (Skt. *Nyāyabindu*; Tib. *Rigs pa'i thigs pa*), the *Drops of Logic* (Skt. *Hetubindu*; Tib. *Gtan tshigs thigs pa*), the *Analysis of Relations* (Skt. *Saṃbandhaparīkṣā*; Tib. *'Brel ba brtag pa*), the *Proof of Other Mental Continuums* (Skt. *Saṃtānāntarasiddhi*; Tib. *Rgyud gzhan grub pa*), and *Reasoning for Debate* (Skt. *Vādanyāya*; Tib. *Rtsod pa'i rigs pa*).

39. Skt. *Bodhisattvacaryāvatāra*; Tib. *Byang chub sems dpa'i spyod pa la 'jug pa*.

40. Bsod nams rtse mo, "Chos la 'jug pa'i sgo zhes bya ba'i bstan bcos," in *Sa skya gong ma rnam lnga'i gsung 'bum dpe bsdur ma las bsod nams rtse mo'i gsung*, vol. 3 (Beijing: Krung go'i bod rig pa dpe skrun khang, 2007), 389–496.

41. For an important survey of the wider historical context, see: Leonard van der Kuijp, *Contributions to the Development of Tibetan Buddhist Epistemology from the Eleventh to the Thirteenth Century* (Weisbaden: Verlag, 1983).

42. A lay disciple (female = upāsikā, male = upāsaka) is technically one who takes refuge in the Triple Gem and vows to keep the five basic precepts (Skt. *pañcaśīla*; Tib. *bslab pa lnga*): no longer to kill, steal, engage in sexual misconduct, lie, or take intoxicants. Furthermore, upon full and new moon days (Skt. *upoṣadha*; Tib. *gso sbyong*), an upāsaka or upāsikā vows to observe a further three vows: to not eat at an inappropriate time (i.e., between noon and the following dawn); to not frolic, dance, sing, or attend performances, or adorn or anoint one's body with garlands, fragrances, fine clothing, jewelry, and the like; and to refrain from resting or sleeping upon high or ostentatious beds.

43. For useful overviews of the Sakya tradition in its broader socio-religious and political context during the thirteenth century, see: Jonathan C. Gold, *The Dharma's Gatekeepers: Sakya Pandita on Buddhist Scholarship in Tibet* (Albany:

State University of New York Press, 2007); Davidson, *Tibetan Renaissance: Tantric Buddhism in the Rebirth of Tibetan Culture*; David Paul Jackson and Sa-skya Paṇḍi-ta Kun-dga'-rgyal-mtshan, *The Entrance Gate for the Wise (Section III): Sa-Skya Paṇḍita on Indian and Tibetan Traditions of Pramāṇa and Philosophical Debate* (Wien: Arbeitskreis für Tibetische und Buddhistische Studien, Universität Wien, 1987); Luciano Petech, *Central Tibet and the Mongols: The Yuan-Sa Skya Period of Tibetan History*, vol. LXV, Serie Orientale Roma (Rome: Instituto italiano per il Medio, 1990); János Szerb, "Glosses on the Oeuvre of Blama 'Phags Pa: On the Activity of the Sa Skya Paṇḍita," Tibetan Studies in Honour of Hugh Richardson: Proceedings of the International Seminar on Tibetan Studies, Oxford, 1979 (Warminster, England: Aris and Phillips, 1979).

44. Skt. *pañcavidyā*; Tib. *rig gnas che ba lnga*; Ch. *wuming* 五明; Mong. *Uqaγan tabun*. In Mahāyāna and tantric literature, bodhisattvas are said to have mastered these five fields of knowledge, which include: grammar and composition, logic, medicinal arts, arts and craft, and, finally, the "inner knowledge" (Skt. *adhyātmavidyā*) of the word of the Buddha (Skt. *buddhavacana*).

45. Gold, *The Dharma's Gatekeepers: Sakya Pandita on Buddhist Scholarship in Tibet*.

46. There is by now a veritable library of European language translations of Sapaṇ's works, including: Gold, *The Dharma's Gatekeepers: Sakya Paṇḍita on Buddhist Scholarship in Tibet*; Yon-tan-bzang-po and Ngawang Samten Chophel, *Teachings on Sakya Pandita's Clarifying the Sage's Intent*, 2nd rev. ed (Kathmandu: Vajra Publications, 2008); Ricardo Canzio, *Sakya Pandita's Treatise on Music (Rol Mo'i Bstan Bcos): With a Commentary by Kunga Sonam* (Kathmandu: Vajra Books, 2019); Migmar Tsering, "Sakya Pandita: Glimpses of His Three Major Works," *The Tibet Journal* 13 (n.d.): 12; Jonathan Stoltz, "Sakya Pandita and the Status of Concepts," *Philosophy East and West* 56 (n.d.): 567; Sakya Pandita, *Ordinary Wisdom: Sakya Pandita's Treasury of Good Advice*, trans. John T. Davenport (Boston: Wisdom Publications, 2000); Sakya Pandita Kunga Gyaltsen, *A Clear Differentiation of the Three Codes: Essential Distinctions among the Individual Liberation, Great Vehicle, and Tantric Systems: The Sdom Gsum Rab Dbye and Six Letters*, SUNY Series in Buddhist Studies, trans. Jared Rhoton (Albany: State University of New York Press, 2002); Pascale Hugon and Sa-skya Paṇḍita Kun-dga'-rgyal-mtshan, *Trésors du Raisonnement: Sa skya Paṇḍita et ses prédécesseurs tibétains sur les modes de fonctionnement de la pensée et le fondement de l'inférence*, Wiener Studien zur Tibetologie und Buddhismuskunde (Wien: Arbeitskreis für Tibetische und Buddhistische Studien, Universität Wien, 2008); David Paul Jackson and Sa-skya Paṇḍi-ta Kun-dga'-rgyal-mtshan, *The Entrance Gate for the Wise*; Leonard W. J. van der Kuijp, "Tibetan Contributions to the 'Apoha' Theory: The Fourth Chapter of the Tshad-Ma Rigs-Pa'i Gter," *Journal of the American Oriental Society* 99.3 (1979): 408–22; Jonathan C. Gold, "Sakya Paṇḍita's Anti-Realism as a Return to the Mainstream," *Philosophy East and West* 64 (2014): 360; David Paul Jackson and Sa-skya Paṇḍi-ta Kun-dga'-rgyal-mtshan, "Sa-Skya Paṇḍita on Indian and Tibetan Traditions of Philosophical Debate: The Mkhas Pa Rnams 'jug Pa'i Sgo, Section III" (PhD diss., University of Washington, 1985); Helmut Eimer and Kun-dga'-rgyal-mtshan, *Sa skya legs bshad: die Strophen zur Lebensklugheit von Sa skya Paṇḍita Kun dga' rgyal mtshan (1182–1251)*, Wiener Studien zur Tibetologie und

Buddhismuskunde (Wien: Arbeitskreis für Tibetische und Buddhistische Studien, Universität Wien, 2014); Sa-skya Paṇḍi-ta and Christopher Wilkinson, *Poetic Wisdom* (North Charleston South Carolina: CreateSpace, 2014); Ananda Dhvaja, *Le Subhāsitaratnandidhi mongol, un document du moyen mongol*, ed. Lajos Ligeti, Bibliotheca Orientalis Hungarica (Budapest: Société Körösi Csoma, 1948); György Kara and Marta Kiripolská, *Dictionary of Sonom Gara's Erdeni-Yin Sang: A Middle Mongol Version of the Tibetan Sa-Skya Legs Bshad: Mongol-English-Tibetan*, Brill's Inner Asian Library (Leiden: Brill, 2009); Artur Przybysławski, *Cognizable Object in Sa Skya Paṇḍita: An Edition and Annotated Translation of the First Chapter of Tshad Ma Rigs Gter by Sa Skya Paṇḍita and the First Chapter of Tshad Ma Rigs Pa'i Gter Gyi Don Gsal Bar Byed Pa by Go Rams Pa*, 1st ed. (Kraków: Jagiellonian University Press, 2018); James E. Bosson, *A Treasury of Aphoristic Jewels: The Subhāṣitaratnanidhi of Sa Skya Paṇḍita in Tibetan and Mongolian* (Bloomington: Indiana University, 1969); and Rhoton, *A Clear Differentiation of the Three Codes*.

47. For a masterful translation and study of one of the earliest sources on the life of Činggis Qan and his descendents, produced in the very heart of the empire he founded, see: Christopher P. Atwood, *The Secret History of the Mongols* (London: Penguin Books 2023).
48. I.e., the Western Xia 西夏; Tib. *Mi nyag*.
49. Though his characterization of Tibet's insularity is overstated, Tyrell Wylie paints a vivid picture of why the Mongols intruded into Tibetan societies so late: "It is not surprising that the Mongols had ignored Tibet until this time. Tibet was presumably as much a terra incognita to the Mongols of the thirteenth century as it was to its other neighbors. Not renowned for fabulous treasures, Tibet's mountainous terrain did not welcome merchants, who had long preferred the caravan routes established over more hospitable ground, thus avoiding the barren wastelands and glacial snows of Tibet. Although the Mongols had controlled His-hsia, contiguous with Tibet, for over a decade, no attempt was made to penetrate the 'Land of the Lamas' from there. The awesome Nan-chan mountain range separating the two countries formed a natural barrier to military movements. When Prince Köden became master of the Kokonor region, a less formidable route into Tibet from the northeast became open to him" (Wylie 1977, 110).
50. Later Tibetan and Mongolian Buddhist historians widely cite a legend about Činggis Qan's correspondence with earlier Sakya forefathers, but the possibility is negated by impossible dating in addition to the lack of any historical evidence.
51. Penghao Sun, "The Birth of an Etiquette Story: Tibetan Narratives of U Rgyan Pa, Qubilai, and the Yuan Government" (PhD diss., Harvard University, 2023), 64.
52. Many traditional Tibetan historians recount how prescient Tibetan delegates surrendered to the Mongols and began paying tribute following Činggis' ascension in 1206. While Giuseppe Tucci accepted the historical veracity of this account, many other earlier historians realized that any substantive Tibetan contact with the Mongol Empire during the life of Činggis Qan was later invention. See: Giuseppe Tucci, *Tibetan Painted Scrolls* (Rome: Libreria dello

Stato, 1949), 9; Richard Howorth, *History of the Mongols from the 9th to the 19th Century*, vol. 4 (London: Longmans, Green & Co., 1927), 128; Luc Kwanten, "Chinggis Khan's Conquest of Tibet: Myth or Reality?," *Journal of Asian History* 8 (1974): 1–20; and Turrell V. Wylie, "The First Mongol Conquest of Tibet Reinterpreted," *Harvard Journal of Asiatic Studies* 37.1 (1977): 106.

53. It must be mentioned that later Tibetan and even Mongolian Buddhist historians almost always misidentify Köden as the ruler of the Mongol empire (ex. Go tan rgyal po) or, worse still, the ruler of China (*rgya nag*). These histories also regularly misidentify his camp at Liangzhou as the court of the Mongol world empire.

54. Anna Tsendina has observed that that in Persian and Chinese sources, Köden surfaces only as a relatively insignificant actor mentioned in passing during narrative concerning intrigues against Qubilai, the enthronement of Möngke, and so forth. See: Anna Tsendina, "Godan Khan in Mongolian and Tibetan Historical Works," *Studia Orientalia* 85 (1999): 245.

55. Christopher Pratt Atwood, *Encyclopedia of Mongolia and the Mongolian Empire* (New York: Facts on File, 2004), 321.

56. For example, Dharmātala's nineteenth-century *Rosary of White Lotuses* records: "In the Iron Rat Year [...] general Dorta [...] together with the royal physician, set out for Tibet with a great army. Marching through the Upper and Lower Do, they killed many Tibetans in the Sog River valley. Their power extended to Gongpo in the east, Belpo in the west and Mon in the south. They killed five hundred monks in Radreng. At that (same) time an earthquake shook the royal temple, killing Soten and five hundred other monks and laymen" (Dharmātala 1989, 165–66).

57. As we might expect, our traditional monastic histories attribute the Mongol re-entry to far more pious reasons. For example, the widely read Pawo Tsuklak Trengwa (Dpa' bo gtsug lag 'phreng ba, 1504–66) leaves the paradox of violent conquest and piety hanging, writing in his 1564 *Scholar's Festival* that "Köden killed many monks and burned the temples, but still he sent an invitation letter for Sapaṇ to come and serve as his lama for the benefit of all Tibetans" (Gtsug lag 'phreng ba, *Dam pa'i chos kyi 'khor lo bsgyur ba rnams kyi byung ba gsal bar byed pa mkhas pa'i dga' ston*, Beijing: Mi rigs dge skrun khang, 1980, 599).

58. Atwood, *Encyclopedia of Mongolia and the Mongolian Empire*, 321. Several scholars have previously described the broader Mongolian geopolitical theater in which Köden's incursions took place; see Wylie, "The First Mongol Conquest of Tibet Reinterpreted"; Szerb, "Glosses on the Oeuvre of Blama 'Phags Pa: On the Activity of the Sa Skya Paṇḍita"; Christopher I. Beckwith, "Tibetan Science at the Courts of the Great Khans," *The Journal of the Tibet Society* 7 (1987): 5–12; Petech, *Central Tibet and the Mongols: The Yuan-Sa Skya Period of Tibetan History*; and Morris Rossabi, *Qubilai Khan: His Life and Times* (Berkeley: University of California Press, 1988).

59. See, for example: Luciano Petech, *Central Tibet and the Mongols: The Yüan Sa-Skya Period of Tibetan History*, Serie Orientale Roma (Rome: Istituto Italiano per il Medio ed Estremo Oriente, 1990), 5–25.

60. For a detailed study of such narratives from the perspective of later Inner

Asian monastic histories, see: Matthew W. King, "Exorcising the Body Politic: The Lion's Roar, Köden Ejen's Two Bodies and the Question of Conversion at the Tibet-Mongol Interface," *Buddhist Studies Review* 38.1 (2021): 45–57.

61. See: Luciano Petech, "P'ags-pa (1235–1280)," in *In the Service of the Khan: Eminent Personalities of the Early Mongol-Yüan Period (1200–1300)*, ed. Igor de Rachewiltz, et al. (Wiesbaden: Harrassowitz, 1993).

62. For a wonderful biography of Qubilai that extensively contextualizes the Tibeto-centered story told in works like Ameshab's, see Morris Rossabi, *Kublai Khan: His Life and Times* (Berkeley: University of California Press, 1988).

63. Christopher Wilkinson has produced three collections of these writings in excellent translation, which readers of Ameshab's history will surely wish to explore: Christopher Wilkinson, trans., *At the Court of Kublai Khan: Writings of the Tibetan Monk Chogyal Phagpa* (Cambridge, MA: Christopher Wilkinson, 2015); Christopher Wilkinson, trans., *Advice to Kublai Khan: Letters by the Tibetan Monk Chogyal Phagpa to Kublai Khan and his Court* (Cambridge, MA: Christopher Wilkinson, 2015); Christopher Wilkinson, trans., *Chogyal Phagpa: The Emperor's Guru*, Sakya Gongma Series (Concord, MA: Suvarna Bhasa Publishing, 2014).

64. The original name of this office was Zongzhi Yuan (總制院). It was renamed Xuanzheng Yuan (宣政院) in 1288.

65. For surveys of how these ideas of shared sovereignty organized trans-Inner Asian religious and political life in the centuries that followed in explicit reference to the memory of Phakpa and Qubilai, see: David Seyfort Ruegg, et al., *The Relationship between Religion and State (Chos Srid Zung 'brel) in Traditional Tibet: Proceedings of a Seminar Held in Lumbini, Nepal, March 2000*, ed. Christoph Cüppers, LIRI Seminar Proceedings Series (Lumbini: Lumbini International Research Institute, 2004); King, *Ocean of Milk, Ocean of Blood: A Mongolian Monk in the Ruins of the Qing Empire*; Johan Elverskog, "Tibetocentrism, Religious Conversion and the Study of Mongolian Buddhism," in *The Mongolia-Tibet Interface: Opening New Research Terrains in Inner Asia*, ed. Uradyn E. Bulag and Hildegard G. M. Diemberger (Boston: Brill, 2007); Sagang Setsen, *The Precious Summary: A History of the Mongols from Chinggis Khan to the Qing Dynasty*; Johan Elverskog, *The Jewel Translucent Sūtra: Altan Khan and the Mongols in the Sixteenth Century*, Brill's Inner Asian Library (Boston: Brill, 2003); Johan Elverskog, *Our Great Qing: The Mongols, Buddhism and the State in Late Imperial China* (Honolulu: University of Hawai'i Press, 2006).

66. Like many of the most impactful Inner Asian religious and literary figures, Ameshab (A mes zhabs) is known by many pseudonyms and shorthands. Some of the most popular are: 'Jam mgon A myes zhabs; A myes zhabs ngag dbang kun dga' bsod nams; Sa skya pa chen po 'jam mgon A mes zhabs ngag dbang kun gda' bsod nams; or A myes zhabs, a variant spelling of A mes zhabs.

67. Lha sras bsod nams rgyal mo.

68. Grags pa blo gros, personal names 'Jam dbyangs bsod nams rgyal mtshan and Grags pa blo gros rgyal mtshan dpal bzang po.

69. Sa skya khri chen.

70. Byams pa dpal ngag dbang bsod nams dbang po, 1559–1621.

71. 'Jam dbyangs mthu stobs dbang phyug.
72. Ngag dbang kun dga' dbang rgyal.
73. Bsod nams dpal bzang, dates unknown.
74. Ngor mkhan chen nam mkha' dpal bzang, 1532–1602.
75. Mus chen sangs rgyas rgyal mtshan.
76. Jan-Ulrich Sobisch, "The 'Records of Teachings Received' in the Collected Works of A Mes Zhabs: An Untapped Source for the Study of Sa Skya Pa Biographies," in *Tibet, Past and Present: Tibetan Studies I* PIATS 2000. (Leiden; Boston; Köln: Brill, 2002), 6.
77. 'Jam mgon a myes zhabs ngag dbang kun dga' bsod nams, *'Dzam gling byang phyogs kyi thub pa'i rgyal tshab chen po dpal ldan sa skya pa'i gdung rabs rin po che ji ltar byon pa'i tshul gyi rnam par thar pa ngo tshar rin po che'i bang mdzod dgos 'dod kun 'byung* (Delhi: Tashi Dorje, 1975), 664–65.
78. Ibid., 6–7.
79. *Dpal ldan sa skya pa'i bla ma dam pa chos kyi rje sems can thams cad kyi ston pa la na med pa rnams la rjes su 'brang ba bdag yang yang phyag bgyi'o.*
80. Ma bzang spun bdun.
81. In the Tibetan, part of the poetic display here is playing with words for "holding" and "bearing" (*'chang; 'dzin*) such things as names, vajras, and malice against the doubled meaning of *khön* (*'khon*) as malice, malevolence, or aberration, but also the family name of the great Sakyapa founders.
82. An epithet of the sun in Indian mythology, wherein seven horses draw it across the sky in a chariot.
83. In this verse the play is off of the doubled meaning of *sakya* (*sa skya*), as meaning literally "gray earth," but then also, of course, the name of the famed monastic institution and Buddhist tradition.
84. Here the reference is to the powerful Mongolian nobility and qaγans of the Mongol Empire and Yuan Dynasty who became patrons and tantric disciples of several Sakya masters.
85. Interlinear note from original text: "The famous heart disciples of the mantra holder Kunga Rinchen were Lodrö (Blo gros) and Sönam Wangpo (Bsod nams dbang po)."
86. Dkon mchog lhun grub, 1497–1557.
87. *Sa skya pa'i gdung rabs ya rabs kha rgyan.*
88. Spyi ring; G.yu ring; G.yu se.
89. Dmu bza' ldem bu.
90. Ma bzang spyi rje.
91. Thog lcam 'ur mo.
92. Dpa' bo stag.
93. Klu lcam bra ma.
94. Klu tsa stag po 'od can.
95. Mon bza' mtso mo rgya.
96. *Rigs sras.*
97. In other words, at the meeting place of a rocky mountain (*g.ya' ri*) and a grassy hill or mountain (*spang ri*).
98. G.ya' spang skyes, lit. "Born at Rock and Grass." This would later become a generic name used by the Sakya hierarchs.

99. Gtsang rab gsal, G.yo dge 'byung, and Dmar sha kya mu ne: three bhikṣus who escaped persecution during the period of fragmentation by fleeing eastward from Central Tibet with donkey loads of Vinaya and Abhidharma scriptures. According to traditional histories, these three first went westward to Ngari, then to Mongolian kingdoms in the north and east. Unable to communicate with their Mongol hosts, they settled eventually in the still-active monastic institutions of the eastern Tibetan principality of Tsongkha.

100. Bla chen gongs pa rab gsal (ca. 832–915), a master of the Vinaya monastic code who preserved its lineage in eastern Tibet during the persecution of Buddhist monasticism in Central Tibet during the period of fragmentation.

101. In other words, they and the kings, lamas, and translators listed in the following sentences helped to end the turbulent period of fragmentation (*sil bu'i skabs*, ca. 847–1264) between the mid-ninth-century assassination of Langdarma and the centralization of religious and political authority under the Sakya and their Mongol patrons in the thirteenth century.

102. *Lha btsun khu dbon*. The king of Ngari, Lha Lama Yeshé Öd (Lha bla ma ye shes 'od), and his nephew Lhatsün Jangchup Ö (Lha btsun byang chub 'od, 947–1019/1024), who centralized political power in Western Tibet, patronized the revitalization of Buddhist institutions and practice, and invited Atiśa to come from India.

103. I.e., the Bengali master Atiśa Dīpaṃkara Śrījñāna (982–ca. 1055) and his Tibetan disciples, including principally the layman Dromtönpa Gyalwa Jungné ('Brom ston pa rgyal ba 'byung gnas, 1004–64).

104. 'Gos khug pa lhas btsas, ca. eleventh century.

105. 'Brog mi lo tsā ba shākya ye shes (ca. 992–1043/1072), 'Gos lo tsā ba gzhon nu dpal (1392–1481), and Mar pa lo tsā ba chos kyi blo gros (ca. 1012–97).

106. Pa tsab lo tsā ba nyi ma grags pa (b. 1055), Rngog lo tsā ba blo ldan shes rab (1059–1109), and Khyung rin chen grags (ca. eleventh century).

107. Rwa lo tsā ba rdo rje grags (1016–1128), 'Bro lo tsā ba shes rab grags pa (ca. twelfth century).

108. *Rgyal rigs; rje'u rigs; dmangs rigs.*

109. ['Khon] dkon pa rje gung stag, also known as Khön Palpoché ('Khon dpal po che), is remembered as a minister of Trisong Detsen (Khri srong lde btsan, 742–96), one of the famed kings of Tibet's Yarlung Empire (which extended, according to tradition, between the advent of the reign of Nyatri Tsenpo in 390 BCE and the assassination of Langdarma in 842 CE).

110. The paternal lineage is identified as originating from the "bone" (*rus*) and the maternal lineage from one's tribe, or sometimes "race" (*rigs*).

111. Tibetan monastic historians have identified these original clans and tribes in many ways. A common list gives the four original clans as *se*, *rmu*, *ldong*, and *stong* and the six tribes as *dbra*, *'gru*, *sdong*, *sgo*, *nu bo*, and *dbal brda*.

112. Spyi ring, G.yu ring, and G.yu se.

113. Si byi le.

114. *Ldong rus chen bco brgyad.*

115. Dmu.

116. Dmu za ldem bu.

117. Ma sang spyi rje. The masang are a class of non-human beings said to have

inhabited Tibetan lands before the arrival of humans.

118. Thog lcam 'ur mo.
119. Thog lha 'od can.
120. Thog tsha dpa' bo stag.
121. Klu lcam bra ma.
122. Klu tsha stag po 'od can.
123. Mon bza' mtsho mo rgyal.
124. G.ya spang skyes.
125. G.yas ru shangs.
126. G.yas spang.
127. Skya rings khrag med. There are numerous demons of all sorts in Tibet, often summarized into the eight classes of gods and spirits (*lha srin sde brgya*); the *srin po* are particularly vicious demons who eat human flesh and live in a southwestern region called Chamara.
128. G.ya 'brum si li ma.
129. 'Khon bar skyes.
130. Btsan bza' lcam bu sgron.
131. Dkon pa rje gung stag.
132. 'Khon ston dpal po che.
133. Gnyan rtse.
134. Glang bza' ne chung.
135. Khri mdzes; Lha legs; Tse lha dbang phyug; Klu yi dbang po tse 'dzin.
136. Here Ameshab moves between the verses and his explanation in a very clearly delineated way that we don't see in much of the rest of the text. We have tried to retain the style while keeping things clear for readers.
137. Klu'i bong po; Rdo rje rin chen.
138. Klu'i dbang po.
139. Ga ring rgyal po.
140. *Rtsis bsdur*. This refers to a letter addressed to Garing from Drakpa Gyaltsen, published as "Ga ring rgyal po la rtsis bsdur du btang ba'i yi ge" and found, for example, on pages 448–51 of volume *Nya* in the *Sa skya bka' 'bum* (Kathmandu: Sachen International, 2006).
141. 'Bro bza g.ya' lon skyed.
142. 'Bro tsha. 'Bro was an important family clan in early Tibet.
143. Mtha' ltag shes rab yon tan.
144. Grom pa.
145. Yon tan 'byung gnas; Tshul khrims rgyal; Gtsug tor shes rab; Dge skyabs; Dge mthong; 'Khon ston bal po; Shākya blo gros.
146. Shes rab tshul khrims; Dkon mchog rgyal po.
147. G.ya' phrug 'khon bar skye.
148. Shel tsha rgyal mo'i gangs.
149. *Bla mtsho*. For more information on this topic, see: Katia Buffetrille, "Reflections on Pilgrimages to Sacred Mountains, Lakes, and Caves," in *Pilgrimage in Tibet*, ed. Alex McKay (Richmond, London: Curzon Press, 1998): 18–34, among many other articles and books on this topic.
150. Sngags 'chang chos kyi rgyal po.
151. I.e., Ngakchang Drakpa Lodrö (Sngags 'chang grags pa blo gros) and

Jamyang Sönam Wangpo ('Jam dbyangs bsod nams dbang po).

152. Mnga' ris.
153. Btsan bza' lcam bu sgron.
154. *Yid 'phrog pa.*
155. Bsam yas.
156. Dgun tha; Dgun smug.
157. Thar gyi ya chang.
158. Gam 'brog; Rgyang 'brog.
159. Stag tshang lo tsā ba shes rab rin chen, 1405–77.
160. Literally, the "good qualities of the contents" (*bcud kyi yon tan*).
161. Literally, the "good qualities of the vessel" (*snod kyi yon tan*).
162. Khri srong lde'u btsan, 742–98 CE.
163. 'Khon dpal bo che.
164. Glang khams pa lo tsā ba.
165. Glang bza' ne chung ma.
166. 'Khon lo tsā ba klu'i dbang po bsrung ba; 'Khon rdo rje rin po che.
167. *Sgra pa sgyur gyi lo tsā ba sad mi bdun*. These men, each of them translators, were famously examined by the Indian abbot Śāntarakṣita, who determined they were suitable candidates for monastic ordination. According to legend, they then became Tibet's first seven Buddhist monks.
168. The first is the aforementioned *Ya rabs kha rgyan*, followed by the much-abbreviated titles: *Nyi lde*, *Mus pa*, and *Ngo mtshar snang ba*.
169. Khri mdzes lha legs; Tshe lha dbang phyug; Klu'i dbang po; Tshe 'dzin.
170. The *Nyidé*, for example, has them as the same person.
171. In the Tibetan, the titles of the succession histories claiming these historical views were added as interlinear notes by some unknown hand. For clarity, we have included those notes in the body of the text, even though there is some redundancy.
172. *Gtsang byams pa'i gdung rabs.*
173. *Gsung rab dgongs gsal.*
174. Lho pa kun mkhyen; Bde ba can ye shes mgon po.
175. Klu'i dbang po bsrungs pa.
176. Mkhan chen Zhi ba 'tsho, ca. 725–88.
177. The specific ordination that Śāntarakṣita conferred was that of a prarajita/pravrajyā (Tib. *rab tu byung ba*), the lower novitiate ordination of a śrāmaṇera (male) or śrāmaṇerikā (female).
178. I.e., "the Protector Lui Wangpo": Klu'i dbang po bsrungs pa.
179. Lui Wangpo's uncle was the aforementioned Lang Khampa Lotsāwa; both are counted among the "seven men to be tested."
180. Bde gshegs go cha bsrungs pa.
181. To clarify, Ameshab is saying that this Khön ancestor ought to be counted among these seven progenitors of Buddhist monasticism in Tibet under the name Deshek Gocha Sungpa and not Lang Khampa Lotsāwa.
182. Yer pa'i brag.
183. 'Bro dgra 'dul; 'Bro bza' g.yang lon skyid.
184. 'Brog gnyan rtse.
185. Mnga' ris mang yul.

186. Mnga' ris gung thang.
187. Srad.
188. Gnyal lo ro.
189. Nyang shab.
190. Ma khrigs sde gsum.
191. Shes rab yon tan.
192. Grom pa g.ya' lung.
193. Khab so stag thog.
194. Yon tan 'byung gnas.
195. Tshul khrims rgyal po.
196. Grom pa.
197. Brdal chang tshang.
198. Gtsug tor shes rab.
199. G.ya' lung.
200. 'Khon dge skyabs.
201. Phyis shab.
202. Shab stod kyi 'khon.
203. Dge mthong.
204. Yang dag [he ru ka]; [Rdo rje] phur bu.
205. Tsha mo rong gi brag.
206. *Dngos grub*. *Siddhi* means "attainment," in the sense of realization produced through successfully practicing the grounds and paths described in the Buddha's teachings.
207. Shākya blo gros.
208. Bya ru lung pa; Shab stod smad.
209. G.ya' lung mkhar stabs.
210. 'Khon rog shes rab tshul khrims; 'Khon dkon mchog rgyal po.
211. Skt. *gōmi upāsaka*, Tib. *gōmi'i dge bsnyen*. This is like the lay anagārikā vows (Tib. *khyim med pa*), or "going forth into homelessness" vows, which include keeping the five precepts (Skt. *pañcaśīla*) plus not eating at the inappropriate time, not dancing or singing or adorning the body, and not sleeping or sitting on high beds. Here celibacy is added to those eight precepts. In the Tibetan tradition, gōmi upāsaka precepts may be taken for a day, months, years, or a lifetime. Keeping these vows may or may not involve wearing monk's robes, though such upāsakas are not technically monks.
212. Zhu ston brtson 'grus.
213. Lo ston rdo rje dbang phyug.
214. Skt. *pāramitāyāna*; Tib. *pha rol tu phyin pa'i theg pa*. In other words, they were acquainted with some of the philosophical traditions (*mtshan nyid kyi skor*) of the general Mahāyāna, in the piecemeal fashion in which these were known in Central Tibet before the eleventh century.
215. Sna 'gyur.
216. Yang dag [he ru ka].
217. [Rdo rje] phur bu.
218. Dkar mo ni zla; Bdud mgon.
219. *Nus pa*.
220. I.e., Beginning with the younger brother of Khön Rok Sherab Tsultrim, the

Khön lineage practiced according to the tantric systems of the New Translation schools.

221. Zhang mo bsod nams skyid.
222. Kun dga' snying po.
223. Tsha rong ma; Jo lcam phur mo.
224. Kun dga' 'bar.
225. Jo lcam 'od sgron.
226. Slo dpon rtse mo; Rje btsun grag pa [rgyal mtshan]; Dpal chen 'od po.
227. Gar phu ma Nyi khri lcam.
228. Sa skya paṇ chen; Zangs tsha bsod nams rgyal mtshan.
229. Mdog stod tsha sna ma Ma gcig kun skyid.
230. 'Phags pa; 'Gro mgon phyag na rdo rje.
231. Sa skya'i chu mdo ma Jo 'bro.
232. Slod dpon rin rgyal.
233. Ma gcig rdo rje ldan.
234. Ye shes 'byung gnas.
235. Ma gcig zha lu ma Mkha' 'gro 'bum.
236. Stag 'bum.
237. Ma gcig khab smad ma Chos srin skyid. This was Sangpo Pal (Bzang po dpal).
238. Bdag nyid chen po.
239. 'Khon dkon mchog rgyal po, 1034–1102.
240. 'Bro'i lung.
241. Dbyang phyug ma.
242. Dkar mo nyi zla lcam sring.
243. 'Brog mi sākya ye shes, ca. 992–1043 or 1072.
244. 'Khyin lo tsā ba.
245. 'Gos lo tsa ba gzhon nu dpal, 1392–1481.
246. O rgyan gyi paṇḍita shes rab gsang ba.
247. Thig le lnga.
248. Rma lo tsā ba dge ba'i blo gros, 1044–89.
249. Mal lo tsā ba blo gros grags pa; Ba ri lo tsa ba rin chen drak (1040–1111); Spu hrang lo tsā ba; Gnam kha'u pa; 'Khon sgyi chu ba; Skyu ra a seng.
250. I.e., stūpas or statues of them, likely with relics inside.
251. Zhang yul 'jag gshong.
252. Bra bo lung.
253. Sa skya gog po.
254. Dpon po ri.
255. Jo bo gdong nag pa.
256. Zhang gzhung gu ra ba dang; Ban de grong bzhi; Lha mi grong bdun.
257. Mon grog.
258. 'Bal grog.
259. Jowo lha gcig, 982–1054.
260. Sbyin pa dpal.
261. Gnam kha'u pa dar ma seng ge.
262. Spyan ras gzigs kha sar pā ni.
263. Ma gcig zhang mo.

264. Kha'u skyed lhas kyi dgon pa.
265. *'od gsal*. Though interpretations differ widely in sūtra and tantric systems, clear light is generally presented as the innate, fundamental nature of mind itself.
266. Dkar gong lung.
267. Chang is a barley wine popular across Tibetan societies.
268. Phru ma.
269. Thugs rje gdong; Yi chad 'phrang. These translate as: "The Face of Compassion [Mountain]" and "The Precipitous Path of Disappointment."
270. Kun dga' snying po, 1092–1158.
271. Phru ma'i bdud 'dul mchod rten.
272. Sngags 'chang chos kyi rgyal po.
273. Phru ma'i dgon gnas.
274. Spyin pa dpal.
275. Kun dga' snying po.
276. Rdo rje phyug mo, who was Könchok Gyalpo's wife.
277. Bya khram.
278. Mkhar sgo lung.
279. Dkar gong lung.
280. *Rigs gsum mgon pa*; Skt. *Trikulanātha*. These are Avalokiteśvara, Mañjuśrī, and Vajrapāni, the embodiments of all the buddhas' compassion, wisdom, and power, respectively.
281. Mnga' ris stod, in the west of the Tibetan plateau.
282. 'Brom ston pa [rgyal ba'i 'byung gnas], 1004–64.
283. 'Brong nu.
284. Dpon po.
285. Phyag 'tshal sgang.
286. Klong gsal mkha' 'gro snyan brgyud.
287. Lit. "They will uphold the Buddha's teachings from the ten [periods] of five [hundred]" (*sangs rgyas bstan pa lnga bcu 'dzin*).
288. *Sa chen la bstod pa*.
289. 'Jam mgon. "The Smooth Protector," an epithet for Mañjuśrī.
290. Sgo rung.
291. Grog po gdung tshugs.
292. Kha'u'i mdo.
293. Zhang gzhung gu ra ba.
294. *Mtho ris yon tan bdun*. These seven qualities are usually listed as: long life, good health, a beautiful physical form, good fortune, high social position, abundant wealth, and great wisdom.
295. I.e., his father passed away.
296. G.yu mkhar mo.
297. 'Phrang; Brag dmar.
298. This is the widely practiced root mantra of Mañjuśrī, embodiment of all the buddhas' wisdom.
299. *Dung gi mi chen po*.
300. Dpe dkar.
301. Jo bo mi g.yo ba (Skt. Acalanātha, the "Immovable Lord").
302. Chu'i srung ba.

303. 'Jam dpal brag khung.
304. *Zhen pa bzhi bral*. Though there are different versions, the one-verse teaching is as follows: "If attached to this life, you are not a Dharma practitioner; / if attached to saṃsāra, you have no renunciation; / if attached to your own welfare, you have no bodhicitta; / if grasping arises, you do not possess the view."
305. Rong ngur smig.
306. Brang ti ba.
307. Yar 'brog khob le.
308. *'brum bu*.
309. A pho phag ston.
310. Bra chung gong kha.
311. Bdud rgyal thod phreng can.
312. Ngur smrig pa brang ti dar ma snying po.
313. Byang chad pa khyung.
314. *Sa sde lnga*. I.e., Skt. *Yogācārabhūmi*; Tib. *Rnal 'byor spyod pa'i sa*.
315. *Sdom rnam gnyis*. This refers to Asanga's *Compendium of the Mahāyāna* (Skt. *Mahāyānasaṃgraha*; Tib. *Theg pa chen po bsdus pa*) and his *Compendium of Abhidharma* (Skt. *Abhidharmasamuccaya*; Tib. *Mngon pa kun btus*).
316. Nyang stod.
317. Khyung rin chen grags.
318. Skt. *Pramāṇaviniścaya*; Tib. *Tshad ma rnam par nges pa*.
319. Skt. *Nyāyabindu*; Tib. *Rigs pa'i thig pa*.
320. Me dig pa.
321. Skt. *Ratnakūṭa Sūtra*; Tib. *'Phags pa dkon mchog brtsegs pa'i mdo*.
322. Skt. *Buddhāvataṃsaka Sūtra*; Tib. *Sangs rgyas phal po che'i mdo*.
323. Skt. *kriyātantra*; Tib. *bya ba'i rgyud*.
324. Skt. *caryātantra*; Tib. *spyod rgyud*.
325. Gzhin rje gshed.
326. Khro bo rnam par rgyal ba.
327. Rnal 'byor chen po'i rgyud.
328. Dpal gsang ba 'dus pa.
329. Sangs rgyas ye shes zhabs.
330. Dpal 'dzin.
331. *Dpal rdo rje gdan bzhi*.
332. *Sangs rgyas mnyam sbyor*.
333. *Sgrub thabs rgya rtsa*.
334. Rnam rgyal mchod rten.
335. Sangs rgyas 'od srungs.
336. Rnam rgyal gyi gzungs.
337. Slob dpon bsod nams rtse mo.
338. Mgon po'i bka' babs bzhi.
339. Rdo mgon yid bzhin gyi nor bu.
340. Bar phug.
341. Grom g.yu rtse 'byid phu.
342. Me lhang tshor.
343. This refers to the *Madhyamakālaṃkāra* of Śāntarakṣita, *Madhyamakāloka* of Ka-

malasila, and *Madhyamakā Satyadvayavibhaṅga* of Jñānagarbha.

344. Gnam kha'u pa [dar ma seng ge].
345. Skt. *Vidyottama;* Tib. *Rig pa mchog gi rgyud legs par grub pa.*
346. Skt. *Subāhupariprcchā;* Tib. *Dpung pa bzang po.*
347. Skt. *Vajrapāṇyabhiṣeka;* Tib. *Phyag rdor dbang bskur ba'i rgyud.*
348. Skt. *Sarvamaṇḍalasāmānyavidhiguhyatantra;* Tib. *Gsang ba spyi rgyud.*
349. Skt. *Dhyanottaratantra;* Tib. *Sam gtan phyi ma.*
350. *Dam tshig gsum bkod.*
351. Skt. *Vairocanābhisa bodhi;* Tib. *Rnam snang mngon byang rgyud.*
352. Skt. *Tattvasaṃgraha;* Tib. *De nyid 'dus pa* [sic. *bsdus pa*].
353. Skt. *Tattvāloka;* Tib. *De nyid snang ba.*
354. Skt. *Kosalālaṃkāratattvasaṃgrahatīka;* Tib. *Ko sa la'i rgyan.*
355. Skt. *Paramādikalpa;* Tib. *Dpal mchog dang po'i rgyud.*
356. *Stong phrag nyi shu rtsa lnga.*
357. *Rdo rje rtsem mo.*
358. *Mgon po kun snang.*
359. Skt. *Sarvadurgatipariśodhanatejorāja;* Tib. *Ngan song sbyong rgyud.*
360. Skt. *Sarvarahasyanāmatantrarāja;* Tib. *Thams cad gsang ba rgyud.*
361. *Rdo rje 'byung ba.*
362. *Khams gsum rnam rgyal.*
363. *Gtsug [gtor chen po bam po] dgu pa.*
364. Skt. *Pradīpoddyotana;* Tib. *Sgron gsal.*
365. *Rim lnga mdo bsre.*
366. Skt. *Caryāmelāpakapradīpa;* Tib. *Spyod bsdus.*
367. Skt. *Svādhiṣṭhānakramaprabheda;* Tib. *Bdag byin gyis brlab pa'i rim pa.*
368. *Sems kyis sgrib sbyong.*
369. Klu'i [byang chub].
370. *Dkyil cho ga nyi shu.*
371. *Sgrub thabs kun bzang.*
372. *Tha ka na,* i.e., *Kun tu bzang po shes bya ba'i sgrub pa'i thabs.*
373. Skt. *Kusumāñjaliguhyasamājanibandha;* Tib. *Snyim pa'i me tog.*
374. *Sgrub thabs bstan pa'i nor rdzas.*
375. Mi bkyod rdo rje.
376. Bsod synoms pa.
377. Sgeg pa'i rdo rje.
378. Zla gsang dpal.
379. *Rnam rtog bde ba.*
380. Skt. *Abhisamayālaṅkāra;* Tib. *Mngon rtogs rgyan.*
381. Skt. *Śikṣāsamuccaya;* Tib. *Bslab pa kun las btus pa.* On the training and practice of bodhisattvas, heavily supplemented by Mahāyāna sūtras.
382. Skt. *Bodhicaryāvatāra;* Tib. *Spyod 'jug.* Śāntideva's masterwork on the gradual training of a bodhisattva.
383. Skt. *Mahāsūtrasamuccaya;* Tib. *Mdo kun las btus pa.*
384. Pu hrang pa gsal snying.
385. 'Khon sgyi chu ba dgra lha 'bar.
386. Srid pa'i rgya mtsho.
387. Bram zer nag po.

388. *Rnal 'byor sbyor phreng.*
389. *Snying po'i skor gyi grub pa sde bco brgyad.*
390. *Zla gsang thig le.*
391. *Sangs rgyas thod pa.*
392. Mar pa lo tsā ba.
393. *Brtag* [*gnyis*].
394. *Ma hā mā yā rgyud.*
395. Bla ma Mnga' ris pa.
396. Bla ma se [ston kun rig], also known as Se 'khar chung ba (1029–1116).
397. Mdog stod.
398. Mkhar chung pa'i rje.
399. Where Lama Setön Kunrik was then based.
400. Ston pa rdo rje 'od; Zhang btsun ra tsa.
401. Tib. *rab tu byung ba*. In the Mūlasarvāstivāda Vinaya tradition followed in Tibet, such ordination involves following thirty-six precepts. Only after a certain probationary period, involving being a junior excluded from many major communal activities of the monastic order, can a novice later take higher (*upasaṃpadā*) ordination.
402. Bla ma mal [lo tsā ba blo gros grags pa].
403. *Gung thang na la rtsel gnas gsar.*
404. *He ru ka mngon 'byung.*
405. [*Rnal 'byor ma'i*] *Kun* [*tu*] *spyod* [*pa*].
406. *Rnal 'byor ma bzhi*[*'i*] *kha sbyor* [*gyi rgyud*].
407. *Mkha' 'gro ma mngon 'byung*. Presumably: *Ḍākinīsarvacittādvayācintyajñānavajravarāhyabhibhavatantrarāja*.
408. Nag po chos drug.
409. Nā ro mkha' spyod.
410. Jo bo rin chen bzang po.
411. Slob dpon ko ka na rgyal ba bzang po.
412. *Mi g.yo ba.*
413. *Phyag na rdo rje.*
414. *Bde mchog sdom 'byung.*
415. Rin chen rdo rje.
416. Skt. *Yuktikāya*; Tib. *Dbu ma rigs tshogs.*
417. Skt. *Sūtrasamuccaya*; Tib. *Mdo kun las btsus pa.*
418. *Bstod pa'i tshogs.*
419. The text only gives "Rtog bdun." This may refer to one of the action tantra ritual texts of the goddess Mārīcī (*'Od zer can ma*) canonized in the Kangyur, such as *Ārya Mārīcī Maṇḍalavidhi Mārīcījāta Dvādaśasahasra Uddhitaṃ Kalpa Hṛdaya Saptaśata* (Tib. *'Phags ma 'od zer can gyi dkyil 'khor gyi cho ga 'od zer can 'byung ba'i rgyud stong phrag bcu gnyis pa las phyung ba'i rtog pa'i snying po bdun brgya pa*).
420. G.yas ru na ma.
421. *Sbyong rgyud*. Presumably, this refers to *Śūnyatāsamādhivajra* (Tib. [*Dpal ngan song thams cad yongs su*] *sbyong* [*ba'i*] *rgyud*.
422. *Rab gnas kyi rgyud*. Presumably, this refers to *Supratiṣṭhatantrasaṁgraha* (Tib. *Rab* [*tu*] *gnas* [*pa mdor bsdus pa'i*] *rgyud*).

423. Bse 'bag nag po 'phur.
424. Lho stod.
425. Pu hrang lo chung.
426. *Bal po bhadanta'i lugs.*
427. Ha ngu.
428. Mchog sred.
429. Mdo khams.
430. 'Bri khung pa'i skyu ra a skye ba.
431. Lha [*sic* Lho] rdo rje snying po.
432. *Sman pa'i zhabs.*
433. *Rin po che'i ljon shing.*
434. Mar me mdzad bzang po.
435. *Dngos grub 'byung ba'i gter.*
436. Skt. *Vajrāmṛtamahā Tantra*; Tib. *Rdo rje bdud rtsi'i rgyud.*
437. *Sems 'dzin brgyad bcu pa.*
438. Skt. *Mañjuśrīnāmasaṃgīti*; Tib. *Mtshan brjod.*
439. *Dus 'khor.*
440. Dge bshes rngog.
441. *Nyi khri snang ba.*
442. Skt. *Prajñāpāramitāpiṇḍārtha*; Tib. *Brgyad stong don bsdus.*
443. Zhang ston.
444. *Bstan pa'i nor rdzas.*
445. Sag thang.
446. Rdzogs chen rtsa mun ti.
447. Jo sras 'od mchog.
448. Se ston rdor 'byung.
449. Dor ka mdo.
450. When a dog sees lungs, apparently, it will act to consume them as quickly as possible without a moment's thought. This Tibetan expression cautions against jumping to action without careful consideration.
451. *Lam skor dgu.*
452. *Phra mo nyi shu rtsa lnga.*
453. Gsang 'dus rtsa rgyud.
454. Mnyam sbyor rtsa rgyud.
455. Bla ma A seng.
456. *Lam 'bras don bsdus ma.*
457. *Sga theng ma*, *Zhu byas ma*, and *Klog skya ma.*
458. Dge bshes Snyag.
459. *Kun gzhi rgyu rgyud.*
460. *Gdan sogs lus dkyil.*
461. *'Chi ltas brtag pa 'chi bslu dang bcas pa.*
462. *'Da' kha ma'i gdams ngag.*
463. *Thig le'i rnal 'byor.*
464. *Phyag rgya'i mtshan nyid.*
465. *Yi ge sgo dgag pa'i man ngag.*
466. *Bar do bzhi.* Referring to the bardo of birth, the bardo of dying, the bardo of the dharmatā, and the bardo of becoming.

467. *Lam dus kyi dbang.*
468. *Tshad ma bzhi.* These include: the nondeceptive śāstras, the nondeceptive scriptures, the nondeceptive lama, and nondeceptive experience.
469. *Gdams ngag drug.*
470. *Rten 'brel lnga.*
471. *Rdo rje mkha' 'gro'i sbyin sreg.*
472. *Grib ma khrus kyis sel ba.*
473. *Tsha tshas sel ba.* Tsatsa are miniature figures, usually of the buddhas and other deities, molded in clay and used as offerings. The preparation of one hundred thousand tsatsa is one of the traditional preparatory practices for long retreat.
474. *Thig le bsrung ba.*
475. *Yig brgya 'don thabs.*
476. *Rlung sbyor bdun gyi lam khrid pa.*
477. *Bha ga'i yi ge bcu bzhi.*
478. *'Khor bzhi'i rgya.*
479. *Sa bcu gsum pa'i sa phyed kyi mngon rtogs.*
480. *'Khor 'das dbyer med.* This indivisibility represents the main view of the Sakya school.
481. *Dbang bzhi'i cho ga'i gnad.*
482. *Mchog dbang gsum gyi yi ge.*
483. *Phyi bskyed rim gyi gdams ngag.*
484. *Bdud rtsi ril bu sgrub thabs.*
485. *'Phrang bdun bsal ba'i man ngag.*
486. *Byung rgyal du mi gtong ba'i gnad bzhi.*
487. *'Byung ba lus 'khrugs rlung dang spyod lam gyis bsal ba.*
488. *Phrin las so gnyis.*
489. *Lam 'bring po.*
490. *Lam bsdus pa.*
491. *Gzhung ji ltar ba bzhin du bkri ba.*
492. *Gnad drug gis bkri ba.*
493. *Gnad bcu gcig gis bkri ba.*
494. *Dbang po rab 'bring gsum gyis bkri ba.*
495. *Lam 'jug ldog.*
496. *Phyag rgya 'jug ldog.*
497. *Shes pas phan 'dogs pa'i man ngag bdun.*
498. *Lam sra ba 'gros dang bcas pa.*
499. *Phyi nang gi mdzad pa bcu gnyis.*
500. *Bla ma'i rnal 'byor.*
501. *Bla ma bod kyi lo rgyus.*
502. *Rgya gar ba'i lo rgyus.*
503. *Bir wa pa'i glu dang bcas pa.*
504. *Tog tse pa'i bsam mi khyab la man ngag lnga.*
505. *Mtsho skyes kyi rnam thar.*
506. *Mtsho skyes kyi zab pa'i tshul dgu.*
507. *Dombi pa'i man ngag bzhi.*
508. *Nag po pa'i gtum mo lam rdzogs.*

509. *Ngag dbang grags pa'i yi ge med pa.*
510. *Klu sgrub kyi mchod rten drung thob.*
511. *Yon po bsrang ba'i man ngag.*
512. *Indra bhūti'i man ngag.*
513. *Rgyud sde spyi'i rnam gzhag.*
514. *Rgyud brtag gnyis kyi bsdus don.*
515. *Brtag gnyis kyi dka' 'grel.*
516. *Gur gyi tho yig zer ba'i rgyud kyi don bsdus.*
517. *Klu'i bshad pa.*
518. *Rtsa'i mngon rtogs.*
519. *Gur gyi bshad pa'i chings.*
520. *Rdo rje snying 'grel gyi yig sna.*
521. *Sgrub thabs mtsho skyes kyi don 'grel.*
522. *Bde mchog rtsa rgyud kyi le 'grel.*
523. *Rtsa rgyud kyi sa bcad.*
524. *Bde mchog nag po pa'i dkyil chog gi tho yig.*
525. *Ras bris la brten pa'i dkyil cho ga.*
526. *Gsang ba'i de kho na nyid kyi don gyi cha gsungs bzhin bris pa.*
527. *O la pa ti'i don bsdus.*
528. *Dde mchog gi rnal 'byor pa'i ro sreg pa'i cho ga.*
529. *O la pa ti'i 'grel pa.*
530. *Gsang ba'i de kho na nyid kyi tshig don bsdus pa'i go 'byed.*
531. *'Jigs byed rtogs bdun gyi tī ka.*
532. *Sgrol ma bcu bdun ma'i dkyil cho ga.*
533. *Man ngag gces bsdus.*
534. *Bha ya na'i srung 'khor.*
535. *Bla ma skyu ra a skyabs la zhu yig.*
536. *Bum gter gzhug tshul gyi man ngag.*
537. *Sgrub thabs mtsho skyes kyi sa bcad.*
538. *Bde mchog rtsa rgyud kyi tī ka mu tig gi phreng ba.*
539. *Bde mchog rtsa rgyud kyi tī ka mu tig gi phreng ba.*
540. *Tshogs bdag (dang) 'dod rgyal.*
541. G.yas ru'i grong chung dgon pa.
542. Brang khang snying pa dgon pa.
543. *Lcags ri phyir mi 'da' ba'i zab mo chos bzhi.*
544. Tshar kha.
545. Dril bu pa.
546. Gron la lcam lha khang.
547. 'Bring mtshams.
548. Zangs sdong.
549. Shab sgo lnga.
550. Lha chen stag tsha.
551. Re ba 'dzu gu.
552. Rdo rje rgyal.
553. Ldan ma.
554. Sgo rum gzims spyil dkar po.
555. The dates seem meaningful here, for the twenty-ninth of the lunar month is

traditionally reserved for extensive ritual practices for the Dharma protectors. The Dharma protector Mahākāla is an accomplice in this narrative of wrathful, sacred violence. The dating thus collapses the killing into a permissible ritual act.

556. Bse mgon chen po.
557. Ngag dbang kun dga' rin chen.
558. Sgo rum.
559. Dbu rtse.
560. Re ba dzu gu.
561. Chos khri thang mo che.
562. *Bzlogs bsad kyi sngags.*
563. Khams pa rdor rgyal; Bde gshegs khams pa rdor rgyal.
564. Phag gru.
565. Rdo rje rgyal po.
566. Sa lo 'Jam pa'i rdo rje.
567. *Sa skya'i gnas bshad.*
568. Slob dpon dpal ldan rtse mo.
569. Singga la'i gling.
570. Byang chub sems dpa' stag.
571. Sgom pa skyi 'bar ba.
572. Rje btsun rin po che.
573. Zhu byas.
574. Dga' ston rdo rje grags.
575. Nags sgom bsod nams rgyal mtshan.
576. Tshar kha'i rnal 'byor pa.
577. Sgom pa 'od grags.
578. Mang chung ma.
579. *Gsung ngag gi chos 'byung chen mo legs bshad 'dus pa'i rgya mtsho.*
580. Zhu byas.
581. Khams pa a seng.
582. Lho pa zhu byas.
583. Klog skya jo sras chos grags.
584. Gnyan phul chung ba.
585. Gtsug tor rgyal po.
586. Mtshan dngos bsod nams rdo rje.
587. Byang sems zla ba rgyal mtshan.
588. Zangs ri phug pa.
589. Khams pa sga theng.
590. Snyag bzhi dar ma dbang phyug rgyal mtshan.
591. Kun dga' 'bar.
592. Jo lcam phur mo.
593. G.ya' lung gi jo mo a 'u ma.
594. Mang mkhar gyi jo mo mang chung ma.
595. Rnam 'grel bcu gcig.
596. Sna ro bande.
597. Stong sgom byang chub shes rab.
598. Mi nyag pra dznyā dzwa la.

599. Zhu brag dmar ba.
600. Yar sbu ba.
601. 'U yug.
602. Phag mo grub pa.
603. La stod pa dkon mchog mkhar.
604. Khams pa rgwa lo.
605. Ne tshe sbal ston.
606. Gshen rdo rje bzang po.
607. *Rje sa chen gyi bstod pa.*
608. Paṇchen mi myag grags rdor.
609. Singga gling gi rnal 'byor.
610. Byang sems stag.
611. Sgom pa skyi 'bar.
612. Rje btsun chen po.
613. Zhus byas songs grub.
614. Nags sgom bsod rgyal.
615. Sgom pa 'od grags.
616. Dga' ston.
617. Mang chung ma.
618. Dpal chen rgwa lo.
619. Zla ba rgyal mtshan.
620. Sgom pa rta rgan.
621. Phag ston.
622. Rgyal tsha tal phug pa.
623. Rta nag.
624. Dbyar ston sbu ma ba.
625. Gshen ston rdor seng.
626. G.yor ston.
627. Gshen ston dgon dkar ba.
628. Zhang ston gsum thog pa.
629. 'On.
630. Brag dmar zhu.
631. Zhang ston spe'i dmar pa.
632. Skyu ra a skyabs.
633. Gnam.
634. Lha brag dkar ston.
635. Lcags kyi rdo rje.
636. Mdzangs ston.
637. Mdza' ne.
638. Gsang phu.
639. Bsod nams rdo rje.
640. Gnyan phul chung ba.
641. Snyag ston dbang rgyal.
642. Rgya sgom tshul khrims grags.
643. 'A 'u ma.
644. Rgwa lo.
645. G.yu brag pa.

646. Zla rgyal.
647. Nyin phug pa.
648. I.e., 'Bri kung kyob pa 'jig rten mgon po, 1143–1217; Stag lung thang pa bkra shis dpal, 1142–1209/1210; and Gling rje ras pa padma rdo rje, 1128–88.
649. Rgyal tsha.
650. Ri ma lce bsgom.
651. Phyag, Gtsang, and Nyang ran.
652. I.e., the ninth month.
653. G.yas ry skya bo kha gdong.
654. Gser mdog can.
655. Zhu byas ngos grub.
656. Dge bshes zangs ri phug pa.
657. Sku 'bum rnam rgyal.
658. Spyin pa dpal.
659. Stug po'i bkod pa'i zhing khams.
660. I.e., the Sakya landscape.
661. I.e., Brahmā, Tib. *Tshangs pa.*
662. sic. Skya bzang, i.e., Skya sang or, alternatively, Skya seng. This is the father of a band of five brothers in the *Mahābhārata* epic.
663. I.e., Indra.
664. I.e., Sakya Monastery.
665. I.e., Indra.
666. Tib. Sa srung dbang po.
667. I.e., the Gaṅgā, or Ganges River.
668. Here, as elsewhere in this praise, "great bliss" is in reference to Sakya Monastery.
669. *'dzin ma.*
670. *Dbang po'i nyer 'tsho,* i.e., the fourteenth century *Sa skya'i rnam thar dbang po'i nyer 'tsho* by Nyamé Drakpa Gyaltshen (Mnyam med grags pa rgyal mtshan).
671. Tsha mo rong pa.
672. Jo lcam phur mo.
673. Kun dga' 'bar.
674. Ma gcig 'od sgron.
675. This refers to the three classes of unexcelled yoga tantra class: father tantras (*pha rgyud*), mother tantras (*ma rgyud*), and nondual tantras (*gnyis med kyi rgyud*). Please see the introduction for more detail.
676. Only *Kun las 'tus* (sic. *bstus*) is given in the text. This is a very common component of the titles of many tantras, and it has been difficult to find other sources that could help determine which was meant here.
677. Mi thub zla ba.
678. Skt. *pramāṇa;* Tib. *tshad ma.*
679. Cha pa chos kyi seng ge, 1109–69. Chapa Chökyi Sengé was a prominent Tibetan Buddhist scholar who greatly influenced the formation of Tibetan Buddhist philosophy.
680. *Gser gyi 'gan 'jir,* an ornamental pinnacle on a building.
681. 'Khon jo sras rtse mo.
682. Khu jo sras ne tso.

683. Rngog jo sras ra mo.
684. Gnyis jo sras 'od ma.
685. *Chos la 'jug pa'i sgo.*
686. Na la rtse.
687. *Srog shing.*
688. Gzims khang snying ma.
689. Jo sras lcags kyi rdo rje.
690. Rmog ston gtsug tor dbon po.
691. Kun 'dar; Kun tu bzang po.
692. Chos mchog.
693. I.e., a layperson.
694. *Sa skya pa chen po la bstod pa.*
695. *Lam 'bras brgyud pa'i gsol 'debs 'brel mar yod pa.*
696. *Rgya sgom tshul khrims grags la springs pa.*
697. *Slob dpon cha pa la bstod pa.*
698. *Rgyud sde spyi'i rnam gzhag.*
699. *Brtag gnyis kyi rnam bshad nyi ma'i 'od zer.*
700. *Sambu ta'i 'grel pa gnad kyi gsal byed de'i sa bcad rab byed gnyis pa'i tī ka.*
701. *Dpal kye rdo rje'i mngon rtogs rgyas pa.*
702. *Dbang chu chen mo.*
703. *Zhi ba'i sbyin sreg.*
704. *Rab gnas bzang po drug pa.*
705. *Bdag med ma'i dbang gi tho yig.*
706. *Dombi he ru ka'i lugs kyi dkyil 'khor gyi cho ga.*
707. *Sbyin sreg gi cho ga'i tī ka.*
708. *Sgrub thabs mtsho skyes kyi tī ka.*
709. *Dkyil chog nas gling ma.*
710. *Bde mchog dril bu pa'i mngon rtogs chung ngu.*
711. *Bde mchog dril bu pa'i dbang gi bya ba'i tī ka.*
712. *Bde mchog Lu yi pa'i mchod phreng.*
713. *Gtsug tor rnam rgyal gyi rtog pa gnyis kyi tī ka.*
714. *Rtog pa gnyis ka'i sa bcad.*
715. *Rdo rje gdan pa'i chos drug.*
716. *Don zhags lha lnga'i bstod pa.*
717. *Bla ma brgyud pa'i lo rgyus.*
718. *Rtog pa'i sa bcad.*
719. *Rtog pa'i tī ka rin chen phreng ba.*
720. *Mi g.yo sngon po'i chu srung.*
721. *Seng ge sgra'i sgrub skor.*
722. *Gtor chen gyi cho ga.*
723. *Spyod 'jug gi tī ka.*
724. *Chos la 'jug pa'i sgo.*
725. *Byis pa bde blag tu 'jug pa.*
726. I.e., exposition, debate, and composition.
727. *Gdung dbyangs ma.*
728. *Chu mig rdzing kha.*
729. Sngags 'chang chos kyi rgyal po ngag dbang kun dga' rin chen.

730. *Rgyab yol.*
731. Chu mig rdzing kha.
732. Sgo rum dpe khang.
733. Rmog ston.
734. Byang sems zla ba rgyal mtshan.
735. Skt. *poṣadha;* Tib. *gso sbyong.*
736. This is a practice required by the Vinaya of reciting verses in thanks for receiving gifts.
737. Skt. *Bodhisattvasaṃvaraviṃśaka;* Tib. *Byang chub sems dpa'i sdom pa nyi shu pa.*
738. Gnyan gtsug tor rgyal po.
739. Zhang tshul khrims grags.
740. Snyag dbang rgyal.
741. Bal po dza ya se na.
742. Lo tsā ba dar ma yon tan.
743. Sum pa lo tsa ba dpal mchog dang po'i rdo rje.
744. Sman zhabs.
745. *Sbyong rgyud.*
746. Skt. *Mañjuśrīnāmasaṃgīti;* Tib. *'Jam dpal mtshan brjod.*
747. Mi g.yo ba'i rtod pa chen po.
748. Skt. *Subāhupariprcchātantra;* Tib. *'Phags pa dpung bzang gis zhus pa zhes bya ba'i rgyud.*
749. In other words, his teaching was done in the context of his Hevajra meditation, which requires a preliminary torma as well as a torma for the meditation session.
750. *Lam 'bras brgyud pa'i gsol 'debs.*
751. *Brtag gnyis kyi 'grel pa dag ldan.*
752. *Rgyud gsum gyi mngon rtogs rin po che'i ljon shing.*
753. *Rgyud sde'i dum bu brgya bcu gsum pa.*
754. *Stong thun sa bcad.*
755. *Rje btsun sa skya pa chen po'i rnam thar.*
756. *Slob dpon rin po che'i rnam thar tshigs bcad ma.*
757. *Rje btsun nyid kyi mnal lam gyi rnam thar.*
758. *Rgyud 'bum gyi dkar chag.*
759. *Bla chen mal gyi chos skor gyi dkar chag.*
760. *Kye rdo rje'i chos skor gyi dkar chag.*
761. *Tshar gsum khug pa'i man ngag.*
762. *Kye rdo rje'i mngon rtogs yan lag drug pa.*
763. *Ba ri lo tsā ba'i lugs kyi kye rdor dpa' gcig.*
764. *Mngon rtogs yan lag drug pa.*
765. *Dga' ston rdo rje grags la gdams pa.*
766. *Kye rdor las bzhi'i sbyin sreg gi cho ga.*
767. *Rdo rje bdag med ma'i mngon rtogs.*
768. *Lam 'bras brgyud pa'i gsol 'debs chung ngu gcig.*
769. *Kye rdo rje'i dkyil 'khor bkra shis.*
770. *Dus tha ma'i cho ga.*
771. *Kye rdo rje'i bstod pa dandaka.*
772. *Bdag med ma'i bstod pa.*

773. *Mi g.yo sngon po la bstod pa.*
774. *Rdo rje gur gyi sa bcad.*
775. *'Grel pa gur rgyan.*
776. *Gur gyi thig gi gsal byed.*
777. *Ku ru kulle'i sgrub thabs.*
778. *Dpal he ru ka'i chas drug.*
779. *Rdor dril gyi mtshan nyid.*
780. *De nyid gsum pa.*
781. *Lla ma lnga bcu pa'i tī ka.*
782. *Rtsa ltung gi 'grel pa 'khrul pa spong ba.*
783. *Dpal he ru ka'i byung tshul.*
784. *Dde mchog lu hi pa'i sgrub thabs.*
785. *Nag po pa'i dkyil chog gi 'grel pa.*
786. *Nag po pa'i dkyil chog.*
787. *Nag po gzhung drug gi sa bcad.*
788. *Dril bu pa'i lo rgyus dang sgrub thabs.*
789. *Tshes bcu'i mchod pa bya tshul.*
790. *Dril bu rim lnga'i khrid yig.*
791. *Phag mo zhal gnyis ma'i sgrub thabs.*
792. *Rdzogs rim sngags kyi de nyid.*
793. *Las bcu'i gdams ngag.*
794. *Mai tri mkha' spyod kyi rgyud kyi dum bu.*
795. *Mai tri mkha' spyod kyi sgrub thabs.*
796. *Nā ro mkha' spyod sgrub thabs.*
797. *Sgoṁ bzlas la brten nas mkha' spyod sgrub thabs.*
798. *Pra dbab pa'i gdams ngag.*
799. *Gnod sbyin mo sgrub pa'i gdams ngag.*
800. *Sman chen po'i bcud len.*
801. *Rdzogs rim rtsa dbu ma'i khrid yig.*
802. *Rnal 'byor ma kun spyod kyi tī ka.*
803. *Tshogs bdag dmar chen gyi sgrub thabs.*
804. *Dgra nag lha bcu gsum ma'i sgrub thabs.*
805. *Rdo rje 'jigs byed kyi bstod pa.*
806. *Yo ga rdo rje 'byung ba'i tī ka.*
807. *Rab gnas don gsal.*
808. *Argha'i cho ga.*
809. *Sbyong rgyud gzhan phan spyi chings.*
810. *Sbyong rgyud kyi sa bcad.*
811. *Kun rig gi cho ga gzhan phan 'od zer.*
812. *Zhan phan nyer mkho.*
813. *Ro sreg gi cho ga dang zhi ba'i sbyin sreg.*
814. *Rigs gsum spyi'i dkyil chog.*
815. *Dpa' bo gcig sgrub kyi rgyud kyi tī ka.*
816. *'Jam dbyangs kyi bstod pa rgyud gsum 'khor lo.*
817. *'Jam dpal mtshan brjod 'don thabs.*
818. *'Jam dbyangs a ra pa tsa na lha lnga dkar po'i mngon rtogs.*
819. *A ra pa tsa na'i dkyil chog.*

820. *Don zhags kyi cho ga.*
821. *Don zhags kyi mandal.*
822. *Brda byang chub sems dpas mdzad pa'i bstod pa.*
823. *Srung ba bri tshul.*
824. *Phyag na rdo rje'i gzungs kyi man ngag rgyas par bshad pa.*
825. *Rdo rje rnam 'joms rgyud kyi tī ka dang sa bcad.*
826. *Dpung bzangs [kyis zhus pa']i rgyud kyi tī ka.*
827. *Sgrol ma spyi sgrub.*
828. *Lha mo nyer gcig so so'i sgrub thabs.*
829. *Bstod pa 'don thabs kyi brjed byang.*
830. *Las tshogs nyi shu rtsa gcig gi gzhung gi tī ka.*
831. *Sgrol ma lus dkyil gyi mngon rtogs mchims chos seng la spring yig tu byas pa.*
832. *Sgrol ma nyin zhi mtshan khro'i sgrub thabs.*
833. *Dug gzhil ba.*
834. *Nor sgrub pa rnams kyi man ngag.*
835. *Mandal bzhi'i gsol 'debs bsdus pa.*
836. *Man bzhi rgyas pa.*
837. *Gnyan gyi sgrol ma yan lag drug pa.*
838. *Phyag 'tshal nyer gcig gi sa bcad.*
839. *Gsal ba'i 'od zer.*
840. *Mkha' lding gi mngon rtogs.*
841. *Sgrub thabs brgya rtsa'i tī ka.*
842. *Shākya'i rgyal po'i gdung rabs.*
843. *Bod kyi rgyal po'i rgyal rabs mdor bsdus ba.*
844. *Rgya bod kyi sde pa'i gyes tshul.*
845. *Dus tshod nges par bzung ba'i rtsis.*
846. *Ga ring rgyal po la rtsis bsdur gyi yi ge.*
847. *Las dang po pa'i chos sbyond rin chen phreng ba.*
848. *Sdom pa nyi shu ba'i 'grel pa.*
849. *Sbyod 'jug gi sa bcad.*
850. *Phyag yig dgu phrugs kyi yi ge.*
851. *Nyams dbyangs chen mo sogs gsung mgur gyi tshogs du ma.*
852. *Sman dpyad rgyal po'i dkor mdzad rnams.*
853. *Gnyags ma.* Named after its requester, Gnyags dbang phyug rgyal mtshan.
854. *Lam 'bras gegs sel mchog dbang gsum grol lam la brten te bskur ba.*
855. *Bsam mi khyab kyi gzhung rin chen 'bar ba.*
856. *Dril bu skor gsum.*
857. *Sbyong rgyud.*
858. *Dpa' bo gcig tu grub pa'i rgyud.*
859. *Phyag 'tshal nyer gcig gi mngon rtogs dang lam gyi yan lag.*
860. *Smra sgo mtshon cha.*
861. *Dpa' bo gcig sgrub kyi dpe bris.*
862. *Glud du gtong ba.*
863. Dbu rtse rnying ma.
864. Bkra shis sgo mang.
865. *Gdung khebs.*
866. Skt. *Śatasāhasrikāprajñāpāramitā;* Tib. *Shes rab kyi pha rol tu phyin pa stong phrag*

brgya pa.

867. Gcung pa ba gug zhi jo 'bum.
868. Mi nyag rgyal rgod, the seventh king of the Minyak.
869. *Bla mchod.*
870. It is difficult to determine what the author may have meant by *dré* (*bre*). A *dré* can be a volume of material, or it can be a vessel for material. Contemporary dictionary definitions range from two pints to one kilogram, a wooden vessel to a quart.
871. Presumably Vārendra, in eastern Bengal.
872. Sgo mtha' yas pa'i blo gros.
873. Skt. *Gṛdhrakūṭaparvata;* Tib. *Bya rgod phung po'i ri.* An important teaching site that in Inner and East Asian Mahāyāna Buddhism is considered to be the the staging ground for the cycle of the Buddha's Mahāyāna teachings, as recorded in such texts as the *Lotus Sūtra* (Skt. *Saddharmapuṇḍarīka Sūtra;* Tib. *Dam pa'i chos padma dkar po'i mdo*) and the Perfection of Wisdom sūtras (Skt. *Prajñāpāramitā;* Tib. *Shes rab kyi pha rol tu phyin pa*).
874. Gcung pa.
875. Nag po tshangs.
876. *Sngags don.*
877. Ston pa sbal ston.
878. *Dpe dbyangs.*
879. Gser gyi mdog can.
880. Gser 'od.
881. Bsod nams mtha' yas.
882. Yon tan mtha' yas.
883. Ru mtshams.
884. Gung ston.
885. Stag.
886. Zhu yas.
887. Dga' ston.
888. Lit. "make suchness into one's cushion."
889. Dbu dgu'i dod lbab dgu rtsegs.
890. I.e., Śākyaśrībhadra (Tib. Shākya shrī), 1127–1225.
891. Shang sreg shing.
892. Nag po 'khun shes.
893. Mon rdo rje rā rdzā.
894. Gnam the'u.
895. Btsan thang rgyal po.
896. Gtsug na rin chen.
897. Mkha' spyod.
898. *Dbyug pa zla ba,* a name for the ninth month.
899. Bde pa can.
900. Skt. *Sahālokadhātu;* Tib. *Mi mjed kyi 'jig rten khams.* A common name for this world system in Mahāyāna Buddhist sources.
901. I.e., Kunga Nyingpo and Sönam Tsemo.
902. Dbang phyug grags; Bshes gnyen grags; Śākya grags pa; Rigs 'dzin grags.
903. Lde ston dkon mchog grags; Dga' ston rdor grags; Sras ston blo gros grags;

'Jigs med grags.

904. Skt. *Vajrapañjaratantra*; Tib. *Rdo rje'i gur rgyud.*

905. Smu chu byang grags; Gtsang ston brtson 'grus grags; Lha thog yon tan; Shes rab rin chen.

906. Rtsis 'dul gzhon seng; Khams kyi 'dzi ston; Dbon ston skyer khang; Jo sras lcags rdor.

907. Dpal chen 'od po.

908. *Brgyud chung nyi ma'i 'od zer.*

909. Ma gcig gar phu ma nyi khri ltsam.

910. Chos rje sa skya pan di ta kun dga' rgyal mtshan.

911. An undated work on Sanskrit prosody attributed to Ratnākaraśānti, translated into Tibetan by Yarlung Lotsāwa Drakpa Gyaltshan (Yar lung lo tsā ba grags pa rgyal mtshan, 1242–1346) and Jangchub Tsemo (Byang chub rtse mo, 1303–80).

912. Dmar ser.

913. Rgyal ba'i lha.

914. Dge 'dun dpal.

915. Skt. *Kāvyādarśa*; Tib. *Snyan ngag me long.*

916. *Dbyangs can mgul rgyan.*

917. *'Chi med mdzod.*

918. Skt. *Anāvilatantrarāja*; Tib. *Rgyud rgyal rnyog pa med pa.*

919. Skt. *Mahākālabhyudayatantra*; Tib. *Mgon po mngon par 'byung ba'i rgyud.*

920. *De nyid 'dus pa 'grel pa.*

921. Skt. *Vajraśekhara*; Tib. *Rdo rje rtse mo.*

922. Skt. *Śaṃvarakhasamatantra*; Tib. *Bde mchog nam mkha' dang mnyam pa'i rgyud.*

923. Skt. *Vajrakrodharājakalpalaghutantra*; Tib. *Rdo rje khro bo'i rgyal po'i rtog pa bsdus pa'i rgyud.*

924. Skt. *Susiddhikaramahātantra*; Tib. *Legs par grub par byed pa'i rgyud chen po.*

925. *Ku mu ti.*

926. Skt. *Abhisamayamuktamala*; Tib. *Mu tig phreng ba.*

927. Tib. *Padma can.*

928. *Rin chen phreng ba'i rnam bshad.*

929. Skt. *Vairocanābhisambodhi*; Tib. *Rnam par snang mdzad mngon par rdzogs par byang chub pa'i rgyud.*

930. Skt. *Āryaguhyamaṇitilakanāmasūtra*; Tib. *'Phags pa gsang ba nor bu thig le zhes bya ba'i mdo.*

931. Skt. *Vajrapātālatantra*; Tib. *Rdo rje sa 'og gi rgyud.*

932. Skt. *Guhyālaṃkāravyūhatantra*; Tib. *Gsang ba rgyan bkod kyi rgyud.*

933. Skt. *Vajramaṇḍālaṃkāratant*; Tib. *Rdo rje snying po rgyan gyi rgyud.*

934. Lho pa kun mkhyen rin chen dpal.

935. *Tsandra pa.*

936. Rgyas pa.

937. Gnas 'jig.

938. Grog mkhar.

939. Nor rgyas.

940. Skt. *Pramāṇasamuccaya*; Tib. *Tshad ma kun las btus pa.*

941. *Tshad ma sde bdun.* These seven texts are: the *Pramāṇavārttika*, the *Pramāṇa-*

viniścaya, the *Nyāyabindu*, the *Hetubindu*, the *Sambandhaparīkṣā*, the *Saṃtānāntarasiddhi*, and the *Vādanyāya*.

942. Skt. *sugata*; Tib. *bde bar gshegs pa*. An epithet for the Buddha Śākyamuni.
943. Sgra gcan gyi gdong, the name of a planet in Indian astronomy.
944. Dus kyi me.
945. Glo bo mkhan chen.
946. Zangs tsha, who was Sakya Paṇḍita's brother (see chapter 6, just below, for Ameshab's account of him).
947. Rgya ma dpon grags.
948. This symbol is popularly known in Tibetan as *sdom brtsom dam pa*.
949. *Nyin re spyod pa dang dus su spyad pa*.
950. *Gso ba zhi byed kyi sman*.
951. *Sbyong byed kyi sman*.
952. 'Tsho byed gzhon nu (Skt. Jīvaka Komārabhacca), a celebrated physician who served the Buddha.
953. *Sdong po bkod pa'i mdo*.
954. Skt. *śrāvakas*; Tib. *nyan thos*; Ch. *shengweng* 聲聞. Literally "hearers" or "listeners," in Mahāyāna doxography śrāvakas were direct disciples of Buddha Śākyamuni or some other historical buddha who chose to disregard the plight of other sentient beings and to exclusively pursue their own liberation from saṃsāra (by becoming an arhat). In this pejorative sense, in Mahāyāna textual cultures śrāvakas are counted alongside pratyekabuddhas, or "solitary realizers" (Tib. *rang sangs rgyas*).
955. Skt. *pratyekabuddhas* (here Tib. *rang rgyal*, or more commonly, *rang sangs rgyas*; Ch. *dujue* 獨覺) are "solitary buddhas," practitioners who achieve arhatship by their own efforts, without being a direct disciple of a buddha (in the lifetime of their liberation).
956. Chos kyi grags pa; Blo gros brtan pa; Shes rab 'byung gnas sās pa; Shi ka ra nanda; Smra ba'i seng ge.
957. Skya'o kha gdangs.
958. Nam mkha' 'bum.
959. Skt. *darśanamārga*; Tib. *mthong lam*.
960. Skt. *Abhisamayālaṃkāra*; Tib. *Mngon par rtogs pa'i rgyan*. Attributed to Maitreya and recorded by Asaṅga (ca. 320–90 CE).
961. Rgyal po nyi ma'i stobs 'phel.
962. Rngog blo ldan shes rab, 1059–1109.
963. *Thub pa dgongs pa rab gsal*.
964. Skt. *Mahāyānasūtrālaṃkāra*; Tib. *Theg pa chen po'i mdo sde'i rgyan*. One of the five treatises attributed to the buddha Maitreya and recorded by Asaṅga.
965. *[Tshad ma] rigs pa'i gter*.
966. Skt. *Abhidharmakośa*; Tib. *Chos mngon pa mjod*.
967. *Rdo rje'i tshig rkang*; *Thub pa dgongs gsal*; *Legs par bshad pa rin po che'i gter*.
968. Skt. *Abhidharmasamuccaya*; Tib. *Chos mngon pa kun las btus pa*.
969. *Mkhas pa 'jug pa'i sgo*; *Shes rab 'phro ba*; *Shes rab la 'jug pa*; *Sgra nyer bsdu*.
970. *Sangs rgyas byang chub sems dpa' la zhu ba'i 'phrin yig*; *Grub mtha' rnam 'byed*; *Pha rol phyin pa'i gzung lugs spyi'i tshogs chos chen mo*.
971. *Bdag med ma'i bstod pa*.

972. *Rdo rje theg pa'i man ngag rten 'brel lnga'i yi ge; Lam sbas bshad dang bla ma'i rnal 'byor; Khrid kyi dkar chag.*
973. *Sdeb sbyor me tog gi chun po; Bde bar gshegs pa'i thugs rje la bskul ba; Snyan ngag mkhas pa'i kha rgyan; Mngon brjod tshig gi gter; Zlos gar rab dga'i 'jug pa; Rol mo'i bstan bcos.*
974. Zhang lo; Chag lo; Glo bo lotsāwa.
975. Rdo rje seng ge.
976. Snye mo sgom chen.
977. *Sgra la 'jug pa.*
978. *Smra sgo'i bsdus don.*
979. *Byis pa bde 'jug gi 'grel pa.*
980. *Yi ge'i sbyor ba.*
981. *Sgra nye bar bsdu ba.*
982. *Sku gzugs kyi bstan bcos.*
983. *Sa brtag pa'i rab byed.*
984. *Yan lag brgyad pa'i don bsdus.*
985. *Sangs rgyas kyi bstod pa; Thub pa'i bstod pa; Spyan ras gzigs kyi bstod pa gnyis; 'Jam dbyangs kyi phyag mtshan ri mo la bstod pa; Bsam yas lhun gyis grub pa'i gnas chen la bstod pa; 'Jam dbyangs kyi bstod pa'i rnam bshad.*
986. *Grub mtha'i rnam 'byed; Thub pa dgongs gsal; Sdom gsum rab dbye; Sems bskyed chen mo lung sbyor dang bcas pa; Chos nyams su blang ba'i rim pa; Chos spyod bcu pa; Zhen pa bzhi bral; Theg pa chen po'i lam gyi rnam gzhag mdor bsdus pa; Bsngo ba'i yon bshad.*
987. *Mkhas pa 'jug pa'i sgo; Gzhung lugs legs dbyad.*
988. *Legs bshad.*
989. *'Phrag byed dka' bo pham bar byas pa'i tshigs bcad; Ba go ra zhes bya ba'i sgra las drangs ba'i tshigs bcas; Blo gsal ba'i skyes bu rnams la ji ltar dri ba'i tshigs bcad; Bdag nyid kyi rnam thar.*
990. *Phyogs bcu'i sangs rgyas dang byang chub sems dpa' la zhu ba'i 'phrin yig; Skyes bu dam pa rnams la springs yig; Bstan pa la dga' ba'i lha rnams la springs yig; Shing kun na bzhugs pa'i dge 'dun rnams la springs yig; Nyi ma spring yig; Glo bo lotsāwa la spring yig; Zhang lotsāwa la gdams pa; 'Od 'jo ba'i dge bshes springs yig; Snye mo sgom chen la springs yig; Do gor ba'i zhus lan; Chag lotsāwa'i zhus lan.*
991. *'Jam dpal gyi sgrub thabs kyi gsal byed; Sgrol ma'i sgrub thabs; Gza' yum gyi mchod pa'i cho ga; Zhi ba 'tsho las brgyud pa'i gza' yum gyi sgrub thabs; Zung 'jug gsal ba'i dkyil 'khor gyi cho ga; Snang ba mtha' yas kyi bsgom don; 'Chi kha ma'i gdams ngag.*
992. *Bla ma'i bstod pa gnyis; Rnal 'byor dbang phyug gi bstod pa; Bde mchog brgyud pa'i bstod pa; Bla ma'i rnal 'byor chen mo; Phyi nang gsang gsum gyi maṇḍal; Lam 'bras kyi khrid kyi dkar chag; Sgrub pa lung sbyin; Rten 'brel lngas yongs su rdzogs pa; Lam sbas bshad rtsa bay an lag dang bcas pa; Grub chen bcu phra mo brgyad dang bcas pa; Aṣṭa'i gzhi bshad; Tshogs kyi 'khor lo'i yi ge; Bdag med ma'i bstod pa'i 'grel ba; Rigs drug gi mtshan don dang ye shes bsre ba'i bshad pa; Bde mchog lhun skyes kyi byin rlabs; Rnam 'joms bir lugs kyi bshad pa; Mchan la sambuṭa; Rdo rje rnam 'joms kyi rgyud; Sdom gsum rab dbye.*
993. 'Phrog byed dga' bo. The Sanskrit equivalent for this figure is never, to our knowledge, glossed in Tibetan sources. Here we follow the majority of secondary sources which give Harinanda for 'Phrog byed dga' bo (and in the *Treasury*) or, in other sources, 'Phrog byed dga' ba.

994. Gser skya.
995. Rgyas pa.
996. Gzegs zan.
997. Grangs can.
998. Rig pa can.
999. Nyin mo long ba.
1000. No lha'i bu.
1001. Byin za.
1002. *Bud med kyi brtul zhugs 'dzin*. Plainly a gendered stereotype about the capacity and conduct of women. Often (but certainly not always) in Inner Asian Buddhist literature and the South Asian tradition upon which it is built, women are characterized as sided closely with saṃsāra and with diminished capacities because of their feminine embodiment. Such associations go back to the stated implications of the Buddha Śākyamuni allowing women to ordain in the monastic saṅgha. We should not forget that such literature, very much including *The Treasury*, was in the premodern period written almost entirely by men for the consumption of other men, usually monastics.
1003. Tib. *dpag tshad*; Ch. *youxun* 由旬. Sometimes translated as a "league," *yojana* is a common unit of measuring space in Buddhist texts. It is, however, difficult to provide an equivalency in more contemporary units. Among other reasons, this is because *yojana* often measure not simply a measure of space, but also the length of time it may take someone to traverse it.
1004. Rkang mig.
1005. A phyi'i 'bum pa.
1006. Dbyid gnyen.
1007. 'Jam pa'i dbyangs shes rab rgya mtsho.
1008. Phyogs kyi glang po.
1009. Srin po ri pa.
1010. Bo dong rin po che brtson 'grus rdo rje.
1011. 'Phags yul. An extremely common referent in Tibetan letters for roughly what we call India today.
1012. Gtsang nags phug pa 'jam dbyangs shes rab 'od zer.
1013. Dge bshes g.yag sde bsod nams bzang po. Also called Yakdepa (G.yag sde pa).
1014. Dpe dkar rgyal po.
1015. Gnyan stod 'dul ba seng ge.
1016. Dbu ma pa shes rab 'bum.
1017. Shar pa shes rab 'byung gnas.
1018. *Rgyas pa'i 'phrin las*.
1019. Smyal zhig 'jam dpal rdo rje.
1020. 'U yug pa rig pa'i seng ge.
1021. Btsad po shākya mgon.
1022. *Mi nyag* (Mong. *Tangγud*; Ch. *Xi xia* 西夏). A cosmopolitan Buddhist empire that existed along the Hexi Corridor in what is today northwestern China. It lasted from 1038 to 1227, when the advancing Mongols laid waste to it on Činggis Qan's orders during a devastating second attack. Činggis Qan himself is said to have died of illness during this campaign.

1023. I.e., Sri Lanka.
1024. Gnam the'u dkar po.
1025. E chen go den.
1026. Tho lo no yon.
1027. Rdor sri mgon; Dbon jo dar ma.
1028. Blo gros rab gsal.
1029. Skt. *Vajracchedikā Sūtra*; Tib. *Rdo rje gcod pa'i mdo*.
1030. Skt. *Mahāyānauttaratantraśāstra*; Tib. *Rgyud bla ma*.
1031. Skt. *Madhyāntavibhāga*; Tib. *Dbus dang mtha' rnam par 'byed pa*.
1032. Skt. *Mūlamadhyamakakārikā*; Tib. *Dbu ma rtsa ba shes rab*.
1033. Bi ji rin chen grags. Sapaṇ's attendant and physician, whom we encounter at length below.
1034. Phru ma pa.
1035. *Zhi gnas*.
1036. Tib. In dra bhu ti.
1037. Skt. *Mahāyānasūtrālaṃkārakārikā*; Tib. *Theg pa chen po mdo sde'i rgyan zhes bya ba'i tshig le'ur byas pa*.
1038. Skt. *Karuṇāpuṇḍarīka*; Tib. *Snying rje pad ma dkar po*.
1039. Mdo khams smad gling kha.
1040. Rdo rje 'chang kun dga' dbang phyug.
1041. *Chis kyi rgyal po sac hen gan*. Qubilai Qaγan (1215–93) was the fifth qaγan of the Mongol Empire founded by his grandfather Činggis Qan (i.e., Genghis Khan). Qubilai became the supreme ruler of the Mongol Empire in 1260 and, after the defeat of the Song Dynasty by Mongol forces, the founder and first emperor of the Yuan Dynasty (Ch. Da yuan 大元; Mong. Dai yuwan ulus) under the reign title Sečen Qaγan (r. 1271–94). As such, Qubilai Qaγan ruled the Mongol Empire at its most expansive territorial reach and was thus one of the most powerful men in world history. Qubilai was involved in interreligious affairs in the Mongol Empire before his reign, such as being charged with pacifying ongoing Daoist-Buddhist conflicts in favor of the Buddhists. For later Tibetan and Mongolian Buddhist historians, very much including our author Ameshab, Qubilai and his imperial entourage became paradigms of devoted disciples and patrons of Tibetan tantric Buddhist masters like Phakpa, whose example was evoked again and again over the centuries in the so-called two system model of unified Dharmic and political authority (Tib. *lugs gnyis*; Mong. *qoyar yosu*), such as in the relationship of the third Dalai Lama, Sönam Gyatso, and Altan Qan of the Tümed.
1042. Sman rtse.
1043. Ch. Guo shi 國師; Tib. Gug srī.
1044. Lha'i bu'i bdud.
1045. Ling chu.
1046. A reminder to readers that here Ameshab follows later Tibetan (and even Mongolian) confusion about the status of Köden within the Mongol Empire. We have dutifully translated Ameshab's identification of him as a "king" (*rgyal po*) but refer readers back to the introduction of this book for a brief historical clarification.
1047. Go yug gan.

1048. E ka 'un.
1049. *Seng ge sgra*. Siṃhanāda, or "Lion's Roar," is a wrathful form of Avalokiteśvara. Siṃhanāda rituals are found throughout the collected works of the early Sakya masters and remain widespread in Inner Asian Buddhism to this day.
1050. Rtogs ldan rgyan po. Could alternatively be read with tokden as a title, and thus as "the realized yogin Gyenpo."
1051. Dog tse pa.
1052. Tib. *dri za*. In this context, gandharvas are celestial musicians, a kind of demigod from Indian cosmology who fly about and perform in the courts of the gods.
1053. Skt. *Vajramālābhidhānamahāyogatantrasarvatantrahṛdayarahasyavibhaṅga*; Tib. *Rdo rje 'phreng ba'i rgyud*.
1054. *Gsang ba'i sny ing po'i rgyud*.
1055. *Phyag rgya chen po thig le*.
1056. *Gug skye*. We have been unable to identify a translation for this term.
1057. Skt. *saṃbhāramārga*; Tib. *tshogs lam*; Ch. *ziliang dao* 資糧道. According to the Indian Mahāyāna tradition, the path of accumulation is counted as the first of the "five paths" that mark the progress of a practitioner from saṃsāra to liberation.
1058. *Rtogs ldan rgyan po la gdams pa phyag rgya chen po'i mig thur*. We find dictionary definitions of *mig thur* as medical instruments used for removing cataracts, but without any other detail. We thus have translated provisionally as above.
1059. Skt. *Suvarṇaprabhāsottamasūtra*; Tib. *Gser 'od dam pa'i mdo*. Well known in Mongolian translation as the *Altan gerel sudur*.
1060. The verse being debated is from chapter 2, verse 43 of the sūtra. It reads: "When sublime, excellent clothes / That can be worn in the cold weather / Are woven from the hair of turtles, / Then seek for a relic of the Bhagavat" (folio 25b in Degé Kangyur vol 89, 19a–151a). This verse is from the translation by Alan Roberts, et al., published in 2023 by 84,000 (https://read.84000.co/translation/UT22084-089-012.html#translation).
1061. *Tshogs chos*. An alternative title for *Clarifying the Sage's Intent*.
1062. Tib. *'u lag*. This is a Tibetan gloss of Mongol *ulaγa*. It is used elsewhere in Tibetan literature to mean more generally "forced labor," and not specifically compulsory service in the trans-imperial equine postal service established by the Mongol Empire. Given the proximity of Sapaṇ to the arms of Mongol authority while (supposedly) writing this letter, we have kept "postal service."
1063. *Dar kha che*. Apparently, a gloss for Mongolian *darγ-a*. We find this glossed more commonly elsewhere in Tibetan as *da ra kha che*.
1064. Sgra dbyangs mi zad pa sgro pa'i rgyal po.
1065. Mchog sbyin dpal.
1066. Slob dpon jo gdan. Joden Monastery is a Kadampa institution from the Lhasa region established in the mid-eleventh century. It is likely that this otherwise unnamed master hailed from there.
1067. Ju gur me mar.
1068. Rdo rang.
1069. Nyi ma'i stobs 'phel.

1070. These are some of the thirty-two major and eighty minor marks, the classical description of the physical body of a buddha.
1071. Dul ba rgyal mtshan.
1072. The Tibetan gives "Zo rog ta," and it is certainly unclear exactly who may have given this gift. Our guess is that the reference might be to Sorγaγtani (Ch. Xianyi Zhuangsheng 顯懿莊聖皇后, ca. 1190–1252). Sorγaγtani was a wife of Tolui who became the supremely powerful daughter-in-law of Čing-gis Qan and mother of Qubilai Qaγan and his powerful brothers. A problem with this attribution is that, while Phakpa would become close to this branch of the Mongolian nobility in the court of Qubilai, here Sapaṇ and Biji are in the court of Köden, the son of Ögedei Qaγan, without any direct interaction with Sorγaγtani. More research is required.
1073. Jo 'bum gug shrī; Mi nyag 'ga'.
1074. Yar lung pa grags pa rgyal mtshan.
1075. *Phyag sor g.yas pa klu shing*. We remain unclear what "nāga tree" (*klu shing*) means in this context.
1076. Ling chu rtser khab.
1077. Bsam yas; Nyang stod rkyang thur; and Shangs sreg shing.
1078. 'U yug pa rig pa'i seng ge.
1079. Zhang btsun rdo rje dpal.
1080. Nā le ndra; Gser mdog can; Skyid tshal; Thub bstan rnam rgyal; Thub bstan yang can; Dbus rtses thang; Byang ngam ring; Dpal sa skya'i thub bstan lha chen.
1081. [Zang tsa] Bsod rnams rgyal mtshan.
1082. Skya'o kha gdangs.
1083. Lcam dral.
1084. Mon grog; 'Bal grog; Sa dkar logs.
1085. Zhing mo che; Mda' rgyang khang.
1086. Zi thang.
1087. Grom stod; Grom smad; Stag thog; Mang mkhar dril chen; Gtsang bar phug; Shab stod smad; Rta nag.
1088. Byang gcung; Khab so; Kom 'dre; Gar phug.
1089. Ra sa.
1090. Na bza' brag phug pa.
1091. Dpal ri; Mdog stod ros; La stod byang.
1092. Rta re rong; brgyud bzang ba; Zangs kyi jo sras.
1093. Ga ring rgyal po.
1094. Mdog gi tsha sna'i 'dab.
1095. Zur khang gi brgya tsho; Rgyal ba dpal.
1096. Ma gcig kun skyid.
1097. 'Gro mgon chos rgyal 'phags pa [blo gros rgyal mtshan].
1098. G.yas ru ngam ring.
1099. Sa ston ri pa.
1100. Glang ri pa.
1101. Bkra shis don grub.
1102. *Sgrub thabs mtsho skyes*.
1103. Skt. *ārya*; Tib. *'phags pa* (phoneticized as "Phakpa" in English); Mong. *ariy-a*,

qutuγtu; Ch. *sheng* 聖. Though there are many ways of identifying a "noble being" or "superior" in different Buddhist schools, in most cases the term refers to someone who has directly (and not merely conceptually or intellectually) perceived the ultimate nature of reality.

1104. Jātaka stories (Tib. *skyes rabs;* Mong. *cadiγ;* Ch. *bensheng jing* 本生經) are a very popular genre of Buddhist moral literature that recount the previous lives of Buddha Śākyamuni as he progressed along the bodhisattva path over the course of many lives.

1105. Na bza' 'phred gsol.

1106. Zul phu.

1107. Shes rab seng ge.

1108. Skyor mo lung pa.

1109. *Chos rgyal mes dpon gsum.*

1110. Srong btsan sgam po (r. 605–50); Khri srong lde'u btsan (r. 754–99); Khri ral pa can (r. 815–38). All three were rulers of the Tibetan Yarlung empire. All are widely memorialized in Inner Asian historiography for playing key roles in bringing the Buddhadharma to Tibetan society, such as by inviting Indian paṇḍits, abbots, tantric masters, and foreign princesses. With such foreign collaboration, these kings are remembered to have founded the first monastery and supported the ordination of the first Tibetan Buddhist monks, erecting the major early statuary and other material culture, patronizing the creation of a Tibetan script suitable to translate Buddhist scriptures, supporting the wrathful tantric subjugation of indigenous Tibetan deities who resisted the arrival of Buddhism, and so on.

1111. Mi la ras pa (1028/40–1111/23). Milarepa is surely the most famous yogin in Tibetan history, as Phakpa notes in this passage; not only among the Kagyü school of Tibetan Buddhism, which was a rival of the Sakyapa in the thirteenth century, but among all Tibetan Buddhist lineages and sects. Milarepa's famous life story, and the collection of vernacular songs of realization attributed to him, have enraptured Inner Asian audiences and practitioners for a millennium with their depiction of personal transformation from wickedness to virtue, perseverance through hardship, and fearlessly naked expressions of enlightenment.

1112. Čabui Qatun (Tib. Dpon mo cha bu). While elsewhere we have translated *dpon mo* as "female leader" and "chieftainess," depending on context, here we chose to translate it as "consort" based on the imperial usage, in whose context the remainder of Phakpa's life will unfold.

1113. *Tshal pa.* Usually in reference to representatives of the Tsalpa Kagyü school of Central Tibet, which during the thirteenth century was based at Tsal Gungthang Monastery (Tshal gung thang) to the south of Lhasa. But here the reference must be specifically to the Second Karmapa, Karma Pakshi, who had been invited to the court of Qubilai and Čabui around 1251, the same year that Phakpa and his brother were invited from Köden's court, before the Qubilai had been installed as supreme qaγan of the Mongol Empire or as emperor of the Yuan Dynasty.

1114. *Kong jo.* The reference is to Gyaza Kongjo (Tib. Rgya bza' kong jo; Ch. Wencheng Gongzhu 文成公主, ca. 623–80), an extended family member of

Emperor Taizong太宗 (598–649) of the Tang Dynasty. As part of reconciliations in the aftermath of military conflicts between Tibetan and Chinese imperials during the mid-650s, the young Kongjo was sent as a wife for either the aforementioned King Songtsen Gampo or his son. In the prevailing historiographical traditions of thirteenth-century Tibetan letters, Kongjo and Songtsen Gampo's Nepalese wife, Bhṛkutī (Bal bza' khri btsun), were memorialized as collaborators in the court's project to establish Buddhist institutionalism in the heart of the Yarlung Empire. As in the account of Phakpa's explanation to Qubilai here, in this memory Kongjo traveled to Tibet with a personal Jowo Śākyamuni statue. So too did Bhṛkutī. The former's statue was housed in the newly built Jokhang Temple (Jo khang) in Lhasa and the latter's at Ramoché (Ra mo che). Also in these prevailing memories, Kongjo is remembered to have divined that a demoness (*srin mo*) pervading the landscape itself was obstructing the establishment of Buddhism in Central Tibet. Based on this divination, the Tibetan court subdued the demoness by pinning her down with a series of temples and other Buddhist architecture.

1115. Gtsang chu mig.

1116. *Bsnyen sgrub*. Literally "approach and accomplishment," here referring to a retreat wherein a practitioner completes a set of hundreds of thousands of mantra recitations, visualizations, and other contemplative and yogic practices associated with a particular yidam meditation deity practice to then become qualified to bestow initiation upon others.

1117. Exactly which polities, or myriarchies (*khri skor*), this may have referred to at the time is unclear, but later Tibetan and Mongolian monastic historians often list the following thirteen (with some variation): Latö Lhowa (La stod lho ba), Latö Jangwa (La stod byang ba), Chumik Shang (Chu mig shangs), Shalu (Zhal lu), Jangdrok (Byang 'brog), Yardrok (Yar 'brog), Drigung ('Bri gung), Tshelpa (Tshal pa), Phakdru (Phag gru), Yazang (G.ya' bzang), Gyama (Rgya ma), Taklung (Stag lung), Chayul (Bya yul).

1118. *Chos dung dkar po rgyang grags*. A *rgyang grags* may refer to an actual unit of space, variously defined (for example, five hundred arm spans). Here the idea seems to be less specific, gesturing instead to an impressive and superhuman measure of space across which the conch's sound may be heard.

1119. Bod phyogs kha gsum.

1120. Skya bo yan.

1121. Literally "black-headed people" (*mgo nag mi*), but here seems to refer in general to humankind.

1122. *Gyad gling rta'i phyogs kha*.

1123. *Rgya mi yur chen mo*.

1124. *Dpal ldan sa skya la bsngags pa snyan ngag dbang po'i nyer mtsho*. Lake Nyer (*Nyer mtsho*) is a salt lake laying nearly 4,500 meters above sea level in today's Gegyé County (*Dge rgye rdzong*), Ngari Prefecture, Tibetan Autonomous Zone.

1125. Tib. Nā lend dra; Ch. Nalantuosi 那爛陀寺.

1126. *Chu klung gi mdo; Rgyan stug po bkod pa'i mdo; 'Dul ba ko sha; Za ma tog bkod pa'i mdo*.

1127. Ngag dbang kun dga' rin chen.

1128. Lhasa Rdzong pa.

1129. Karma Pakshi hailed from Dergé in Kham, in the eastern Tibetan cultural region, and became retroactively known as the Second Karmapa. Though he spent much of his early life in retreat, Karma Pakshi traveled widely because of regional disturbances and military conflicts. In his travels, Karma Pakshi became widely known as a miracle worker and accomplished siddha, a reputation that apparently reached Qubilai, who was not yet crowned supreme qaγan of the Mongol Empire. Invited the same year as Phakpa and Chana Dorjé, Karma Pakshi is said to have met Qubilai at Rongyul Sertö (Rong yul gser stod) and resided in the company of the Mongol prince for some five years. He later visited the court of Qubilai's brother Möngke Qaγan (r. 1251–59), then the leader of the Mongols. There he is said to have participated in interreligious debates between Daoists, Chinese, Buddhists, Nestorian Christians, and Confucians. It is said that because of his association with the Mongols as a teacher, or *baγsi* (Ch. *boshi* 博士), that this lama acquired his name: Karma Pakshi.

1130. The most common enumeration of these five buddhas, found across most tantric systems known to the New Translation (*Gsar ma*) schools of Inner Asia, including the Sakya, derives from the *Sarvatathāgatatattvasaṃgraha* tantric corpus. This system, which is likely the one readers of this text would have understood Lama Phakpa to be referencing, lists the buddhas Vairocana, Akṣobhya, Amitābha, Ratnasambhava, and Amoghsiddhi as members of the "five families" (Skt. *kula*; Tib. *rigs lnga*): Tathāgatakula, Vajrakula, Padmakula, Ratnakula, and Karmakula.

1131. Ch. *dishi* 帝師; Tib. *ti srī*. There had long been a tradition of appointing "state preceptors" (Ch. *guoshi* 國師; Mong. *gosi, güüsi*) in imperial China going back to at least the northern Qi Dynasty in the sixth century. The position of tishi, however, was an innovation of Qubilai Qaγan born from the emergent patronage of Sakya and other Tibetan Buddhist masters and lineages favored in the Mongol courts of the Yuan.

1132. *Bande [g]shed bskyed.*

1133. *'Tsher 'babs pa* is in general a rather obscure term for "stay the night," but apparently still lives on in certain Khampa dialects.

1134. Ch. *xiyu* 西域. The "western regions" is an old term from the Chinese chronicle tradition referring to the western reaches of Chinese dynasties, in the eastern portions of what we today gloss as Central Asia (such as the Tarim Basin and Xinjiang in the contemporary PRC), but also including many polities and societies in what we now gloss as Tibet.

1135. *'Ja' sa mu tig ma.* Though the chronology is difficult to follow here, this particular edict was sent with Phakpa and Chakna when, in 1264, Qubilai ordered them back to Central Tibet in order to exert Mongol sovereignty.

1136. *'Ja' sa bod yig.*

1137. *Chim gir rgyal po'i khrims lugs.*

1138. I.e., Mong. *darγ-a*, as we have seen above.

1139. *Ri rgyu ma byed.* The sense seems to be that since whatever one finds upon a mountain is ownerless, one may simply take it as one's own.

1140. Sometimes spelled Tengri, Tngri (Tib. *gnam mchod pa*) is considered either a singular or a multitude of high divinities in Mongolian tradition, including (as in this reference) to the statecraft of Činggis Qan and the political, legal, and ritual structure of the Mongol Empire and the Yuan Dynasty. According to Mongolian historical traditions, it was Tngri who commanded that a young Temujin unite rival Mongolian clans and lead a world empire as Činggis Qan, and the famous religious tolerance of the Mongol Empire was largely conceived and implemented in a Tngrist frame (where all religions, with their only apparent differences, were considered instances of an overarching Tngri).

1141. Gshong tho.

1142. Klu dbang grags pa.

1143. Readers will by now recognize in these verses the characteristic Tibetan confusion about Mongol succession. Ögedei was Köden's father, not his brother as stated here, and Qubilai was not Köden's heir, but his uncle (son of Ögedei's brother, Tolui).

1144. *Sigs.*

1145. Here Čabui is referred to in Tibetan as *cha bu ga bstun.* We find no common or sensible Tibetan usage for "gatun" (*ga bstun*), but recognize that it is likely a Tibetan transliteration of Mongolian *qatun*, meaning queen, or, more appropriately, the consort of a qaγan.

1146. Ska ba dpal brtsegs.

1147. U rgyan gha na.

1148. Grom pa.

1149. Ljang yul, i.e., Yunnan Province 云南省.

1150. *Sku 'bum.* Literally "100,000 images," the name of an important (and later) monastery in Amdo, as well as several important stūpas across Inner Asia. As in the episode below about Phakpa's return to Sakya and visiting Drakpa Gyaltsen's reliquary, this is in reference to a reliquary stūpa for Sapaṇ. This is presumably Sapaṇ's reliquary stūpa at the "Emanated Temple" (Sprul pa'i sde) in Liangzhou, known today as The White Pagoda Temple (Ch. Baitasi白塔寺).

1151. 'U yug pa.

1152. While Ameshab does not make this clear, Phakpa Lama and Qubilai had not yet met. They would rendezvous in Kaiping (known later as Shangdu), Qubilai's capital, in 1254.

1153. Snye thang [dgon].

1154. Grags pa seng ge.

1155. Dri ma med pa'i dpal.

1156. 'Brug.

1157. Skam mchu ba.

1158. Ling chu rtse.

1159. Jo gdan byang pa bsod nams rgyal mtshan.

1160. Yar lung pa byang chub rgyal mtshan.

1161. Dbu rgan.

1162. Mang ra ba mkhan po Spro.

1163. Gnam phar ba Rtshul rin.

1164. Skt. *Prasannapadā*; Tib. *Tshig gsal.* Candrakirtī's (ca. 600–50 CE) commentary on Nāgārjuna's *Fundamental Treatise on the Middle Way.*

1165. *The Sūtra of Individual Liberation* (Tib. *So sor thar pa'i mdo*), which outlines monastic discipline.
1166. *'Dul ba mdo [rtsa ba].*
1167. Ldong.
1168. *Gshin rje gshed brda bzhi.*
1169. *Rdor dbyings.*
1170. In their fullest reference for New Translation-period Tibetan exegetes, the "Collection of Middle Way Reasoning" (Skt. *Yuktikāya*; Tib. *Rigs tshogs*) encompasses six of Nāgārjuna's works: *Fundamental Treatise on the Middle Way* (Skt. *Mūlamadhyamakakārikā*; Tib. *Dbu ma rtsa ba'i tshig le'u byas pa*; Ch. *Zhong lun* 中論), *Sixty Stanzas on Reasoning* (Skt. *Yuktiṣaṣṭikā*; Tib. *Rigs pa drug cu pa*; Ch. *Liushisong ruli lun* 六十頌如理論), *Seventy Stanzas on Emptiness* (Skt. *Śūnyatāsaptati*; Tib. *Stong pa nyid bdun cu pa*), *Refutation of Objections* (Skt. *Vigrahavyāvartanī*; Tib. *Rtsod pa bzlog pa*; Ch. *Huizheng lun* 迴諍論), *Extended Explanation* (Skt. *Vaidalyaprakaraṇa*; Tib. *Zhib mo rnam par 'thag pa*), and *Garland of Jewels* (Skt. *Ratnāvalī*; Tib. *Rin chen phreng ba*; Ch. *Baoxingwang zheng lun* 寶行王正論).
1171. "The Collection of Praise" (Skt. *Stavakāya*; Tib. *Bstod tshogs*) consists of four homages attributed to Nāgārjuna, also known as "The Four Praises" (Skt. *Catuḥstava*; Tib. *Bstod pa bzhi*): *Homage to the Supramundane One* (Skt. *Lokātītastava*; Tib. *'Jig rten las 'das par bstod pa*), *Homage to the Peerless One* (Skt. *Niraupamyastava*; Tib. *Dpe med par bstod pa*), *Praise to the Inconceivable One* (Skt. *Acintyastava*; Tib. *Bsam gyis mi khyab par bstod pa*), and *Praise of the Ultimate One* (Skt. *Paramārthastava*; Tib. *Don dam par bstod pa*).
1172. *Thos pa rgya mtsho ma.*
1173. It is difficult to follow Ameshab's timeline in places, but we have determined that this is in reference to Phakpa's famous defeat of rival Daoist masters in debate, at Qubilai's behest, in 1258.
1174. Shākya bzang po, d. 1270. Under the title pönchen (*dpon chen*), for twenty years Shākya Sangpo served as regent of Sakya Monastery after Sakya Paṇḍita and his nephew departed for the courts of Köden in 1244. The pönchen was a new institution during this period, in which a Mongol-appointed official would reside in Tibet as an imperial authority, while the imperial preceptor (such as Phakpa) would reside at court to minister to the imperial familiar and manage Buddhist affairs in the empire.
1175. Gser thog chen mo.
1176. Bkra shis sgo mang mchod rten.
1177. Glo po lo tsā ba shes rab rin chen.
1178. Mchims nam mkha' grags.
1179. Gsang ba gnyan 'od srung mgon po.
1180. Che ras pa.
1181. Yon tan dpal.
1182. Sgyer bu ba tshogs sgom kun dga' dpal.
1183. Zhang zhung pa rdo rje 'od zer.
1184. Rin po che skyob pa dpal.
1185. Rang dben dmar pa rnal 'byor dbang phyug rgwa lo.
1186. Nyi ma dpal.

1187. E pa zhang mngon pa ba rin chen rdo rje.
1188. Brag phug pa 'bum pa 'od zer.
1189. Mdog glo ba 'dul 'dzin shākya byang chub.
1190. Dbang phyug brtson 'grus.
1191. Rong ri lung phug pa'i gsang sngags pa chos kyi mgon po.
1192. Rdzil bu ba'i dge shes stag ston shes rab 'od zer.
1193. Dbus sde pa slob dpon sangs rgyas 'bum.
1194. Dge bshes 'Bras khud pa.
1195. Dar ma seng ge.
1196. Bcom ldan ral gri.
1197. *Gdungs rabs ya rabs kha rgyan.*
1198. 'Dam.
1199. A ti sha mar me mdzad dpal ye shes, 982–1054.
1200. 'Brom ston rgyal ba'i 'byung gnas, 1004–64.
1201. I.e., the great Kadampa geshé Potawa Rinchen Sal (Po to ba rin chen gsal, 1027–1105).
1202. I.e., Sharawa Yönten Drak (Sha ra ba yon tan grags, 1070–1141).
1203. Stabs kha ba. The reference is a little unclear, though likely to the twelfth-century master Tapkha Darma Drak (Stabs kha dar ma grags).
1204. Zhang ston.
1205. Dgon chen po.
1206. Jo bo yab sras kyi bka' srol chig rgyun.
1207. Rwa sgreng dgon. Also known in English as Reting Monastery.
1208. 'Jam ser.
1209. *Theg chen gsal ba'i yig sna.*
1210. *Lung bsdu ba.*
1211. *Kon mchog sgron ma.*
1212. Skt. *Āryatriskandhaka Sūtra*; Tib. *Phung po gsum pa'i mdo.*
1213. Glang thang pa; Shar pa; Sne zur ba; Bya yul ba; Stod lung pa.
1214. Ston pa dkon mchog seng ge.
1215. Dril bu pa. One of the eighty-four mahāsiddhas (Tib. *grub thob chen po*), or "great adepts" of tantric Buddhist lineage as memorialized in Tibet by the thirteenth century. Ghaṇṭāpa was, and remains, particularly associated with one of the three main lineages of Heruka-Cakrasaṃvara practices in the Sakya, Kagyü, and Geluk schools.
1216. Ma chen mo.
1217. Ston gzhon; Dge sling.
1218. Mar 'gro.
1219. Mngon pa ba.
1220. Phya ru ba.
1221. 'Chad dka' ba, i.e., Ye shes rdo rje (1101–1175). A renowned Kadampa master and author of the famous *Seven-Point Mind Training* (*Blo sbyong don bdun ma*).
1222. *Nor bu'i 'phreng ba.* Likely a commentary on the *Abhisamayamuktamala.*
1223. *Ngan song sbyor ba gnyis.*
1224. Skt. Bhaiṣajyaguru; Tib. Sman lha; Ch. Yaoshi rulai 藥師如來. An important buddha in Mahāyāna textual, visual, and ritual cultures.
1225. Tib. Tshogs gdag; i.e., Gaṇeśa.

1226. Skt. *yānas*; Tib. *theg pa*; Ch. *sheng* 乘. A common rhetorical term in Mahāyāna (the "Great Vehicle") doxography, referring to the multiple "vehicles" in which followers of the Buddha's teachings, and indeed even non-Buddhist practitioners, may advance gradually along the path to enlightenment.

1227. Sne'u thog.

1228. Ston pa chos mgon.

1229. This may be in reference to the "Lopön Joden" who appears in Biji's account of the final days of Sakya Paṇḍita.

1230. 'Dul 'dzin chos mgon.

1231. Dbu ru.

1232. The following record of questions and answers reads in places as if they were in the first-person voice of Phakpa and Namkha Bum, but then in other places they slip into third-person summary. We have left the text as it appears and tried to clarify changes in voice and perspective as they arise.

1233. Skt. *śamatha*; Tib. *zhi gnas*; Ch. *zhi* 止. Also often translated as "quietude" and "serenity." Calm abiding is the result of gradual training in concentration (Skt. *samādhi*; Tib. *ting nge 'dzin*; Ch. *sanmei* 三昧). It is the perfection of one form of meditative cultivation that supplies the single-minded and long-term focus and stability required for developing insight into the nature of reality and the destruction of the afflictions (Skt. *kleśa*; Tib. *nyon mong*; Ch. *fannao* 煩惱) that bind sentient beings in saṃsāra, or cyclic existence.

1234. Referring to "aspirational bodhicitta" (Skt. *praṇidhicittotpāda*; Tib. *smon pa'i sems bskyed*; Ch. *yuan puti xin* 願菩提心), where one declares one's intention to become enlightened to liberate all sentient beings, and what the Tibetans translated as "engaged bodhicitta" (Skt. *prasthānacittotpāda*, lit. "generating the intention to embark"; Tib. *'jug pa'i sems bskyed*; Ch. *xing puti xin* 行菩提心), where one follows through on this aspiration by pursuing self-cultivation toward enlightenment.

1235. Mkha' ru ba.

1236. Lama Phakpa and Namkha Bum likely counted these ten "Dharma activities" (Skt. *dharmacarya*; Tib. *chos spyod*; Ch. *faxing* 法行) in a tradition based on Maitreya's fourth-century text, *Distinguishing the Middle from the Extremes*. These ten are listed as: (1) writing (Skt. *lekhana*; Tib. *yi ge 'bri pa*; Ch. *shuxie* 書寫); (2) homage (Skt. *pūjā*; Tib. *mchod pa*; Ch. *gongyang* 供養); (3) giving (Skt. *dāna*; Tib. *sbyin pa*; Ch. *shita* 施他); (4) learning (Skt. *śravaṇa*; Tib. *nyan ba*; Ch. *tingwen* 聽聞); (5) reading (Skt. *vācana*; Tib. *klog pa*; Ch. *pidu* 披讀); (6) understanding (Skt. *udgrahaṇa*; Tib. *'dzin pa*; Ch. *shouchi* 受持); (7) instructing (Skt. *prakāśana*; Tib. *rab tu ston pa*; Ch. *kaiyan* 開演); (8) reciting (Skt. *svādhyāya*; Tib. *kha 'don byed pa*; Ch. *fengsong* 諷誦); (9) contemplation (Skt. *cintana*; Tib. *sems pa*; Ch. *siwei* 思惟); and (10) meditation (Skt. *bhāvanā*; Tib. *sgom pa*; Ch. *xiuxi* 修習).

1237. *Gnyen po kun tu spyod pa'i stobs*, lit. "the power of completely engaging in the antidote."

1238. Skt. *Gurupañcāśikā*; Tib. *Bla ma lnga bcu pa*. Attributed to Aśvaghoṣa (Rta dbyangs, ca. tenth century), this work became a standard reference for all Tibetan Buddhist traditions during and since the New Translation period.

In poetic verse, it outlines correct guru devotion and student conduct in the context of tantric practice.

1239. Tib. *Rnam par snang mdzad*; Ch. *Dari rulai* 大日如來.

1240. Rnam par snang mdzad gang chen mtsho.

1241. Skt. Cittamātra; Tib. Sems tsam; Ch. Weizin 唯心. An alternative name for the Yogācāra philosophical school, which holds that the sensory world is dependent upon the mind and that the phenomenal world is a projection of mind.

1242. The Madhyamaka, or Middle Way school (Tib. Dbu ma pa; Ch. Zhongguan 中觀) is one of two major Mahāyāna philosophical schools (along with Yogācāra). Derived from the works of Nāgārjuna (ca. second century CE), proponents of Madhyamaka argue that reality is untainted by the two extreme views of "eternalism" (Skt. *śāśvatadṛṣṭi*; Tib. *rtag lta*; Ch. *changjian* 常見) and "nihilism" (Skt. *ucchedadṛṣṭi*; Tib. *chad lta*; Ch. *duanjian* 斷見).

1243. Gcung mos pa.

1244. Skt. Sadāprarudita; Tib. Rtag tu ngu; Ch. Changti [pusa] 常啼[菩薩]. An oft-referenced protagonist of the famous *Perfection of Wisdom in Eight Thousand Lines* (Skt. *Aṣṭasāhasrikāprajñāpāramitā*; Tib. *Sher phyin brgyad stong pa*; Ch. *Xiaopin bore jing* 小品般若經), Ever-Weeping is a bodhisattva intent on studying with qualified gurus who practices exemplary generosity in the form of giving his own bodily flesh to beggars and the needy.

1245. I.e., you are uninterested in taking initiation but interested in practicing Mantra Vehicle rituals.

1246. This is Atiśa's famous *Bodhipathapradīpa* (Tib. *Byang chub lam gyi sgron ma*), which he wrote soon after his arrival in Tibet in 1042. Tibetan monastic historians characterized the composition of this work as a response to the improper practice of tantra in Tibet following the collapse of the Yarlung Empire. Specifically, Atiśa is said to have written this work as a step-by-step guide for his Tibetan disciples to train in the foundational, exoteric practices of the Mahāyāna as the basis for proper tantric practice.

1247. *Tsha tsha*. These are miniature molded figures of deities, stūpas, auspicious signs, and the like, which are made from clay and other impressionable media and sometimes mixed with ashes and relics, as is referenced in this question.

1248. Stong lung pa.

1249. Skt. *Suhṛllekha*; Tib. *Bshes pa'i spring yig*. One of two famous letters sent to kings attributed to Nāgārjuna. The bulk of this letter advises the king on how to live virtuously as a layman.

1250. One of the "three realms of [saṃsāric] existence" according to Buddhist cosmology (Skt. *traidhātuka*; Tib. *khams gsum*; Ch. *san jie* 三界). The other two realms are the form realm (Skt. *rūpadhātu*; Tib. *gzugs khams*; Ch. *se jie* 色界) and the formless realm (Skt. *ārūpyadhātu*; Tib. *gzugs med khams*; Ch. *wuse jie* 無色).

1251. Skt. *tathāgatagarbha*; Tib. *bzhin gshegs pa'i snying po*; Ch. *rulaizang* 如來藏). Can be translated literally as "womb of the tathāgatas," in reference to the potential to achieve buddhahood that several Mahāyāna schools claim is fundamental to the mind of sentient beings currently imprisoned in saṃsāra.

1252. Gangs pa she'u.

1253. A chupa is a knee-length, often wool-lined garment that remains common in Tibetan societies.

1254. Tib. *yongs su mya ngan las 'das pa chen po*; Ch. *da banniepan* 大般涅槃.
1255. Tib. Don yod zhags pa; Ch. Bukong juansuo 不空羂索. Considered an alternative tantric form of Avalokiteśvara.
1256. Dpal ldan ngan song.
1257. *Rnam dag snying po.*
1258. *Snying po de bzhin gshegs pa.*
1259. Glang ri thang pa, 1054–1123.
1260. *Blo sbyong tshig brgyad ma*. A key "mind transformation" (Tib. *blo sbyong*) text in the Kadampa tradition. The eight verses are pithy reminders and aspirations to eliminate self-cherishing, cultivate the cherishing of others, abandon worldly attachments, and recognize the illusory nature of reality.
1261. In other words, the stages of the path is the most important practice.
1262. *Dbu ma bden chung.*
1263. *Dbu ma man ngag.*
1264. Rin chen sgang pa.
1265. Spyil phu ba.
1266. Mu mu ne.
1267. Chos 'phags.
1268. Tib. Jim gyim; Ch. Zhenjin 真金, 1243–86. Though he died eight years before his father, Čingkim was a popular member of the Mongolian imperial household and well trained in the Confucian tradition. He was in time appointed Qubilai's principal heir. For example, the latter appointed his son the prince of Yan (燕王) in 1262 and crown prince (皇太子) in 1273. Lama Phakpa was a tutor and friend of Čingkim who wrote his famous *Illuminating the Knowable* (Tib. *Shes bya rab gsal*) for the Mongol prince.
1269. *Ku mud da'i tshal*. According to some reference works, the kumudu is the Sanskrit name for *Nymphaea pubescens*.
1270. Shākya bzang po.
1271. Kun dga' bzang po.
1272. Rin chen sgang bla brang; Lha khang bla brang; Dus mchod bla brang. The history of these important Sakya institutions are Ameshab's subjects later in this text, which will be translated into English in the forthcoming second volume of this work.
1273. Shel dam ling drug ma.
1274. Mi nyag rgya rgod rgyal po.
1275. *Gnam gyi 'og sa'i steng na rgya gar lha'i sras po sprul pa'i sangs rgyas yi ge rtsom mi rgyal khams 'jags su 'jug pa po gnas lnga rig pa'i pandi ta 'phags pa ti shrī.*
1276. Rma gu ra.
1277. Sbom ra lha.
1278. Rma chu. This is the Tibetan name for the Yellow River (Huang he 黄河).
1279. While Ameshab here refers to Čingkim as "emperor" (Tib. *rgyal po*), this is either a misunderstanding or misprint of *rgyal po* for *rgyal bu*, meaning prince. Qubilai's son in fact never assumed his father's position. Dying eight years before his father, Čingkim was given the temple name Yuzong (裕宗) and posthumously appointed as emperor Wenhui Mingxiao (文惠明孝). Čingkim's son Temür succeeded Qubilai in 1294 as the sixth qaγan of the

Mongol Empire and the second emperor of the Yuan dynasty under the reign title Öljiyetü Qaγan.

1280. Chu mig ring mo.
1281. Yon khri chings sangs.
1282. Spelled *chings sangs* in this text, but more commonly *ching sang* or *phying sang*.
1283. Skt. *vidhyādhara*; Tib. *rig pa'i 'dzin pa*; Ch. Chiming持明. This term has many references in different kinds of Buddhist and non-Buddhist traditions in South Asia. Here the reference is to tantric masters (though it can also refer to tantric deities) whose mastery of secret mantra has transformed them into "holders" of tantric knowledge.
1284. *Dbyangs tshangs pa'i 'brug sgra.*
1285. Bing bing ka'u si.
1286. Mdo khams sgang.
1287. Stag thog gzhis mo che.
1288. Sgo mang.
1289. That is, the ordination of fully ordained monks and nuns, and novice monks and nuns, respectively.
1290. 'Dul 'dzin chos kyi mgon po, i.e., "the upholder of the Vinaya, Chökyi Gönpo."
1291. Rje yang dgon pa.
1292. 'U yug.
1293. *Jo gdan*. Though spelled the same as the personal name of Lopön Joden, whom we have encountered already, here "joden" apparently is in reference to a particular bureaucratic position in the Mongol imperial administration. We have been unable to determine what exactly this was, or whether "joden" glosses a specific Mongolian term (while confusingly retaining the Tibetan spelling for Joden Monastery). More research is required.
1294. Shangs lta bu.
1295. *Lam 'bras bla ma brgyud pa'i gsol 'debs.*
1296. *Rgyud kyi bla ma brgyud pa'i gsol 'debs.*
1297. *'Jigs byed brgyud pa'i gsol 'debs.*
1298. *Ba ri brgyud pa'i gsol 'debs.*
1299. *Bla ma'i mtshan 'bum.*
1300. *Sku'i spyod pa la spel ba che chung gnyis.*
1301. *Bla ma'i spyi bstod me tog gi phreng ba.*
1302. *Chos rje la gsol ba 'debs pa blo chen ma.*
1303. *Chos rje la bstod cing gsol ba 'debs pa.*
1304. *Bla ma la bstod pa ri bo rtse lngar sbar ba.*
1305. *Chos rje la bstod pa bstod dbyangs rgya mtsho.*
1306. *Śākya'i rgyal po la bstod pa.*
1307. *'Jam dpal la mtshan don gyi sgo nas bstod pa.*
1308. *Ri bo rtse lnga'i bstod pa.*
1309. *Bstan pa'i 'khor lo'i bstod pa.* "Wheel of the Teachings" is an epithet for Mañjuśrī.
1310. *'Jam dbyang la bstod pa gnyis.*
1311. *Spyan ras gzigs kyi bstod pa.*
1312. *Byams pa'i bstod pa.*

1313. *Gnas brtan bcu drug gi bstod pa.*
1314. *Dkon mchog gsum gyi bstod pa.*
1315. *Mchog brgyad kyi bstod pa.*
1316. *Bdag med lha mo bco lnga'i bstod pa.* Nairātmyā is the consort of Hevajra.
1317. *Khro bcu'i bstod bskul.* These are in the maṇḍala of Vajrakīlaya.
1318. *Bde mchog gi dkyil 'khor gyi bstod pa.*
1319. *Tshe dpag med kyi bsod pa.*
1320. *Barna sha ba rī'i bstod pa.*
1321. *'Od zer can gyi bstod pa.*
1322. *'Dod pa'i lha la bstod pa.* Kāmadeva is a god with sovereignty over the desire realm.
1323. *Srung ba lnga'i lha rnams la bstod pa.*
1324. *Srung ba lnga'i dkyil 'khor gyi lha la bstod pa.*
1325. *Mi g.yo ba'i bstod pa.*
1326. *Gur mgon lcam dral gyi bstod pa.*
1327. *Gdong bzhi ba'i bstod pa.*
1328. *Bla ma'i bstod pa me tog phreng ba.*
1329. *Brgyud pa'i phreng ba.*
1330. *Thun mong ma yin pa'i gsol 'debs kyi 'bru 'grel.*
1331. *Bla ma'i gsol 'debs phyogs bcu dus gsum ma rnams mdzad.*
1332. *Bla ma'i rnal 'byor.*
1333. *Bla ma la mandal 'bul ba'i cho ga.*
1334. *Lam 'bras kyi gzhung bshad.*
1335. *'Pho ba'i yi ge.*
1336. *Dag pa gsum gyi khrid.*
1337. *Dril bu pa'i rim lnga.*
1338. *Snang ba mtha' yas kyi bsgom don.*
1339. *Zab mo snang ba.*
1340. *Phyag rgya chen po bsgom pa'i man ngag.*
1341. *Phyag rgya chen po yan lag bdun ldan rnams mdzad.*
1342. *Kye rdor bsdus don.*
1343. *Dag chung.*
1344. *Ljon chung.*
1345. *Brtag gnyis kyi mchan.*
1346. *Gur gyi le 'grel.* The reference here is to the *Ḍākinīvajrapañjara Tantra,* which the Sakya by Phakpa's time considered to belong to the Hevajra tantric corpus.
1347. *Sambu ta'i sab cad.*
1348. *Rdo rje sems dpa'i bsgom bzlas.*
1349. *Dpa' gcig srung 'khor dang bcas pa yid bzhin nor bu.*
1350. *Yan lag pa.*
1351. *Bdag 'jug jim gyim ma dang dpal 'byung ma gnyis.*
1352. *Bdag 'jug la ltos pa'i dbang gi tho yig.*
1353. *Lam dus kyi dbang.*
1354. *Mchog gsum yi ge.*
1355. *Lus dkyil.*
1356. *Tshogs 'khor bdud rtsi bum pa.*

1357. *La shu'i don du mdzad pa'i tshogs 'khor.*
1358. *Bdud rtsi ril bu sgrub thabs.*
1359. *Bdag med ma'i sgrub thabs.*
1360. *Dus 'khor thugs dkyil gyi sgrub thabs.*
1361. Nag po pa.
1362. *Mchod phreng.*
1363. *Sgrub thabs rim pa gsal ba.*
1364. *Thabs kyi rim pa tshogs bsags bcu gsum pa.*
1365. *Rig ma bcu drug.*
1366. *Pho nya bcu'i bskul.*
1367. *Mngon rtogs.*
1368. *Lha lnga'i sgrub thabs.*
1369. *Lhan skyes rnal 'byor bcu pa.*
1370. *Jo sras phag mchu'i don du mdzad pa gcig.*
1371. *Za byed rdo rje mkha' 'gro'i sbyin sreg.*
1372. *Bde mchog gi bkra shis.*
1373. *Phag mo mngon byung gi mngon rtogs.*
1374. *Nā ro mkha' spyod kyi sgrub thabs che chung gnyis.*
1375. *Lha bcu bdun ma'i sgrub thabs.*
1376. O rgyan sgrol ma.
1377. 'Jigs pa brgyad skyob sgrol ma.
1378. Phyag drug sgrol ma.
1379. *Mi bskyod pa'i dkyil chog.*
1380. *'Jam pa'i rdo rje'i mngon rtogs kyi bsdus don.*
1381. *Ye shes zhabs kyi lo rgyus.*
1382. *Lha bcu dgu'i sgrub thabs.*
1383. *Dgra nag gi sgrub thabs.*
1384. *Sgrub thabs 'jigs med rnam rol.*
1385. *Lhan skyes rnams.*
1386. *Sngags thun mong.*
1387. *Bla ma lnga bcu pa'i bsdus don.*
1388. *Rtsa ltung gi 'grel pa dam tshig rab gsal.*
1389. *Spyod rgyud nas bshad pa'i tshe dpag med.*
1390. *Mi 'khrugs pa'i sbyin sreg.*
1391. Rnam 'joms.
1392. 'Jam dpal dpa' bo grub pa.
1393. Seng ge sgra.
1394. Rta mgrin khyung gshog can.
1395. Rnam rgyal gdugs dkar.
1396. Ri khrod ma.
1397. Spyan ma.
1398. Gza' yum.
1399. *Rig ma bcu drug gi tshigs bcad gnyis.*
1400. *Mtshams spyod.*
1401. *Gza' dang rgyu skar la gsol ba gdab pa.*
1402. *Rgyud sde'i dkar chag.*
1403. *Bdag nyid kyis chos gsan pa'i dkar chag.*

1404. *Chos spyod bcu la spel ba.*
1405. *Chos spyod bcu pa.*
1406. *Slob dpon chen po'i don du mdzad pa'i sems bskyed.*
1407. *Theg mchog gsal ba.*
1408. *Las 'bras gsal ba'i me long.*
1409. *Bden gnyis rnam nges.*
1410. *Theg pa chen po'i man ngag.*
1411. *Bu mor in chen gyis zhus pa'i mdo'i bsdus don.*
1412. *Zab mo mdo lnga'i sdom.*
1413. *Rgyud bla'i bsdus don.*
1414. *Theg pa'i rnam dbye.*
1415. *Lam gyi snying po.*
1416. *Zab mo nyams su len tshul.*
1417. *Theg chen gsal ba'i 'grel pa 'thad ldan rnams.*
1418. *Gdams pa bdud rtsi'i thig le.*
1419. *Yan lag bdun gyi gtam.*
1420. *Rga shi med pa'i lam rab bdun pa.*
1421. *Skyo ba'i gtam.*
1422. *Snyigs ma'i gtam.*
1423. *Ka kha la spel ba.*
1424. *Mgon g.yag la bstod pa.*
1425. *Zin shing btul ba'i tshigs bcad.*
1426. *Gtsang kha ma.*
1427. *Sman tshe ngo bltas pa la bsngags pa rnam.*
1428. *G.yag sde pa'i dris lan.*
1429. *Dris lan rnam nges.*
1430. *Grags rin gyi zhus lan.*
1431. *Ston pa brtson 'grus kyi dris lan.*
1432. *Dpon blo gros seng ge'i zhus lan.*
1433. *Rgyal po la gdams pa.*
1434. *Ji mig de mur la gtam du bya ba nor bu'i phreng ba.*
1435. *Mangga la gtam du bya ba bkra shis kyi phreng ba.*
1436. *Rgyal bu mo no gan la spring yig.* Here the Tibetan has reversed the first two syllables in the Mongolian name of Qubilai's fourth son.
1437. *Ho go la gdams pa.*
1438. *De gu bho ga la gdams pa.*
1439. *The mu 'o ga la gdams pa.*
1440. *Dpon mo punda rī ka la gdams pa.*
1441. *Rgyal po jim gyim la gdams pa gsum.*
1442. *A tsa ra la gdams pa.*
1443. *Bla ma ldong gi gdan sar bkur ba.*
1444. *Grags bzang la springs pa.*
1445. *Bod yul gyi dge 'dun spyi la bkur ba.*
1446. *Tshwa rong pa la springs pa.*
1447. *Ji big la springs pa.*
1448. *Rgyal bu la springs pa chos gtam dgu pa.*
1449. *Rwa dbon la bkur ba.*

1450. *Ral gri la springs yig.*
1451. *Spyi bo lhas pa la bkur ba.*
1452. *Khro phu ba la bkur ba.*
1453. *Chag lo la bkur ba.*
1454. *Chos 'khor phyi ma'i dus su dbus kyi mtshan nyid pa spyi la bkur ba.*
1455. *Dbus kyi bka' gdams pa spyi la bkur ba.*
1456. *Stag lung pa la bkur ba.*
1457. *Dbus kyi sgom chen pa rnams la bskur ba.*
1458. *Rgyal bu ji big la springs pa.*
1459. *Grags bzang la springs yig.*
1460. *Ston gzhon la bkur ba rnams.*
1461. Skt. *Avataṃsaka Sūtra*; Tib. *Mdo phal po che*; Ch. *Huayan jing* 華嚴經.
1462. This was Qubilai's second son with consort Čabui.
1463. A rog ches.
1464. Dur rgan dur mi.
1465. Bla ma grags pa 'Od zer.
1466. Bla ma bkra shis dpal.
1467. Zhang dkon dpal.
1468. Kun blo.
1469. La ru ba; Nyen chen pa; Sru lung pa; Gsal la ba 'od zer 'bum; Dbus pa sangs 'bum.
1470. Dpal gyi ri.
1471. Rig pa'i rgyal mo rma bya chen mo.
1472. Grags pa gzhon nu.
1473. 'Jam dbyangs sngong po.
1474. Rin chen mdzod dgon.
1475. Shang grud.
1476. Brgya tsho ba.
1477. Lha sa rdzong pa.
1478. Rje btsun dam pa Kun dga' grol mchog.
1479. Smon 'gro.
1480. Sngags 'chang ngag dbang kun dga' bsod nams.
1481. Ti shrī grags pa 'od zer.
1482. Dpal brtsegs bsrung.
1483. Sa ston ri.
1484. Palden (*dpal ldan*).
1485. Phakpa (*'phags pa*).
1486. Zas gtsang. Śuddodana was the Buddha Śākyamuni's father.
1487. 'Gro ba'i mgon Phyag na rdo rje.
1488. G.ya ru mdog gi gad lo.
1489. Mdog stod tshan.
1490. Ma gcig kun skyid.
1491. A bow and arrow, a sword, and a spear.
1492. Phyag mda' bsgrub chu.
1493. Sa len dbang.
1494. Gser tham thong phyi.

1495. G.yas g.yon gyi khrims ra.
1496. Me kha bdun. In this passage we read the reference to Mekhadun as being a daughter of Qubilai, but in other sources and in a section below, she is identified (correctly) as the daughter of Köden Ejen.
1497. Chos skor.
1498. Sgo rum dpe khang.
1499. Zangs tsha bsod nams rgyal mtshan, 1184–1239.
1500. Chu mdo ba.
1501. Rje btsad.
1502. Ma gcig jo 'gro.
1503. Slop dpon rin chen rgyal mtshan.
1504. Me tog ra ba.
1505. Shing kun.
1506. Slob dpon ma mdo sde.
1507. Mus su go.
1508. Mus chen rgyal mtshan dpal bzang.
1509. Chu mdo.
1510. Shab Jo 'gro ma.
1511. Mnga' ris gung thang.
1512. Lha gcig mdzes ma.
1513. Bsod nams 'bum.
1514. Jo mo gling.
1515. Nyi ma 'bum.
1516. Bkra shis brtsegs pa dpal.
1517. Jo lcam hor mo; Jo mo hor lcam.
1518. Rin chen 'byung gnas.
1519. Brgya tsho dpon drung.
1520. Lha gcig mdzes ma.
1521. Rdo rje gdan.
1522. Ye shes 'byung gnas.
1523. Shar pa shes rab 'byung gnas; Shar pa rdo rje 'od zer.
1524. Hu dkar che.
1525. Ljang yul.
1526. Ser snang.
1527. We would expect the reference here to be to Mekhadun, Köden Ejen's betrothed daughter, as above. Mangala was one of Phakpa's disciples, as above, and this is likely a typo in the Tibetan text.
1528. Ma gcig ldan tsha chos 'bum.
1529. Mkha' 'gro 'bum.
1530. Sku zhang rnga sgra.
1531. Gnas drug lha khang.
1532. Lha chen dpal 'bar.
1533. *Sku tshad bcu gsum sogs mang du*. It is unclear what exact measure or unit is being referenced here.
1534. Bla ma ye shes rin chen pa.
1535. Pre mandal.

1536. Jo mo stag 'bum.
1537. In other sources, this child is often named Dharmabhadra or Ratnapāla-rakṣita.
1538. Shar pa 'jam dbyangs rin chen rgyal mtshan.
1539. Zhal bdag; Gser thog; G.yu thog.
1540. Thig khang.
1541. Ma gcig khab smad sma; Jo mo 'bum me.
1542. Bdag nyid chen po bzang po dpal.
1543. Bo dong er.
1544. Khab smad.
1545. I.e., we will run out of good options for the dungsé leaders of the Khön succession lineage and be required to appoint dungsé from more marginal and far removed branches of the family tree.
1546. Sman rtse.
1547. Ch. 苏州; Tib. Zo chu.
1548. *'jam chen.* This measure of space is unclear. However, in the passages just below, Sangpo Pal's travels are measured by *jel-lam* (*'jal lam*). This suggests that *'jam chen* (great *jam*) in this passage may have been a contraction of the first part of *'jal* with the ending of *lam* to become *'jam.*
1549. Ch. 杭州; Tib. Ham chu.
1550. Kun dga' 'od zer.
1551. Shar pa 'Jam dbyangs chen po, 1258–1306.
1552. Ag gleng.
1553. *Sic.* thigs khang.
1554. Blo chen; Snur ye shes rgyal mtshan.
1555. Yar brog.
1556. Dbon nag.
1557. *Gug śrī.*
1558. Shes rab dpal; O bu.
1559. Dam pa hre po.
1560. Sga a gnyan dam pa.
1561. Bong sna can.
1562. This is Gyasa Kongjo (Tib. Rgya bza' kong jo; Ch. Wencheng Gongzhu文成公主), the aforementioned seventh-century bride of Songtsen Gampo.
1563. Rje btsad po thang tha'i dzung. Kongjo's father, the famous Tang dynasty emperor Taizong (太宗), 598–649.
1564. Kyin chang hau.
1565. Spos ldan.
1566. As mentioned already, this famous narrative is derived from the *Avataṃsaka Sūtra.*
1567. Gzhi thog bla sbrang. One of the labrang residences of Ṣakya. Ameshab explores the histories of all these residences, which were fully established by Sangpo Pal's many children, in great detail later in volume 2 of this translation.
1568. A mo gha dhwa dza śrī pā la.
1569. 'Phags pa kun [dga'] blo [gros rgyal mtshan].
1570. Mus sras.

Bibliography

Ahmad, Zahiruddin. *Sino-Tibetan Relations in the Seventeenth Century.* Roma: Istituto Italiano per il Medio ed Estremo Oriente, 1970.

Ananda Dhvaja. *Le Subhāsitaratnandidhi Mongol: Un Document du Moyen Mongol.* Edited by Lajos Ligeti. Bibliotheca Orientalis Hungarica. Budapest: Société Körösi Csoma, 1948.

Atwood, Christopher Pratt. *Encyclopedia of Mongolia and the Mongolian Empire.* New York, NY: Facts on File, 2004.

———. *The Secret History of the Mongols.* London: Penguin Books, 2023.

Beckwith, Christopher I. "A Study of the Early Medieval Chinese, Latin and Tibetan Historical Sources on Pre-Imperial Tibet." PhD diss., Indiana University, 1978.

———. *The Tibetan Empire in Central Asia: A History of the Struggle for Great Power among Tibetans, Turks, Arabs, and Chinese during the Early Middle Ages.* Princeton, NJ: Princeton University Press, 1993.

———. "Tibetan Science at the Courts of the Great Khans." *The Journal of the Tibet Society* 7 (1987): 5–12.

Bosson, James E. *A Treasury of Aphoristic Jewels: The Subhāṣitaratnanidhi of Sa Skya Paṇḍita in Tibetan and Mongolian.* Bloomington: Indiana University, 1969.

Canzio, Ricardo. *Sakya Pandita's Treatise on Music* (*Rol mo'i bstan bcos*). Kathmandu: Vajra Books, 2019.

Cuevas, Bryan J., and Kurtis R. Schaeffer, eds. *Power, Politics, and the Reinvention of Tradition: Tibet in the Seventeenth and Eighteenth Centuries.* PIATS 2003. Brill's Tibetan Studies Library. Leiden: Brill, 2006.

Cüppers, Christoph, ed. *The Relationship between Religion and State (Chos Srid Zung 'brel) in Traditional Tibet: Proceedings of a Seminar Held in Lumbini, Nepal, March 2000*. LIRI Seminar Proceedings Series. Lumbini: Lumbini International Research Institute, 2004.

Davidson, Ronald M. *Indian Esoteric Buddhism: A Social History of the Tantric Movement*. New York: Columbia University Press, 2002.

———. *Tibetan Renaissance: Tantric Buddhism in the Rebirth of Tibetan Culture*. New York: Columbia University Press, 2005.

Debreczeny, Karl, and Gary Tuttle, eds. *The Tenth Karmapa and Tibet's Turbulent Seventeenth Century*. Chicago: Serindia Publications, 2016.

Dharmatāla. *Dharmatala's Annals of Buddhism*. Śta-Pitaka Series: Indo-Asian Literatures. New Delhi: Sharada Rani, 1975.

Eimer, Helmut, and Kun-dgav-rgyal-mtshan. *Sa skya legs bshad: die Strophen zur Lebensklugheit von Sa skya Paṇḍita Kun dga' rgyal mtshan (1182–1251)*. Wiener Studien zur Tibetologie und Buddhismuskunde. Wien: Arbeitskreis für Tibetische und Buddhistische Studien, Universität Wien, 2014.

Elverskog, Johan. *Our Great Qing: The Mongols, Buddhism and the State in Late Imperial China*. Honolulu: University of Hawai'i Press, 2006.

———. *The Jewel Translucent Sūtra: Altan Khan and the Mongols in the Sixteenth Century*. Brill's Inner Asian Library. Leiden/Boston: Brill, 2003.

———. "Tibetocentrism, Religious Conversion and the Study of Mongolian Buddhism." In *The Mongolia-Tibet Interface: Opening New Research Terrains in Inner Asia*. PIATS 2003. Edited by Uradyn E. Bulag and Hildegard G. M. Diemberger. Leiden/Boston: Brill, 2007.

Farrow, G. W., I. Menon, and Kṛṣṇavajrapāda. *The Concealed Essence of the Hevajra Tantra: With the Commentary Yogaratnamālā*. 1st ed. Delhi: Motilal Banarsidass Publishers, 1992.

Gold, Jonathan C. "Sakya Paṇḍita's Anti-Realism as a Return to the Mainstream." *Philosophy East and West* 64 (2014): 360–74.

———. *The Dharma's Gatekeepers: Sakya Pandita on Buddhist Scholarship in Tibet*. Albany: State University of New York Press, 2007.

Grags pa rgyal mtshan and Sa skya Paṇḍita. *An Overview of Tantra and Related Works*. Translated by Christopher Wilkinson. Sakya Gongma Series. Concord: Suvarna Bhasa Publishing, 2014.

———. *The Hermit King*. Translated by Christopher Wilkinson. Sakya Gongma Series. Concord: Suvarna Bhasa Publishing, 2014.

Howorth, Richard. *History of the Mongols from the 9th to the 19th Century*. Vol. 4. London: Longmans, Green & Co., 1927.

Hugon, Pascale, and Sa-skya Paṇḍi-ta Kun-dga'-rgyal-mtshan. *Trésors du Raisonnement: Sa skya Paṇḍita et ses prédécesseurs tibétains sur les modes de fonctionnement de la pensée et le fondement de l'inférence: édition et traduction annotée du quatrième chapitre et d'une section du dixième chapitre du Tshad ma rigs pa 'i gter*. Wiener Studien zur Tibetologie und Buddhismuskunde. Wien: Arbeitskreis für Tibetische und Buddhistische Studien, Universität Wien, 2008.

Ishihama, Yumiko. "The Notion of 'Buddhist Government' (chos srid) Shared by Tibet, Mongol, and Manchu in the Early 17th Century." In *The Relationship between Religion and State (chos srid zung 'brel) in Traditional Tibet: Proceedings of a Seminar held in Lumbini, Nepal, March 2000*. Edited by Christoph Cüppers, 15–31. Lumbini: Lumbini International Research Institute, 2004.

Jackson, David Paul, and Sa-skya Paṇḍi-ta Kun-dga'-rgyal-mtshan. "Sa-Syka Paṇḍita on Indian and Tibetan Traditions of Philosophical Debate: The Mhkas Pa Rnams 'jug Pa'i Sgo, Section III." PhD diss., University of Washington, 1985.

———. *The Entrance Gate for the Wise (Section III): Sa-Skya Paṇḍita on Indian and Tibetan Traditions of Pramāṇa and Philosophical Debate*. Wien: Arbeitskreis für Tibetische und Buddhistische Studien, Universität Wien, 1987.

'Jam mgon a myes zhabs ngag dbang kun dga' bsod nams. *'Dzam gling byang phyogs kyi thub pa'i rgyal tshab chen po dpal ldan sa skya pa'i gdung rabs rin po che ji ltar byon pa'i tshul gyi rnam par thar pa ngo tshar rin po che'i bang mdzod dgos 'dod kun 'byung*. Delhi: Tashi Dorje, 1975.

Kara, György, and Marta Kiripolská. *Dictionary of Sonom Gara's Erdeni-Yin Sang: A Middle Mongol Version of the Tibetan Sa-Skya Legs Bshad: Mongol-English-Tibetan*. Brill's Inner Asian Library. Leiden: Brill, 2009.

King, Matthew. "Exorcising the Body Politic: The Lion's Roar, Köden Ejen's Two Bodies and the Question of Conversion at the Tibet-Mongol Interface." *Buddhist Studies Review* 38.1 (2021): 45–57.

———. *Ocean of Milk, Ocean of Blood: A Mongolian Monk in the Ruins of the Qing Empire*. New York: Columbia University Press, 2019.

Kwanten, Luc. "Chinggis Khan's Conquest of Tibet: Myth or Reality?" *Journal of Asian History* 8 (1974): 1–20.

Losang Tadrin (Blo bzang rta mgrin). *The Amazing Golden Book: The Great Elucidation Upon the Legends of Great Northerly Mongolia. Byang phyogs chen po hor gyi rgyal khams kyi rtogs brjod kyi bstan bcos chen po ngo mtshar gser gyi deb ther*. In *Gsung 'bum / Blo bzang rta mgrin*, 2:43–490. New Delhi: Mongolian Lama Guru Deva, 1975.

Onoda, Shunzō. "The Chronology of the Abbatial Successions of the gSang phu sNe'u thog Monastery," *Wiener Zeitschrift für die Kunde Südasiens* 33 (1989):203–13.

Petech, Luciano. *Central Tibet and the Mongols: The Yüan Sa-Skya Period of Tibetan History*. Serie Orientale Roma. Rome: Istituto Italiano per il Medio ed Estremo Oriente, 1990.

———. "'P'ags-pa (1235–1280)." In *In the Service of the Khan: Eminent Personalities of the Early Mongol-Yüan Period (1200-1300)*. Edited by Igor de Rachewiltz, et al. Wiesbaden: Harrassowitz, 1993.

'Phags-pa Blo-gros-rgyal-mtshan and Christopher Wilkinson. *At the Court of Kublai Khan: Writings of the Tibetan Monk Chogyal Phagpa*. Cambridge: Christopher Wilkinson, 2015.

Phakpa Lodrö Gyaltsen ('Phags pa blo gros rgyal mtshan). *Advice to Kublai Khan: Letters by the Tibetan Monk Chogyal Phagpa to Kublai Khan and His Court*. Translated by Christopher Wilkinson. Cambridge, MA: Christopher Wilkinson, 2015.

———. *Chogyal Phagpa: The Emperor's Guru*. Translated by Christopher Wilkinson. Sakya Gongma Series. Concord: Suvarna Bhasa Publishing, 2014.

Pommaret, Françoise. *Lhasa in the Seventeenth Century: The Capital of the Dalai Lamas*. Brill's Tibetan Studies Library. Leiden: Brill, 2003.

Przybysławski, Artur, Go-rams-pa Bsod-nams-seng-ge, and Sa-skya Paṇḍi-ta Kun-dga'-rgyal-mtshan. *Cognizable Object in Sa Skya Paṇḍita: An Edition and Annotated Translation of the First Chapter of Tshad Ma Rigs Gter by Sa Skya Paṇḍita and the First Chapter of Tshad Ma Rigs Pa'i Gter Gyi Don Gsal Bar Byed Pa by Go Rams Pa*. 1st ed. Kraków: Jagiellonian University Press, 2017.

Rossabi, Morris. *Khubilai Khan: His Life and Times*. Berkeley: University of California Press, 1988.

Sa skya paṇḍi ta Kun dga' rgyal mtshan. *Poetic Wisdom*. Translated by Christopher Wilkinson. Sakya Gongma Series. Concord: Suvarna Bhasa Publishing, 2014.

Sa skya paṇḍi ta Kun dga' rgyal mtshan, John T. Davenport, Sallie D. Davenport, and Losang Thonden. *Ordinary Wisdom: Sakya Pandita's Treasury of Good Advice*. Boston, MA: Wisdom Publications, 2000.

Sagang Sechen. *The Precious Summary: A History of the Mongols from Chinggis Khan to the Qing Dynasty*. Translated by Johan Elverskog. New York: Columbia University Press, 2023.

Sakya Pandita Kunga Gyaltshen. *A Clear Differentiation of the Three Codes: Essential Distinctions among the Individual Liberation, Great Vehicle, and Tantric Systems: The Sdom Gsum Rab Dbye and Six Letters*. Translated by Jared Rhoton. SUNY Series in Buddhist Studies. Albany: State University of New York Press, 2002.

Shashibala. "Hevajra in Buddhist Literature, Imperial Ceremonies and Art." In *Written Treasures of Bhutan: Mirror of the Past and Bridge to the Future*. Edited by John A. Ardussi and Sonam Topgay, 1:357–80. Proceedings of the First International Conference on the Scriptural Heritage of Bhutan. Thimphu: National Library of Bhutan, 2008.

Smith, E. Gene. "The Early History of the 'Khon Family and the Sa skya School." In *Among Tibetan Texts: History and Literature of the Himalayan Plateau*. Edited by E. Gene Smith. Boston: Wisdom, 2001.

Snellgrove, David L., and Kṛṣṇācāryapāda. *The Hevajra Tantra: A Critical Study*. London Oriental Series. London: Oxford University Press, 1976.

Sobisch, Jan-Ulrich. *Hevajra and Lam 'bras Literature of India and Tibet as Seen through the Eyes of A-Mes-Zhabs*. Contributions to Tibetan Studies. Wiesbaden: Reichert, 2008.

———. "The 'Records of Teachings Received' in the Collected Works of A Mes Zhabs: An Untapped Source for the Study of Sa Skya Pa Biographies." In *Tibet, Past and Present: Tibetan Studies I* [PIATS 2000]. 1:161–81. Leiden/Boston/Köln: Brill, 2002.

Sonam Tsemo (Bsod nams rtse mo). *Admission at Dharma's Gate*. Translated by Christopher Wilkinson. Sakya Gongma Series. Concord: Suvarna Bhasa Publishing, 2014.

———. *Entranceway to the Dharma. Chos la 'jug pa'i sgo zhes bya ba'i bstan bcos*. In *Sa skya gong ma rnam lnga'i gsung 'bum dpe bsdur ma las bsod nams rtse mo'i gsung*, 3:389–496. Beijing: Krung go'i bod rig pa dpe skrun khang, 2007.

Stearns, Cyrus. *Luminous Lives: The Story of the Early Masters of the Lam 'bras in Tibet*. Boston: Wisdom Publications, 2002.

———. *Taking the Result as the Path: Core Teachings of the Sakya Lamdre Tradition*. Library of Tibetan Classics. Boston: Wisdom Publications, 2006.

Stoltz, Jonathan. "Sakya Pandita and the Status of Concepts." *Philosophy East and West* 56 (2006): 567–82.

Sun, Penghao. "The Birth of an Etiquette Story: Tibetan Narratives of U Rgyan Pa, Qubilai, and the Yuan Government." PhD diss., Harvard University, 2023.

Szerb, János. "Glosses on the Oeuvre of Blama 'Phags Pa: On the Activity of the Sa Skya Paṇḍita." In *Tibetan Studies in Honour of Hugh Richardson: Proceedings of the International Seminar on Tibetan Studies Oxford 1979*. Warminster: Aris & Phillips, 1979.

Tauscher, Helmut. "Remarks on Phya pa Chos kyi seng ge and his Madhyamaka Treatises." *The Tibet Journal* 34/35, no. 3/2 (2009–10):1–35.

Thuken Losang Chökyi Nyima. *The Crystal Mirror of Philosophical Systems: A Tibetan Study of Asian Religious Thought*. Translated by Geshé Lhundub Sopa. The Library of Tibetan Classics 25. Boston: Wisdom Publications, 2009.

Tsendina, Anna. "Godan Khan in Mongolian and Tibetan Historical Works." *Studia Orientalia* 85 (1999): 245–48.

Tsering, Migmar. "Sakya Pandita: Glimpses of His Three Major Works." *The Tibet Journal* 13 (1988): 12.

Tucci, Giuseppe. *Tibetan Painted Scrolls*. Roma: Libreria dello Stato, 1949.

van der Kuijp, Leonard W. J. *Contributions to the Development of Tibetan Buddhist Epistemology from the Eleventh to the Thirteenth Century*. Weisbaden: Verlag, 1983.

———. "The Monastery of Gsang-phu ne'u-thog and Its Abbatial Succession from ca. 1073 to 1250," *Berliner indologische Studien* 3 (1987):103–27.

———. "Tibetan Contributions to the 'Apoha' Theory: The Fourth Chapter of the Tshad-Ma Rigs-Pa'i Gter." *Journal of the American Oriental Society* 99:3 (1979): 408–22.

Venturi, Federica. "Creating Sacred Space: The Religious Geography of Sa Skya, Tibet's Medieval Capital." PhD diss., Indiana University, 2013.

Willemen, Charles. *The Chinese Hevajratantra: The Scriptural Text of the Ritual of the Great King of the Teaching, the Adamantine One with Great Compassion and Knowledge of the Void.* 1st Indian ed. Buddhist Traditions. Delhi: Motilal Banarsidass Publishers, 2004.

Wylie, Turrell V. "The First Mongol Conquest of Tibet Reinterpreted." *Harvard Journal of Asiatic Studies* 37.1 (1977): 103–33.

Yon-tan-bzang-po and Ngawang Samten Chophel. *Teachings on Sakya Pandita's Clarifying the Sage's Intent.* 2nd rev. ed. Kathmandu: Vajra Publications, 2008.

Žamcarano, Cyben Žamzaranovič, and Rudolf Loewenthal. *The Mongol Chronicles of the Seventeenth Century.* Wiesbaden: Harrassowitz, 1955.

Index

A

Abhidharma, 57, 65, 66, 133, 153, 322n99
Amazing Treasury, The (Ameshab)
  advice on studying, 32
  composition of, 1–4, 22–25, 324n171
  opening homage, 29–31
Ameshab Ngakwang Kunga Sönam, 1, 11, 19–22, 320n66
  on writing *Amazing Treasury*, 22–24
Ascertaining Valid Cognition (Dharmakīrti), 12
Atiśa Dīpaṃkara Śrījñāna, 10, 61–62, 322nn102–3. See also *Bodhipathapradīpa* (Atiśa)
attachment, 255, 260, 261, 357n1260
attainments (*siddhi*), 7, 113, 325n206
Avadhūtipa, 177
Avalokiteśvara, 59–60, 86, 89, 90, 153, 199, 213, 327n280, 327n1255, 347n1049

B

bardos, 247–48, 331n466
Bari Lotsāwa, 64, 66, 67
Biji, 186–90, 269
blessings, 185, 240, 253, 274
bliss, 7, 95, 105, 143, 148, 166, 167, 168, 177, 178, 203, 277, 336n668
bodhicitta, 117, 144, 180, 239, 241–42, 244, 257–58, 261, 328n304, 355n1234
Bodhipathapradīpa (Atiśa), 356n1246
bodhisattva vow, 230, 239–41, 242, 258, 275
bodhisattvas, 145, 242, 243, 244, 254, 317n44, 329n381
body, 265
  of buddhas, 141, 159, 210, 250–51, 260, 348n1070
  emptiness of, 177
  of gods, 262–63
  of higher rebirth, 220, 269
  illusory, 7
  offering, 201, 202
  purification of, 267
  suffering of, 188
  vows of, 316n42, 325n211
buddha nature, 163, 263, 356n1251
Buddha Śākyamuni, 170, 215, 240, 250, 251, 265, 343n942, 343n954. *See also* Jātaka stories
buddhas, 140, 141, 162, 180, 244, 250–51, 253–54, 260, 275, 327n280, 351n1130. *See also* Buddha Śākyamuni, five buddha families

C

Čabui Qatun, 201–2, 215, 217, 349n1112
calm abiding (*śamatha*), 134, 166–68, 241, 355n1233
Chakna Dorjé, 17, 18, 291–93
Chapa Chökyi Sengé, 12
China, 9, 181, 351n1131
  Ming-dynasty, 21–22
  Song-dynasty, 15
  See also Qing Empire
Chiring, 33–35
Chögyal Phakpa Lodrö Gyaltsen, 2, 8, 13, 17, 18, 144–45, 310–11
  accomplishments of, 225–38
  birth of, 197–98
  compositions by, 280–85
  and Dharma Drakpa Sengé, 220–24
  disciples of, 285–86
  magical displays of, 206–7

and Mongolian Empire, 199–203, 208–10, 272–80
and Namkha Bum's questions, 239–70
passing of, 287–90
and Sangpo Pal, 305–6
and "Sapaṇ's White Dharma Conch Shell," 205–6
Chomden Raldri, 277–78
Činggis Qan, 14, 19, 345–46n1022, 352n1140
Čingkim, 272, 357n1268
clairvoyance, 84, 113, 241, 279–80, 285
Clarifying the Intention of the Discourses, 44
Clear Differentiation of the Three Vows (Sapaṇ), 160–61, 169, 327n280
Commentary on Valid Cognition (Dharmakīrti), 144, 161–62, 164
compassion, 90, 95, 143, 213, 243, 255, 327n280
Compendium of Training (Śāntideva), 258, 264–65
concentration (*samādhi*), 82, 134, 148, 246, 256, 278–79, 355n1233. *See also* meditation
contemplation, 127, 167, 246, 355n1236
conventional truth, 130, 161–62, 163–64

D

Dalai Lamas, 1, 18, 19, 21, 22, 346n1041
death, 140, 154, 156, 178, 231, 247–49, 263, 268. *See also* rebirth
debate, 14, 103, 110–11, 136, 138, 150–51, 156–57, 175, 225, 337n726, 351n1129, 353n1173
demons, 30, 97, 107, 172–73, 211, 240–41, 323n127
Desi Karma Tenkyong Wangpo, 2
devotion, 50, 76, 81, 122, 123, 211, 243, 250, 253, 355–56n1238
Dharma, 70, 73, 91–92, 117–18, 142, 170, 182, 208–9, 216, 217, 228, 243, 252
centers, 10
in China, 181
downfall of, 137, 328n304
protectors, 50, 54–55, 61–62, 84–85, 283, 308, 333–34n555
relatives, 247
supramundane, 182
teachers, 145
transmission to Tibet, 1–2, 5, 34–35, 71
See also ten Dharma activities; "Two Systems"
Dharma Drakpa Sengé, 220–24
dharmadhātu, 160–61, 162–63
dharmakāya, 162, 191, 254, 260, 268
Dharmakīrti, 137. See also *Ascertaining Valid Cognition*; *Commentary on Valid Cognition*
Dharmapālarakṣita, 301–2
Diamond Cutter Sūtra, 162
Distinguishing the Middle from the Extremes, 163
Distinguishing What Is True from What Is False (Sapaṇ), 165
Dorta Darqan, 15, 16
Drakpa Gyaltsen. *See* Jetsun Drakpa Gyaltsen
Drokmi Lotsāwa Śākya Yeshé, 6, 8, 9

E

Eight Verses of Thought Transformation (Thangpa), 268, 357n1260
elimination of other, 163
empowerments, 178, 201–2, 247, 254, 256, 258–59, 261
emptiness, 142, 166, 175
and bliss, 168, 177, 178, 277
Entranceway to the Dharma (Tsemo), 12
Ever-Weeping (bodhisattva), 271
Extra Supplement to the Amazing Treasury of the Precious Sakya Lineage (Trinlé Rinchen), 24

F

Fifty Verses on the Guru, 247
five buddha families, 250, 351n1130
five fields of knowledge, 130–33, 135–36, 317n44
Friendly Letter (Nāgārjuna), 262, 356n1249
Fundamental Verses on the Middle Way, The (Nāgārjuna), 164–65

G

gandharvas, 347n1052
Garland of Vajras Tantra, 176
Geluk school, 1, 6, 10, 13, 19, 22, 354n1215
Geshé Yakdé Sönam Sangpo, 155

Ghaṇṭāpa, 232, 354n1215
gods, 41, 96, 172–73, 214, 262–63, 323n127, 359n1322
Great Perfection teachings, 9
Guhyasamāja Tantra, 215n18
Gyaza Kongjo, 200, 349–50n1114, 364n1562

H

Hevajra Tantra, 6–9, 176, 178, 314n13, 338n749

I

ignorance, 30, 95, 96, 143, 215
impermanence, 161, 268
individual beings, 249
Introduction to the Bodhisattva's Way of Life, 162–63, 264–65

J

Jangchup Ö, 322n102
jātaka stories, 128, 349n1104
Jetsun Drakpa Gyaltsen, 11, 12–13, 108, 118–20, 122–23
  birth of, 107
  compositions by, 111–13
  dreams of, 114–17
  passing of, 121
  training of, 109–10
Jinpa Pal, 59
Jowo Śākyamuni statue, 266

K

Kadampa tradition, 10, 230, 231, 257, 357n1260
Kagyü tradition, 6, 8, 10, 16, 349n1111, 349n1113, 354n1215
karma, 105, 166, 169, 226, 242, 248–50, 251–52, 268, 280
Karma Pakshi, 8, 200, 349n1113, 351n1129
  and Chögyal Phakpa, 206–7
Khampa Dorjé Gyal, 85
Khön Dorjé Rinchen, 40, 43–45
Khön Gekyab, 48, 50
Khön Getong, 48
Khön Könchok Gyalpo, 4–5, 11, 50, 53, 54–57, 59, 60–61, 78
  passing of, 63, 64
Khön Lui Wangpo, 43–46
Khön Palwo Ché, 42–43
Khön Rok Sherab Tsultrim, 50, 53
Khön Shākya Lodrö, 49
Khön Sherab Yönten, 46
Khön Tön Belpo, 50
Khön Tsuktor Sherab, 47
Khön Tsültrim Gyalpo, 47
Khön Yönten Jungné, 46
Khöndung Gyana Vajra Rinpché, 11
King Devarāja, 204–5
King Dharmapāla, 204–5
Köden Ejen, 2, 15, 16, 17–18, 159–60, 171–74, 180–81, 182, 214
Könpa Jé Gungtak, 35

L

Lama Shang, 76–78
Lamdré method, 5, 6, 8, 76–81, 156
Lamp for the Path of Enlightenment, 258–59, 268
Lang Khampa Lotsāwa, 45
lay disciples, 316n42, 356n1249
liberation, 95, 166, 177, 205, 274, 343, 343n954, 347n1057
Lineage Succession of the Khön, The (Drakpa Gyaltsen), 43–44
listening, 202, 286, 295, 307
Lords of the Three Families, 34
  prophesies concerning, 61–63
Lui Wangpo Sungpa, 268, 315n31

M

Machik Shangmo, 59, 60, 61, 65–66
Madhyamaka school, 12, 167, 356n1242
Mahākāla, 333–34n555
mahāmudrā, 165, 167, 168, 174–80, 256
Mahāyāna, 12, 174, 240, 243, 244, 251, 275, 355n1226. *See also* Perfection Vehicle
Mal Lotsāwa Lodrö Drakpa, 9, 72–74
Mañjuśrī [Mañjughoṣa], 23, 33, 34–35, 62–63, 64–65, 95, 106, 140, 143, 180, 199, 240–41, 264–65, 327n280, 327n298
Mantra Vehicle, 254–55, 256–59, 265
Marpa Chökyi Lodrö, 8
masang, 322–23n117
meditation, 7, 56, 82, 83, 104, 165–68, 209, 245, 246, 268, 355n1236
  bodhicitta, 242
  deities, 114, 241, 350n1116

generation and completion stage, 257–58
Hevajra, 338n749
mahāmudrā, 174, 175, 177, 178
See also calm abiding (*śamatha*); vipaśyanā
meditative accomplishment, 113
merit, 93, 210, 214, 217, 220, 228, 247, 279–80
accumulating, 104, 144, 189, 244–46, 255–57, 261
dedicating, 261
Milarepa, 199, 349n1111
mind, 165, 166, 179, 202, 255, 267, 356n1241, 356n1251
of clear light, 6–7
of enlightenment, 177–78, 241–42, 266
of stable mental engagement, 241
Mind Only school (Cittamātra), 252, 356n1241
Möngke Khan, 8
Mongolian Empire, 1, 2, 13–19, 214–15, 279, 315n24, 346n1041
and Sakya Paṇḍita, 158–70
and Tibet, 318–19n52, 318n49, 319nn56–57
Mount Pönpo, 10–11
Mount Wangpo, 91–92
Muchen Sangyé Gyaltsen, 21

N

Nāgārjuna, 165–66, 176, 287, 353n1171, 356n1242, 356n1249. *See also individual works*
Nairātmyā, 5
Nālandā Monastery, 5, 204
Nam Khaupa [Darma Sengé], 59–60, 61, 67–68
Namkha Bum, 141
Namri Songtsen, 4, 314n7
New Translation (Gsar ma) period, 5, 6, 9, 10, 13, 19, 53, 56, 76, 326n220, 351n1130, 353n1170, 356n1238. *See also* Geluk school; Kagyü tradition; Sakya tradition
Ngakchang Chökyi Gyalpo, 45
Ngakwang Künga Rinchen, 85
Ngakwang Kunga Tekchen Pelbar, 11
Ngakwang Kunga Wangyal, 21
Ngok Lekpai Sherab, 12
noble beings, 163, 169, 249, 349n1103. *See also* bodhisattvas; buddhas

O

offerings, 95, 201, 216, 242, 276, 278, 287, 332n473
funerary, 261
to images, 262
torma, 267
Ögedei Qaγan, 14, 15, 16, 214
Old Translation period, 9, 53, 54, 56
ordination, 324n167, 324n177, 330n401. *See also* vows
Ornament Adorning the Mouths of the Noble, The (Könchok Lundrup), 33–34, 39, 53–54, 227
Ornament for Clear Realization, 142, 343n960
Ornament of the Mahāyāna Sūtras, 145, 166–67, 343n964

P

Padmasambhava, 45, 46, 61, 62, 89, 219
Palchen Öpo, 124, 125
paths and grounds, 142, 177–79, 251, 347n1057
Pawo Tak, 37
"Pearl Edict" (Qubilai Qaγan), 208–10
Perfection of Wisdom Sūtra in Eight Thousand Lines, 271
Perfection Vehicle, 133–34, 175, 254–58, 325n214. *See also* Mahāyāna
Phakpa Lodrö Gyaltsen. *See* Chögyal Phakpa Lodrö Gyaltsen
Poetic Power of Lake Nyer, 204
Power of Sustenance, The, 98
Praise to Sachen (Sönam Tsemo), 62–63
Prajñākaragupta, 137–38
pratyekabuddhas, 254, 343n954–55
purification, 205, 245, 246–47, 266–67

Q

Qing Empire, 1, 21. *See also* China
Qubilai Qaγan, 2, 8, 169–70, 214–15, 217, 291, 293, 346n1041
and Chögyal Phakpa, 199–203
Quintessential Instructions on the Middle Way, 268

R

Ratna Vajra Rinpoché, 11

Ratnabhadra, 303
rebirth
female, 345n1006
in formless realm, 166
higher, 63, 205, 220, 327n294
lower, 165, 251–52
See also bardos
recitation, 244, 245, 246
Reciting the Names of Mañjuśrī, 178, 179, 254
refuge, 95, 205, 243–44, 247, 267, 283, 316n42. *See also* Triple Gem
retreat, 261, 266–67, 332n473, 350n1116
Rinchen Gyaltsen, 295–97
Rinchen Sangpo, 5
Rosary of White Lotuses (Dharmātala), 319n56

S

Sachen Kunga Nyingpo, 9–10, 11, 58, 84–86, 91–98, 99
birth of, 59–63
compositions by, 79–81
disciples of, 87–89
and Lamdré, 76–78
passing of, 90
qualities of, 82–83
training of, 63–75
Sakya Monastery, 91–98, 273, 336n668
founding of, 63
Sakya Paṇḍita Kunga Gyaltsen, 2, 12, 13–14, 126
accomplishments of, 151–91
birth of, 127
and China, 181
and Chögyal Phakpa, 197, 199
compositions by, 146–50
and Drakpa Gyaltsen, 121
and mahāmūdra, 174–80
and Mongolian Empire, 16–18, 158–70, 173, 182–86, 279
passing of, 171–72, 186–90, 269
praises of, 137–45
"Sapaṇ's White Dharma Conch Shell," 205
training of, 128–36
Sakya tradition, 1–4, 22, 25
"celestial family of the Khön Sakyapa," 53–57
five forefathers of, 11–13
founding of, 4–11, 53
Khön celestial family, 54–57
Khön family lineage, 1–2, 4–11, 30, 39–51, 96 (*See also individuals*)
lineage from gods, 33–38
and Mongolian Empire, 18–19, 315n24
See also Khön family lineage
Sakya Trizin (title), 11–13
Śākyaśrībhadra, 159
saṃsāra, 117, 143–44, 167, 177, 179, 180, 210, 213, 255, 263–64, 328n304, 345n1002, 355n1233
Samyé Monastery, 157–58
Sangphu Neuthok Monastery, 12
Sangpo Pal
accomplishments of, 306–10
birth of, 305
passing of, 311–12
Sankarānanda, 138
Śāntarakṣita, 45, 324n167
Śāntideva, 264–65
Saraha, 179–80
Secret Mantra Vehicle, 132–35
self-grasping, 143–44, 151, 213, 357n1260
Se[tön Kunrik], 70
"seven brothers of Masang," 36–37
Shākya Lodrö, 50
Sharpa Jamyang Chenmo, 307
Short Truth of the Middle Way, 268
"Sijilé siblings," 36
six perfections, 235, 245–46, 255–56, 257
six-syllable mantra, 265
Sönam Gyaltsen, 193–95
Sönam Tsemo, 11–12, 100, 102–6
birth of, 99, 101
Songtsen Gampo, 199, 314n7
śrāvakas, 254, 343n954
Śrī Ghānaśrīna, 139
Sthiramati, 137
stūpas, 67, 219, 260–61, 352n1150
Sublime Continuation, 163
suffering, 143–44, 163, 213, 263, 286
Supplement to the Amazing Treasury of the Precious Sakya Lineage (Sönam Drakpa), 24

T

Takpo Öchen, 37
Taming Mara Stūpa, 61
Tangut Empire, 14

tantric practices, 6–7, 71, 175, 336n675, 355–56n1238, 356n1246. *See also individual tantras*
Tashi Döndrup, 198
ten Dharma activities, 245–46, 258, 266–67, 355n1236
ten excellent qualities of land, 42
thoughts, 76, 168, 177, 178
 blocking, 165
 nonconceptual, 104, 188
 and wisdom, 180
Tibet, 2–3, 9, 11, 183, 200–201, 318–19n52, 318n49, 349n1110
 Dharma in, 34–35
 Empire period, 4
 Phakmodru Dynasty, 19–20
"Tibetan Language Edict, The" (Phakpa), 210–18
Tngri, 210, 216, 352n1140
Tokden Gyenpo, 174–80
transmission, 5, 9, 259–60
Treasury of Abhidharma, 163–64
Treasury of Knowledge, The, 160
Tri Ralpachen, 199
Triple Gem, 169, 185, 210, 242, 243–44, 326n42. *See also* refuge
Trisong Detsen, 4, 42, 199, 268
Tsang Desi Karma Tenkyong Wangpo, 1
Tsang-Mongol war, 1, 22
tsatsa, 260, 356n1247
Tsultrim Gyalpo, 49
"Two Systems," 9, 19

U
ultimate truth, 130, 140, 162, 163–64, 349n1103

V
Vādisiṃhaḥ, 138–39
Vairocana, 250–51
Vajra Verses (Virūpa), 11
Vajrapāṇi, 10, 62, 199, 291, 327n280
vidhyādhara, 276, 358n1283
vipaśyanā, 165, 166–68
virtues, 144, 164, 169, 240, 253, 269, 349n1111
Virūpa, 5, 82
visualization, 134, 253, 280, 282, 350n1116
vows, 249, 316n42, 325n211
 See also bodhisattva vow; ordination
Vulture Peak, 115, 341n873

W
Whispered Lineage of the Ḍākinīs of Luminous Space (Padmasambhava), 62
White Dharma Conch [that Sounds] from Afar, The, 204–6
White Lotus of Compassion Sūtra, 167–68
wisdom, 6–7, 23, 29, 34–35, 64, 117, 132, 156, 220, 253, 255, 256, 265, 327n280, 327n294
 of buddha, 327n298
 coemergent, 176–78
 realizing selflessness, 143–44
 secret, 258–59
 and thoughts, 180
Wisdom at the Moment of Death Sūtra, 179
Wondrous Precious Treasury Fulfilling All Wishes, The, 32
wrong views, 84, 150–51, 252, 255, 356n1242

Y
Ya Chang, 41–42
Ya Pangkyé, 40
Yaktruk Khön Barkyé, 40–41
Yapang Kyé, 38
Yeshé Jugné, 298–99
Yeshé Öd, 322n102
Yuring, 33–34, 35
Yusé, 33–34, 36

Z
Zhangtön Chöbar, 9

ABOUT THE AUTHORS

AMESHAB NGAKWANG KUNGA SÖNAM (A myes zhabs ngag dbang kun dga' bsod nams, 1597–1659) was the long-serving twenty-seventh throne holder of the Sakya lineage of Tibetan Buddhism. Deeply trained in his tradition, Ameshab was ordained as a monk around 1618 and undertook extensive scholastic study. After the death of his father and brother, however, in 1620 Ameshab returned his vows and was enthroned as Sakya Trizin. In the decades that followed, Ameshab widely promoted the transmission of the Sakya tradition and mediated peace amid rising military conflict in Central Tibet. A prodigious historian, Ameshab wrote impactful histories of the Sakya school; the Lamdré, or "Path and Result," tradition; and the *Hevajra Tantra*, which were read for centuries in Tibet and across the Inner Asian Buddhist world.

KHENPO KUNGA SHERAB was born in Lhoka, near Lhasa, Tibet, and is a monastic scholar and teacher. He is the author of several studies in Tibetan on the Abhidharma and on Middle Way philosophy. He holds several advanced monastic degrees, including the Madhyamaka diploma, and shastri, acharya, and khenpo degrees from Dzongsar Institute for Advanced Studies in Buddhist Philosophy and Research, India. Following his monastic education, in addition to taking on teaching roles at Dzongsar, from 2000 to 2008 Khenpo Kunga served as abbot of Zurmang Monastery in Sikkim, India while teaching continuously at Dharma centers around Asia. In 2014, he received an MA and then, in 2023, a PhD in Buddhist studies from the University of Toronto. His major English-language academic work to date has examined the cultural history of practices used to identify incarnate lamas between the thirteenth and twentieth centuries. He has long been involved in teaching Buddhist meditation and philosophy in settings as diverse as traditional Tibetan monastic colleges, interfaith institutes, Dharma centers across North America and Asia, as well as university classrooms. Since 2017, he has served as Buddhist chaplain at Warkworth Correctional Institute, in addition to serving other prisons in southwestern Ontario, Canada. Since 2010, Khenpo Kunga has worked as a team member on various international research projects examining Tibetan Buddhist history with colleagues in Canada, the United States, and Asia.

MATTHEW W. KING is Professor of Transnational Buddhism at the University of California, Riverside. He specializes in Inner Asian Buddhism with a special focus on the Tibet-Mongol interface during the Yuan and Qing periods. He has published widely on the history of Buddhist scholasticism, medicine, and institution building, and on political theory in Inner Asia. He has also explored the history of Inner Asian Buddhist interactions with circulating intellectual traditions during this period, including European natural philosophy and humanism, biomedicine, nationalism, state socialism, and Buddhist Studies. His first book, *Ocean of Milk, Ocean of Blood: A Mongolian Monk in the Ruins of the Qing Empire* (Columbia University Press, 2019), won several awards, including the American Academy of Religion's 2020 award for Best Book in Textual Study. His most recent book is *In the Forest of the Blind: The Eurasian Journey of Faxian's Record of Buddhist Kingdoms* (Columbia University Press, 2022).

What to read next from Wisdom Publications

The Sakya School of Tibetan Buddhism
A History
Dhongthog Rinpoche
Translated by Sam van Schaik

Since its 1976 publication in Tibetan, Dhongthog Rinpoche's history of the Sakya school of Tibetan Buddhism has been a key reference for specialists in Tibetan studies.

Ornament to Beautify the Three Appearances
The Mahāyāna Preliminary Practices of the Sakya Lamdré Tradition
Ngorchen Könchok Lhundrup
Translated by Cyrus Stearns
Foreword by His Holiness the Sakya Trichen

The first book of a two-volume set of works written by Ngorchen Könchok Lhundrup (1497–1557) to explain the Lamdré teachings, the most important system of tantric theory and practice in the Sakya tradition of Tibetan Buddhism.

Ordinary Wisdom
Sakya Pandita's Treasury of Good Advice
Translated by John Davenport

"A sterling translation of one of the most loved books of the Tibetan Buddhist tradition."—Gehlek Rinpoche

The Bodhisattva Path from Ground to Fruition
Commentary on Sakya Paṇḍita's Clarifying the Sage's Intent
His Holiness the 42nd Sakya Trizin

Discover profound teachings on the Buddhist path from His Holiness the 42nd Sakya Trizin Ratna Vajra, one of Tibetan Buddhism's most prominent leaders.

Taking the Result as the Path
Core Teachings of the Sakya Lamdré Tradition
Translated by Cyrus Stearns

"*Taking the Result as the Path* represents a major breakthrough by bringing these teachings to light with the full blessings of the Sakya masters. This collection will be an invaluable resource for practitioners of the Lamdré system."—*Buddhadharma*

Freeing the Heart and Mind (3 volumes)
His Holiness the Sakya Trichen

This trilogy is "required reading" for any Sakya practitioner, and will also be deeply inspiring for Buddhists of all traditions.

A History of Buddhism in India and Tibet
An Expanded Version of the Dharma's Origins Made by the Learned Scholar Deyu
Translated by Dan Martin

"This book is a treasure and a work of great service to those of us who are fascinated by Tibet's history and culture. Martin's translation—a massive achievement—allows readers to access a fascinating thirteenth-century Tibetan Buddhist history that has become a touchstone in Tibetan studies. The introduction is superb, and the notes throughout the work, in Martin's inimitable voice, include some great insights into this text's many delights and riddles." —Brandon Dotson, associate professor and director, Department of Theology and Religious Studies, Georgetown University

Luminous Lives

The Story of the Early Masters of the Lam 'bras Tradition in Tibet

Cyrus Stearns

"A seminal manuscript history of its earliest practitioners and masters, and a detailed description of the Lam 'bras teachings."—*Tricycle*

About Wisdom Publications

Wisdom Publications is the leading publisher of classic and contemporary Buddhist books and practical works on mindfulness. To learn more about us or to explore our other books, please visit our website at wisdom.org or contact us at the address below.

Wisdom Publications
132 Perry Street
New York, NY 10014 USA

We are a 501(c)(3) organization, and donations in support of our mission are tax deductible.

Wisdom Publications is affiliated with the Foundation for the Preservation of the Mahayana Tradition (FPMT).